LEGAL HANDBOOK FOR EDUCATORS

FIFTH EDITION

ANTHONY F. BROWN, LL.B., LL.M., M.ED.

THOMSON

™

CARSWELL

National Library of Canada Cataloguing in Publication
Brown, Anthony F., 1953-
    Legal handbook for educators / Anthony F. Brown.—5th ed.
Includes index.
First-3rd eds. published under title: Legal handbook for school
    administrators.
ISBN 0-459-24134-6

1. Educational law and legislation—Ontario.
2. School management and organization—Law and legislation—Ontario.
I. Brown, Anthony F., 1953- . Legal handbook for school
administrators. II. Title.

KEO770.B76   2004   344.713'07 C2004-900686-X
KF4119.B76 2004

The paper used in this publication meets the minimum requirements of American National Standard for Information Sciences - Permanence of Paper for Printed Library Materials, ANSI Z39.48-1984.

One Corporate Plaza, 2075 Kennedy Road, Scarborough, Ontario M1T 3V4
Customer Service:
Toronto 1-416-609-3800
Elsewhere in Canada/U.S. 1-800-387-5164
Fax 1-416-298-5094

Dedication

To Catherine, Lisa and Sebastian

Table of Contents

List of Statutes and Regulations

STATUTES

Canadian Charter of Rights and Freedoms (being Part I of the Constitution Act, 1982 [en. by the Canada Act, 1982 (U.K.), c. 11, Sched. B])
Child and Family Services Act, R.S.O. 1990, c. C.11
Education Act, R.S.O. c. E.2, ss. 264, 265, 286
Statutory Powers Procedure Act, R.S.O. 1990, c. S.22
Teaching Profession Act, R.S.O. 1990, c. T.2
Trespass to Property Act, R.S.O. 1990, c. T.21
Youth Criminal Justice Act, S.C. 2002, c. 1

REGULATIONS

Access to School Premises, O. Reg. 474/00
Collection of Personal Information, O. Reg. 521/01
Continuing Education, R.R.O. 1990, Reg. 285
Electronic Meetings, O. Reg. 463/97
General, O. Reg. 72/97
Identification and Placement of Exceptional Pupils, O. Reg. 181/98
Opening or Closing Exercises, O. Reg. 435/00
Operation of Schools—General, R.R.O. 1990, Reg. 298
Principals and Vice-Principals—Redundancy and Reassignment, O. Reg. 90/98
Professional Misconduct, O. Reg. 437/97
Pupil Representation on Boards, O. Reg. 461/97

Regulation made under the Teaching Profession Act
School Councils, O. Reg. 612/00
School Year Calendar, R.R.O. 1990, Reg. 304
Supervisory Officers, R.R.O. 1990, Reg. 309
Teacher Performance Appraisal, O. Reg. 99/02
Teachers Qualifications, O. Reg. 184/97

Introduction to the Fifth Edition

This edition of the *Legal Handbook for Educators* continues the original purpose of the book, namely to explain in a clear and concise way the areas of education law that are most relevant to school administrators, educators and parents. It is intended to be a handy resource that summarizes pertinent legislation and provides easy access to the statutory and regulatory provisions most relevant to understanding the legal environment of schools and school boards. Of course, this information is not a substitute for advice from a lawyer about a particular issue that you may encounter. In addition to a general update to reflect new legislation, this edition reflects substantial changes to the law in areas such as expulsion and suspension, reporting child abuse, denial of access to school premises, and the *Youth Criminal Justice Act*.

Since publication of the First Edition, the field of education law has expanded in breadth and complexity. Several well-qualified writers and lawyers have taken up the mission of expanding the legal resources available to school principals and others, in such areas as human rights, employment law, collective bargaining, sexual misconduct, school violence, and discipline. The remarkable "body" of education law becomes very obvious from a perusal of Carswell's *Annotated Education Act*, and it is noteworthy that education law is now receiving more attention in law schools. All of this academic activity merely reflects what the reader has known all along-that the pursuit of a better understanding of education law is both important and enjoyable, and that there is a thirst for information and dialogue in order to understand the legal challenges faced in our schools.

Indeed, the legal challenges faced in Ontario are similar to those encountered in schools across the globe. Bullying, discipline, sexual misconduct, and issues about freedom of expression (of teachers and students) continue to challenge educators and lawyers. Another issue involves deciding when a student's conduct justifies depriving him or her of the right to attend school. Does "zero tolerance" ensure that our schools are safe, and does this policy detrimentally affect certain minorities in a disproportionate way? Further, in a world where financial constraints force boards to make tough choices, challenges include trying to find reasonable limits on providing programs and services for exceptional children without infringing their rights under human rights legislation or the *Charter of Rights and Freedoms*. We can all learn from the experience of other jurisdictions in dealing with these and other issues.

I wish to express my thanks to the many readers who have used the *Legal Handbook for Educators* over the years. I hope that you will continue to find it a useful resource and a good starting point for your legal research. My sincere thanks to Julia Gulej, Product Development Manager, Ken Mathies, Product Process Manager, and to all of the editorial and production staff at Carswell for their patience and assistance throughout the process of revising the *Handbook*. Finally, words are completely inadequate to express my gratitude to Catherine for her support and encouragement, having so often set aside her own needs and precious time so that I could write.

1

The *Education Act*: An Overview

The *Education Act* and its many regulations provide the statutory basis for how education is delivered to pupils who are enrolled in the publicly-funded school system in Ontario. Aside from its sheer size, part of the reason why the Act seems a bit overwhelming is that it contains provisions that are deeply rooted in legislative history (e.g. teachers' duties) to which various new bits and pieces have been added in a mostly ad hoc manner. In addition, it is often necessary to have separate sections dealing with a single topic in respect of the four types of district school board. None of the Act makes much sense unless the reader is familiar with the definitions in section 1, and yet this is a section people often ignore. In addition, the regulations made under the Act are as important to our understanding of the law as the Act itself.

This chapter is intended to give you an answer to the question: "What is the *Education Act* about?" It provides a general overview of the Act and some of its regulations, and explains many of the key provisions that relate to the operation of boards and their schools. I have not dealt in detail with certain narrow, highly specialized areas such as education development charges because these would be of limited interest to most readers. If you are researching a specific issue, it is important to refer to the wording of the relevant provisions in the legislation because there could be exceptions to the usual rules that cannot be covered here. Some of the provisions of the Act are reproduced within the text for easy reference. In addition, some regulations are included in this book for easy reference. As a means of dealing with the length and complexity of the Act, I have used a "question and answer" format to focus on its components. I hope this approach is useful.

Unless otherwise noted, all section references are to the *Education Act*.

1.1 SCHOOL BOARDS

(a) What is a School Board?

According to our Constitution, Canadian provinces have exclusive jurisdiction over education. A school board is a corporation that exercises powers that have been delegated to it by the province. It is run by elected members (trustees) and has the legal capacity to sue and be sued in its own name. The legal structure for education governance in Ontario reflects the Constitutional rights of Roman Catholics to have separate schools, and the section 23 *Charter* educational rights of the French linguistic minority.

The *Education Act* refers to two distinct kinds of "boards": District School Boards and School Authorities.

District School Boards

There are four types of District School Board:

- English-language public
- English-language separate
- French-language public
- French-language separate.

In total, 129 "old" school boards were "merged" into 72 district school boards on January 1, 1998. This was accomplished by Ontario Regulation 460/97. The boards' areas of jurisdiction are set out in Ontario Regulation 185/97 as amended by Ontario Regulations 278/97, 80/98 and 213/98. The number and distribution of trustees are determined by Ontario Regulation 412/00. Board names are set out in Ontario Regulation 486/00. In 1998, District School Boards took over the assets, liabilities and employees of the old board or boards that preceded them (s. 58.5). Old boards were *merged* into District School Boards, not amalgamated. A district school board may not have more than 22 or fewer than five members (s. 58.1(10)).

School Authorities

The *Education Quality Improvement Act, 1997* did not create School Authorities as *new* corporate entities. A "school authority" is the new name that describes any of the following:

- a board of a district school area
- a board of rural separate school
- a board of a combined separate school zone
- a board of a secondary school district (i.e. James Bay Lowlands Secondary School District)
- a hospital board (established under s. 68 of the *Education Act*)
- a Protestant separate school board.

Unlike a district school board, a school authority is responsible for provision of education to the linguistic minority within its jurisdiction. Members of hospital boards are appointed by the Minister of Education and Training pursuant to section 68 of the *Education Act*; they are not elected.

(b) What is a "Supported" School Board?

The notion of a "supported" board is relevant in relation to the transition during 1998 from old boards to District School Boards as a result of the *Education Quality Improvement Act, 1997* and the *Fewer School Boards Act, 1997*. A "supported" board is a district school board whose assets, liabilities and employees were temporarily "parked" at a "designated" board until such time as the Education Improvement Commission ordered a transfer of the assets, liabilities or employees to the supported board. Because the designated boards (in most cases, an English-language board) had "predecessors" that existed on December 31, 1997, they already had an organizational and administrative infrastructure. In many cases, the supported board (usually a French-language board) had to start from the beginning in an organizational sense, and therefore could not assume assets, liabilities and employees on January 1, 1998. Regulation 460/97 lists supported and designated district school boards.

(c) What Authority Does a School Trustee Have?

A trustee may vote and act as a member of the board but has no individual authority over education within the board's jurisdiction. Unless authorized by, and acting on behalf of the board, trustees should not issue orders or directions to staff. Obviously, a trustee is free to perform many functions in his or her role, including visiting schools, talking to parents, staff, pupils and others, and voicing his or her opinions on education issues. This is quite a different matter from purporting to act on behalf of the board as a whole and from usurping the role of teachers and administrators.

A school board exercises powers delegated to it by the province or guaranteed to it under the Constitution. A board should always be sure of its legal authority to act. A board may exercise only those powers that are conferred on it by or under a statute, and may do those things that are necessarily incidental to the exercise of those powers.

1.2 TRUSTEE ELECTIONS

(a) Who Can Be Elected as a Trustee of a District School Board?

A school trustee is referred to in the *Education Act* as a "board member". A board member is a person elected by "electors" to serve on a school board. You will find the definition of "public school elector" and "separate school elector" in the *Municipal Elections Act, 1996* because most school board elections are held in accordance with the provisions of that Act as well as the provisions of the *Education Act*. The *Education Act* specifically provides that a board member may also be referred to as a "trustee". These terms are often used interchangeably (s. 1(12)).

In order to be elected as a trustee you must be qualified to vote for members of the board and you must be resident anywhere in the board's jurisdiction. Election of district school board members is done in the same manner as the elections of members of a council of a municipality (ss. 58.6 and 58.7). You can vote if you reside in the jurisdiction or if you are an owner or tenant, or the spouse of an owner or tenant of residential land in the jurisdiction at any time during the "qualification period" (which begins on the Tuesday after Labour Day and ends on voting day) (s. 17 *Municipal Elections Act, 1996*). Under subsection 1(10) of the *Education Act*, on voting day you must be at least 18 years old, a Canadian citizen and not prohibited from voting under the *Municipal Elections Act, 1996* or otherwise by law. The *Municipal Elections Act, 1996* prohibits the following from voting:

- a person who is serving a sentence of imprisonment in penal or correctional institution

- a corporation
- a person acting as an executor, trustee or other representative capacity except as a voting proxy
- a person who was convicted of a corrupt practice described in subsection 90(3) of the *Municipal Elections Act, 1996* within four years of the election in respect of which he or she was convicted.

(See s. 1 and s. 219 of the *Education Act.*)

The number of members to be elected to a district school board is determined by Ontario Regulation 412/00. The *Education Act* says that a district school board cannot have fewer than five members or more than 22 members (excluding native representatives) (s. 58.1(10)(11)).

The English-language public district school board is to be elected by persons who are not separate school supporters and are not qualified to be electors for a French-language district school board (or who do not exercise their right to be a French-language board elector). The English-language separate school board is to be elected by persons who are separate school supporters and are not qualified to be electors for a French-language district school board. The French-language public district school board is to be elected by persons who are not separate school supporters and are qualified to be electors for a French-language district school board. The French-language separate school board is to be elected by persons who are separate school supporters and are qualified to be electors for a French-language district school board. (See generally s. 58.9.) (With respect to electors for French-language district school boards, see also s. 58.8.) (See also s. 54 with respect to resident Roman Catholics who are not separate supporters but want to be on a "preliminary list" of voters.)

(b) When Are Elections Held?

Regular elections are held on the second Monday in November in the year of an election. Elections are held every three years.

(c) Who Cannot Hold Office?

Under section 219 of the Act, you cannot be elected or act as a trustee if

- you are employed by any school board in Ontario (unless on unpaid leave under s. 219(5))
- you are the clerk, treasurer, deputy clerk or deputy treasurer of a

municipality or upper-tier municipality, all or part of which is included in the area of jurisdiction of the district school board or the school authority
- you are an Ontario MPP, Federal MP or Senator
- you are otherwise ineligible or disqualified under any Act. (E.g. under the *Municipal Conflict of Interest Act* or under s. 230.12(3) of the *Education Act.*)

It is an offence to act as a trustee while disqualified (s. 213).

See generally s. 219 of the *Education Act* and sections 29 and 30 of the *Municipal Elections Act, 1996.*

(d) What if a Trustee Leaves the Board's Jurisdiction?

A trustee must remain a "resident" of the board's jurisdiction in order to remain qualified as a trustee.

(e) Can a Person Run For More Than One Seat on a Board?

No. You can only run for one seat on the board (s. 219(10)). You cannot hold more than one office election to which is governed by the *Municipal Elections Act, 1996.*

(f) What Happens When a Trustee Quits During His or Her Term?

A trustee can resign with the consent of a majority of the other board members, unless it would reduce the board to below quorum (s. 220). After the resignation, the remaining board members must decide whether to fill the vacancy by appointing a person to the board or by holding a by-election. The appointment must be made within 60 days of the vacancy. The board cannot hold an election to replace the trustee if the vacancy occurs after April 1 in a regular election year (ss. 221-228).

(g) When Does a Seat Become Vacant?

Section 219(11) of the Act states that the seat of a member who is not qualified or entitled to act as a member of the board is vacated. Section 220 provides that a member of a board vacates his or her seat on the board if he or she:

- is convicted of an indictable offence-the vacancy cannot be filled until the time for taking any appeal has elapsed or until the final determination of any appeal; if the conviction is quashed, then the seat is deemed not to have been vacated
- absents himself or herself from three consecutive meetings of the board, without being authorized by board resolution
- ceases to hold the qualifications required to act as a member
- becomes disqualified under section 219(4); i.e. becomes an employee of the board, becomes a clerk, treasurer, deputy clerk or deputy treasurer of a municipality or upper-tier municipality sharing jurisdiction with the board, becomes a member of the Legislative Assembly, or the Senate or the House of Commons, or becomes otherwise ineligible or disqualified under any Act
- fails to be physically present in the board's meeting room for at least three regular board meetings in a 12-month period.

Section 221 provides how the board is to fill a vacancy. The members may appoint a person within 60 days of the vacancy, if a majority of members remains in office in order to make the appointment. Alternatively, if a majority does remain, they may hold a by-election provided that the vacancy occurs in a year in which there is no regular election, or before April 1 in a year of a regular election, or after the new board is organized in the year of a regular election. (If no majority remains to make an appointment or to choose an optional by-election, the Act provides that a by-election must be held.) A member appointed or elected to fill a vacancy does so for the remainder of the term of the member who vacated the office.

1.3 RUNNING THE BOARD

(a) When Does a Trustee Have a Conflict of Interest?

The *Municipal Conflict of Interest Act* is the statute that governs conflict of interest for trustees. In a strictly legal sense, "conflict of interest" for a school trustee is confined to direct, indirect and deemed *pecuniary* interest. The onus is on the trustee to declare if he or she has a conflict of interest in a matter under consideration by the board, or by a committee of which the trustee is a member. The declaration must be recorded in the minutes. Having made such a declaration, the trustee must not vote on the matter, attempt to influence the vote, or participate in the discussion of the matter. If the meeting is in closed session, the trustee must leave the meeting during consideration of the matter, and have this fact recorded in the minutes.

If a trustee is absent from a meeting that dealt with a matter in respect of which the trustee has a conflict of interest, the trustee must disclose the interest at the next meeting of the board or committee that the trustee attends, and must not vote on, influence, or discuss the matter.

A trustee has an *indirect interest* in a matter if,

(a)   the trustee or his or her nominee is a shareholder in, or a director or senior officer of, a corporation (that is not publicly-traded) that has a pecuniary interest in the matter;
(b)   if he or she has a controlling interest in, or is a director or senior officer of, a publicly-traded corporation that has a pecuniary interest in the matter;
(c)   is a member of a body that has a pecuniary interest in the matter; or
(d)   is a partner of a person or is in the employment of a person or body that has a pecuniary interest in the matter.

The direct or indirect pecuniary interest of a parent or the spouse, same-sex partner, or any child of the trustee is *deemed* to be the pecuniary interest of the trustee, if known to the trustee.

The *Municipal Conflict of Interest Act* has a list of "exceptions" that do not constitute a pecuniary interest. For example, a pecuniary interest "in common with electors generally", or that is "so remote or insignificant in its nature that it cannot reasonably be regarded as likely to influence the member" does not have to be declared under the Act.

What happens if a trustee fails to declare a conflict of interest at a meeting? The trustee cannot be forced to declare an interest or to leave the meeting during discussion of a matter. After the fact, the only remedy is an expensive, cumbersome and risky one. An "elector" may apply (within six months) to a judge of the Ontario Court (General Division) for a determination of the question of whether the Act has been complied with. If a contravention of the Act is found to have occurred, the trustee's seat can be declared vacant, the person can be prohibited from serving as trustee for seven years and, where appropriate, an order for restitution can be made. If the Court finds that the Act was contravened through "inadvertence or error of judgment", the trustee is not subject to having his or her seat declared vacant or to being disqualified from running again.

(b) Can the Provincial Government "Take Over" a School Board?

Yes, the Province can assume control over the administration and operations of a school board in certain circumstances. Provincial control has three stages: investigation, direction and supervision.

Ensuring Compliance by Boards

The *Education Quality and Accountability Act, 1997,* amended the *Education Act* with provisions (s. 230 to s. 230.19) that allow the Minister of Education to intervene in situations where the Minister has concerns that the board may have done something or omitted to do something that contravenes specific sections of the Act that impose obligations on the board in respect of:

- prescribed courses of study and curriculum guidelines
- plans for co-instructional activities
- class size
- minimum teaching time—elementary
- minimum teaching time—secondary
- trustee honoraria and expenses
- application of funds contrary to the Legislative Grant Regulations.

In addition, a school council or a supporter of the board can complain to the Minister that the board has passed a motion or resolution indicating an intention to violate the above statutory requirements (s. 230.1(1)).

The Minister may direct an investigation of the board in response to his or her own concerns or in response to a complaint. If the report of the investigator discloses evidence of non-compliance or that the board will likely be in non-compliance, the Minister may issue directions to the board to address the matter. If the board fails to comply with the direction, the Minister may seek a vesting order from the Ontario Cabinet, giving the Ministry charge and control over the administration of the affairs of the board and the Act gives the Minister extensive powers in this regard (s. 230.5 to s. 230.17), including dismissing any officer or employee of the board who fails to obey an order, direction or decision of the Minister.

These "compliance" provisions were enacted to address the fact that the Minister had few practical means to force school boards to comply with the Act, short of taking them to court or withholding grants. Moreover, it provided a specific vehicle for persons to "complain" to the Minister.

Procedurally, the provisions share much in common with those found at section 257.30 to section 257.52, but the latter provisions do not have a complaint section and they are specifically designed to address situations in which the Minister has concerns about a board's financial affairs.

Investigation Where There are Financial Concerns

The Minister of Education can direct an investigation of the financial affairs of a board if:

- the financial statements or auditor's report indicate that the board had a deficit
- the board fails to make a debenture or interest payment on time
- the board fails to meet any other debt or liability on time
- the Minister has concerns about the board's ability to meet its financial obligations. (See s. 257.30(1).)

Direction

On receiving the investigator's report, Minister may give directions to the board to address its financial affairs. If it fails to comply with the Minister's directions, or if the investigator's report recommends assumption of control, the Lieutenant Governor in Council may make an order vesting in the Ministry control and charge over the administration of the affairs of the board (s. 257.31(2), (3)).

Supervision

The Act sets out very extensive supervision powers of the Minister (s. 257.30 to s. 257.52). However, a supervision order does not authorize the Minister to interfere with or control the denominational aspects of a Roman Catholic board or Protestant separate school board, or the linguistic or cultural aspects of a French-language district school board. It does give the Minister control over staffing, budgeting, accounting/auditing systems, borrowing, and disposition of assets. The order is revoked when the board is no longer in debt or when otherwise specified by the Lieutenant Governor in Council. Thus, supervision is not of indefinite duration.

The power to supervise a board is not new. Very similar provisions respecting both municipalities and school boards have been found in the *Municipal Affairs Act*, (Part III), since the 1930s. The amendments in the

Education Quality Improvement Act, 1997 essentially transferred the supervision powers into the *Education Act*. The need for supervision reflects the fact that school boards are a form of local government, created by provincial statute. They are legally prohibited from budgeting for a deficit. If they run into financial difficulty, the province must be able to step in, investigate, and if necessary, assume control.

(c) How Much Do Trustees Get Paid?

The maximum annual honorarium for a district school board member is $5,000 (s. 191(2)). A chair or vice-chair may receive an additional honorarium of up to $5,000. Members may also be reimbursed for out-of-pocket expenses. A board may no longer provide insured benefits to its members. Board members are not considered "employees" of the board, and are not entitled to employment-related benefits such as severance. The *Education Act* provides that honoraria for members of school authorities, including the chair and vice-chair, may be established by regulation. Until a regulation is made, school authorities are limited to what they were paying in 1996.

(d) Are Board Meetings Open to the Public?

Meetings of the board and its committees are open to the public (s. 207). The location of a board meeting is determined by the board (ss. 208(2) and (6)). The public may be excluded when a committee of the board (including committee of the whole) is considering an item that is one of the following:

- the security of the property of the board
- disclosure of intimate, personal or financial information about a board or committee member, an employee, a prospective employee of the board, a pupil or a pupil's parent or guardian
- acquisition or disposal of a school site
- decisions about negotiations with employees
- litigation affecting the board

Trustees and board employees must also comply with the *Municipal Freedom of Information and Protection of Privacy Act*. Disclosure of certain confidential items outside the confines of a closed meeting could result in an offence being committed under that Act. All trustees (and employees) should be provided with information about their obligations under the legislation. They should also be aware that the *Education Act* requires that student records be kept secret (s. 266).

A person who is guilty of "improper conduct" at a board meeting may be expelled from it by the presiding officer (s. 207(3)). It is an offence to disrupt a meeting from which one has been expelled (s. 212(2)).

Subject to specific statutory exceptions, a board is entitled to determine its own procedures for meetings. These are usually set out in the board's by-laws. For example, the board may determine the rules and time limits for presentations by delegations. If the board is conducting a "hearing" (e.g. expulsion hearing) it must adhere to the applicable provision of the *Education Act* and the *Statutory Powers Procedure Act*.

(e) Can a Board Hold Electronic Meetings?

The *Education Quality Improvement Act, 1997*, gave district school boards the authority to hold electronic meetings. This was a timely change, given the huge geographic area of many of these boards. Ontario Regulation 463/97 states that every district school board shall develop a policy providing for the use of electronic means for holding meetings of the board and its committees. The policy must be consistent with any policies or guidelines issued by the Minister about electronic meetings. The board's policy must provide that a board member or a pupil representative shall be provided with the means of participating in meetings by electronic means and must be able to hear and be heard by all the other participants (see s. 3 of O. Reg. 463/97).

Subject to Ministry policies and guidelines, the board shall determine whether the *public* is to be able to participate by electronic means, and if so, the extent and manner of participation. In all cases, it is vital that precautions be taken so that persons who are not eligible to attend closed meetings do not have access to them through electronic means.

Section 229 of the Act requires members to be physically present at a meeting of the board at least three times during each twelve-month period commencing December 1st. The board can increase this minimum number. The board chair (or designate), at least one other member and the director of education (or designate) must be physically present in the meeting room of the board. At *committee* meetings the chair of the committee (or designate) and the director (or designate) must be physically present at the meeting. (Section 5, O. Reg. 463/97.) Except where a meeting is closed in accordance with the *Education Act*, the meeting room of the board or a committee must be open to those who wish to attend.

See generally sections 8(1)[3.6], 208.1, and 229 of the *Education Act*.

1.4 OTHER VOICES

(a) Do Pupils Have a Right to Serve on a School Board?

Yes, the appointment or election of at least one pupil representative is required. The *Education Act* gives boards specific authority in this respect. Section 8(1)[3.5] says that the Minister of Education may "establish policies and guidelines for the development and implementation of board policies dealing with the representation on boards of the interests of pupils and require boards to comply with the policies and guidelines". The Lieutenant Governor in Council may make regulations providing for representation on boards, by peer election or by appointment, of the interests of pupils in Grades 7 and 8 and in secondary school. A pupil representative may be reimbursed for out-of-pocket expenses in connection with his or her duties. A pupil representative is not a member of the board and is not entitled to be present at a *closed* meeting of the board or board committee (s. 55).

Ontario Regulation 461/97 deals with pupil representation. Every board must have a policy on pupil representation. A board *must* have at least one pupil representative but may have more than one. The board's policy is to specify whether the representative is to be selected by peer election or by appointment, and the election or appointment procedures. While pupil representatives cannot vote in or attend closed meetings, they are otherwise to be afforded the same opportunity to participate at meetings of the board and its committees as board members are.

(b) How are Native Persons Represented on a School Board?

Section 188 of the *Education Act* used to provide for the appointment of one or two trustees (depending on proportion of enrolment of native pupils to all pupils) to be appointed by a band, band council or education authority that had an agreement (commonly referred to as a "tuition agreement") with a board to provide education to native pupils. Part of section 188 was repealed by the *Education Quality Improvement Act, 1997*, and a new regulation-making power was enacted under which the Lieutenant Governor in Council may make regulations providing for native representation on school boards. Ontario Regulation 462/97, filed on December 11, 1997, deals with native representation. In large part, it mirrors the requirements that were formerly contained in section 188. Where a board has one or more tuition agreements under s. 188 of the Act, the *council* of the band may appoint one person to "represent the interests of the Indian pupils". The person appointed is deemed to be an elected member of the board. If the tuition agreement(s) only covers elementary pupils, the representative may not vote on secondary school issues. If the tuition agreement(s) only covers secondary pupils, the representative may not vote on elementary school issues. Two native representatives may be appointed if the native pupils covered by the agreement(s) represent over 25 per cent of the total average daily enrolment of the board.

The right to appoint a native trustee only arises if there is one or more agreements between the band council and the board. There is no legal obligation upon the board to enter into any such agreement. There is also no requirement that the appointed representative be of native ancestry. However, a person appointed to a Roman Catholic board must be a Roman Catholic and at least 18 years of age. A person appointed to a French-language district school board must be a French-language rights holder and at least 18 years of age.

1.5 EDUCATION FINANCE

(a) Where Does the School Board Get its Money from?

A district school board gets revenue from:

- residential property tax revenue from its school supporters
- business property tax revenue shared between coterminous boards on the basis of pupil enrolment
- provincial grants
- education development charges
- other sources such as non-resident tuition fees, lease or sale of property, donations, interest income, transfer from reserves, and cafeteria revenue.

(b) What Kinds of "Grants" Are There?

There are three components to the current funding model:

- Foundation Grant
- Special Purpose Grants
- Pupil Accommodation Grant.

Foundation Grant

The Foundation Grant is intended to cover the basic cost of providing education to a pupil for one school year. It is allocated on a per-pupil basis and this annual amount is the same for all boards across Ontario. The amount for secondary school pupils is higher than that for elementary school pupils because it costs more to deliver secondary school education. The Foundation Grant covers:

- salaries and benefits for classroom teachers, occasional (i.e. supply) teachers and professional development for teachers
- salaries and benefits of teachers' assistants
- text books and learning materials
- classroom supplies
- classroom computers
- salaries and benefits for school librarians and guidance counsellors
- professional and para-professional support staff
- salaries and benefits for additional teachers who teach while others are on "preparation time" (i.e. not in the classroom)
- salaries and benefits for teacher consultants
- salaries and benefits for school principals and vice-principals and others involved in school administration
- local priorities amount.

The government calculates what boards should be spending on these items and then establishes an annual amount that is used in the annual Grant Regulation.

Special Purpose Grants

Special Purpose Grants reflect the additional costs of meeting the special needs of pupils or the special circumstances of boards:

- Special Education Per Pupil Amount, which goes to every board to cover the cost of providing additional assistance to the majority of pupils with special needs
- Intensive Support Amount (ISA), which covers the needs of specific pupils who require high-cost assistance

- Learning Opportunities Grant to cover the cost of educating pupils who are at greater risk of academic failure because of their social or economic circumstances; this is based on four factors: family income, parental education, recent immigration and aboriginal status
- Geographic Circumstances Grant for boards with small schools or which qualify as "remote and rural".
- Language Grant, which supports:
  - French as a first language
  - French as a second language
  - Native language
  - English as second language and English skills development
  - Actualisation Linguistique en Français and Perfectionnement du Français
- Early Learning Grant for use to support programs in Grades 1 to 3 in areas where the board does not offer Junior Kindergarten (Junior Kindergarten funding comes from the Foundation Grant, other Special Purpose Grants, and the Pupil Accommodation Grants)
- Continuing Education Grant (including elementary international language programs Adult ESL, and prior learning assessment)
- Teacher Qualification and Experience Grant, which cushions the cost of having teachers on staff whose qualifications and experience result in higher than average salary costs
- Transportation Grant, which covers the cost of transporting pupils to and from school
- School Board Administration and Governance Grant, which is intended to cover the cost of operating board offices and central facilities, including salaries and benefits for directors, supervisory officers, clerical support, and trustee honoraria and expenses
- Learning Opportunities Grant, for early literacy, remedial literacy and mathematics, and students at risk.

Pupil Accommodation Grant

The Pupil Accommodation Grant has the following components:

- New Pupil Places, to acquire new space for pupils if the board has exceeded its capacity
- School Renewal, to cover the cost of repairing and renovating schools
- School Operation, to cover such things as heating, lighting, maintaining and cleaning schools

- Capital Debt Servicing, to help boards meet debt service costs arising from previous capital debt commitments.

(c) What Is a "Classroom" or "Non-Classroom" Expenditure?

CLASSROOM EXPENDITURES	NON-CLASSROOM EXPENDITURES
• classroom teachers • occasional teachers • teacher assistants • textbooks and learning materials • computers • professional and para-professional support • library and guidance • staff development	• preparation time • principals and vice-principals • department heads • school secretaries • trustees • directors and supervisory officers • board administration • school operations • continuing education • transportation

(d) Who Decides How Much Education Tax I Have to Pay? Where Does the Money Go?

The Minister of Finance establishes a single tax rate to be applied to the residential assessment base of each municipality for school purposes. The tax rate is applied to the assessment of residential property and collected by each municipality in the area of jurisdiction of the board, on behalf of the board. The amount is forwarded to the board designated by the occupant of the property (English-language public; English-language Roman Catholic; French-language public; French-language Roman Catholic; Protestant Separate). If there is no municipal organization in the area and the area is not otherwise attached to a municipality, then one of the boards, usually the English-language public board, collects the taxes and distributes them to each board having jurisdiction in the area.

Roman Catholics may designate themselves as separate school supporters. French-language right-holders may designate themselves as French-language school supporters. If tax support is not specifically designated, the occupant is deemed to be an English-language public school supporter. Private corporations can designate residential taxes to separate or French language boards to the extent that the corporation's shares are owned by individuals with these designation rights. Partnerships can designate residential taxes to separate or French language boards to the extent of the interest in the assets of the partnership of the partners with these designation rights.

With respect to business property, the Minister of Finance may prescribe tax rates for different classes of business property (e.g. commercial, industrial, pipe line). The rates are applied to the business assessment in each municipality and forwarded to the school boards on the basis of their pupil enrolment. The "enrolment shares" are determined by the Ministry using enrolment data. Different tax rates may be prescribed in different municipalities. Property classes are defined in the *Assessment Act*. Different tax rates are possible for different business and residential classes. Municipalities are to remit taxes at least four times per year (s. 257.11).

Calculation of Grant

Grants to school boards are calculated in accordance with the annual Grant Regulation, which contains numerous formulas and tables to be used by the business officials of the board. From the total possible grant receivable by the board, the board must subtract the revenue gained from residential and business property taxes. The resulting difference is the board's "grant entitlement". The total amount of money that a board gets is no longer dependent on the wealth of the local assessment base. In some areas, however, a bigger proportion the board's revenue is raised locally than in other areas. Under the "old" funding system, the school board had to levy a provincially prescribed mill rate but was also able to raise taxes beyond the provincial mill rate (i.e. above the "ceiling"). The *Education Act* no longer enables a board to set its own tax rates or determine how much money to requisition from the municipality for school purposes.

Education Development Charges

School boards that lack capacity (i.e. classroom space) within their existing schools and need new sites for schools because of residential development may impose education development charges on residential and non-residential land undergoing development. The statutory provisions that deal with education development charges were moved from the *Development Charges Act* to the *Education Act* as a result of the *Education Quality Improvement Act, 1997* (See ss. 257.53 to 257.105). Pupil accommodation grants are intended to cover capital costs other than new site acquisitions.

(e) Does the *Education Act* Guarantee Fair Funding?

The *Education Act* (ss. 234(2) and (3)) says that a regulation governing grants for educational purposes must ensure that the legislation and regulations operate in a *fair and non-discriminatory* manner,

* as between English-language public boards and English-language Roman Catholic boards
* as between French-language public district school boards and French-language Roman Catholic district school boards
* and so as to respect the rights given by section 23 of the *Canadian Charter of Rights and Freedoms.*

(f) What Is "Enveloping"?

"Enveloping" describes the requirement that a school board must spend its money for the purpose or purposes for which it is intended. For instance, a board may not use "classroom" money for non-classroom purposes. This would infringe a condition upon which the grant was given by the province and could lead to the Minister withholding part of the board's grant money. Within the envelope, the board may exercise its discretion as to how the money is spent.

(g) How Are School Trustees Held Financially Accountable?

Every year, the treasurer of the board must prepare the financial statements of the board. Two copies of the statements, along with the auditor's report, are sent to the Minister. These statements and the auditor's report must be made public (s. 252(2)). Publication in the local newspaper is the usual method.

Every board must have one or more auditors (s. 253(1)). They are appointed for up to five years. Their duties may be prescribed by the Minister of Education and by the school board. An auditor has a right of access to all records of the board and can require any information and explanation that in the auditor's opinion may be necessary to enable the auditor to carry out his or her duties. It is an offence for a trustee or board officer not to co-operate with the auditor by withholding information and access to records (s. 253(6)). An auditor has a right to attend any meeting of the board or a committee of the board.

The Minister has extensive powers to obtain information from a board. Under section 8(1) [27.1], the Minister may require a board,

(a)   to prepare any report that the Minister may require,
(b)   to submit, in the form directed by the Minister, a copy of the report to the Ministry and to such other persons as the Minister may direct,
(c)   to attach a copy of the report to the financial statements of the board referred to in section 252.

The Minister may also designate a provincial supervisory officer or other person to have access to any school and to the books and records of a board or a school (s. 286(5)).

There are many financial safeguards in the *Education Act* that govern the use of public money by the board. For instance, the Act prescribes, through regulation, the kinds of securities that a board may invest in. The Act sets out a board's investment powers, including how it may borrow its capital and reserve funds to finance current needs. The government may, by regulation, provide for "debt, financial obligation and liability limits for boards or classes of boards" (s. 242). "Current borrowing" by boards, to meet their day-to-day financial needs and debt charges, is permitted by section 243, but a board may not borrow more money than it expects to receive in the year, according to its estimates. School boards may issue debentures. In the case of a Roman Catholic school board, this includes a "mortgage" (ss. 244 and 245). Boards may also borrow money or incur debt for permanent improvements. The details on this are prescribed in the regulations made under s. 247 of the Act. There are also stringent requirements about how a board may dispose of a school or school site. (See s. 194 of the Act and O. Reg. 444/98.)

The Minister may withhold grants from a board that is not in compliance with the *Education Act* and regulations or any other Act that is assigned to the Minister.

(h) Can a Board Incur a Deficit?

A board is required to prepare and adopt estimates of its revenues and expenditures. In doing so, it "shall ensure that its estimated expenditures do not exceed its estimated revenues" (s. 231(2)). Section 231(1)(g) says that the estimates "shall not provide for any deficit" except that the board must provide in its estimates for a deficit that occurred in the previous fiscal year or that is projected to occur from the previous fiscal year.

Therefore:

(1) a board may not intentionally provide for, or estimate for, a deficit and
(2) if a deficit does occur, it must be dealt with in the estimates for the next fiscal year.

(i) Does the Board Get a Financial Windfall if There is a Strike or Lock-Out?

No, a board does not get a windfall when it does not have to pay the salary of teachers or other employees who are on strike or are locked out. The board must calculate the savings that result from the strike in accordance with Ontario Regulation 486/98 and must place that amount in its reserves. At the end of the fiscal year, the reserve amount is brought into the board's general revenues for that fiscal year and will be off-set against its grant entitlement. (See s. 233.)

2

Going to School

The *Education Act* governs who has a right to go to school and who *must* go to school. This is an important distinction; just because a person has a right to attend school does not mean he or she must attend. The Act only *requires* children who are of "compulsory school age" to attend school unless they are legally excused from attending. Logically, the right to attend is different for elementary and secondary schools. For example, the age limit to attend elementary school is 21 years; there is no age limit to attend secondary school (although some pupils may be directed to continuing education courses, and pupils may be required to pay a fee after seven years in secondary school). There are minimum age limits only in respect of when a board *must* admit a pupil to school.

2.1 THE RIGHT TO ATTEND SCHOOL

(a) Where Do I Have a Right to Attend School?

The *Education Act* uses many words to say that you can attend school where you and your parent or guardian live. Actually, it isn't quite that simple, as this chapter explains. Here's the legal labyrinth:

(b) Elementary School Attendance

You have a right to attend elementary school if you are "qualified to be a resident pupil" of a board. The following steps will help you determine if you are "qualified":

Step One — How Old Are You?

IF ENTERING GRADE ONE	IF ENTERING KINDERGARTEN	IF ENTERING JUNIOR KINDERGARTEN
If you attain 6 years of age during the year you can enter school in September of that year. You can stay in school until the last school day in June in the year in which you attain 21 years of age (s. 33).	If you attain 5 years of age during the year you can enter school in September of that year. You can stay in school until the last school day in June in the year in which you attain 21 years of age (s. 34).	If you attain 4 years of age during the year you can enter school in September of that year (if JK is offered). You can stay in school until the last school day in June in the year in which you attain 21 years of age (s. 34).

Step Two — Where Do You Live?

The person must reside in the board's jurisdiction and a parent or guardian of the person must reside in the board's jurisdiction (s. 33).

Step Three — Additional Requirements

French-language public DSB	English-language public DSB or public school authority	French-language separate	English-language separate (or Roman Catholic school authority)
1. Must be a French-speaking person (see definition below). 2. Parent or guardian is either not a tax supporter or, if entitled to be a tax supporter, directs support to the French-language public board.	1. Parent or guardian must *not* be a separate school supporter or French-language board supporter.	1. Must be a French-speaking person. 2. Parent or guardian must be Roman Catholic. 3. Parent or guardian must direct tax to the French-language separate board.	1. Parent or guardian must be Roman Catholic. 2. Parent or guardian must direct tax support to the English-language separate board.

Step Four — Enrolment

To be a "pupil", you have to enrol in a school operated by the board (or in another board's school under an arrangement between the two boards) (s. 33(6)).

(c) Secondary School Attendance

You have a right to attend secondary school if you are "qualified to be a resident pupil" of a board in respect of secondary school. The following steps will help you determine if you are "qualified". There is no specified age requirement for attending secondary school.

French-language public DSB	English-language public DSB	French-language separate DSB	English-language separate DSB
(A) Person and parent/guardian reside in board's jurisdiction *and* the parent or guardian is either not a tax supporter or, if entitled to be a tax supporter, directs support to the French-language public board.	(A) Person and parent/guardian reside in board's jurisdiction *and* the parent/guardian is not a separate school supporter or a French-language DSB supporter	(A) Person and parent/guardian reside in the board's jurisdiction *and* the parent/guardian directs tax support to the board (Must be Roman Catholic and a French-speaking person to direct support to the board)	(A) Person and parent/guardian reside in the board's jurisdiction *and* the parent/guardian directs tax support to the board (Must be Roman Catholic to direct support to the board)
or	or	or	or
(B) Person is a tax supporter of the board (therefore French-speaking), resides in the board's jurisdiction, *and* is the owner or tenant of separately assessed residential property in the board's jurisdiction	(B) Person is a tax supporter of the board, resides in the board's jurisdiction *and* is the owner or tenant of separately assessed residential property in the board's jurisdiction	(B) Person is a tax supporter of the board, (therefore Roman Catholic) resides in the board's jurisdiction *and* is the owner or tenant of separately assessed residential property in the board's jurisdiction	(B) Person is a tax supporter of the board (therefore Roman Catholic), resides in the board's jurisdiction *and* is the owner or tenant of separately assessed residential property in the board's jurisdiction
or	or	or	or
(C) Person is over 18 years of age, has resided in the board's jurisdiction for 12 months immediately before admission, and is not a tax supporter of any board.	(C) Person is over 18 years of age, has resided in the board's jurisdiction for 12 months immediately before admission, and is not a tax supporter of any board.	(C) Person is over 18 years of age, has resided in the board's jurisdiction for 12 months immediately before admission, and is not a tax supporter of any board.	(C) Person is over 18 years of age, has resided in the board's jurisdiction for 12 months immediately before admission, and is not a tax supporter of any board.
Person must be a French-speaking person.		Person must be a French-speaking person. Parent/guardian must be Roman Catholic under (A). Person must be Roman Catholic under (B) and (C).	Parent/guardian must be Roman Catholic under (A). Person must be Roman Catholic under (B) and (C).

Enrolment and Admission — Secondary School

To be a "pupil", you have to enrol in a secondary school operated by the board (or in another board's school under an arrangement between the two boards) (s. 36(5)).

A pupil will be admitted to secondary school if the pupil has been promoted from "elementary school" (a defined term) (s. 41(1)).

A person who has not been promoted from elementary school shall be admitted if the principal of the secondary school is satisfied that the applicant "is competent to undertake the work of the school" (s. 41(2)).

If you are refused admission to secondary school by the principal, you may appeal the principal's decision to the school board (s. 41(3)).

Definitions

"French-speaking person" means a child of a person who has the right under subsection 23(1) or (2), without regard to subsection 23(3), of the *Canadian Charter of Rights and Freedoms* to have his or her children receive their primary and secondary school instruction in the French language in Ontario.

Note that the "person" being defined is the child, but the child's rights depend upon whether his or her parents have section 23 *Charter* rights. Section 23 of the *Charter* states:

23(1) Citizens of Canada
- (a) whose first language learned and still understood is that of the English or French linguistic minority population of the province in which they reside, or
- (b) who have received their primary school instruction in Canada in English or French and reside in a province where the language in which they received that instruction is the language of the English or French linguistic minority population of the province

have the right to have their children receive primary and secondary school instruction in that language in that province.

(2) Citizens of Canada of whom any child has received or is receiving primary or secondary school instruction in English or French in Canada, have the right to have all their children receive primary and secondary school instruction in the same language.

(3) The right of citizens of Canada under subsection (1) and (2) to have their children receive primary and secondary school instruction in the language of the English or French linguistic minority population of a province
- (a) applies wherever in the province the number of children of citizens who have such

a right is sufficient to warrant the provision to them out of public funds of minority language instruction; and

(b) includes, where the number of those children so warrants, the right to have them receive that instruction in minority language education facilities provided out of public funds.

Education Act, section 1:

"guardian" means a person who has lawful custody of a child, other than the parent of the child.

"separate school supporter" means an English-language Roman Catholic board supporter or a French-language separate district school board supporter.

"English-language Roman Catholic board supporter" means a Roman Catholic,

(a) who is shown as an English-language Roman Catholic board supporter on the school support list as prepared or revised by the assessment commissioner under section 16 of the *Assessment Act*, or

(b) who is declared to be an English-language Roman Catholic board supporter as a result of a final decision rendered in proceedings commenced under the *Assessment Act*,

and includes his or her Roman Catholic spouse.

"English-language public board supporter" means a person who is an owner or tenant of residential property in the area of jurisdiction of a board and who is not,

(a) a separate school supporter,

(b) a French-language public district school board supporter, or

(c) a Protestant separate school board supporter.

"French-language separate district school board supporter" means a Roman Catholic French-language rights holder,

(a) who is shown as a French-language separate district school board supporter on the school support list as prepared or revised by the assessment commissioner under section 16 of the *Assessment Act*, or

(b) who is declared to be a French-language separate district school board supporter as a result of a final decision rendered in proceedings commenced under the *Assessment Act*,

and includes his or her Roman Catholic spouse if the spouse is a French-language rights holder.

"French-language public district school board supporter" means a French-language rights holder,

(a) who is shown as a French-language public district school board supporter on the school support list as prepared or revised by the assessment commissioner under section 16 of the *Assessment Act*, or

(b) who is declared to be a French-language district school board supporter as a result of a final decision rendered in proceedings commenced under the *Assessment Act*,

and includes his or her spouse or same-sex partner if the spouse or same-sex partner is a French-language rights holder.

Is there a Right to Attend Continuing Education Courses?

A board is not required to offer continuing education courses or classes. (International languages at the elementary level offered in accordance with Reg. 285 are an exception.) If continuing education is offered, a person is entitled to enrol in a credit course or class if the principal is satisfied that the person is competent to undertake the work of the course or class (s. 41(6)).

(d) Special Attendance Rules

Switching from a School Authority to a District School Board for Secondary Education

If you are qualified to be a resident pupil in a school authority that only provides elementary education and is *not* a *public* school authority, you have a right to attend secondary school provided by a public district school board that shares geographic jurisdiction with the school authority. This is designed to protect the secondary school attendance rights of pupils who are attending an elementary school operated by a rural separate school board, combined separate school board, or Protestant separate school board. (However, attendance under this section at a French-language public district school board is still conditional upon the person being a French-speaking person.) (Subsections 36(6), (7).)

Non-Resident Secondary School Pupils Switching Boards

If
(i)   you are 18 years of age or older,
(ii)   you have been promoted or transferred to secondary school,
(iii) you would qualify as a resident pupil of a board except for the fact that you do not reside in the board's jurisdiction,
(iv) you reside in the jurisdiction of another school board,

then:

the other board, (i.e. where you reside) must admit you, without fee, to a secondary school of the same type (English-language public, French-language public, English-language Roman Catholic, French-language Roman Catholic), if its supervisory officer certifies that it can accommodate you (s. 37).

Going to a More Accessible Elementary School

If you are qualified as a resident pupil for elementary school, you may attend an elementary school of the same type (English-language public, French-language public, English-language Roman Catholic, French-language Roman Catholic) at another board that is nearer to your residence than the school you are required to attend in your "home" board. For this to apply, your home board's school must be at least 3.2 kilometres from your residence, and 0.8 kilometres from the point from which transportation is provided (s. 35).

Going to a More Accessible Secondary School

If you are qualified as a resident pupil to attend secondary school, you may attend a secondary school of the same type (English-language public, French-language public, English-language Roman Catholic, French-language Roman Catholic) at another board if it is more accessible than any secondary school at your "home" board. This attendance right is conditional upon a supervisory officer certifying that the receiving board can accommodate you (s. 39(1)(a)).

You may also use this provision to go to a secondary school at another board in order to take secondary courses that you need to get your diploma, to enter university or college or to enter a trade, profession or calling, presumably because your "home" board does not offer the courses (s. 39(1)(b)). However, this does not apply if your home board has made an agreement with another board to provide the relevant subjects (s. 39(4)).

Living on Tax-Exempt Land

A person who resides on tax-exempt land is not treated as a true "resident" of a board. The person shall be admitted by the board to an accessible school (if otherwise qualified) if the board has space for the person "for the current year". This person can be charged fees in accordance with the annual "Calculation of Fees" regulation. (See s. 46.)

However, if the person or his/her parent or guardian is assessed for education taxes for the board, then he or she can qualify as a resident pupil (and therefore must be admitted in the usual manner). For example, if you live on Crown land but your parent owns or rents a property in the board's jurisdiction on which education taxes are assessed, then you are eligible to qualify as a resident pupil.

There are special attendance rights for people who reside on Defence property owned by Canada (s. 46.1) to enable them to attend school without payment of a fee in the municipality where the defence establishment is located.

Sole Support Parent

If a person is supported by only one parent and the parent

(1)   resides in Ontario in a residence that is not assessed for school purposes, and
(2)   boards the person in a residence

then the person (if otherwise qualified as a resident pupil) is deemed to be qualified to be a resident pupil in the area where the residence is located, and in accordance with the tax support of the residence (s. 45).

(This does not include a children's residence under Part IX of the *Child and Family Services Act*.)

Ward of Children's Aid Society or Training School

If a child is in the care of or a ward of a Children's Aid Society or a ward of a training school, he or she can attend school in the jurisdiction where he or she resides. The child must be otherwise qualified to be admitted to elementary or secondary school.

Child in Custody of a Corporation or Society

A child who is in the custody of a "corporation" or "society" and who does not have a right to attend the school where the corporation or society has sent him or her, shall be admitted to the school if there is sufficient accommodation for the current year (assuming that the child is otherwise qualified to be admitted). The regulations may prescribe fees to be paid by the corporation or society to the board.

What is the "Seven Year" Rule for Charging Fees?

Where a pupil has completed elementary school and has attended one or more secondary schools for a total of seven or more years, the board may charge the pupil a fee under the regulations (s. 38). This section is often misunderstood to mean that you have a right to attend secondary school for only seven years. In fact the limitation is only as to whether a fee may be charged. In some jurisdictions, this resulted in adults attending school for reasons that had nothing to do with obtaining a diploma or qualifying for post-secondary school entry. In 1996, the Legislature enacted provisions that would make it easier for a board to redirect an adult pupil into continuing education courses. These provisions are found in section 49.2. They include protection for exceptional pupils who have been placed in a day school program, and for pupils who need courses not offered in the continuing education program for the purpose of obtaining a secondary school diploma, to qualify for admission to a university or college of applied arts and technology, or to enter a trade, profession or calling.

Can a Child Attend School Even if His or Her Parent is Unlawfully in Canada?

Yes, a person who is otherwise entitled to be admitted to school and who is less than 18 years of age cannot be refused admission because the child's parent or guardian is unlawfully in Canada (s. 49.1).

(e) Movement of Secondary School Pupils between Public and Separate Boards

When separate school boards were given the right to have public funding in order to "extend" their secondary school to offer all secondary grade levels, the *Education Act* provided that there would be "open access" at the secondary school level for public school pupils and separate school pupils. This basic concept was preserved in the amendments found in the *Education Quality Improvement Act, 1997*, and are now found in section 42 of the *Education Act*. To make sense of them, it is important to refer to the definitions of the different kinds of "boards" in the *Education Act*. Some terms include "school authorities" and some do not.

Open access occurs where the boards are coterminous, i.e. share part or all of their (geographic) areas of jurisdiction. It only applies to secondary education.

RESIDENT PUPIL OF:		MAY ATTEND:
English-language public board	→	English-language Roman Catholic board
French-language public DSB	→	French-language separate DSB
English-language Roman Catholic board	→	English-language public board
French-language separate DSB	→	French-language public DSB
French-language separate DSB	→	English-language public board
French-speaking person — pupil of English-language public board	→	French-language separate DSB
French-language public DSB	→	English-language separate DSB
French-speaking person — pupil of English-language separate DSB	→	French-language public DSB

(f) Movement between French-Language and English-Language Boards

The *Education Act* provides for movement between French-language district school boards and English-language district school boards that are coterminous. However, a qualified resident pupil of an English-language board who is not a French-speaking person has no right to transfer to a French-language district school board. Movement under section 43 is permitted at the elementary and secondary level. Section 43 covers only public-to-public and separate-to-separate transfers.

RESIDENT PUPIL OF:		MAY ATTEND:
French-speaking person – pupil of English-language public board	→	French-language public DSB
French-language public DSB	→	English-language public board
French-speaking person – pupil of English-language Roman Catholic board	→	French-language separate DSB
French-language separate DSB	→	English-language Roman Catholic board

What Happens if a Person has Moved into a Residence but has not had Time to Change Tax Support?

If you move into a residence that is assessed for the "wrong" type of tax support for the school that you want to attend, you can still attend the school if you file a notice of change of support for the following year. For example, to attend a separate school, you must be a separate school supporter. If you move into a residence that is assessed for public school purposes and you are past the deadline to change your tax support to the separate school board, you can still attend a separate school if you file the notice for next year (s. 44).

Can a Board Admit a Person Even if He or She Does Not Have the Right to Attend One of its Schools?

As can be seen from the above references, the *Education Act* covers many situations in which a board either "shall" or "may" admit a person to school. What happens if the Act does not specifically cover a situation? A board has considerable discretion to admit a person to its schools where there is no provision in the Act that specifically covers the circumstances.

For example, section 32(2) states:

Despite the other provisions of this Part, but subject to subsection 49(6), where it appears to a board that a person who resides in the area of jurisdiction of the board is denied the right to attend school without the payment of a fee, the board, at its discretion, may admit the person from year to year without the payment of a fee.

Note, this covers persons who are resident in the board's jurisdiction.

Section 49(5) states:

A board may admit to a school that it operates a person whose admission with or without the payment of a fee is not otherwise provided for in this Act but who, except as to residence, is qualified to attend such school, and may, at its discretion, require the payment by or on behalf of a person of the fee, if any, payable for the purpose under the regulations.

Note, this covers persons who are not resident in the board's jurisdiction, and permits discretion as to whether or not a fee will be charged. The fee is calculated in accordance with the applicable regulation.

A French-language district school board may admit persons who are not French-speaking persons (s. 293). A school authority that operates a French-language instructional unit also has this discretionary power.

Must a Board Charge a Fee to a Non-Resident?

There are several instances where a board has the discretion as to whether or not to charge a fee to a non-resident pupil. However, if a board admits a person who is a temporary resident within the meaning of the

Immigration and Refugee Protection Act (Canada) or a person who is in possession of a study permit under that Act, the board *must* charge the person the maximum fee calculated under the regulations (s. 49(6)), subject to specific exceptions for diplomats, refugees and others set out in section 49(7).

2.2 COMPULSORY SCHOOL ATTENDANCE

(a) Does a Child Have to Go to School?

Thus far, this chapter has discussed whether a person has a right to go to school. But does anyone have a right to make you go to school? Yes. Every child of compulsory school age must attend school unless legally excused from attendance. Compulsory school age is often referred to being between ages "6 and 16". The statutory provisions are slightly different. To paraphrase:

    (a) If a child turns six on or before the first school day in September, he or she must start attending school commencing with the first school day in September of that school year. The child must attend school until he or she turns 16. There is no obligation to finish out the school year once the child turns 16.

    (b) If a child turns six after the first school day in September, he or she must start attending school from the first school day in September of the *next following* school year. The child must attend school until the *last school day in June* in the year in which he or she turns 16. The child finishes the school year, but has no obligation to start the next September even though his or her 16th birthday lies somewhere between September and December.

(b) What are the "Legal Excuses" for Not Attending School?

Children have devised many excuses for not showing up for school, but the *Education Act* has the "official" list (s. 21(2)(a)-(h)).

    (a) the child is receiving satisfactory instruction at home or elsewhere;

The Act does not define "satisfactory instruction". It is a duty of a board, through its local school attendance counsellor, to ensure that all children of compulsory school age in the board's jurisdiction attend school unless legally excused.

A board has a duty to find out if absent children are being educated. Because parents, in the absence of a legal excuse, have the obligation to send their children to school (s. 21(5)), they should take reasonable steps to satisfy board officials that their child is legally excused. The Supreme Court of Canada has confirmed the need for parents to comply with compulsory education laws. *R. v. Jones*, 69 N.R. 241, [1986] 2 S.C.R. 284, (*sub nom. Jones v. R.*) 31 D.L.R. (4th) 569, [1986] 6 W.W.R. 577, 47 Alta. L.R. (2d) 97, 73 A.R. 133, 28 C.C.C. (3d) 513, (*sub nom. Jones v. R.*) 25 C.R.R. 63, 1986 CarswellAlta 181, 1986 CarswellAlta 716 (S.C.C.)). However, a board official does not have a right to enter any premises without the occupier's consent to discover if satisfactory instruction is being delivered.

Being educated "elsewhere" usually means that the child is enrolled in a private (independent) school.

> (b) the child is unable to attend school by reason of sickness or other unavoidable cause;

Note: if medical reasons require that a child be educated at home, the principal can arrange "home instruction" to be provided by a board teacher (s. 11(11), Reg. 298). This should not be confused with "home schooling". Home instruction is provided by the board.

> (c) transportation is not provided by a board for the child and there is no school that the child has a right to attend situated,
>   (i)   within 1.6 kilometres from the child's residence measured by the nearest road if the child has not attained the age of seven years on or before the first school day in September in the year in question, or
>   (ii) within 3.2 kilometres from the child's residence measured by the nearest road if the child has attained the age of seven years but not the age of ten years on or before the first day of school in September in the year in question, or
>   (iii) within 4.8 kilometres from the child's residence measured by the nearest road if the child has attained the age of ten years on or before the first school day in September in the year in question;
> (d) the child has obtained a secondary school graduation diploma or has completed a course that gives equivalent standing;
> (e) the child is absent from school for the purpose of receiving instruction in music and the period of absence does not exceed one-half day any week;
> (f) the child is suspended, expelled or excluded from attendance at school under any Act or under the regulations;
> (g) the child is absent on a day regarded as a holy day by the church or religious denomination to which the child belongs; or
> (h) the child is absent or excused as authorized under this Act and the regulations.

For example, parents may temporarily withdraw a child from school with the permission of the principal (s. 23(3), Reg. 298).

If a child *under* compulsory school age enrols in an elementary school (e.g. in junior kindergarten), then the obligation to attend school (unless legally excused) applies during the period for which he or she is enrolled as if the child were of compulsory school age (s. 21(4)).

(c) Can a Child be Excluded from School if He or She is Not Immunized?

Yes. The *Immunization of School Pupils Act* (s. 3) says that the medical officer of health can order a person who operates a school (i.e. a board or a private school operator) to suspend a pupil until the pupil has completed the "prescribed program of immunization" in respect of diseases designated under the Act, or until the parent of the pupil has filed:

*   a current statement of medical exemption or
*   a statement of conscientious belief or
*   a statement of religious belief.

The suspension is for 20 days, and may be repeated until the statutory conditions are satisfied (immunization or valid exemption).

If there is an outbreak, or risk of outbreak, of a designated disease in a school, the medical officer of health can order that a pupil be excluded from attendance at school if the pupil has not been immunized or granted an exemption under the Act. The order lasts until it is rescinded (s. 12).

If the medical officer of health makes a suspension or exclusion order, the parent and pupil (if 16 or 17 years old) must be advised of their entitlement to a hearing before the Health Services Appeal and Review Board. No hearing is required *before* an order is made by the medical officer of health.

Regulation 645 prescribes the contents of the record of immunization, and the required immunization schedule for designated diseases. It also contains the forms for obtaining an exemption, and for transferring records between schools if the pupil moves.

Under the *Education Act* (s. 265), a principal must report cases of suspected communicable disease in the school to the board and the local medical officer of health. A principal must refuse to admit to school a person whom he or she believes is infected with or exposed to a communicable disease, until the person has been medically "cleared".

(d) Who is the School Attendance Counsellor?

Every board must have one or more school attendance counsellors. Boards may share a school attendance counsellor. The counsellor has jurisdiction and is responsible for the enforcement of compulsory school attendance of every child who is required to attend school and who is qualified to be a resident pupil of the board, or is or has been enrolled during the current school year in a school operated by the board (other than a pupil under the jurisdiction of a person appointed under s. 119 of the *Indian Act*). The counsellor must inquire into every case of failure to attend school within his or her knowledge, or when requested to do so by the appropriate supervisory officer, the principal of a school or a ratepayer. The counsellor is responsible for instituting the prosecution of habitually absent children under section 30(5) of the *Education Act*. The parent or guardian of a child of compulsory school age can also be prosecuted for not sending the child to school.

Education Act, R.S.O. 1990, c. E-2:

30(1) Liability of parent or guardian — A parent or guardian of a child of compulsory school age who neglects or refuses to cause the child to attend school is, unless the child is legally excused from attendance, guilty of an offence and on conviction is liable to a fine of not more than $200.

(2) Bond for attendance — The court may, in addition to or instead of imposing a fine, require a person convicted of an offence under subsection (1) to submit to the Minister of Finance a personal bond, in a form prescribed by the court, in the penal sum of $200 with one or more sureties as required, conditioned that the person shall cause the child to attend school as required by this Part, and upon breach of the condition the bond is forfeit to the Crown.

(3) Employment during school hours — A person who employs during school hours a child who is required to attend school under section 21 is guilty of an offence and on conviction is liable to a fine of not more than $200.

(4) Offences by corporations — Subsections (1) and (3) apply with necessary modifications to a corporation and, in addition, every director and officer of the corporation who authorizes, permits or acquiesces in the contravention is guilty of an offence and on conviction is liable to the same penalty as the corporation.

(5) Habitually absent from school — A child who is required by law to attend school and who refuses to attend or who is habitually absent from school is guilty of an offence and on conviction is liable to the penalties under Part VI of the *Provincial Offences Act* and subsection 266(2) of this Act [Ontario Student Record is privileged] applies in any proceeding under this section.

(6) Proceedings under subs. (5) — Proceedings in respect of offences under subsection (5) shall be proceeded with only in accordance with such subsection.

(7) Reference to provincial counsellor for inquiry — Where, in a proceeding under this section, it appears to the court that the child may have been excused from attendance at school under subsection 21(2), the court may refer the matter to the Provincial School Attendance Counsellor who shall direct that an inquiry shall be made as provided in subsection 24(2) which subsection shall apply with necessary modifications except that the Provincial School Attendance Counsellor shall, in lieu of making an order, submit a report to the court.

1997, c. 31, s. 12

3

Statutory Roles and Responsibilities

This chapter explains the statutory roles and responsibilities of pupils, parents, teachers, directors of education, supervisory officers, the Ontario Teachers' Federation, the Education Quality and Accountability Office, and the Ministry of Education and Training. The roles of the Ontario College of Teachers, teachers' unions, and local school attendance counsellors are covered elsewhere in this book. The roles of the various "players" in education can only be properly carried out if there is cooperation. Education is rarely a topic upon which there is universal agreement, but somehow the Ministry, boards, unions, parents and ratepayers have sustained a system which, despite its flaws, still serves society and children well. It has done this through partnership, albeit at times a grudging one. Sometimes it is important to remind ourselves of the obvious: no one player can function in the absence of respect for the role of the other partners.

3.1 SCHOOL BOARDS

The powers and duties of school boards are numerous. They include such matters as negotiating collective agreements; being the "employer" of teachers and of many other persons who dedicate themselves to education; setting local funding priorities; ensuring that their huge budgets are spent wisely; and ensuring the construction, maintenance and repair of schools. Much of the *Education Act* is about telling boards how to exercise their powers, and although many sections of the Act deal with the duties and powers of school boards, two sections are particularly important: section

170 prescribes what a board *shall* do and section 171 prescribes what a board *may* do. For example, a board *must* hire a principal and an adequate number of teachers for each school, and must provide textbooks, instruction, and special education. It *may* provide junior kindergarten, evening classes, pupil transportation, day nurseries, etc. A board must ensure that every school under its charge is conducted in accordance with the *Education Act* and the regulations, and it must do anything that a board is required to do under any provision of the *Education Act* or any other Act (s. 170(1)[10] and [18]).

There are, of course, many other statutes that affect school boards, including, for example, the *Occupational Health and Safety Act, Day Nurseries Act, Human Rights Code, Labour Relations Act,* and *Employment Standards Act.*

More information about school boards is found in Chapter 1 in the context of an overview of the *Education Act.*

3.2 PUPILS

Pupils of compulsory school age must attend school unless they are legally excused from attendance (See Chapter 2 for details on attendance obligations.) Under Regulation 298, section 23, pupils must attend their classes punctually, respect school property, take required tests, and study diligently. Self-discipline and courtesy are also required by the regulation, which further states that pupils must accept the discipline that a kind, firm and judicious parent would exercise. They are responsible to the principal of their school for their conduct (a) on the school premises, (b) on out-of-school activities that are part of the school program, and (c) while traveling on a school bus. They are not permitted to do fund-raising or canvassing on school property without the board's consent. They are entitled to have a pupil representative on the school board, in accordance with Ontario Regulation 461/97.

Under the *Education Quality and Accountability Office Act, 1996*, section 4(6), a pupil is required to take a test administered under that Act, unless exempted in accordance with directives issued by the Education Quality and Accountability Office.

Under the *Tobacco Control Act*, pupils are prohibited from smoking on school property.

(a) Provincial Code of Conduct (Excerpts)

Guiding Principles

- All participants involved in the publicly funded school system—students, parents or guardians, volunteers, teachers and other staff members—are included in this Code of Conduct whether they are on school property, on school buses, or at school- authorized events or activities.
- All members of the school community are to be treated with respect and dignity, especially persons in positions of authority.
- Responsible citizenship involves appropriate participation in the civic life of the school community. Active and engaged citizens are aware of their rights, but more importantly, they accept responsibility for protecting their rights and the rights of others.
- Members of the school community are expected to use non-violent means to resolve conflict. Physically aggressive behaviour is not a responsible way to interact with others.
- The possession, use, or threatened use of any object to injure another person endangers the safety of oneself and others.
- Alcohol and illegal drugs are addictive and present a health hazard. Ontario schools will work cooperatively with police and drug and alcohol agencies to promote prevention strategies and, where necessary, respond to school members who are in possession of, or under the influence of, alcohol or illegal drugs.
- Insults, disrespect, and other hurtful acts disrupt learning and teaching in a school community. Members of the school community have a responsibility to maintain an environment where conflict and difference can be addressed in a manner characterized by respect and civility.

Student and Parent Responsibilities under the Code

Students are to be treated with respect and dignity. In return, they must demonstrate respect for themselves, for others, and for the responsibilities of citizenship through acceptable behaviour. Respect and responsibility are demonstrated when a student:

- comes to school prepared, on time, and ready to learn
- shows respect for themselves, for others, and for those in authority
- refrains from bringing anything to school that may compromise the safety of others

- follows the established rules and takes responsibility for his or her own action.

Parents play an important role in educating their children and have a responsibility to support the efforts of school staff in maintaining a safe and respectful learning environment for all students. Parents fulfill this responsibility when they:

- show an active interest in their child's school work and progress
- communicate regularly with the school
- help their child be neat, appropriately dressed, and prepared for school
- ensure that their child attends school regularly and on time
- promptly report to the school their child's absence or late arrival
- become familiar with the Code of Conduct and school rules
- encourage and assist their child in following the rules of behaviour
- assist school staff in dealing with disciplinary issues.

3.3 PARENTS

Parents must ensure that their child (of compulsory school age) goes to school unless the child is legally excused (see Chapter 2). Parents have the right to see their child's Ontario Student Record. They can request corrections to inaccurate information in the record, and may ask to have information removed which is "not conducive to the improvement of instruction" of their child (s. 266(4)). If their child is suspended by a principal, they have the right to appeal the suspension to the school board. If their child might be expelled, the board must hold an expulsion hearing, and parents are a "party" at such a hearing.

If a parent wants to remove a pupil from school temporarily, the parent must make a request in writing to the school principal (s. 23, Reg. 298).

Parents have a key role in providing input into the identification and placement of their child as an "exceptional" pupil under the *Education Act* and Ontario Regulation 181/98. (Please see chapter on Special Education.)

Once a pupil reaches the age of 18 years, the legal rights and responsibilities of a parent or guardian are vested in the pupil. See section 1(2) of the *Education Act*. (This assumes that the person is not otherwise legally incapacitated.)

(a) School Councils

Section 170(1)[17.1] of the Act requires a school board to establish a school council for each school that it operates, in accordance with the regulations. Section 170(3) permits the government to make regulations respecting school councils. Section 265(3) requires a school principal to consult the school council at least once in each school year respecting the school plan for co-instructional activities that the principal is required to implement under section 265(2).

Ontario Regulation 612/00 governs school councils. It states that the purpose of a school council is, "through active participation of parents, to improve pupil achievement and to enhance the accountability of the education system to parents" (s. 2(1)). A council's primary means of achieving its purpose is by making recommendations in accordance with the regulation to the principal of the school and to the board (s. 2(2)). A board must solicit the views of school councils with respect to establishing or amending board policies and guidelines that relate to pupil achievement or to the accountability of the education system to parents. This includes fundraising, codes of conduct, dress codes, funding of councils by the board, reimbursement of members' expenses, and conflict resolution processes to be used by the council. Boards must also consult councils about the development and implementation plans for new education initiatives that relate to pupil achievement or accountability, about board action plans for improvement based on reports from the Education Quality and Accountability Office, and about the process and criteria applicable to the selection and placement of principals and vice-principals (s. 19). A board must consider and respond to recommendations from a school council (s. 21).

The council must meet at least four times during the school year. Its meetings are open to the public and must be held in a location that is accessible to the public (s. 12). It is entitled to meet at the school. A school council may not be incorporated (s. 17). The council may engage in fund raising activities in accordance with board policy (s. 22). The council must consult with parents about matters under consideration by the council (s. 23). It must also file an annual report on its activities to the principal and the board, copies of which must be provided by the principal to parents of pupils in the school (s. 24).

Under section 3 of the Regulation, a school council must be composed of the following people:

- Parents who have a child enrolled in the school. The number of parent representatives is to be determined in accordance with the school council by-law, or if there is no by-law, then in accordance with board policy. Parent representatives must form a majority of the council. Section 4 sets out requirements concerning the election of parent representatives, which must be held within the first 30 days of each school year. Election is by secret ballot. The principal must give written notice of the election to parents at least 14 days before the election.

- The principal of the school. The principal is not entitled to vote at council meetings. Everyone else gets a single vote (s. 14). The principal may delegate his or her duties as a council member to a vice-principal of the school (s. 18(1)).

- One teacher employed at the school, other than the principal or vice-principal, elected by other teachers at the school within the first 30 days of the school year.

- One other person employed at the school, other than the principal, vice-principal or any other teacher, elected by persons employed at the school other than a principal, vice-principal or any teacher, within the first 30 days of the school year.

- In a school with one or more secondary grades, a pupil enrolled in the school who is appointed by the student council or, if there is no student council, elected by pupils enrolled in the school within the first 30 days of the school year.

- If a school does not have secondary grades, the school council may include a pupil appointed by the principal if the principal determines after consulting with the members of the council that it should include a pupil.

- A community representative appointed by members of the school council. The council's by-law may specify that two or more community representatives can be appointed, provided that parents remain a majority on the council. A community representative cannot be employed at the school, but may be employed elsewhere by the board provided this is revealed to the council before the person's appointment.

- One person appointed by an association that is a member of the Ontario Federation of Home and School Associations, the Ontario Association of Parents in Catholic Education, or *Parent Partenaires en Education*, if the association that is a member of the Ontario

Federation of Home and School Associations, the Ontario Association of Parents in Catholic Education, or *Parent Partenaires en Education* is established in respect of the school.

Pupil representatives are not required to be appointed or elected in a school established primarily for adults. Members of the board cannot serve on a school council (s. 3(7)).

A council member holds office until the first meeting of the school council in the next school year, and he or she may be re-elected or reappointed if still qualified.

The school council shall have a chair, or if permitted by its by-laws, it may have co-chairs (s. 8). The chair or a co-chair must be a parent representative. A person on the council who is employed by the board cannot be a chair or co-chair. The by-laws may determine whether the council shall have other officers.

A council member shall not receive remuneration for serving as a member, but may be reimbursed for expenses (s. 11).

The Ontario Ministry of Education publishes an extensive Guideline to assist school councils, which is available on its website.

(b) Medical Information

Common sense dictates that parents should provide sufficient information about their children to enable school staff to respond to medical emergencies, medication requirements, allergic reactions, etc. If this information is not supplied, the school can hardly be held liable for not responding appropriately in situations where the information would have made a difference. For example, peanut allergies and bee-sting allergies may require instantaneous response should an allergic reaction occur. This requires full disclosure of information about the child's allergy and the steps to be taken should an emergency occur during school activities.

(c) Immunization

A pupil is required to be immunized against certain designated diseases, in accordance with the *Immunization of School Pupils Act*. Parents must ensure that their children are immunized in order for them to be admitted to school, unless the child is exempt for medical reasons or as a matter of religious or conscientious belief. (Please see Chapter 2.)

3.4 TEACHERS

The job of a teacher is to teach. The term "teach" is not defined in the *Education Act*. However, one glance at the dictionary shows that "teach" can have different interpretations, including "direct", "instruct", "train", "guide", "discipline", "school", "tutor", "coach", "show how", and "cause to know". Teaching can occur by precept, example or experience. Unless the context of a particular statutory or regulatory provision requires otherwise, "teach" means exactly what we commonly understand it to mean in schools, and we should therefore use its ordinary dictionary meaning interpreted in the overall context of education legislation and the realities of how schools operate.

In the context of Ontario education law, our understanding of what a teacher does is enhanced if we look at how the *Education Act* and regulations describe the *duties* of a teacher. Although these prescribed duties tell a teacher what his or her legal obligations are, they paint a mere sketch of what a teacher actually does during the day. The picture is partly completed by the teacher's collective agreement and local employment policies of the board.

(a) Teachers' Duties

"Teachers' duties" are prescribed in the *Education Act* (primarily s. 264) and section 20 of Regulation 298, with respect to teachers employed by school boards. (Regulation 298 is included in the Appendices.) A teacher may be assigned these statutory and regulatory duties by a board and can also be assigned other duties. A collective agreement may impose duties on a teacher and may limit the duties that a teacher must perform. For example, a collective agreement could state that a teacher must fill in for absent teachers ("on-call" time), but may limit the time spent supervising pupils outside the classroom. The agreement may limit the average number of pupils that a teacher can be required to teach in one day ("pupil-teacher contact"), or impose other "workload" restrictions and requirements.

Further duties are prescribed in the *Teaching Profession Act* regulation and in the *Ontario College of Teachers Act, 1996*. These apply to teachers, not as employees, but by virtue of their membership in the Ontario Teachers' Federation and the College. A teacher's duty under the *Ontario College of Teachers Act, 1996* is to avoid doing things that will result in disciplinary measures being taken by the College because of misconduct or incompetence. There is also a duty to pay prescribed fees, to provide information required by the College, and to fulfill ongoing education requirements. More information about the College is found in Chapter 4.

A teacher also has duties as a member of the Ontario Teachers' Federation. The regulation made under the *Teaching Profession Act* prescribes a member's duties to his or her pupils, to educational authorities, to the public, to the Federation, and to fellow members. A member is required to "strive at all times to achieve and maintain the highest degree of professional competence and to uphold the honour, dignity, and ethical standards of the teaching profession" (*TPA* Reg. s. 13). Other ethical requirements are prescribed in sections 14 to 18 of the regulation under the *Teaching Profession Act*. The regulation is included in the Appendices.

It is a teacher's professional duty to report suspected child abuse. The *Child and Family Services Act* says that a person who has reasonable grounds to suspect that a child has suffered or is at risk of suffering the kinds of harm or other situations described in section 72(1) of the *CFSA* (e.g. physical, sexual, emotional) shall immediately report the suspicion and the information to a Society. A teacher or principal who fails to report a suspicion commits an offence under section 72(4) of the Act.

3.5 PRINCIPALS

As a group, principals and vice-principals underwent significant change because of the *Education Quality Improvement Act, 1997.* They are not permitted to bargain collectively. In response, many have joined associations that provide a range of services to their members, including professional development, insurance, lobbying, and employment representation. Ontario Regulation 90/98 provides some protection to principals and vice-principals who are declared redundant. It says that the board must find them another position for which they are qualified. If the position is not in a bargaining unit, their salary is maintained at its current level for a minimum of one year.

The *Education Quality Improvement Act, 1997* did not significantly change the statutory duties of principals (although it added duties in respect of such matters as allocating teaching time (s. 170.2(5)) and assigning duties to teachers prior to the start of the school year (s. 171(1)(3)). The Act did not alter the fact that principals and vice-principals are "teachers" under the *Education Act* (with the exception of the collective bargaining provisions in Part X.I). They are still required to be members of the Ontario College of Teachers. They are excluded from mandatory membership in the Ontario Teachers' Federation. The *Education Act* specifically states that principals and vice-principals may be assigned to teach (s. 287.1).

A principal's primary duties are to:

1.   organize and manage the school
2.   be in charge of, and supervise, the instruction of pupils
3.   maintain proper order and discipline of pupils.

Everything else that a principal is required to do flows from these three components. This includes the suspension of pupils, granting credits, promoting and admitting pupils, arranging home instruction, assisting and evaluating teachers, inspecting the school, and ensuring the health and comfort of pupils. The following list contains more examples of a principal's duties:

• recommend to the Minister that diplomas be granted
• retain on file all courses of study used in the school
• ensure appropriate "condition and appearance" of the school and the care of all teaching materials and other school property
• hold fire and emergency drills
• assign suitable quarters to pupils to eat lunch
• record pupil attendance in the register
• receive pupil absence notes from parents or guardians
• deal with trespassers and anyone who disrupts the pupils
• ensure supply teachers are in place if regular teachers are absent
• ensure school announcements and advertisements comply with board policy
• ensure that the board approves any canvassing or fund-raising activity involving pupils and that pupils are adequately supervised
• inspect school premises weekly
• report lack of attention on the part of school maintenance staff
• allocate instructional time to teachers
• report on necessary repairs
• instruct pupils in the care of school premises
• refuse admission to the school of any person suspected of being infected with or exposed to a communicable disease
• report to the board and Medical Officer of Health if he or she suspects the existence of a communicable disease in the school
• promote and maintain cooperation of the school with others in the community
• serve on the school council and provide information to it as required by the Minister

- ensure parent/guardian consents are obtained for field trips, athletics and extra-curricular activities
- ensure the proper handling of each pupil's Ontario Student Record (OSR)
- ensure compliance within the school with respect to privacy and freedom of information, *Youth Criminal Justice Act* confidentiality, and *Education Act* confidentiality provisions pertaining to pupils and/or staff
- ensure rights of young persons are not violated during an investigation by the principal of potentially criminal activity
- ensure compliance with the policies of the board and the ministry respecting the administration of medication to pupils
- fulfill other duties assigned by the board.

The above list contains many of the legal responsibilities of a principal, some of which the principal may choose to delegate to a vice-principal. While each school must have a principal, there is no requirement to appoint vice-principals.

The "real" job of a principal includes such additional matters as:

- attend countless meetings with supervisors, parents, trustees, union representatives, police, Children's Aid, lawyers, insurance adjusters, the clergy, teachers, support staff, school nurses, volunteers, other principals, and pupils
- interview people for job vacancies
- be a "curriculum leader"
- take professional development courses
- coach sports
- be a role model for staff, pupils and the community
- serve on committees and organize staff meetings
- manage school funds
- help organize school assemblies, school fairs, school trips, concerts, professional activity days, parent interview days, student photographs, etc.
- document accidents on the premises affecting pupils, staff and visitors
- deal with vandalism at the school.

3.6 DIRECTOR OF EDUCATION AND SUPERVISORY OFFICERS

(a) Director of Education

A district school board must employ a supervisory officer as a Director of Education. Two or more school *authorities* may agree to appoint a Director of Education with the approval of the Minister, and they cannot abolish the Director's position without the approval of the Minister.

The Director is the chief executive officer and the chief education officer of the board, and must be a supervisory officer who qualified as such as a teacher. The *Education Act* states that the Director shall, within policies established by the board, develop and maintain an effective organization and the programs required to implement the board's policies (s. 283(2)). He or she is required to make an annual report to the board, with a copy to the Minister (s. 283(3)). The Minister may establish policies and guidelines respecting the roles and responsibilities of Directors of Education and supervisory officers (s. 8(1)[3.4]).

(b) Supervisory Officer

A district school board may employ "such other supervisory officers as it considers necessary to supervise all aspects of the programs under its jurisdiction" (s. 279). It does not have to obtain the Minister's approval to hire the Director or any other supervisory officer. It must confirm with the Minister that a person it wants to appoint as a supervisory officer in fact holds the qualifications of a supervisory officer, namely the "supervisory officer's certificate". This certificate is issued by the Ministry. In the case of "academic" supervisory officers, it is issued if the Ontario College of Teachers confirms that the person has completed the supervisory officer's qualification program.

The term "supervisory officer" is defined in the *Education Act* as:

> . . . a person who is qualified in accordance with the regulations governing supervisory officers and who is employed,
>   (a) by a board and designated by the board, or
>   (b) in the Ministry and designated by the Minister
>
> to perform such supervisory and administrative duties as are required of supervisory officers by [the *Education Act*] and the regulations . . .

The person must be qualified (hold a certificate), be employed by a board or the Ministry, and be designated to perform supervisory officers' duties. The board must designate the "title and area of responsibility" of each supervisory officer and can assign the person duties in addition to those prescribed in the Act and regulations (s. 285(1)).

School *authorities* must appoint one or more supervisory officers. They are permitted to share the services of a supervisory officer with another board, or to agree to use a Ministry supervisory officer (s. 284).

The statutory duties of a supervisory officer are prescribed in section 286 of the *Education Act*, which can be found in the Appendices.

The *Education Act* also has many references to actions or decisions being made by the "appropriate supervisory officer". For example, he or she must decide whether to support a school principal if there is a dispute with a parent about the removal or correction of information in a pupil's Ontario Student Record (s. 266(5)). A supervisory officer's job is full-time, and the Minister must consent before he or she takes on any other job or office while employed as a supervisory officer (s. 286(4)).

A supervisory officer can only be suspended or dismissed by a board for "neglect of duty, misconduct or inefficiency" (s. 287(1)). Regulation 309 (s. 8) says that a board shall not suspend or dismiss a supervisory officer without first giving the supervisory officer reasonable information about the reasons for the suspension or dismissal and an opportunity to make submissions to the board. Submissions can be made orally or in writing. The suspension and dismissal requirements in Regulation 309 reflect the common law right to be "heard". The duty of fairness obliges a board to give a supervisory officer reasonable advance notice that a suspension or dismissal is being considered, along with complete information about the allegations against the supervisory officer. The supervisory officer must have an opportunity to respond to the allegations and to provide all relevant information to the board before it considers the matter. The same considerations apply to the dismissal of a teacher, subject to the applicable collective agreement. They also apply to a principal or vice-principal.

An employment contract between a board and a supervisory officer may deal expressly with the rights and obligations of the parties if the employment relationship is to be terminated for any reason. Because Regulation 309 prescribes a minimum standard of fairness, the contract could contain other conditions, such as notice periods and severance payments that do not derogate from the rights contained in the regulation.

Some of the leading cases dealing with procedural fairness are:

- *Nicholson v. Haldimand-Norfolk (Regional Municipality) Commissioners of Police* (1978), [1979] 1 S.C.R. 311, 88 D.L.R. (3d) 671, 78 C.L.L.C. 14, 181, 23 N.R. 410, 1978 CarswellOnt 609, 1978 CarswellOnt 609F (S.C.C.)
- *Kane v. University of British Columbia*, [1980] 1 S.C.R. 1105, 18 B.C.L.R. 124, [1980] 3 W.W.R. 125, 31 N.R. 214, 110 D.L.R. (3d) 311, 1980 CarswellBC 1, 1980 CarswellBC 599 (S.C.C.)
- *Martineau v. Matsqui Institution (No.2)* (1979), [1980] 1 S.C.R. 602, 13 C.R. (3d) 1 (Eng.), 15 C.R. (3d) 315 (Fr.), 50 C.C.C. (2d) 353, 106 D.L.R. (3d) 385, 30 N.R. 119, 1979 CarswellNat 626, 1979 CarswellNat 2 (S.C.C.)
- *Cardinal v. Kent Institution*, [1985] 2 S.C.R. 643, [1986] 1 W.W.R. 577 24 D.L.R. (4th) 44, 63 N.R. 353, 69 B.C.L.R. 255, 16 Admin. L.R. 233, 23 C.C.C. (3d) 118, 49 C.R. (3d) 35, 1985 CarswellBC 402, 1985 CarswellBC 817 (S.C.C.)
- *O.E.C.T.A. v. Essex (County) Roman Catholic Separate School Board* (1987), (*sub nom. English Catholic Teachers' Assn. (Ontario) v. Essex County Roman Catholic Separate School Board*) 18 O.A.C. 271, 58 O.R. (2d) 545, 36 D.L.R. (4th) 115, 28 Admin. L.R. 39, 34 C.R.R. 146, 1987 CarswellOnt 944 (Ont. Div. Ct.), leave to appeal refused (1988), (*sub nom. English Catholic Teachers' Assn. (Ontario) v. Essex County Roman Catholic Separate School Board*) 51 D.L.R. (4th) vii, 65 O.R. (2d) x, 32 O.A.C. 80 (note), 93 N.R. 325 (note), 39 C.R.R. 384 (note) (S.C.C.)
- *S.E.P.Q.A. v. Canada (Human Rights Commission)*, 89 C.L.L.C. 17,002, [1989] 2 S.C.R. 879, 62 D.L.R. (4th) 385, 100 N.R. 241, 11 C.H.R.R. D/1, 1989 CarswellNat 701, 1989 CarswellNat 877 (S.C.C.)
- *Knight v. Indian Head School Division No. 19*, [1990] 1 S.C.R. 653, 69 D.L.R. (4th) 489, [1990] 3 W.W.R. 289, 30 C.C.E.L. 237, 90 C.L.L.C. 14,010, 43 Admin. L.R. 157, 83 Sask. R. 81, 106 N.R. 17, 1990 CarswellSask 146, 1990 CarswellSask 408 (S.C.C.).

In *Knight*, the Supreme Court of Canada considered the dismissal of the Director of Education of a school board. L'Heureux-Dubé J. commented at page 500 on the circumstances giving rise to the duty of fairness:

> The existence of a general duty to act fairly will depend on the consideration of three factors: (i) the nature of the decision to be made by the administrative body; (ii) the relationship existing between that body and the individual; and (iii) the effect of that decision on the individual's rights.

L'Heureux-Dubé J. also referred in her judgment to Sopinka J. in the *Syndicat* case wherein Sopinka J. states at page 425:

> Both the rules of natural justice and the duty of fairness are variable standards. Their content will depend on the circumstances of the case, the statutory provisions and the nature of the matter to be decided.

At page 512, L'Heureux-Dubé J. stated further:

> It must not be forgotten that every administrative body is the master of its own procedure and need not assume the trappings of a court. The object is not to import into administrative proceedings the rigidity of all the requirements of natural justice that must be observed by a court, but rather to allow administrative bodies to work out a system that is flexible, adapted to their needs and fair. . . . [I]f it can be found that the respondent indeed had knowledge of the reasons for his dismissal and had an opportunity to be heard by the board, the requirements of procedural fairness will be satisfied even if there was no structured "hearing" in the judicial meaning of the word.

A board may offer the opportunity to have a "hearing" if it believes that this would be the best way of ensuring that a person is fairly treated. A "hearing" involves the right to appear personally before the tribunal, to be represented by an agent or counsel, to introduce evidence and call witnesses, and to cross-examine witnesses under oath. The *Education Act* requires a board to notify a supervisory officer of its decision to suspend or dismiss, with reasons.

(c) Redundancy

If a supervisory officer's position is declared redundant by a board, he or she has some protection under Regulation 309. The supervisory officer must be given at least three month's notice of the redundancy. He or she must be transferred to another position for which he or she is qualified with supervisory and administrative responsibilities as similar as possible to those of his or her previous position. He or she must be paid for at least a year after the transfer with no reduction of salary (Reg. 309, s. 7(2)).

3.7 THE EDUCATION QUALITY AND ACCOUNTABILITY OFFICE

The Education Quality and Accountability Office is a corporation without share capital established by the *Education Quality and Accountability Office Act, 1996* as a Crown Agency, to do the following:

- evaluate the quality and effectiveness of elementary and secondary school education

- develop tests and require or undertake the administering and marking of tests of pupils in elementary and secondary schools
- develop systems for evaluating the quality and effectiveness of elementary and secondary school education
- research and collect information on assessing academic achievement
- evaluate the public accountability of boards and collect information on strategies for improving that accountability
- report to the public and to the Minister of Education on the results of tests and generally on the quality and effectiveness of elementary and secondary school education and on the public accountability of boards
- make recommendations on any matter related to the quality and effectiveness of elementary and secondary school education or to the public accountability of boards.

The Minister may delegate powers and duties to the Office that it needs for the "carrying out of its objects". The Minister may also issue directives and policies that the Office is obliged to follow. The objects of the Office can be added to by regulation.

The Office is covered by the *Freedom of Information and Protection of Privacy Act*. It has a board of directors (seven to nine persons) and a chief executive officer appointed by the Lieutenant Governor in Council. It may charge fees for its goods and services. For example, it could obtain revenue by selling its testing material to other countries.

The Office may require school boards to administer tests to pupils, to mark them, and to report the results. It can require boards to provide information, including personal information. Pupils are required to take any test administered by a board on behalf of the Office. The Office may issue directives about exempting pupils from tests. Parents of children enrolled in publicly funded schools do not have the legal right to elect not to have their child take a test administered on behalf of the Office.

It is a duty of a teacher to "co-operate and assist in the administration of tests under the *Education Quality and Accountability Office Act, 1996*". (Reg. 298, s. 20(j).)

3.8 THE ONTARIO TEACHERS' FEDERATION

The Ontario Teachers' Federation (OTF) was formally established in 1944 by the *Teaching Profession Act*. Its objects are:

- to promote and advance the cause of education
- to raise the status of the teaching profession
- to promote and advance the interests of teachers and to secure conditions that will make possible the best professional service
- to arouse and increase public interest in educational affairs
- to cooperate with other teachers' organizations throughout the world having the same or like objectives
- to represent all members of the pension plan established under the *Teachers' Pension Act* in the administration of the plan and the management of the pension fund.

The OTF is governed by a board of governors representing its affiliated bodies: Elementary Teachers' Federation of Ontario (whose members were formerly members of the Federation of Women Teachers' Associations of Ontario or the Ontario Public School Teachers' Federation), the Ontario Secondary School Teachers' Federation, the Ontario English Catholic Teachers' Association and l'Association des enseignantes et des enseignants franco-ontariens.

All teachers employed to teach by a school board, other than principals and vice-principals, are required to be OTF members. As of March 31, 1998, this includes occasional teachers.

The pension representation function performed by OTF requires that it represent all members of the teachers' pension plan. This includes supervisory officers, principals, vice-principals, some private school teachers, and others. The representation function is actually carried out by the OTF executive under section 9 of the *Teaching Profession Act*. The executive may appoint persons to the pension board, enter into agreements under the *Teachers' Pension Act*; and agree to changes to the Schedule to that Act.

3.9 THE MINISTRY OF EDUCATION

In respect of elementary and secondary education, the Minister of Education is responsible for administering various statutes, including the *Education Act, Education Quality and Accountability Office Act, 1996*, and the *Ontario College of Teachers Act, 1996*. There are very few things that the Minister is *required* to do under these statutes, but there are many things that the Minister *may* do and does do. The primary functions are:

- prescribing curriculum, courses of study, diploma requirements, and approved textbooks

- issuing money to school boards in accordance with the grant regulations
- policy development and education reform.

Some other key areas within the Ministry are

- special education
- French-language education
- Native education
- schools for the blind, deaf and deaf-blind, and demonstration schools for the learning disabled
- adult education
- religious education
- school board governance and compliance
- finance policy.

The Minister of Finance is responsible for establishing education property tax rates for residential and business property. The Minister of Labour and the Minister of Education have a shared role in respect of teachers' collective bargaining issues, because of the tie between the *Education Act* and the *Labour Relations Act, 1995*.

The Minister does not have the power to intervene in local employment issues, human rights complaints, school bus transportation disputes, or other local matters. The Minister is not "vicariously" liable for the conduct or negligence of board employees because the Minister does not employ, hire, supervise, evaluate or discipline them.

4

Governing the Teaching Profession

The teaching profession is controlled and influenced in different ways by several organizations, chiefly the Ontario College of Teachers, the Ontario Teachers' Federation, the teachers' unions, and the Ministry of Education. Among these, it is the College that is charged with the mandate of governing the teaching profession and protecting the public interest with respect to the profession. This chapter provides information about laws that affect teachers as members of a profession. It also includes information about the qualifications a person needs to become qualified as a teacher.

4.1 THE ONTARIO COLLEGE OF TEACHERS

(a) When Did the Ontario College of Teachers Start Operating?

On June 27, 1996, the *Ontario College of Teachers Act, 1996* (*OCTA*) received Royal Assent. It is now fully proclaimed in force. Any person who held valid Ontario teaching certification on May 20, 1997 was deemed to hold a certificate of qualification and registration issued by the College. Anyone who was enrolled in a faculty of education on May 20, 1997, and who fulfilled the requirements for an Ontario Teacher's Certificate was deemed to be entitled to a certificate of qualification and registration issued by the College. (Sections 62 and 63 *OCTA* and s. 58, O. Reg. 184/97.)

The Council had its first meeting on May 1 and 2, 1997.

(b) How to Contact the College

The phone number for the Ontario College of Teachers is (416) 961-8800.
Toll free in Ontario: 1-888-534-2222.
The fax number is (416) 961-8822.

The address is:

Ontario College of Teachers
121 Bloor Street East
Toronto, ON
M4W 3M5

The Web Site is www.oct.ca.

Services are provided in French and English.

The regular publication of the College is "Professionally Speaking".

(c) What is the "Register"?

The Register is a list of all members of the College. Any person may
inspect the Register and, for a fee, may obtain a copy of any part of it. A
College by-law deals with how a member can change his or her name on
the register.

Before hiring a teacher, a board should contact the College to confirm that
the person is on the Register as a member in good standing with the appropriate basic and additional qualifications.

The Register contains information about each member's teaching qualifications. It also reveals if a member's certificate has been suspended,
revoked or cancelled. The by-laws also permit the removal of certain information from the register. For example, if conditions had been placed upon
the member's certificate and were subsequently removed, then the
Register would be amended to remove any reference to the condition.

(d) Who Decides on the "Fees"?

The members of the College establish their fees through by-laws approved by their Council. Aside from the annual membership fee, there are also fees for:

- registration
- evaluation of qualifications obtained outside Ontario or outside Canada
- penalty for late payment of annual fee
- reinstatement of suspended membership
- reinstatement of revoked membership
- registration appeal
- duplicate certificate
- duplicate tax receipt
- statement of good standing.

(e) What is the Role of the College?

The mandate of the College is set out in a series of "objects" in section 3 of the *Ontario College of Teachers Act, 1996*. The objects are as follows:

(1) To regulate the profession of teaching and to govern its members.

(2) To develop, establish and maintain qualifications for membership in the College.

(3) To accredit professional teacher education programs offered by post-secondary educational institutions.

(4) To accredit ongoing education programs for teachers offered by post-secondary educational institutions and other bodies.

(5) To issue, renew, amend, suspend, cancel, revoke and reinstate certificates of qualification and registration.

(6) To provide for the ongoing education of members of the College, including professional learning required to maintain certificates of qualification and registration.

(7) To establish and enforce professional standards and ethical standards applicable to members of the College.

(8) To receive and investigate complaints against members of the College and to deal with discipline and fitness to practise issues.

(9) To develop, provide and accredit educational programs leading to certificates of qualification additional to the certificate required for membership, including but not limited to certificates of qualification as a supervisory officer, and to issue, renew, amend, suspend, cancel, revoke and reinstate such additional certificates.

(10) To communicate with the public on behalf of the members of the College.

(11) To perform such additional functions as are prescribed by the regulations.

The College is a body corporate without share capital, with all the powers of a natural person. The *Corporations Act* and *Corporations Information Act* do not apply to the College except as specified in the Act or regulations.

(f) Who Runs the College?

The College is governed by a Council composed of 17 members elected by the members of the College and 14 persons appointed by the Lieutenant Governor in Council. (See s. 4 of the Act and O. Reg. 345/96).

The term for Council members cannot exceed three years, except if permitted by regulation (s. 5, Act). Elections are held every three years. Appointments by the government are of different lengths, so that some members are appointed for one year, two years or three years. No person can be a Council member for more than ten consecutive years.

The College has several committees, one of which is the Executive Committee (s. 15, Act). This Committee can be delegated powers and duties by the Council, but it cannot make, amend or revoke a by-law or regulation (s. 16, Act). The Council must meet at least four times a year. An annual meeting of the membership of the College must be held (s. 13).

The Chief Executive Officer of the College is the "Registrar".

(g) How Can the College Make a Regulation?

It is not always the government that makes regulations. Self-governing bodies are often given this power. The College's regulation-making powers are listed in section 40 of the Act, which can be found in the Appendices. Note that the Minister of Education has the opportunity to *review* any College regulation before it is made, and the regulation must be *approved* by the Lieutenant Governor in Council. For this reason, College regulations are presented to the Legislation/Regulations Committee of Cabinet and then to Cabinet for approval. They are then signed by the Lieutenant Governor. The regulations made by the College are gazetted in the Ontario Gazette.

To date, the key regulations include:

* Ontario Regulation 184/97 — on teachers' qualifications, essentially replacing the now-revoked Regulation 297

- Ontario Regulation 437/97 — which defines "professional miscon-
  duct"
- Ontario Regulation 72/97 — a general regulation setting out various
  administrative and organizational matters for the College
- Ontario Regulation 293/00 — election of council members
- Ontario Regulation 270/01 — Professional Learning.

(h) What is in the By-laws?

The College has by-laws to govern its administration and operations.
These include the following:

- establishing the fees for membership and services
- the calling of regular and special Council meetings
- meeting procedures, including the taking of minutes
- naming officers of the College (Chair, Vice-Chair, Registrar and
  other officers as determined from time to time)
- electing the Chair and Vice-Chair of the Council, and filling vacancies of these positions
- responsibilities of the Registrar
- Standing Committees:
  - Finance (five persons)
  - Standards of Practice and Education (nine persons)
- Special Committees:
  - Quality Assurance (five persons)
  - Election (five persons)
  - Nomination (five persons)
  - Human Resources Committee (five persons)
- dealing with vacancies on Committees
  This by-law outlines how an elected member of the Council can be
  suspended or disqualified from serving on the Council or its committees. It states how and when a vacancy must be filled. Vacancies
  are filled by appointment by the Executive Committee, and its decision is placed before the Council for confirmation at its next regular
  meeting. Note that Ontario Regulation 72/97 has specific provisions
  dealing with disqualification and vacancies on Council and statutory
  committees.
  Persons appointed by the Lieutenant Governor in Council are not
  "elected" Council members, and their removal and replacement is
  not within the scope of the by-law.
- committee reports
- appointing signing officers for College documents

- banking and finance, including investments and borrowing
- audit
- indemnifying Council members and College employees for acts done in the execution of their duties
- purchasing liability insurance and property insurance
- conducting the annual meeting
- delegating to Executive Committee all the powers and duties of the Council (note, this cannot include the power to make or change by-laws or regulations)
- conflict of interest

  This requires all members of Council and officers of the College to disclose any conflict of interest that they may have in any matter coming before the Council or a committee. They shall not participate in the discussion or vote on a matter where they have a conflict of interest. A member or officer has a conflict when he or she makes a decision or is present when a decision is made or participates in making a decision in the carrying out of his or her role that may directly or indirectly confer a benefit on the member or officer or any person with whom the member or officer does not deal at arm's length, and at the same time knows that in making the decision there is the opportunity to further his or her private interest or the private interest of a party with whom the member or officer does not deal at arm's length. There is no conflict of interest when approving resolutions relating to remuneration of Council, indemnification of Council members, or the acquisition of insurance relating to indemnification of Council members.

- Code of Ethics for Council — members must:
    - comply with the *Ontario College of Teachers Act*, the regulations and the College by-laws
    - familiarize themselves with the Act, regulations, by-laws and any other records and documents that may be necessary for the performance of the duties of their office
    - take part in the committee work of the College and serve actively during their term of office on any committees to which they have been appointed
    - ensure that confidential matters coming to their attention as members of the Council are not disclosed by them except as required for the performance of their duties or as directed by the Council or the Chair
    - recognize the distinction between their corporate and individual authority as council members and conduct themselves accordingly with College staff, members of the College and the public

- •   exercise care, diligence, skill and prudence in carrying out the business of the College
- •   conscientiously perform duties on behalf of the officers of the College, as requested
- •   seek to enhance the public perception of the College and the profession of teaching
- information to be provided to the College by a member: business and home address and phone number, name, birth date, social insurance number, gender, name (and former names if any), name on the Ontario Teacher's Certificate if any, language preference (English or French), country of citizenship, other countries where the member is authorized to teach.
- persons wishing to register must provide a report of a Criminal Reference Check.
- the by-laws also prescribe the standards of practice (By-law No. 32.01) and ethical standards (By-law No. 32.02) for the teaching profession.

4.2 COMPLAINTS AND DISCIPLINE

(a) Who Can Complain About a Member?

A complaint about a member of the College is sent to the Registrar. Under section 26 of the Act, a person may make a complaint regarding the conduct or actions of a member if the person is:

- •   a member of the public
- •   a member of the College
- •   the Registrar
- •   the Minister of Education.

(b) How is a Complaint Processed?

The usual situation involves a person who has called the College to find out whether a complaint should be filed and, if so, how. College staff work with the person to find out if it is a matter that is within the jurisdiction of the College, i.e. involves professional misconduct, incompetence or fitness to practise. In many instances, the issue can and should be resolved at the local level of the school board. If the person still wishes to file a complaint, College staff will provide information on how to do so.

1.   A complaint must be filed with the Registrar in the format prescribed in the by-laws. It must be in writing, and must provide the name of the member who is the subject of the complaint, along with a description of the conduct or actions of the member.

2.   The matter is referred to the "Investigation Committee" (see s. 25 and s. 26). The Committee can refuse to consider and investigate a complaint if, in its opinion,
     (a)   the complaint does not relate to professional misconduct, incompetence or fitness to practise, or
     (b)   the complaint is frivolous, vexatious or an abuse of process.

3.   The College notifies the member about the complaint and the member has 30 days to respond in writing to the Investigation Committee.

4.   The member's response is shared with the complainant.

5.   A College investigator attempts to gather pertinent information and documents for consideration by the Investigation Committee.

6.   The Investigation Committee reviews the complaint, the member's response and relevant information gathered by the Investigator.

(c) What Happens at the Investigation Committee?

The Investigation Committee "need not" hold a hearing or even afford an opportunity to make oral or written submissions. It must give its decision in writing to the member and the complainant, with reasons for the decision. It must use its best efforts to make a decision within 120 days of the filing of the complaint with the Registrar.

The Committee may:

•   refer the matter to the Discipline Committee
•   choose not to refer the matter to the Discipline Committee
•   caution or admonish the member against whom the complaint is filed
•   take such action as it considers appropriate in the circumstances (consistent with the Act, regulations and by-laws).

(d) What Happens at the Discipline Committee?

The Discipline Committee is required to have at least 11 members, at least four of whom must be government-appointed Council members.

While most matters before the Discipline Committee will have been referred there by the Investigation Committee, it is possible for the Council or the Executive Committee to refer matters directly to the Discipline

Committee for a hearing. When such a direct referral is made, the Council or Executive Committee may also order the Registrar to suspend the member or impose terms, conditions or limitations on the member's certificate, if it is of the opinion that the actions or conduct of the member exposes or is likely to expose students to harm or injury (s. 29(3)). No hearing need be held before a direct referral is made. However, a member is to be given notice of the direct referral and 14 days to make written submissions about it, before the referral is made. The 14-day period does not apply if the Council or Executive Committee is of the opinion that the delay would be inappropriate in view of the risk of harm or injury to students. Any matter that has been referred directly by the Council or the Executive Committee must be dealt with expeditiously by the Discipline Committee.

When a matter is referred to the Discipline Committee, it must hear and determine the matter. After a hearing, it can:

(1)   find a member guilty of professional misconduct as defined in the regulations, or

(2)   find a member to be incompetent if, in its opinion, the member has displayed in his or her professional responsibilities a lack of knowledge, skill or judgment, or disregard for the welfare of a student of a nature or extent that demonstrates that the member is unfit to continue to carry out his or her professional responsibilities, or that a certificate held by the member under the *Ontario College of Teachers Act* should be made subject to terms, conditions or limitations (s. 30).

Upon finding a member incompetent or guilty of professional misconduct, the Discipline Committee can make an order:

- directing the Registrar to revoke any certificate of the member
- directing the Registrar to suspend any certificate of the member for a stated period not to exceed 24 months
- directing the Registrar to impose specified terms, conditions or limitations on any certificate of the member
- directing that the imposition of a penalty be postponed for a specified period and not be imposed if specified terms are met within that period.

If the finding is one of professional misconduct (i.e. not incompetence), there are additional measures that can be taken by the Discipline Committee. It may make an order:

- requiring that the member be reprimanded, admonished or counselled

- imposing a fine on the member (up to $5,000 payable to the Minister of Finance)
- directing publication of its order against the member
- fixing costs to be paid by the member.

The parties before the Discipline Committee are the College and the member whose conduct or actions are being investigated (s. 32(2)). Hearings are conducted in public unless the Committee orders that the public be excluded for any of the reasons listed in subsection 32(7), e.g. a civil or criminal proceeding could be prejudiced. The Act sets out various procedural requirements in section 32, including the right of a party to see all documents, before the hearing, that will be used at the hearing. Where the Act does not deal specifically with a procedural item, the *Statutory Powers Procedure Act* will apply (e.g. right to cross-examine witnesses and to be represented).

Under Part VI of the Act, the Discipline Committee also has the duty to hear applications for reinstatement of membership, or for variation of its previous orders. These hearings are closed to the public. The parties are the College and the applicant. The Council or Executive Committee may, without a hearing, make an order removing a suspension or reinstating a member (s. 34).

A decision of the Discipline Committee may be appealed to Divisional Court (s. 35).

(e) What does the Fitness to Practise Committee Do?

A complaint about a member usually infers that the member has deliberately done something wrong. However, the member's alleged failings as a professional may not be a matter of "fault". The Fitness to Practise Committee has the duty to hear matters referred to it by the Investigation Committee, or directly by Council or the Executive Committtee, or on an application for reinstatement or variation. It may, after a hearing, find a member to be incapacitated if, in its opinion, the member is suffering from a physical or mental condition or disorder such that the member is unfit to continue to carry out his or her professional responsibilities or that a certificate held by the member should be made subject to terms, conditions or limitations. Upon finding a member to be incapacitated, it may make an order:

- directing the Registrar to revoke any certificate of the member

- directing the Registrar to suspend any certificate of the member for a stated period not to exceed 24 months
- directing the Registrar to impose specified terms, conditions or limitations on any certificate of the member
- directing that the imposition of a penalty be postponed for a specified period and not be imposed if specified terms are met within that period.

The Fitness to Practise Committee will follow many of the same procedures as the Discipline Committee in ensuring that the member receives a full and fair hearing. However, due to the nature of the matters being considered, its hearings are closed to the public. The member can request that the hearing be open. The Committee can refuse this request if it is satisfied that it should be closed for any of the reasons specified in subsection 32(9), e.g. safety of a person may be jeopardized, ongoing civil or criminal proceedings, etc.

Pursuant to subsection 33(14), the Fitness to Practise Committee also has the duty to hear applications for variation of its orders or for reinstatement of a revoked or suspended certification. The procedures outlined in section 33 apply.

4.3 GENERAL REGULATION

Ontario Regulation 72/97, made pursuant to the *Ontario College of Teachers Act, 1996*, covers a number of different operational and administrative matters.

(a) Annual Membership Fees

Section 2 requires a board, private school and the Ministry of Education (for members employed by the Provincial Schools Authority) to submit the annual membership fee to the College on behalf of members in their employ, and authorizes them to deduct the fee from the member's salary. The fee must be submitted no later than 35 days after the due date specified for the year in the College by-laws. The employer's deadline can be delayed by the College if the employer is facing extraordinary circumstances that warrant an extension. The employer may be required to pay interest on dues in arrears. Members whose employers do not submit fees on their behalf must pay the annual fee directly. The College can and will suspend a member who has not paid his or her dues.

(b) Quorum at Council Meetings

Council quorum is 16 members of Council, at least four of whom are appointees of the Lieutenant Governor in Council (s. 5).

(c) Disqualification of Council Members

Elected Council members can be disqualified:

- if found to be guilty of professional misconduct, incompetent, or unfit to practise
- for failure without cause to attend:
  - three consecutive meetings of Council
  - three consecutive meeting of a committee on which he or she serves, or
  - at least half the meetings of Council in a 12-month period
- for failure to attend a hearing of a panel of a committee on which he or she serves
- if he or she fails or ceases to meet the criteria under which he or she was elected to the Council (see criteria in O. Reg. 293/00).

(d) Vacancies on Council

A vacancy occurs when a member dies, resigns or is disqualified from sitting on Council (s. 7).

If the vacancy occurs within six months of the end of the elected member's term of office, the Council may leave the seat vacant or fill the seat by appointment. If the vacancy is more than six months from the end of the term, the seat must be filled by appointment. There are provisions about how the appointments are to be made (ss. 8 to 10). If vacancies bring the Council below quorum, then an election to fill the vacancies must be held (s. 11). The newly-appointed or elected person fills the seat until the end of the former member's term.

(e) Statutory Committees

The *Ontario College of Teachers Act, 1996* (s. 15), prescribes the College's "statutory committees":

- Executive Committee

- Investigation Committee
- Discipline Committee
- Registration Appeals Committee
- Fitness to Practise Committee.

Ontario Regulation 72/97 provides for the appointment of a chair of each committee by Council. A vice-chair is elected by the committee members. The College Council determines the number of members of each committee provided that this does not conflict with conditions set out in subsections 25(1), 27(1) and 28(1) of the Act (s. 14).

The quorum of the Investigation Committee, Discipline Committee and Fitness to Practise Committee is a majority; the quorum of the Executive Committees is four; the quorum of the Registration Appeals Committee is three; and in all cases, at least one member present must be a government-appointed Council member (s. 15). There are procedures for filling vacancies on the statutory committees (s. 16), and for the calling of meetings (s. 17).

(f) Executive Committee

The Executive Committee comprises the chairs of:

- Fitness to Practise Committee
- Discipline Committee
- Registration Appeals Committee
- Investigation Committee
- Standards of Practice and Education Committee
- Finance Committee
- Accreditation Committee.

The chair and vice-chair of Council must be on the Executive Committee, and the chair of the Council is the chair of Executive Committee. There are also provisions, in section 19, that ensure that the Executive Committee has both elected and government-appointed members.

(g) Investigation Committee

In considering a complaint under the Act, the Investigation Committee will work in "panels" of at least three members selected by the Committee chair (s. 21).

(h) Discipline Committee

In performing its duties under the Act, the Discipline Committee will work in "panels" of at least three members selected by the Committee chair (s. 22).

(i) Registration Appeals Committee

The Registration Appeals Committee is composed of five members, at least two of whom are elected and at least two of whom are government-appointed. In performing its duties under the Act, the Committee will work in "panels" of at least three members selected by the Committee chair (s. 24).

(j) Fitness to Practise Committee

In performing its duties under the Act, the Fitness to Practise Committee will work in "panels" of at least three members selected by the Committee chair (s. 25).

(k) Collection of Information

Section 26 of the Regulation lists organizations for the purposes of section 47(1) of the Act, from which the College may require information, including personal information. These are:

- private schools
- colleges of applied arts and technology
- universities
- Ontario Teachers' Pension Plan Board
- Ontario Teachers' Federation
- Affiliates of the Ontario Teachers' Federation.

4.4 ROLE OF THE MINISTER

(a) Teachers' Qualifications

The government no longer has a *direct* role in deciding what is necessary in order for a person to become a teacher or to obtain additional teaching qualifications. The College has jurisdiction to determine *how* a person may obtain basic and additional teaching qualifications. The *Education Act* states that (except as otherwise provided in or under the *Education Act*) a person must be a member of the College in order to be employed or act as a teacher in an elementary or secondary school. The Minister, with the approval of the Lieutenant Governor in Council, may make regulations prescribing the qualifications of teachers. (A "teacher" is defined as a member of the College.) For example, Regulation 298 requires that a principal must have "principal's qualifications", and a special education teacher must have additional qualifications to teach special education.

(b) Review

The Minister has the power to review the activities of the Council of the College and require the Council to provide reports and information. The Minister may require the Council to do anything that, in the opinion of the Minister, is necessary or advisable to carry out the intent of the *Ontario College of Teachers Act, 1996*. The Minister may also require the College to make, amend or revoke a regulation (s. 12). This power reflects the fact that, although the government has delegated some of its control over "education" to the College, education remains fundamentally a responsibility of the provincial government in accordance with the Canadian Constitution. However, an attempt to use this power to interfere with the day-to-day operations of the College would be contrary to the policy behind establishing the College in the first place, namely that teachers should govern themselves.

(c) Members' Duties

In the *Education Act* and Regulation 298, the government prescribes duties of teachers and principals. However, the College, not the Minister, may discipline a teacher for professional misconduct or incompetence. (Of course, the teacher's employer will likely be involved as well.) The College, not the Minister, may prescribe a code of ethics for members. It should be kept in mind that not all members work for school boards. Some members work for private schools, the provincial government, the teachers' unions, and the faculties of education. Some members are not employed.

(d) Suspension

The College may suspend a person's membership. A person may not teach for a school board while under suspension. The government may prescribe, by regulation, the consequences of having one's membership suspended, or of having terms, conditions or limitations placed upon a certificate of qualification (s. 11(1)[26.1], *Education Act*).

(e) University Faculties of Education

The government provides funding to faculties of education, but the College "accredits" the faculties' programs of professional education for teaching candidates.

(f) Supervisory Officers

The government issues the "Supervisory Officer's Certificate". However, under Regulation 309, to obtain a certificate as an "academic" (as opposed to "business") supervisory officer, a person must show the Ministry that he or she has "additional qualifications" as a supervisory officer issued by the College. The College does not issue the Supervisory Officer's Certificate; it issues "additional qualifications" to members who have completed the prescribed qualifications in Part V of Ontario Regulation 184/97. Regulation 309 also prescribes the requirements to obtain a Business Supervisory Officer's Certificate.

4.5 TEACHERS' QUALIFICATIONS

Section 262 of the *Education Act* states:

Except as otherwise provided in or under this Act, no person shall be employed in an elementary or secondary school to teach or to perform any duty for which membership in the College is required under this Act unless the person is a member of the Ontario College of Teachers.

Clause 170(1)[12] of the Act states that a board shall

appoint for each school that it operates a principal and an adequate number of teachers, all of whom shall be members of the Ontario College of Teachers.

Therefore, once it is determined that a person is being hired to "teach", that person must be a "teacher" as defined in the *Education Act*, i.e. a member of the Ontario College of Teachers. An exception to this rule occurs when a board obtains the Minister's permission to hire a "temporary teacher" (i.e. a person who is not a College member) on a "Letter of Permission".

Regulation 298 specifies whether any additional qualifications are required for a teacher to teach in a specific position or subject.

(a) What is "Teaching"?

The *Education Act* does not define "teach". The duties of a teacher are outlined in the Act and Regulation 298 (s. 20), and they give some indication of what a teacher does. As discussed in Chapter 3, the meaning of the word "teach" is broad. It depends to a certain extent upon our intuitive sense of what the profession of teaching entails in the school system, i.e., the systematic or regular imparting of knowledge, skills or values to one or more pupils, following a course of study and curriculum, usually followed by an evaluation of the pupil's academic progress.

(b) What is "Differentiated Staffing"?

Differentiated staffing refers to the staffing of teaching positions with persons who do not hold teaching qualifications. It is not permitted in Ontario. However, boards are permitted to hire persons to assist teachers in a variety of ways, and there is no law that requires a teacher to be physically present in his or her classroom all the time, provided that the pupils are adequately supervised. As discussed above, there is no absolute way of saying when a person has ceased to act as a teaching assistant and has assumed a teaching role. The role and responsibilities of assistants should be clearly defined by the school board in consultation with the appropriate unions.

(c) What is the Role of the Minister of Education Respecting Qualifications?

The Minister has jurisdiction over:

*   whether a given position or subject requires additional teaching qualifications beyond the basic certificate (e.g. principalship, special education, French-language education)
*   granting supervisory officer certificates (academic and business). In

the case of academic supervisory officers, the person must produce the necessary evidence of completion of the College's program leading to an additional qualification as a supervisory officer

- granting letters of permission to boards to hire unqualified persons to teach on a temporary basis up to 1 year (s. 8(1)[10])
- excluding individuals on a case-by-case basis from the need to meet some or all of the qualification requirements by accepting equivalent qualifications (see s. 8(1)[14]). This power is rarely exercised.

(d) What is the Role of the Ontario College of Teachers Respecting Qualifications?

The Ontario College of Teachers has jurisdiction over:

- how a person obtains a certificate of qualification as a teacher
- how to obtain additional teaching qualifications, including principals' qualifications and academic supervisory officers' qualifications
- accreditation of university faculty of education programs as leading to the granting of a College certificate
- suspension, revocation and cancellation of certificates
- imposing terms, conditions and limitations on certificates
- granting temporary letters of approval to boards. These authorize a board to assign or appoint a teacher to a position or subject for which the teacher does not hold the qualifications required by the regulations made under the *Education Act* for teaching the subject or holding the position. See section 50 of Ontario Regulation 184/97.

Regulation 297 (now revoked) formerly prescribed the forms for the "Ontario Teacher's Certificate" and other teaching qualifications. Ontario Regulation 184/97 does not prescribe the forms of the College's certificates. Instead, these forms are prescribed by by-law. This makes it easier to change the form should the need arise. Like Regulation 297, Ontario Regulation 184/97 prescribes how a teacher may obtain "additional basic" qualifications and "additional" qualifications. It also contains several schedules setting out what qualifications can be obtained in the pre-service (faculty) program of professional education and those that can be obtained as additional qualifications.

(e) What is a "Certificate Of Qualification and Registration"?

A certification of qualification and registration is a certificate granted by the College that has two components:

1. a certificate of registration as a member of the College
2. a certificate of qualification showing the holder's basic and additional teaching qualifications.

The "Ontario Teacher's Certificate" and a "Ontario Teacher's Qualifications Record Card" are things of the past. The permanent letter of standing, provisional letter of standing and temporary letter of standing are also relegated to history.

Under Ontario Regulation 184/97, the College may grant:

1. Certificate of Qualification
2. Certificate of Qualification (interim) — granted pending completion of teaching experience requirement
3. Certificate of Qualification (restricted) — restricts what the holder is permitted to teach, e.g. native language
4. Certificate of Qualification (limited) — limited in duration
5. Certificate of Qualification (limited, restricted) — combination of #3 and #4 above.

Among the "old" certificates issued by the Ministry, the closest parallels for the new certificates are as follows (for the matching numbers above):

1. Ontario Teacher's Certificate
2. Temporary Letter of Standing
3. Permanent Letter of Standing
4. Provisional Letter of Standing (limited in duration)
5. Provisional Letter of Standing (limited in duration and restricted as to what course or program could be taught).

Teachers who held valid Ministry certificates on May 20, 1997 were automatically entitled to be granted an equivalent certificate of qualification and registration by the College. Persons enrolled in a faculty of education during 1997-98 were similarly protected upon successful completion of their program.

(f) Obtaining a Certificate of Qualification

All candidates for a certificate of qualification must comply with section 2 of Ontario Regulation 184/97 which requires the candidate to submit the following documents to the Dean of a college or faculty of education or the Director of a school of education in Ontario:

(1)   certificate of birth or baptism certificate or other acceptable proof of date and place of birth
(2)   a marriage certificate or other acceptable proof of marriage, if a candidate wants to use her married name
(3)   a change of name certificate where applicable
(4)   evidence of the person's academic or technological qualifications
(5)   basis for the person's presence in Canada, where not born in Canada
(6)   proof of freedom from active tuberculosis.

(g) Routes to the Certificate of Qualification

Teacher Training Obtained in Ontario

If a candidate's training as a teacher was obtained in Ontario, there are three routes to obtain an unrestricted, non-limited Certificate of Qualification:

(1)   the candidate has an acceptable university degree (or equivalent) or technological qualifications (as defined)

AND has completed a program of professional education (s. 3, Reg. 184/97)

AND has passed the qualifying test under section 10.1 of the *Education Act*, where applicable (s. 3(b), Reg. 184/97)

OR

(2)   the candidate is of native ancestry and has a Secondary School Graduation diploma (or equivalent standing)

AND has completed a program of professional education with concentration in the primary and junior divisions (see s. 6, Reg. 184/97).

A person who completes this program is qualified to teach in the primary and junior divisions.

OR

(3)   the person has an acceptable university degree (or equivalent) or technological qualifications

AND has completed the first session of a program of professional education followed by a year of successful teaching experience in Ontario on a limited certificate, followed by a second session of the program of professional education, followed by a second year of successful teaching on a limited certificate, followed in some cases by a third session of a program of professional education and a third year of teaching on a limited certificate. What this means is that the person is taking his or her professional education as a teacher over two or three summers and is working as a teacher pending completion of the program. The teaching experience can be obtained at a board, private school, school for the blind or deaf, school operated for Indian pupils by the Federal government or by a band council, band or education authority (s. 9, Reg. 184/97).

Where Teacher Training is Obtained Outside Ontario

If a candidate has completed an acceptable program of professional education *outside Ontario* and submits to the Registrar the information required under section 12, the candidate can be issued an interim certificate of qualification valid for six years from the date of issue (s. 13, Reg. 184/97). In circumstances defined in section 13.1, a limited interim certificate may be issued. Candidates must also pass the qualifying test under section 10.1 of the *Education Act.*

(h) Routes to Other Certificates of Qualification

If a person does not have the qualifications to obtain an unrestricted Certificate, he or she may be able to obtain a restricted Certificate for teaching certain kinds of classes. (A restricted Certificate is converted into a Certificate of Qualification under s. 27, Reg. 184/97.)

(1)   For a Certificate of Qualification (Restricted to teaching the deaf), a candidate must:
   •   have impaired hearing
   •   an acceptable university degree (or equivalent), and
   •   have completed an approved teacher education program for teaching the deaf (s. 19).

There are further provisions for persons who take their teacher education

outside Ontario — essentially they teach under a limited, restricted certificate which can be converted into a Restricted certificate after teaching the
deaf in Ontario for ten months (s. 19(5), Reg. 184/97).

(2)   For a Certificate of Qualification (Restricted to teaching classes of
       pupils who are trainable retarded), the candidate must:
       •   have the Special Education — Part I (TTR) additional qualifi-
            cation and one of three diplomas specified in the Ontario
            Regulation 184/97 (Diploma in Pre-School Education from
            Ryerson Polytechnic University; Diploma in Child Study,
            University of Toronto; Diploma in Early Childhood Education
            from a College of Applied Arts and Technology)
       •   obtain a limited, restricted Certificate for one year
       •   complete one year of successful teaching in a trainable retarded
            class
       •   obtain Special Education — Part II (TTR)
       •   complete a second year of teaching on a limited Certificate
       •   apply for a Certificate of Qualification (Restricted to teaching
            classes for the Trainable Retarded).

(3)   For a Certificate of Qualification (Restricted to teaching Native lan-
       guage as a second language) (NSL), the candidate must:
       •   have fluency in the Algonquin or Iroquoian language
       •   complete the first session of a program for teachers of NSL
       •   obtain a limited, restricted Certificate to enable him or her to
            teach NSL for one year
       •   complete one year of teaching experience in NSL
       •   complete the second session of a program for teachers of NSL
       •   obtain an extension of the limited, restricted Certificate for
            another year
       •   complete a second year of teaching experience in NSL
       •   complete the third session of a program for teachers of NSL
       •   apply for a Certificate of Qualification (Restricted to teaching
            NSL).

5

Special Education

Ontario Regulation 181/98 sets out the requirements for special education identification, placement and review committees, appeal boards, Individual Education Plans, parent guides, and other important aspects of special education law in Ontario.

5.1 IDENTIFICATION PLACEMENT AND REVIEW

(a) What is Special Education?

According to section 1 of the *Education Act*, a "special education program" means an educational program for an exceptional pupil that:

- is based on and modified by the results of continuous assessment and evaluation
- includes a plan with specific objectives and an outline of educational services that meets the needs of the exceptional pupil.

The term "special education services" means:

- facilities
- resources

including support personnel and equipment necessary for developing and implementing a special education program.

A board has a statutory duty to provide special education programs and services for its exceptional pupils, or to enter into an agreement with another board to provide them (s. 170).

(b) Who is an Exceptional Pupil?

According to section 1 of the Act, an "exceptional pupil" means a pupil whose behavioural, communicational, intellectual, physical or multiple exceptionalities are such that he or she is considered to need placement in a special education program by [an Identification, Placement and Review Committee] of the board

> (a) of which the pupil is a resident pupil,
> (b) that admits or enrols the pupil other than pursuant to an agreement with another board for the provision of education, or
> (c) to which the cost of education in respect of the pupil is payable by the Minister.

(c) What is an IPRC?

An IPRC is a "special education *identification, placement* and *review* committee".

A board must have one or more IPRC committees (s. 10, O. Reg. 181/98).

(d) Who Serves on an IPRC?

Each committee must have three or more persons. One of the members must be:

(a)   a principal employed by the board
(b)   a supervisory officer employed by the board, or
(c)   a supervisory officer whose services are used by the board (i.e. in a sharing arrangement with another board, or through agreement with the Ministry).

A principal or supervisory officer appointed to the committee may designate another principal or supervisory officer to act in his or her place on the committee (See s. 11, O. Reg. 181/98).

(e) How is a Pupil Designated as "Exceptional"?

A pupil becomes "exceptional" when an IPRC identifies the pupil as exceptional.

(f) How is an IPRC Initiated?

An IPRC is initiated by:

(1)　the principal of the pupil's school (with written notice to the parent) or

(2)　by the pupil's parent, by written request to the principal.

The parent must receive a copy of the "parent guide" which the board is obliged to produce that explains the special education process set out in the regulation and provides parents with other pertinent information as required by section 13 of Ontario Regulation 181/98.

At least ten days written notice of the time and place of the IPRC's meeting must be given to a parent of the pupil, and to the pupil if 16 or more years of age.

Communications required under the regulation must be done through braille, large print or audio-cassette formats upon request.

A board shall also initiate an IPRC for a pupil who is leaving a provincial demonstration school.

> A parent of a pupil and a pupil (if 16 years of age or more) are entitled to be *present and participate* in all committee discussions about the pupil and to be *present* when the IPRC's identification and placement decisions are made [s. 5(1), O. Reg. 181/98]. A parent or pupil who has a right to be present at or participate during an IPRC's discussion also has a right to have a representative present at the discussion to speak on the person's behalf or otherwise support the person.

(g) What Does the IPRC Do?

The IPRC decides whether to identify a pupil as exceptional and, if so, what the pupil's placement should be.

The committee:

* must obtain and consider an educational assessment of the pupil
* may obtain and consider a health assessment or psychological assessment
* shall consider any information about the pupil submitted by the parent and the pupil (if 16 years of age or older)

- shall consider any information submitted to it that it considers relevant
- may interview a pupil who is under 16 years of age with parental consent.

The IPRC may discuss any proposal for special education services or programs, and shall do so if the parent or pupil (16+) requests. The IPRC may make recommendations regarding special education programs and services but it cannot make decisions about them.

INTEGRATION
Before considering placement in a special education class, the IPRC must consider whether placement in a regular class, with appropriate special education services, would meet the pupil's needs and is consistent with parental preferences. If such a placement would meet the pupil's needs and is consistent with parental preferences, the IPRC must decide in favour of a regular class placement.

(h) What Happens Pending a Meeting or Decision of an IPRC?

Pending a meeting or decision, the board is not required to provide a "placement" but it must provide an "education program" for the pupil that is appropriate to the pupil's "apparent strengths and needs". It must consider a regular classroom setting, as above, before considering a special education classroom. "Appropriate education services" must be provided. These "interim" rules also apply pending a meeting of an appeal board or a decision of a school board under Ontario Regulation 181/98. (Unless there already was a placement and the parent is appealing a review decision, in which case the new placement is stayed, irrespective of what type of placement it is.)

(i) How Does a Parent Hear about the IPRC's Decision?

As soon as possible after the decision is made, the chair of the IPRC must send a written statement of the decision to the parent, the pupil (if 16 years of age or older), the principal and the "designated representative" of the board that established the IPRC. The designated representative is the Director of Education (or secretary if there is no Director).

The decision must state whether the committee has identified the pupil as exceptional. If the pupil is identified as exceptional, the statement of decision will include:

- the IPRC's description of the pupil's strengths and needs
- the categories and definitions of any exceptionalities identified
- the IPRC's placement decision
- the IPRC's recommendations, if any, regarding special education programs and services

If the placement is in a *special education class*, the IPRC must give the reasons for this decision.

(j) How Does a Parent Respond to the Decision?

A parent may request a meeting with the IPRC within 15 days of receiving its decision. This is an opportunity to seek clarification about the decision and the basis on which it was made, and to provide comments on the decision. The request must be in writing to the principal who made the referral (or to the designated representative in the case of a referral from a demonstration school). The principal (or representative) must then arrange a meeting as soon as possible. After the meeting, the IPRC chair must send out a notice indicating if any changes to the IPRC decision were made as a result of the meeting. If so, a revised decision is sent out with the notice. The notice and revised decision, if any, are sent to the persons who received the original decision.

(k) When is a Placement Decision Implemented?

A board must implement an IPRC placement decision as soon as possible after (1) the parent has consented in writing to the placement or (2) after the time for appealing the decision has expired (with notice of implementation to the parent).

(l) How are IPRC Decisions Updated?

There is a procedure for reviewing an identification or placement. The principal may request a review. The parent of the pupil may request a review at any time after the placement has been in effect for three months (and not more often than once in every three-month period).

The designated representative of the board that is providing the program may request a review. This is to ensure that there is a review at least once in each school year, but is unnecessary when the parent has indicated that the annual review can be dispensed with.

The principal has 15 days to inform the parent of the approximate date of the review meeting. The principal decides which of the board's IPRCs shall deal with the review. If it is providing services to the pupil on behalf of another board, the purchasing board must be invited to send a representative to be present at the review committee and participate in its discussions.

The committee may decide that it is satisfied with the current identification and placement, or that the identification or placement should be changed. It will notify the parent, pupil (if 16+), principal, designated representative of the board, and (where applicable) representative of the purchasing board.

If a change is recommended, the statement of decision must state:

(a)   the reasons for the change to the identification and/or placement
(b)   whether the pupil should continue to be identified as exceptional
(c)   if the pupil is to continue to be identified as exceptional,
    (i)   the placement decision
    (ii)   description of pupil's strengths and needs
    (iii)   categories and definitions of the exceptionalities identified
(d)   if placement is in a special education class, the reason for this placement decision.

As is the case with the original IPRC decision, the parent has a right to request a meeting to discuss a decision made by an IPRC that has conducted a review. After this meeting, a notice is sent by the chair indicating whether any changes to the decision were made as a result of the meeting. If changes are made, they must be reflected in a revised written statement of decision.

The board must implement any changes to a pupil's placement as soon as possible, after the parent consents to the changed placement or after the time to appeal the decision has expired (with notice to the parent).

5.2 APPEALS

(a) How is the Decision of an IPRC Appealed?

If a parent is dissatisfied with the decision of an IPRC or a review IPRC, a parent may file a notice of appeal, requiring a hearing by a "special education appeal board". The appeal board comprises:

- one member selected by the board
- one member selected by the parent
- a chair jointly selected by the other two members (or, if they cannot agree, by the appropriate district manager of the Ministry of Education).

No member of an Appeal Board may be:

- a trustee of the providing or purchasing board
- an employee of the providing or purchasing board
- an employee of the Ministry of Education and Training
- a person with prior involvement in the matter.

(b) What Can be Appealed?

A parent can appeal an identification or placement decision of an IPRC made under Part IV of the regulation or the identification or placement decision made after a review by an IPRC under Part V of the regulation.

A parent can appeal:

- a decision that a pupil is exceptional
- a decision that a pupil is not exceptional
- a decision on placement.

An appeal is filed with the secretary of the school board.

It must be filed within 30 days of the parent receiving the IPRC's statement of decision. If a meeting was requested after the statement of decision was received, then the appeal period is 15 days after receiving notice of the outcome of the follow-up meeting.

The parent's notice of appeal should indicate which of the decisions is being appealed and must include a statement setting out the nature of the disagreement.

(c) What is the Appeal Procedure?

- The parent and the pupil (if 16+) are "entitled to be present at and participate in all discussions about the pupil at the meeting held by the special education appeal board" (s. 5(2), O. Reg. 181/98).
- At least 10 days written notice of the time and place of the appeal board's meeting must be given to a parent of the pupil, and to the pupil if 16 or more years of age.
- The chair of the IPRC whose decision is being appealed must provide the appeal board with the statement of decision, and the records, assessments and other documents considered by the IPRC.
- The chair of the appeal board arranges for a meeting of the appeal board to "discuss the matters under appeal".
- Notice of the meeting is given to the parent and pupil (if 16+ years).
- The meeting is to take place at a convenient place, no later than 30 days after the day on which the chair is selected unless parent and the Director of Education (i.e. designated representative) agree to an extension.
- The meeting is to be conducted in an "informal manner".
- The appeal board may invite any person who in the opinion of the chair, may be able to contribute information.
- The appeal board shall invite a purchasing board to sent a representative to the meeting.
- When the appeal board is satisfied that the "opinions, views and information" that bear on the appeal have been sufficiently presented to it, it shall end the meeting.
- Within three days of ending the meeting, the appeal board shall:
  (a) agree with the IPRC and recommend that its decisions be implemented, or
  (b) disagree with the IPRC and make a recommendation to the school board about the pupil's identification, placement or both.

(d) Who Gets the Statement of Recommendations of the Appeal Board?

The statement of recommendations of the Appeal Board are sent to:

- the parent
- the pupil (if 16+)
- the chair of the IPRC committee
- the principal where the pupil is placed
- the designated representative (director/secretary) of the board

- the designated representative (director/secretary) of the purchasing board if any.

Reasons must accompany the written statement of the recommendations.

(e) What Does the Board Do with the Recommendations?

Within 30 days of receiving the appeal board's written statement, the school board must consider the recommendations. It shall decide what action to take with respect to the pupil and must then inform:

- the parent
- the pupil (if 16+)
- the chair of the IPRC committee
- the principal where the pupil is placed
- the designated representative (director/secretary) of the board
- the designated representative (director/secretary) of the purchasing board if any.

Notice of its decision is given in writing. The school board is not limited to the actions that the appeal board recommended or could have recommended.

The school board's decision is implemented:

- once the parent consents to the decision in writing
- after 30 days have passed since the parent received notice of the decision, if no appeal of the school board's decision to the Special Education Tribunal has been commenced under section 57 of the *Education Act*
- after an appeal under section 57 of the *Education Act* has been either dismissed or abandoned.

(f) Does the Appeal Board Actually Decide Anything?

No. The appeal board makes recommendations, which the school board must then consider in deciding the pupil's identification and/or placement.

(g) Can the School Board's Decision be Appealed?

Yes, a parent may appeal an identification or placement decision of a school board to a **Special Education Tribunal**. One or more special education tribunals may be established by the Lieutenant Governor in Council. As a result of the amendments contained in the *Education Quality Improvement Act, 1997*, there is no longer any need for parents to file for leave to appeal prior to obtaining a hearing before the Special Education Tribunal. Therefore, there are no longer any *Regional* Special Education Tribunals.

Education Act, R.S.O. 1990, c. E.2, ss. 57(3)-(5)

57.(3) Right of Appeal — Where a parent or guardian of a pupil has exhausted all rights of appeal under the regulations in respect of the identification or placement of the pupil as an exceptional pupil and is dissatisfied with the decision in respect of the identification or placement, the parent or guardian may appeal to a Special Education Tribunal for a hearing in respect of the identification or placement.

57.(4) Hearing by Special Education Tribunal — The Special Education Tribunal shall hear the appeal and may,
(a)   dismiss the appeal; or
(b)   grant the appeal and make such order as it considers necessary with respect to the identification or placement.

57.(5) Decision final — The decision of the Special Education Tribunal is final and binding on the parties to the decision.

1997, c. 31, s. 31

5.3 INDIVIDUAL EDUCATION PLAN

(a) What is an "Individual Education Plan"?

Every exceptional pupil must have an Individual Education Plan (IEP) developed for him or her. The IEP must include:

(a)   specific educational expectations for the pupil
(b)   an outline of the special education program and services to be received by the pupil
(c)   a statement of the methods by which the pupil's progress will be reviewed.

If the pupil is 14 years of age or older, the IEP must include a plan for transition to appropriate post-secondary school activities, such as work, further education and community living. Therefore, when a pupil becomes 14 years of age, his or her IEP will have to be changed to include a transition plan. In developing the transition plan, the principal shall consult with the community agencies and post-secondary institutions that the principal considers appropriate. A pupil identified solely as gifted does not require a transition plan.

The IEP is developed by the principal in consultation with the parent and the pupil if 16 years of age or older. It must take into consideration any recommendations of the IPRC or Special Education Tribunal about special education programs or services. It must be completed within 30 days of the placement. The parent and pupil (16+) are entitled to a copy of the IEP.

After an IPRC review, the board notifies the principal of the need to review the pupil's IEP to determine whether it needs to be updated. The review of the IEP must be completed within 30 days of the principal receiving the notice, and must involve the parent and pupil (16+). It must take into consideration any recommendations of the IPRC or Special Education Tribunal about special education programs or services. If the IEP does not include a transition plan, and the pupil is 14 years old or will become 14 years old during the school year, the principal must ensure that a transition plan is developed and included in the IEP.

The pupil's IEP is kept in the pupil's Ontario Student Record, unless the parent objects in writing.

MALPRACTICE ALERT!

Lawsuits based on "education malpractice" have not met with success in Canadian courts or in United States appellate courts. However, school boards in the United States have been successfully sued where they have failed to fulfil the requirements in a special education pupil's Individual Education Plan written pursuant to the United States legislation.

6

Teacher-School Board
Collective Bargaining

It is beyond the scope or purpose of this book to discuss in detail collective bargaining by teachers and boards. The *School Boards and Teachers Collective Negotiations Act* governed their collective negotiations from 1975 until the end of 1997. During this time, collective agreements and collective negotiations became increasingly sophisticated and comprehensive. As a result of the *Education Quality Improvement Act, 1997*, teachers and boards now bargain in accordance with the *Education Act* which incorporates the provisions of the *Labour Relations Act, 1995*. The *Labour Relations Act, 1995* has certain features such as "fair representation" and expedited arbitration that were not in the *School Boards and Teachers Collective Negotiations Act*. Certain other employment-related matters were also changed, including the removal of the requirement to have "permanent", "probationary", and "continuing education" contracts.

The following chart indicates the major statutory changes that resulted from the *Education Quality Improvement Act, 1997* in respect of collective bargaining and the employment relationship between teachers and school boards.

6.1 STATUTES

OLD	NEW
School Boards and Teachers Collective Negotiations Act	*Education Act*
	Labour Relations Act
Teaching Profession Act	
Regulation under Teaching Profession Act	
Labour Relations Act (occasional teachers)	

6.2 APPLICATION

OLD	NEW
The *School Boards and Teachers Collective Negotiations Act* applied to school boards and teachers employed by boards on permanent, probationary or continuing education teachers' contracts ("statutory contracts"). This included principals and vice-principals but not supervisory officers or instructors in teacher-training institutions. A person had to have a statutory contract with the board if the person was hired to teach. If the board did not provide a contract to a teacher, the person was deemed to have a permanent teacher's contract.	Part X.I of the *Education Act* applies to boards and teachers "employed to teach". "Teacher" in the *Education Act* means "member of the Ontario College of Teachers'. But Part X.I of the *Education Act* (which governs collective bargaining) has a special definition of "teacher" for collective bargaining purposes that: (i) includes teachers employed by the board to teach (this also includes occasional teachers), and (ii) excludes supervisory officers, principals, vice-principals and instructors at teacher-training institutions. "Employed to teach" is not confined to classroom teachers. If the legislature had intended to include only classroom teachers, it would have said so, as it did in the "teaching time" provisions in section 170.2. However, a person is not a "Part X.I teacher" solely because he or she is a certificated teacher (i.e. member of the Ontario College of Teachers). Inclusion of a person in a teachers' bargaining unit involves an examination of what the person does. Does the person "teach"? The answer will depend on: (i) a comparison of the person's duties with a teacher's duties under the *Education Act* and regulations (ii) past practice of the board in dealing with similar positions (iii) legal precedent.

6.3 TEACHERS' BARGAINING UNITS

OLD	NEW
The *School Boards and Teachers Collective Negotiations Act* did not refer to "bargaining units'. The "unit" was comprised of the teachers who were members of the "branch affiliate", as determined by OTF by-law. According to the by-law: In public boards, female elementary school teachers belonged to the branch affiliate representing members of the Federation of Women Teachers' Associations and male elementary school teachers belonged to the branch affiliate representing members of the Ontario Public School Teachers' Federation. Public secondary school teachers were represented by the branch affiliate of the Ontario Secondary School Teachers' Federation. In separate school boards, teachers were represented by the branch affiliate of the Ontario English Catholic Teachers' Association. Most French-language teachers were represented by l'Association des enseignantes et des enseignants franco-ontariens.	The *Education Act* defines the teachers' bargaining units. It does not provide any choice about belonging to a unit. Each district school board has a separate unit for elementary teachers, secondary teachers, elementary occasional teachers and secondary occasional teachers. An elementary unit is composed of teachers who are assigned to one or more elementary schools or to perform duties in respect of such schools all or most of the time. A secondary unit is composed of teachers who are assigned to one or more secondary schools or to perform duties in respect of such schools all or most of the time. (See *O.S.S.T.F., District 14 v. Kawartha Pine Ridge District School Board,* [2003] O.L.R.B. Rep. 819 (Ont. L.R.B.) for an interpretation of these provisions by the Ontario Labour Relations Board.) Occasional teachers are in an elementary or secondary unit if they are on the roster of occasional teachers for the elementary or secondary panel of the board. A teacher can be a member of more than one occasional teachers' bargaining unit. Teachers working for school authorities have one elementary unit for teachers of French-speaking pupils and one unit for teachers who do not teach French-speaking pupils. There are also separate units for occasional teachers (French-language and other than French-language). The James Bay-Lowlands Board has one secondary teachers' unit and one unit for its secondary occasional teachers. Hospital boards provide education to both elementary and secondary pupils, so their bargaining unit structure is closer to that of the district school boards.

6.4 JOINT BARGAINING

OLD	NEW
Joint bargaining by branch affiliates and boards was permitted.	Bargaining units at the same board may bargain together, either for one agreement or for different agreements.

Bargaining units at the same board that are represented by the same bargaining agent may combine into one unit with the consent of the board.

Different boards and the bargaining agents at those boards may all agree to bargain jointly. For instance, this would permit a form of regional bargaining. |

6.5 TEACHERS' BARGAINING REPRESENTATIVE

OLD	NEW
The appropriate "branch affiliate" of an affiliate of the Ontario Teachers' Federation (OTF), as determined by OTF by-law, was the teachers' representative.

Occasional teachers could choose to unionize under the *Labour Relations Act*. They were not "teachers' as defined in the *Teaching Profession Act* and were not covered by the *School Boards and Teachers Collective Negotiations Act*. | The bargaining representative is determined by the *Education Act*, not OTF by-law.

1. English-language, public elementary teachers – Elementary Teachers' Federation of Ontario

2. English-language public secondary school teachers – the Ontario Secondary School Teachers' Federation

3. English-language separate school teachers – Ontario English Catholic Teachers' Association

4. French-language school teachers – l'Association des enseignantes et des enseignants franco-ontariens.

These agents also represent members of elementary and secondary occasional teachers' bargaining units. Occasional teachers no longer have a choice as to whether to be represented by a union.

Note that the union is the provincial body. The union will, in turn, decide upon its own structure for local representation. |

6.6 SCOPE OF BARGAINING

OLD	NEW
A provision of an Act or regulation prevailed over a provision in a collective agreement if there was a conflict.	In the case of conflict, the *Education Act* and regulations prevail over a collective agreement.
The *School Boards and Teachers Collective Negotiations Act* could not be construed so as to prejudicially affect the rights and privileges with respect to the employment of teachers enjoyed by Roman Catholic and Protestant separate school boards under the *Constitution Act, 1867.*	The *Education Act* and the *Labour Relations Act* shall not be interpreted so as to adversely affect any right or privilege guaranteed by section 93 of the *Constitution Act, 1867* or section 23 of the *Canadian Charter of Rights and Freedoms.*
There were few other statutory restrictions on the scope of bargaining, except:	There are few statutory restrictions on the scope of bargaining. Restrictions include:
• terms of statutory contracts were set by regulation	The *Labour Relations Act* contains certain items that are deemed to be in collective agreements (e.g. one year minimum) and has restrictions on what can be in collective agreements (e.g. agreement cannot discriminate on prohibited grounds under the *Human Rights Code*).
• minimum one-year collective agreement, ending on August 31st.	
Teachers' pensions are non-negotiable because boards do not contribute to them.	Seniority protection is provided for principals and vice-principals who elected to continue teaching by the March 31, 1998 deadline in section 277.11 of the *Education Act.*
	Except with permission of the Minister, a board shall not exceed the prescribed board-wide average class size for elementary school classes (currently 24.5 pupils) and secondary classes (currently 21 pupils, subject to a board resolution increasing it to 22 under s. 170.1(4)).
	Minimum teaching time requirements for elementary and secondary classroom teachers (s. 170.2 and s. 170.2.1, *Education Act*).

6.6 Scope of Bargaining – *Continued*

OLD	NEW
	In some respects, the scope of bargaining has been *increased* because, as of September 1, 1998:
	• teachers' permanent, probationary, continuing education contracts cease to have effect (Note: these contracts contained important provisions, including termination dates, that are now resolved locally)
	• there is more latitude to negotiate a probationary period within a two-year maximum for all newly-hired teachers
	• 20 days sick leave provisions are repealed (by previous amendments to the Act)
	• jury and witness leave provisions are repealed
	• quarantine leave provisions are repealed.

6.7 BARGAINING PROCESS

OLD	NEW
Notice to Bargain respecting agreement for following September: • must meet if notice given • must make effort to reach an agreement • voluntary interest arbitration or final offer selection were available • fact finding mandatory if at impasse in September • mandatory last offer and strike vote prior to strike • unilateral changes by school board possible sixty days after fact finding report made public.	Notice to bargain is given within the period of 90 days before the collective agreement ceases to operate (s. 59, *LRA*). The parties must bargain in good faith. A conciliation officer is appointed at the request of either party. The Minister of Labour decides whether to appoint a conciliation board or mediator, or whether to issue a "No board" report. A strike or lock-out is permitted if no collective agreement is in operation and 7 days have elapsed after the day the Minister has released or is deemed to have released to the parties the report of a conciliation board or mediator, or if 14 days have elapsed after the release or deemed release of a "no board" report by the Minister (s. 79, *LRA*). Unilateral changes to terms and conditions of employment are permitted in accordance with section 86 of the *Labour Relation Act*. Voluntary interest arbitration permitted.

6.8 FACT FINDING

OLD	NEW
Fact finders were appointed by the Education Relations Commission to report on the state of negotiations, including the items agreed upon and the items still outstanding. They were permitted to make non-binding recommendations to the parties.	There is no "fact finding" process under the *Labour Relations Act, 1995*.

6.9 STRIKES

OLD	NEW
Strikes were permitted if certain steps were taken first: collective agreement expired, fact finding concluded, last offer vote taken, strike vote taken, five days strike notice. "Work to rule" was specifically included in definition of "strike", with provision that teachers were to be paid during a work to rule.	Strikes are permitted if certain conditions are fulfilled: expired collective agreement; conciliation; conciliation board or mediator's report or "no-board" report; strike vote. No provision protecting salary during work to rule. "Strike" is defined in the *Education Act* as follows: **277.2(4) Strike**—For the purposes of subsection (1), (a) the definition of **"strike"** in section 1 of the *Labour Relations Act, 1995* does not apply; and (b) **"strike"** includes any action or activity by teachers in combination or in concert or in accordance with a common understanding that is designed or may reasonably be expected to have the effect of curtailing, restricting, limiting or interfering with, (i) the normal activities of a board or its employees, (ii) the operation or functioning of one or more of a board's schools or of one or more of the programs in one or more schools of a board, including but not limited to programs involving co-instructional activities, or (iii) the performance of the duties of teachers set out in the Act or the regulations under it, including any withdrawal of services or work to rule by teachers acting in combination or in concert or in accordance with a common understanding. However, for the purpose of section 19 (see below), "strike" follows the definition found in the *Labour Relations Act, 1995:*

6.9 Strikes – *Continued*

OLD	NEW
	1(1) "strike" includes a cessation of work, a refusal to work or to continue to work by employees in combination or in concert or in accordance with a common understanding, or a slow-down or other concerted activity on the part of the employees designed to restrict or limit output.

6.10 LOCK-OUT

OLD	NEW
A board could lock out teachers only in response to a strike.	Right to lock out occurs at same time as the right to strike. No pre-condition that the teachers be engaged in a strike.

6.11 CLOSING OF SCHOOLS DURING STRIKE

OLD	NEW
A school or schools could be closed during a teachers' strike and the teachers in the affected school did not get paid.	A school or schools may be closed during a teachers' strike or a lock-out and the teachers in the affected school do not get paid, section 19 *Education Act*. A school or schools may be closed if the board is of the opinion that (a) the safety of pupils may be endangered during the strike or lock-out; (b) the school building or the equipment or supplies in the building may not be adequately protected during the strike or lock-out; or (c) the strike or lock-out will substantially interfere with the operation of the school.

6.12 TRIBUNAL

OLD	NEW
Education Relations Commission — a Crown agency appointed as a neutral body to perform certain functions such as monitoring and assisting negotiations, gathering pertinent data, etc. It had very limited power to intervene in parties' negotiations.	Ontario Labour Relations Board — a neutral tribunal with extensive power to enforce the *Labour Relations Act* and hear applications for rulings on various issues. The Education Relations Commission was "continued" despite the repeal of the *School Boards and Teachers Collective Negotiations Act* in order to continue to advise the government as to when a strike or lock out by or of board employees will jeopardize completion of courses of study by students (s. 57.2).

6.13 DUTY OF FAIR REPRESENTATION

OLD	NEW
No express provision mandating fair representation by unions.	Fair representation of union members is mandated by section 74 of the *Labour Relations Act, 1995*.

6.14 FEDERATION FEES (UNION DUES)

OLD	NEW
Determined by regulation under the *Teaching Profession Act*, as made by the Board of Governors of the Ontario Teachers' Federation and approved by the Lieutenant Governor in Council. Boards were required to remit fees to OTF, which distributed the fees to the appropriate affiliate.	Mandatory dues check-off for union dues.

6.15 *TEACHING PROFESSION ACT*

OLD	NEW
Definition of "teacher" included principals and vice-principals. It had the effect of excluding occasional teachers because they did not have statutory teachers' contracts.	Definition of "teacher" in the *Teaching Profession Act* now excludes principals and vice-principals. It includes teachers employed to teach, including occasional teachers.

6.16 PRINCIPALS AND VICE-PRINCIPALS

OLD	NEW
Principals and vice-principals were "teachers" and were therefore covered by the collective agreement.	Principals and vice-principals are excluded from Part X.I of the *Education Act* and from the *Labour Relations Act*. Therefore, they have no right to belong to a union or be represented by a union.
	They are able to form and belong to a local or provincial association. Objects of the association may include representing members in respect of terms and conditions of employment. However, this is not "collective bargaining" and there is no statutory obligation upon a school board to deal with principals and vice-principals through their association.
	They are excluded from the *Teaching Profession Act* definition of "teacher", but not prevented by legislation from being a voluntary member of the Ontario Teachers' Federation.

6.17 TERMINATION AND DISMISSAL

OLD	NEW
A "board of reference" could be granted to a teacher or board by the Minister where it appeared that a "permanent" teacher's contract was improperly terminated. Most collective agreements contain "just cause" clauses in respect of the dismissal and discipline of teachers. Termination and dismissal were usually grieved, instead of using the board of reference route.	The provisions in the *Education Act* dealing with "boards of reference" were repealed on August 31, 1998. Termination and dismissal matters should therefore be covered in collective agreements.

6.18 PROBATION

OLD	NEW
Probationary teachers were given a "probationary teacher's contract". Maximum probationary period was: • one year if the teacher had at least three years of teaching experience in an elementary or secondary school in Ontario • two years if the teacher had less than three years teaching experience in an elementary or secondary school in Ontario.	Probationary contracts under Regulation 310 ceased to have effect on August 31, 1998. Maximum probationary period for newly hired teachers is two years (s. 261).

7

Negligence

This chapter covers the main concepts of the law of negligence as it applies in the school setting. The fear of being sued is prominent in the minds of many principals and teachers. A little fear is perhaps a good thing because it forces us to take a preventative approach. There is no room for complacency. However, an unreasonable or unfounded fear not only creates stress, but also results in limitations upon the programs which are conducted in our schools. We tend to hear of the high profile cases where a board and its employees have been found negligent and huge compensation has been awarded. We do not hear of the lower profile cases which are often successfully defended. The hundreds of reported school negligence cases show that if a teacher has taken normal precautions and has used common sense in the instruction and supervision of students, the court is not likely to make a finding of negligence in a lawsuit resulting from an accident at school.

There is no duty upon teachers to foresee every conceivable accident. There is no duty to supervise every student every minute of the school day. However, teachers do have a duty to act as a careful parent would act and to foresee the risks that a careful parent would foresee. In the gym, shop, laboratory, outdoors, etc., there are obviously special dangers to be guarded against and any competent teacher will be aware of these dangers.

Teachers are under a duty to ensure that adequate safety precautions are taken, that safety equipment is used and that pupils are fully aware of the dangers involved in a given activity. This is particularly important in the science laboratory, the technical shop and in physical and outdoor education. If it can be shown that pupils were properly instructed, warned of possible dangers, and adequately supervised (given their skill, age and experience), then the teacher and board will reduce the possibility of being found liable.

7.1 DEFINITION OF NEGLIGENCE

Although written in 1856, the following definition still conveys a general idea of what we understand negligence to be today: "Negligence is the omission to do something which a reasonable man, guided upon those considerations which ordinarily regulate the conduct of human affairs, would do, or doing something which a prudent and reasonable man would not do. The defendants might have been liable for negligence, if, unintentionally, they omitted to do that which a reasonable person would have done, or did that which a person taking reasonable precautions would not have done." (*Blyth v. Birmingham Water Works Co.* (1856), 156 E.R. 1047, 11 Exch. 781 (Eng. Exch.) at 784 [Exch.].)

In more modern terms, negligence may be described as the failure to use reasonable care. That is, it is the doing of something that a reasonably prudent person would not do, or the failure to do something that a reasonably prudent person would do under like circumstances. A negligent act is viewed as the cause of damage if it "directly and in natural and continuous sequence produces or contributes substantially to producing such damage, so it can reasonably be said that if not for the negligence, the loss, injury or damage would not have occurred. Negligence may be a legal cause of damage even though it operates in combination with the act of another, a natural cause, or some other cause if the other cause occurs at the same time as the negligence and if the negligence contributes substantially to producing such damage." (See www.lectlaw.com/def2/n010.htm.)

7.2 ELEMENTS OF NEGLIGENCE

As a general rule, a person will not be found liable for negligence unless the plaintiff is able to prove four essential elements.

(1)   There must be a duty of care on the part of the defendant toward the plaintiff.
(2)   There must be a breach of the duty of care owed by the defendant to the plaintiff.
(3)   There must be actual damage or loss sustained by the plaintiff.
(4)   The breach of duty must be the proximate cause of the damage or loss.

The onus of proof is on the plaintiff is to prove his or her case upon a "balance of probabilities", rather than "beyond a reasonable doubt".

7.3 THE STANDARD OF CARE

"The standard of care to be exercised by school authorities in providing for the supervision and protection of students for whom they are responsible is that of the careful or prudent parent . . . . It is not, however, a standard which can be applied in the same manner and to the same extent in every case. Its application will vary from case to case and will depend upon the number of students being supervised at any given time, the nature of the exercise or activity in progress, the age and the degree of skill and training which the students may have received in connection with such activity, the nature and condition of the equipment in use at the time, the competency and capacity of the students involved, and a host of other matters which may be widely varied but which, in a given case, may affect the application of the prudent parent-standard. . . ." (*Myers v. Peel (County) Board of Education),* [1981] 2 S.C.R. 21, 123 D.L.R. (3d) 1, 17 C.C.L.T. 269, 37 N.R. 227, 1981 CarswellOnt 579, 1981 CarswellOnt 612 (S.C.C.) at 31-32 [S.C.R.].)

"[T]he schoolmaster was bound to take such care of his boys as a careful father would take of his boys, and there could not be a better definition of the duty of a schoolmaster. Then he was bound to take notice of the ordinary nature of young boys, their tendency to do mischievous acts, and their propensity to meddle with anything that came in their way." (*Williams v. Eady* (1893), 10 T.L.R. 41 (Eng. C.A.) at 42.)

"I do not suggest that it is the duty of a school teacher or a supervisor to keep pupils under supervision during every minute while they are in attendance at school. . . . He must guard the pupils against danger that could reasonably be foreseen." (*Toronto (City) Board of Education v. Higgs* (1959), [1960] S.C.R. 174, 22 D.L.R. (2d) 49, 1959 CarswellOnt 91 (S.C.C.) at 181 [S.C.R.].) See also *Misir v. Children's Rehabilitation Centre of Essex County,* [1989] O.J. No. 1653 (Ont. Dist. Ct.).

7.4 DANGEROUS ACTIVITIES

The fact that a teacher permits his or her students to participate in a potentially dangerous activity is not, in itself, negligence. However, the standard of care taken must be appropriate to the activity, whether it be sports, outdoor education, laboratory experiments, etc. In each case, the teacher is expected to guard against the reasonably foreseeable dangers of the activity.

For example, in *Brost v. Tilley School District*, 1955 CarswellAlta 31, 15 W.W.R. 241, [1955] 3 D.L.R. 159 (Alta. C.A.), the school board and principal were found liable for failing to provide supervision where a 6-year old girl was injured after being pushed too high on a swing set by another student. The Court found that there was a failure "to exercise the degree of care the law required of them to safeguard the small pupils in the use of the swings. . ..It was a thing quite foreseeable that this accident or some such accident would happen sooner or later." (At para. 1.)

7.5 PHYSICAL EDUCATION

Many school negligence lawsuits arise out of accidents in the gymnasium or on the sports field. An accident may result from faulty or inadequate equipment. In other instances, a pupil may have incurred injuries because he or she was not adequately trained in the activity, or was not properly supervised. The *Thornton* case outlines the expected standard of care to be exercised by teachers:

(1)   The exercise must be suitable to the student's age and condition (mental and physical).
(2)   The student must be progressively trained to do the exercise properly and avoid danger.
(3)   The equipment must be adequate and suitably arranged.
(4)   The performance of the exercise must be properly supervised, having regard to its inherently dangerous nature.

See *Thornton v. Prince George Board of Education*, [1976] 5 W.W.R. 240, 73 D.L.R. (3d) 35, 1976 CarswellBC 214 (B.C. C.A.), varied [1978] 2 S.C.R. 267, 3 C.C.L.T. 257, [1978] 1 W.W.R. 607, 19 N.R. 552, 83 D.L.R. (3d) 480, 1978 CarswellBC 370, 1978 CarswellBC 554 (S.C.C.).

7.6 ASSUMPTION OF RISK IN SPORTS

A person who participates in a game or sport assumes the inherent risks of participation. This assumes that the player is of an age and experience to be aware of the inherent risks. Dangers which are not inherent, or which are unreasonable, are not assumed. A player does not assume the risk of being intentionally injured and does not assume that other players will act with wanton disregard for his or her safety.

In the case of *Thomas v. Hamilton (City) Board of Education* (1994), 20 O.R. (3d) 598, 85 O.A.C. 161, 1994 CarswellOnt 1203 (Ont. C.A.), which involved very serious injuries sustained by a pupil during a school football game, the Ontario Court of Appeal had this to say about pupils consenting to participate in dangerous sports:

> The appellant does not take the position that football is so inherently dangerous a game that high school students should not be permitted to participate in it. Nor does the appellant contend that his high school should not have participated in junior and senior football programs. This latter issue arose because many of Scott Park's players have part-time employment with the result that they are not available for practice on Fridays.
>
> The appellant participated in his high school's junior football program of his own free will. He was aware of the risk of injury, even serious injury, that is inherent to participation in a contact sport such as football. However, he did not, through his consent to participate (and that of his mother), assume all risk of injury to the extent that the school authorities were relieved of the duty of care that they owed to him.
>
> The appellant was not incapacitated, let alone obviously incapacitated, as was the case in *Crocker v. Sundance Northwest Resorts Ltd.*, [1988] 1 S.C.R. 1186, 51 D.L.R. (4th) 321. He had his mother's consent, and his family doctor's certificate stating that he was fit to play football. He knew football was a contact sport which carried with it the risk of serious injury. He wore a "horse collar" because he was aware of the fact that his neck was exposed to injury. He said, as the trial judge noted in his reasons for judgment, that even if he had specifically contemplated the risk of a catastrophic neck injury, he would probably have continued to play.
>
> The appellant was appropriately and progressively coached. He was an excellent athlete who excelled in a number of sports, including football. His equipment was adequate. The injury he sustained occurred during a routine play and, although the consequences of his injury were, and continue to be, devastating, the injury came within the ambit of those risks inherent in a contact sport such as football. He did not, of course, give a consent which would overcome negligent conduct on the part of the Board or his coaches. However, I agree with the trial judge that neither the Board nor the coaches were negligent and that the appellant and his mother "consented to the normal risks of the game". I am not prepared to say that the trial judge was wrong in reaching that conclusion. (20 O.R. (3d) 598, at p. 619.)

A duty of care is also owed to spectators at sports activities. For example, in *Plumb (Guardian ad litem of) v. Cowichan School District No. 65* (1993), 1993 CarswellBC 239, [1993] B.C.J. No. 1936, 83 B.C.L.R. (2d) 161, (*sub nom. Plumb v. Board of Education of Cowichan School District No. 65*) 33 B.C.A.C. 300, (*sub nom. Plumb v. Board of Education of Cowichan School District No. 65*) 54 W.A.C. 300 (B.C. C.A.), the plaintiff was struck in the eye by a ball while a spectator of a game of catch being played by fellow students. There was no evidence that the students were acting in a foolish manner or "goofing off". The ball was simply mis-thrown. The appellate court approved the following analysis by the trial judge (at para. 7):

> Was the standard of conduct of the participant, as accepted and expected by the spec-tator, that which the sport permitted and involved? A person attending a game or com-petition takes the risk of any damage caused to him by any act of a participant done in the course of and for the purpose of the game or competition, notwithstanding that such act might involve an error of judgment or lapse of skill, unless the participant's conduct was such as to evidence a reckless disregard of the spectator's safety or was deliberately intended to injure someone whose presence was known so that it was a departure from the standards which might reasonably be expected in anyone pursuing the competition or game.

7.7 Injuries and First Aid

If a pupil is injured at school or during a school activity, first aid must be administered if the injury so requires. This means that the supervising staff member must be able to provide first aid, or ensure that someone else is available to administer it. Even if the school staff are not negligent with respect to the occurrence of an accident, they can be found liable if first aid is not administered, or if it is administered incompetently.

Where necessary, proper medical attention must be secured. Parents must be notified and a written record made concerning the accident. Boards have their own internal procedures to be followed in the event of an acci-dent.

Prior to the administration of any medical or first aid procedure, the con-sent of the pupil must be obtained. If the pupil does not have the capacity to consent (for example, is too young to understand) then the consent of a parent or guardian must be obtained. Ideally, both the pupil and the parent will indicate their consent, in writing. The matter of obtaining a consent in the event that an emergency might arise should be dealt with in advance, usually at the beginning of the school year. Only in absolute emergencies should medication or first aid be administered by school staff without prior informed consent.

7.8 Activities Before or After the School Day

Normally, the board is legally responsible for the safety of its pupils only during school hours or during authorized out-of-school activities. The board may be legally responsible for pupils who arrive early or leave late if it has allowed the pupils to do so. Unless it is made very clear to parents and pupils, on a consistent basis, as to when the school or school yard is open, the board may be found liable for accidents which occur outside the normal hours. Once parents and pupils are aware of the hours during which the school or playground is officially open, the board will not normally be found liable for injuries during non-school related activities by persons on the property outside those hours. However, as an "occupier" of premises as defined in the *Occupier's Liability Act*, a board has a statutory duty of care toward persons coming onto the premises, regardless of whether they are pupils at its schools.

It is well established as a general rule that the board is not responsible for accidents on the way to and from school. However, if a board arranges pupil transportation, it could be found liable if pupils are injured while being transported or after being let off a school bus. Depending on the facts and the transportation arrangements, the board, the driver and the bus charter company could be found liable. However, in *Baldwin v. Erin District High School Board*, 1961 CarswellOnt 137, [1961] O.R. 687, 29 D.L.R. (2d) 290 (Ont. C.A.), affirmed [1962] S.C.R. vii, 36 D.L.R. (2d) 244 (S.C.C.), a school board was able to defended itself successfully. The Ontario Court of Appeal held that the board was not liable for injuries to students arising from a school bus accident where the bus was operated by an independent contractor and the board had no control, or entitlement to assert control, over the manner of driving the bus or the hiring of the drivers.

Liability may arise where a student is sent home in circumstances where there is foreseeable danger, such as during a severe storm, or where a young pupil is sent home alone without the usual supervision, as for example, by an older brother or sister.

7.9 PAST PRACTICE

In defending a negligence claim, the defendant may try to show that he or she was following a well established practice with respect to the alleged negligent act or omission. However, if the practice itself is negligent, it is not a defense to say that it has always been done a certain way.

7.10 VICARIOUS LIABILITY AND FIDUCIARY DUTY

(a) Vicarious Liability

In many instances, the defendants in a tort action are the teacher involved, the principal (whether directly involved or not) and the school board. The plaintiff's lawyer will issue a statement of claim against everyone who is potentially liable because one cannot always predict how a judge or jury will find or apportion liability.

Where an employee is found to have been negligent or to have committed an intentional tort such as assault or battery, the school board, even though it may not be at fault itself, may be held vicariously liable for the employee's conduct. Thus, for example, if a board fails to provide adequate supervision, it may be found liable for direct negligence. However, if the board does provide adequate supervision, but an individual teacher negligently harms a student, the board may be held vicariously liable for the teacher's breach of the duty of care.

In recent years, the issue has arisen as to institutional liability for physical and sexual assault committed by staff members upon children in their care. The "test" for vicarious liability in these circumstances was articulated by the Supreme Court of Canada in *B. (P.A.) v. Curry*, 1999 CarswellBC 1264, 1999 CarswellBC 1265, [1999] S.C.J. No. 35, (*sub nom. B. v. Curry*) 99 C.L.L.C. 210-033, 43 C.C.E.L. (2d) 1, 62 B.C.L.R. (3d) 173, (*sub nom. P.A.B. v. Children's Foundation*) 124 B.C.A.C. 119, (*sub nom. P.A.B. v. Children's Foundation*) 203 W.A.C. 119, (*sub nom. P.A.B. v. Children's Foundation*) 241 N.R. 266, 174 D.L.R. (4th) 45, [1999] 8 W.W.R. 197, [1999] L.V.I. 3046-1, 46 C.C.L.T. (2d) 1, [1999] 2 S.C.R. 534 (S.C.C.). While it is clear that an employer is vicariously liable for an employee's acts authorized by the employer, the real issue is their liability for unauthorized acts, such as sexual assault. The defendant Curry was employed as a residence counsellor by the Children's Foundation in British Columbia. He was expected and permitted to act very much in the role of a parent toward the young children under his care, and he took advantage of this position of control in order to engage in sexual misconduct.

The Supreme Court of Canada held (at para. 46) that the ". . .test for vicarious liability for an employee's sexual abuse of a client should focus on whether the employer's enterprise and empowerment of the employee materially increased the risk of the sexual assault and hence the harm.. . .This requires trial judges to investigate the employee's specific duties and determine whether they gave rise to special opportunities for wrongdoing. Because of the peculiar exercises of power and trust that pervade cases such as child abuse, special attention should be paid to the existence of a power or dependency relationship, which on its own often creates a considerable risk of wrongdoing."

In *T. (G.) v. Griffiths*, 1999 CarswellBC 1262, 1999 CarswellBC 1263, [1999] S.C.J. No. 36, (*sub nom. J. v. Griffiths*) 99 C.L.L.C. 210-034, (*sub nom. G.T.-J. v. Griffiths*) 241 N.R. 201, 174 D.L.R. (4th) 71, 124 B.C.A.C. 161, 203 W.A.C. 161, 63 B.C.L.R. (3d) 1, [1999] L.V.I. 3046-2, [1999] 9 W.W.R. 1, 46 C.C.L.T. (2d) 49, 44 C.C.E.L. (2d) 169, [1999] 2 S.C.R. 570 (S.C.C.), released at the same time as Curry, the Supreme Court of Canada found that a Boy's and Girl's Club was not vicariously liable for sexual assault committed by an employee. The employee took advantage of his position with the Club to make friends with children, but whatever power he used to achieve his ends was not conferred by the Club, nor was it characteristic of the type of enterprise that the Club put into the community. See also *G. (E.D.) v. Hammer* (cited below), in which the trial judge held that a school board was not vicariously liable for the sexual misconduct of a school janitor toward a young female student. This finding was not appealed to the appellate courts in this case because the *T. (G.) v. Griffiths* (cited above) made it clear that the appeal would be unsuccessful on this ground. (See also *B. (K.L.) v. British Columbia*, 2003 CarswellBC 2405, 2003 CarswellBC 2406, 18 B.C.L.R. (4th) 1, 19 C.C.L.T. (3d) 66, 230 D.L.R. (4th) 513, [2003] 11 W.W.R. 203, 2003 SCC 51 (S.C.C.) in which the Supreme Court of Canada held that the Province was not vicariously liable for sexual abuse committed by foster parents, although it was held directly liable for negligence in the placement and supervision of the children.)

(b) Fiduciary Duty

The concept of vicarious liability is different from that of liability for "breach of fiduciary duty". To begin with, vicarious liability does not require a finding of fault on the part of the employer, whereas "fault" is required to find a breach of fiduciary duty. In *G. (E.D.) v. Hammer*, 2003 CarswellBC 2407, 2003 CarswellBC 2408, 18 B.C.L.R. (4th) 42, 19 C.C.L.T. (3d) 38, 230 D.L.R. (4th) 554, [2003] 11 W.W.R. 244, 2003 SCC 52 (S.C.C.), the Supreme Court of Canada recognized that a school board does have a fiduciary duty toward its pupils, but held that, in the circumstances, it did not breach that duty. The issue in this case was the nature and scope of the fiduciary duty. The Court rejected the argument that the board's fiduciary duty meant that it had a duty to act in the "best interests of the child". In drawing a parallel to parental fiduciary duty, the Court noted (at para. 23):

> The maxim that parents should act in their child's best interests may help to justify particular parental fiduciary duties, but it does not constitute a basis for liability. The cases on the parental fiduciary duty focus not on achieving what is in the child's best interest, but on specific conduct that causes harm to children in a manner involving disloyalty, self-interest, or abuse of power—failing to act selflessly in the interests of the child.

Turning to the board's fiduciary duty, the Court stated (at para. 24):

> Fiduciary obligations are not obligations to guarantee a certain outcome for the vulnerable party, regardless of fault. They do not hold the fiduciary to a certain type of outcome, exposing the fiduciary to liability whenever the vulnerable party is harmed by one of the fiduciary's employees.

In the *Hammer* case, the Court found that the only person at fault was the school janitor. There was no act or omission on the part of the board that might amount to breach of its fiduciary duty, and the board had no reason to suspect that the janitor was engaged in any inappropriate behaviour with the children. See also *B. (K.L.) v. British Columbia* (cited above).

7.11 EDUCATIONAL MALPRACTICE

In a lawsuit for "education malpractice" the plaintiff will allege that he or she has suffered damages because the school board did not fulfill its duty to educate the plaintiff. For example, some persons have claimed damages because they graduated from school without the necessary skills to get a job. To date, education malpractice claims have been unsuccessful in Canada and the United States. The courts recognize that a child's failure to achieve age-appropriate learning outcomes is subject to many variables that affect an individual's ability to learn, including his or her innate intelligence, home environment, language barriers, and nutrition. See, for example, *Hicks v. Etobicoke (City) Board of Education* (November 23, 1988), Doc. 306622/87, [1988] O.J. No. 1900 (Ont. Dist. Ct.), where a claim for education malpractice was struck by the Court as disclosing no reasonable cause of action. See also *Haynes (Guardian ad litem of) v. Lleres* (March 10, 1997), Doc. Vancouver 969025, [1997] B.C.J. No. 1202 (B.C. Prov. Ct.), where the Court dismissed a negligence claim alleging inadequate implementation of an education program after finding that it was in effect asserting education malpractice. "Educational malpractice" is distinguishable from negligence that a court *will* recognize, such as misdiagnosis of a child's learning disability, school yard accidents resulting from lack of supervision, or harm caused by improper first aid.

In addition to the difficulty of actually proving all of the constituent elements of negligence in court (duty, breach of duty, damages, proximate cause), the plaintiff is faced with the reluctance of judges to second-guess the professional judgment of educators in matters of pedagogy. Some courts in the United States have said that even if negligence were proved, they would reject the claim on the basis that allowing it would be contrary to public policy. However, if a very strong fact situation were to arise in which the plaintiff could prove "gross negligence" by the board or its employees, we may yet see a successful lawsuit based on educational malpractice.

7.12 TALKING TO PARENTS AND OTHERS

Children are hurt at school as a result of accidents and as a result of intentional actions such as bullying, taunting, extortion, and assault. After an accident or other incident, parents must be informed by the school about any actual or suspected injury to their child as soon as possible. Regardless of how an accident or incident occurred, or who may be at fault, sympathetic communication of clear information to parents by the appropriate school or board official will be appreciated by any concerned parent. Lack of communication may lead to hostility and a greater chance of being sued. However, it is important to be aware that statements by board representatives can be used by a plaintiff in a lawsuit against the board. Therefore, there are limits to what should be said. The board's insurer is responsible for investigating accidents in accordance with the board's insurance policy. Board staff must be careful not to jeopardize the proper handling of a insurance investigation, or indeed, of a police investigation (e.g. of suspected assault).

Principals and teachers:

- should not admit liability for any accident or other incident that occurs on school property
- should not give oral or written statements to parents or opposing lawyers or insurance adjusters
- should cooperate with the insurance adjuster and lawyer who represent the school board
- should keep detailed notes on any incident resulting in suspected or actual personal injury or loss of property
- should not share any insurance reports or personal notes with parents unless permitted to do so by the board's insurer

- should immediately inform senior administration and the board's insurer about the accident or other incident, using the board-approved forms and procedures. (Note: Injuries to employees at the workplace must be reported by the employer as required by the *Workplace Safety and Insurance Act, 1997.*)

8

School Administration

This chapter contains practical information about a variety of topics that are of particular importance in respect of the administration and operation of schools.

8.1 THE SCHOOL YEAR AND SCHOOL CALENDAR

(a) What is a "School Day"?

To know what a school day is, you have to know what the "school year" and "school holidays" are.

A "school day" is a day that is within the "school year" and is not a "school holiday". A school day is either an instructional day or a professional activity day. An instructional day can be an examination day.

(b) How Long is the School Day?

The minimum length of the instructional program of each school day for pupils of compulsory school age is five hours (300 minutes), excluding recesses and scheduled intervals between classes.

The length of the instructional program may be reduced for pupils in special education programs.

The instructional program cannot be scheduled to start earlier than 8:00 a.m. or end later than 5:00 p.m. The Minister may permit exceptions to this.

A board may establish the length of the instructional program on each school day for pupils in junior kindergarten and kindergarten.

(c) How Long is the Lunch Break?

The lunch break for pupils and teachers is a minimum of 40 consecutive minutes. The lunch break is a scheduled interval between classes — it is part of the school day. A pupil's scheduled lunch break need not coincide with the lunch break for any other pupil or any teacher. Similarly, a teacher's scheduled lunch break need not coincide with the lunch break of any other teacher or any pupil (s. 3(5), (5.1), (5.2), Reg. 298).

(d) Are Recesses Required?

In the primary and junior division, there must be a morning and afternoon recess of not less than 10 minutes and not more than 15 minutes.

In the intermediate and senior divisions, the principal may, with the board's approval, provide for recesses or for intervals between periods.

(e) When is a School Supposed to be Open for the Day?

The board may determine when its school buildings and playgrounds will be open to its pupils. However, schools must be open to pupils during the period beginning 15 minutes before classes begin for the day and ending 15 minutes after classes end for the day.

(f) What is a School Year?

Regulation 304 contains the requirements for a school year, which are reflected in the board's school calendar(s). A board may obtain permission from the Minister to have a school calendar or calendars that modify the usual requirements.

(g) What are the Usual Legal Requirements for a School Year Calendar?

A school year must have at least 194 school days and shall commence on or after September 1st and end on or before June 30th.

(h) What is an Instructional Day?

An instructional day is a day on which the pupils are required to be in attendance at school. Examination days are also instructional days.

No more than 10 examination days may be scheduled on a school calendar. (Section 11(7.1) of the *Education Act.*) This also applies to "modified" calendars — please see below.

(i) What is a Professional Activity Day?

A professional activity day is a school day on which pupils do not attend school and which is scheduled for teachers to engage in professional activities.

"Professional activity" *includes* evaluation of the progress of pupils, consultation with parents, the counselling of pupils, curriculum and program evaluation and development, professional development of teachers and attendance at educational conferences (s. 1(1), Reg. 304). The use of the word "includes" indicates that this list is not exhaustive.

No more than four professional activity days may be scheduled on a school calendar (s. 11(7.1), *Education Act*). This applies to all school calendars, including "modified" calenders.

A board must annually evaluate the activities that take place on professional activity days (s. 8 Reg. 304).

(j) What is a "Modified" School Calendar?

A modified school calendar for a school or schools is one that does not adhere to the regular calendar requirements. For instance, it might have a start date earlier than September 1st or it might end later than June 30th. It could have less than 194 school days, or more. It could involve "year-round schooling".

If a board wants to have a modified calendar, it must submit it by March
1st for approval by the Minister, for the following school year. If the
Minister has not approved the requested calendar, or a revised request, by
April 15th, the board must resubmit a calendar (by May 1st) that is not
modified (i.e. complies with the "usual" requirements).

(k) Can a Board Change a School Calendar After it is Filed?

A board may change the date of a professional activity day or an examination day. It must notify the parents and the Minister of the change
(ss. 6(1) and (2), Reg. 304). Any other changes must be approved by the
Minister (s. 6(3), Reg. 304).

(l) How Does the Community Learn About the School Calendar?

The school calendar or calendars for the board's schools must be published
each year. The board must ensure that copies are available at the beginning
of the school year for parents and pupils. The information must also indicate "in a general manner" the nature of the professional activities to be
conducted on professional activity days.

(m) Is Remembrance Day a School Holiday?

No, Remembrance Day is not a school holiday. However, Remembrance
services must be held by the school on Remembrance Day, at the school
or in conjunction with a community service (s. 9, Reg. 304).

(n) What are the School Holidays?

According to subsection 2(4) of Regulation 304, school holidays are:

* Every Saturday and Sunday
* Canada Day (if school is open in July)
* Labour Day
* Thanksgiving Day (or a day appointed by the Governor-General or
  Lieutenant Governor as a public holiday)

- Christmas Vacation — two weeks (14 consecutive days commencing on the Monday next following the Friday preceding the 21st day of December, but when the 21st day of December is a Thursday or a Friday, commencing on the Monday next following)
- March Break — one week (five consecutive days commencing on the Monday next following the Friday preceding the 14th day of March)
- Good Friday
- Easter Monday
- Victoria Day.

These holidays can be changed in a modified school year calendar, with Ministerial approval.

(o) May a Pupil be Absent on Other Days?

The *Education Act* prescribes the circumstances under which a pupil may be excused from attendance at school (s. 21(2)). For example, a pupil may be absent on a religious holy day.

Boards often try to avoid scheduling key school events that coincide with high holidays of the major religions of persons within their jurisdiction.

Alternative arrangements for examinations should be provided to any pupil who cannot write an examination on the normal date for religious reasons.

8.2 VISITORS AND TRESPASSERS

(a) Who has the Right to Visit a School?

A parent or guardian may visit the school that his or her child is attending and a member of the board may attend a school that is operated by the board. A member of the Assembly (i.e. Ontario Legislature) may visit a school in the member's constituency. A member of the clergy may visit a public school in the area where the member has pastoral charge. A member of the clergy of the Roman Catholic Church may visit a Roman Catholic school in the area where the member has pastoral charge. These provisions are in section 50 (public) and section 53 (Roman Catholic) of the *Education Act*.

(b) What Can a School Do About Trespassers on School Property?

Subject to an appeal to the school board, a principal has the duty to refuse to admit to the school or classroom a person whose presence in the school or classroom would in the principal's judgment be detrimental to the physical or mental well-being of the pupils (s. 265(1)(m), *Education Act*). It is an offence to wilfully interrupt or disquiet the proceedings of a school or class. There is a maximum fine of $200 upon conviction (s. 212(1)).

The *Education Act* provides another tool for keeping unwanted persons out of schools or for restricting the purposes for which they are permitted to enter or remain on the premises. Section 305 permits the Minister of Education to make regulations governing access to school premises, specifying classes of persons who are permitted to be on school premises, and specifying the days and times at which different classes of persons are prohibited from being on school premises.

Subsection 305(2) prescribes a blanket prohibition against any person entering or remaining on school premises unless authorized to be there under the regulation. Moreover, a board may, by policy, prohibit any person from entering or remaining on school premises:

305(2) No person shall enter or remain on school premises unless he or she is authorized by regulation to be there on that day or at that time.

305(3) A person shall not enter or remain on school premises if he or she is prohibited under a board policy from being there on that day or at that time.

305(4) The principal of a school may direct a person to leave the school premises if he or she believes that the person is prohibited by regulation or under a board policy from being there.

It is an offence to contravene a prohibition in the regulation.

It is noteworthy that the starting point in section 305 is that persons may not be on school premises and must find something in the regulation that lets them enter or remain there. The law then permits a school board to prohibit persons from being on school premises, implying that they would otherwise be permitted by the regulation to be there at a given time or on a given day.

Turning to Ontario Regulation 474/00, we see that the following persons are permitted to be on school premises on any day and at any time:

1.   a person enrolled as a pupil in the school
2.   a parent or guardian of such a pupil

3.   a person employed or retained by the board
4.   a person who is otherwise on the premises for a lawful purpose.

The first three of the above items are logical. The fourth item permits persons on the school premises if they are there for a lawful purpose. "Lawful purpose" is not defined. Presumably, trespassers are not on the premises for a lawful purpose, but they are already excluded from the property under the *Trespass to Property Act*.

It remains for the school board devise a policy to place limits on the access that will be permitted to any of the four classes of persons listed above. The prohibition can be a blanket prohibition covering all days and times, or it may define the day and time during which it applies. It could, for example, permit members of the general public to have access to the school yard during the evenings and weekends, but prohibit access during school hours.

Ontario Regulation 474/00 also states that a person is not permitted to remain on school premises if his or her presence is detrimental to the safety or well-being of a person on the premises, in the judgment of the principal, a vice-principal, or another person authorized by the board to make such a determination (s. 3(1)). This provision should be compared to section 265(1)(m) of the *Education Act*, which states that a principal has a duty, subject to an appeal to the board, to refuse to admit to the school or classroom a person whose presence in the school or classroom would, in the principal's judgment, be detrimental to the physical or mental well-being of the pupils.

Ontario Regulation 474/00 is broader in that it refers to protecting the well-being of persons, not exclusively pupils. It gives the principal, vice-principal, and other authorized persons the power to exclude others from the school, whereas section 265(1)(m) is confined to principals and is stated as a "duty". In addition, there is no right of appeal to the school board under the Regulation, whereas there is under section 265(1)(m). Both provisions can be used to exclude pupils from school under appropriate circumstances. In my view, neither provision should be used as substitute for the suspension and expulsion provisions in the Act. Moreover, if a principal wishes to temporarily exclude a pupil from school because the pupil's presence is detrimental to the well-being of other pupils, he or she should do so under section 265(1)(m) because it provides a right of appeal. Deprivation of the right to attend school should always have an avenue of appeal to the board, and must be preceded by as thorough an investigation of the facts as is possible in the circumstances.

Ontario Regulation 474/00 also provides that a person is not permitted to remain on school premises if a policy of the board requires the person to report his or her presence on the premises in a specified manner and the person fails to do so (s. 3(2)). Therefore, for example, if a person fails to report to the school office upon entering the school, where there is a policy that requires reporting, the principal has the authority to ask the person to leave.

The *Trespass to Property Act* says that a school board has the rights and duties of an occupier in respect of its school sites. A "school site" means "land or premises or an interest in land or premises required by a board for a school, school playground, school garden, teacher's residence, caretaker's residence, gymnasium, offices, parking areas or for any other school purpose" (s. 1, *Education Act*).

Under the *Trespass to Property Act* the offence of trespassing consists of any of the following, where the person is not acting under a right or authority conferred by law:

(a)   Entering premises when entry is prohibited. Entry may be prohibited by means of notice to that effect. The Act also presumes that entry is prohibited in some circumstances without notice (e.g. property enclosed in a manner that indicates the occupier's intention to keep persons off the premises).

(b)   Engaging in an activity on premises when the activity is prohibited. An occupier may give notice as to the restricted or prohibited activities on the premises (e.g. no hardball; no skateboarding; no swimming).

(c)   Failing to leave the premises immediately after being directed to do so by the occupier of the premises or a person authorized by the occupier.

Notice under the *Trespass to Property Act* may be given orally, in writing, by means of signs, or by means of a marking system.

A police officer, or the occupier, or a person authorized by the occupier, may arrest without warrant any person he or she believes on reasonable and probable grounds to be trespassing in contravention of the Act. If the person making the arrest is not a police officer, he or she must promptly call for a police officer and deliver the person arrested to the police officer. If the suspected trespasser is off the premises, only a police officer may make an arrest under the Act. A person placed under arrest has certain rights under the *Charter of Rights and Freedoms*, including the right not to be arbitrarily arrested or imprisoned, the right to retain and instruct counsel, and the right to be informed of the reason for arrest. Infringement of these rights may result in the arrested person being acquitted at trial.

The *Trespass to Property Act* gives an occupier the right to obtain a judgment for up to $1,000 in damages against a convicted trespasser. Where granted, such a judgment extinguishes the right to seek damages in a civil lawsuit arising out of the same facts.

8.3 STUDENT RECORDS

(a) Are Pupil Records Confidential?

Yes, the information in a pupil's record is confidential. Certain information about a pupil is required to kept in the pupil's Ontario Student Record (OSR). Not all information about a pupil is contained in the OSR. The requirements about OSR contents are contained in the Ontario Student Record Guideline which is issued by the Minister under the authority of paragraph 8(1)[27] of the *Education Act*. A pupil has one official OSR, and if the pupil transfers from one school to another school within Ontario, the OSR is sent to the receiving school. The OSR is not transferred out of Ontario (see s. 6 of the OSR Guideline). Section 266 of the Act only applies to the contents of an OSR. It says that a pupil's Ontario Student Record is "privileged" for the information and use of the supervisory officers, the principal and teachers of the school for the improvement of the instruction of the pupil. The record is not available to any other person *except*:

(a)   the pupil
(b)   the pupil's parent or guardian if the pupil is a minor
(c)   the local medical officer of health
(d)   a Ministry-appointed person who is hearing a dispute about the contents of a record under subsection 266(5)

unless the parent or guardian (of a pupil who is a minor), or the pupil (if the pupil is an adult,) has given written permission to make the record available. A "guardian" includes a person designated by a Children's Aid Society, where the society has custody of the child.

The local medical officer of health is only entitled to the following limited information from the record:

•   the pupil's name, address, telephone number
•   the pupil's birth date

- the name, address and telephone number of the pupil's parent or guardian.

The school principal may divulge information from the OSR if he or she is making a report that is required under the *Education Act* or regulations. Section 266 does not prevent the principal from compiling and delivering information that is required by the Minister or the board.

The school principal may also divulge information from the OSR if he or she is making a report:

(1)   for an educational institution, a pupil or a former pupil in respect of an application for further education, or
(2)   for a pupil or former pupil in respect of an application for employment,

if a written request for the report is made by the former pupil, the adult pupil or the parent/guardian of the pupil who is a minor.

The principal of the pupil's school and the school board may use the OSR for the purpose of a disciplinary proceeding against the pupil instituted by the principal.

Except as permitted in section 266, every person must "preserve secrecy in respect of the content of a record that comes to the person's knowledge in the course of his or her duties or employment" (s. 266(10)). The information in the person's knowledge cannot be communicated to any other person except:

- as may be required in the performance of his or her duties, or
- with the written consent of the parent or guardian of the pupil where the pupil is a minor, or
- with the written consent of the pupil where the pupil is an adult.

No person can be required in any trial or other proceeding to give evidence in respect of the content of a record except where the record has been introduced as evidence as provided in section 266. Unless the written permission of the parent/guardian or adult pupil is obtained, the record is not admissible in evidence for any purpose in any trial, inquest, inquiry, examination, hearing or other proceeding, except to prove the establishment, transfer, maintenance, retention or transfer of the record (s. 266(2)). The exception to this is a hearing held under subsection 266(5) by a Ministry-appointed person.

(b) How Can a Parent Get Information Removed from a Record?

Much of the information in a pupil's OSR is included because the OSR Guideline gives the principal no choice about the matter. However, disputes do arise about some information that a school has included in the OSR. An adult pupil, or the parent or guardian of a pupil who is a minor, may request the removal of information in a record if he or she is of the opinion that the information is inaccurately recorded or is not conducive to the improvement of instruction of the pupil. A request must be in writing and must ask the principal to correct the alleged inaccuracy or to remove the impugned information from the record. If the principal refuses to comply with the request, the person making the request may, in writing, require the principal to refer the request to the appropriate supervisory officer. The supervisory officer must:

(1)   require the principal to comply with the request, or
(2)   submit the record and the request to a person designated by the Minister.

The person designated by the Minister, usually an experienced education officer, must hold a hearing. The principal and the person making the request are the parties at the hearing. The designated person decides the matter and his or her decision is final and binding upon the parties.

(c) Does a Non-Custodial Parent Have Access to a Child's OSR?

Even if separated or divorced, a parent has a right of access to their child and this includes the right to be given information about the child's education (s. 20, *Child and Family Services Act* and s. 16, *Divorce Act*). This right can be restricted by a court order dealing with custody and access. If such an order exists, a copy of it should be provided to the child's school so that school staff are aware of it. The staff are not, however, responsible for *enforcing* the terms of custody orders, and if problems arise, it is up to the parent to enforce the order.

(d) Can a Court Order that a Student Record be Disclosed?

As noted above, unless there is a consent of the parent/guardian or adult pupil to release information that is contained in the pupil's record, the record is not admissible in evidence for any purpose in any trial, inquest, inquiry, examination, hearing or other proceeding, except to prove the establishment, transfer, maintenance, retention or transfer of the record (s. 266(2)). If a principal receives a summons in a civil proceeding to produce a student record, and there is no written consent for the release of the record, he or she should (subject to advice from the board solicitor) respond to the summons by attending court, and should explain (directly or through counsel) to the court that the *Education Act* prohibits the release of the record. The court may nevertheless order that the OSR be produced to the requesting party, which may then seek to adduce the record as evidence.

In proceedings under federal legislation, such as the *Criminal Code* (Canada), the rules are different. If a summons is issued under federal legislation, it takes precedence over the non-disclosure provisions in section 266 of the *Education Act*. Principals must therefore obey a search warrant, and they must obey a summons to attend a court with documents. The judge may be asked to make a determination of the relevance of the documents before admitting them as evidence. The principal is normally summoned to testify that the student records are what they purport to be. The principal should, through counsel, seek permission of the court to leave a copy of the OSR with the court, rather than the original.

Pursuant to the *Child and Family Services Act*, a court may order the principal of a school to produce the OSR for inspection and copying by a Children's Aid Society if the court is satisfied that the record contains information that may be relevant to whether the child is suffering abuse or is likely to suffer abuse and the person in control of the record has refused to permit a society director to inspect it. The OSR should not be released to a Children's Aid Society without an appropriate court order (assuming no written permission has been given by a parent or guardian).

(e) Freedom of Information and Protection of Privacy

The *Municipal Freedom of Information and Protection of Privacy Act* governs the use, collection and storage of information, including personal information, by municipalities, school boards and many other institutions. It is based upon two fundamental principles. The first is that the public has the right to have access to records held by these institutions. The second is that personal information should be protected to ensure privacy. The right to see public records is subject to a number of specific exemptions that permit a board to refuse public disclosure. These include:

- records of meetings that are authorized by law to be held in private
- advice or recommendations to the board
- law enforcement records
- information received in confidence from another government
- information from a third party containing trade secrets or scientific, technical, commercial, financial or labour relations information
- information which might prejudice the economic, financial, competitive, or negotiating interests of an institution
- information covered by solicitor-client privilege
- information which if made public, may seriously threaten the safety or health of an individual
- personal information.

Some of the exemptions do not apply if there is a compelling public interest in disclosure of the record. The Information and Privacy Commissioner has the power to decide whether or not information should be disclosed to the person requesting the information.

A "record" means any record of information however recorded, whether in printed form, on film, by electronic means or otherwise, and includes:

(a)   correspondence, a memorandum, a book, a plan, a map, a drawing, a diagram, a pictorial or graphic work, a photograph, a film, a microfilm, a sound recording, videotape, a machine readable record, any other documentary material, regardless of physical form or characteristics, and any copy thereof and

(b)   subject to the regulations, any record that is capable of being produced from a machine readable record under the control of an institution by means of computer hardware and software or any other information storage equipment and technical expertise normally used by the institution.

Oral communications are not records because they are not recorded or retrievable in physical form.

"Personal information" means recorded information about an identifiable individual, including:

(a)   information relating to the race, national or ethnic origin, colour, religion, age, sex, sexual orientation or marital or family status of the individual

(b)   information relating to the education or the medical, psychiatric, psychological, criminal or employment history of the individual or information relating to financial transactions in which the individual has been involved

(c)   any identifying number, symbol, or other particular assigned to the individual

(d)   the address, telephone number, fingerprints or blood type of the individual

(e)   the personal opinions or views of the individual except if they relate to another individual

(f)   correspondence sent to an institution by the individual that is implicitly or explicitly of a private or confidential nature, and replies to that correspondence that would reveal the contents of the original correspondence

(g)   the views or opinions of another individual about the individual

(h)   the individual's name if it appears with other personal information relating to the individual or where the disclosure of the name would reveal other personal information about the individual.

A school board cannot *collect* personal information, directly or indirectly, unless it has the legal authority to do so, and unless the person has been informed that the information will be collected. Under section 32 of the *MFOIPPA, disclosure* of personal information is permitted, for example,

- when there is an oral or written consent by the individual
- when the disclosure is for the purpose for which it was obtained or a consistent purpose
- when disclosure between employees is on a need-to-know basis for job related purposes
- when there are compelling or compassionate circumstances
- when assisting or aiding law enforcement
- when complying with an Act, regulation, by-law or collective agreement
- to the individual's union representative with consent or pursuant to a collective agreement
- to the Chair of the Management Board of Cabinet
- to the Information and Privacy Commissioner and the Provincial and Federal Governments to facilitate auditing of shared cost programs.

The provisions in the *Education Act* and OSR Guideline with respect to the confidentiality, retention and storage of a pupil's student record apply in conjunction with provisions of the *Municipal Freedom of Information and Protection of Privacy Act*. Boards must comply with both statutes, although in case of conflict, the privacy legislation prevails. Under the *Municipal Freedom of Information and Protection of Privacy Act*, a consent for the release of personal information is obtained from persons 16 years of age or older. This does not, however, operate to deprive parents of pupils who are 16 or 17 years old from having access to their child's student record during years 16 and 17.

8.4 DISCIPLINE, SUSPENSION AND EXPULSION

(a) Who is Responsible for Student Discipline?

Proper conduct in the school is the responsibility of the pupil. If the pupil fails to exercise self-discipline and fails to be courteous to fellow students and to teachers, then the principal and teachers have the authority to discipline the pupil. A pupil must accept such discipline as would be exercised by a "kind, firm and judicious parent" and is responsible to the principal of the school for his or her conduct on the school premises, on out-of-school activities that are part of the school program, and while travelling on a school bus (s. 23, Reg. 298).

The principal of a school has the statutory duty to maintain proper order and discipline in the school (s. 265, Act) He or she must report any serious neglect of duty or infraction of the school rules by a pupil to the pupil's parent or guardian (s. 11, Reg. 298). A teacher has a duty to maintain, under the direction of the principal, proper order and discipline in the teacher's classroom and while on duty in the school and on the school grounds (s. 264, Act). A teacher must cooperate with the principal and other teachers to establish and maintain consistent disciplinary practices in the school (s. 20, Reg. 298).

(b) Suspension and Expulsion

Any decision to impose discipline upon a pupil involves a determination of (1) whether the pupil is actually guilty of certain conduct, (2) whether that conduct constitutes grounds for suspension, expulsion, or lesser discipline, under the *Education Act* or board policy, and (3) the severity of the discipline, if any, that should be imposed. The *Safe Schools Act, 2000* ("Bill 81") amended the *Education Act* with respect to the suspension and expulsion of pupils and introduced the concepts of "mandatory" and "discretionary" suspension and expulsion. The mandatory grounds for suspension and expulsion purportedly implement the concept of "zero tolerance" by removing a principal's or board's discretion as to the severity of the discipline where they are satisfied that certain infractions have occurred. However, much of that discretion was returned in the form of the "mitigating factors" regulations, discussed below.

Under the legislative scheme, there are at least ten different kinds of suspension or expulsion-related decisions that can be made with respect to an individual pupil:

Initial Imposition of Discipline:

- one-day suspension (principal or teacher)
- extension of teacher-imposed suspension
- short suspension over one day
- long-term suspension to maximum of 20 days
- limited expulsion
- full expulsion.

Post-Imposition Process:

- review (the powers and duties of the "reviewer" are set by board policy)
- suspension appeal to school board
- limited expulsion appeal
- full expulsion appeal.

Suspension

(i) Mandatory Suspension

Section 306(1) of Act lists infractions that constitute mandatory grounds for suspension from school and all school-related activities if committed while at school or while engaged in a school-related activity. They are mandatory in the sense that school officials and school boards are required to impose a suspension when they are satisfied that an infraction has been committed. The grounds for mandatory suspension are:

- uttering a threat to inflict serious bodily harm on another person
- possessing alcohol or illegal drugs
- being under the influence of alcohol
- swearing at a teacher or another person in a position of authority
- committing an act of vandalism that causes extensive damage to school property at the pupil's school or to property located on the premises of the pupil's school
- engaging in another activity that, under a policy of a board, is one for which a suspension is mandatory.

Ontario Regulation 106/01 provides for mitigating factors. It states that a mandatory suspension is not mandatory if:

(a)   the pupil does not have the ability to control his or her behaviour
(b)   the pupil does not have the ability to understand the foreseeable consequences of his or her behaviour or
(c)   the pupil's continuing presence in the school does not create an unacceptable risk to the safety or well-being of any person.

The meaning of such terms as "threat", "serious bodily harm", "swearing", "extensive damage", and "person in a position of authority" are open to differing interpretations and therefore may result in inconsistent application of the law, even among schools of the same board. Indeed, the Minister of Education has the power under subsection 306(11) to "issue policies and guidelines to boards to assist principals and teachers in interpreting and administering" the mandatory suspension and expulsion provisions.

A principal has a duty to suspend a pupil who commits an infraction for which suspension is mandatory unless a teacher has already suspended the pupil. A principal must also suspend a pupil if he or she believes the pupil may have committed an infraction for which expulsion is mandatory. A mandatory suspension may not exceed 20 days or be for less than one day. Both the maximum and minimum duration can be varied by regulation, and different "standards" may be established for different circumstances and different classes of persons. If a teacher observes a pupil committing an infraction that requires a mandatory suspension, the teacher must either suspend the pupil or refer the matter to the principal. A suspension by a teacher cannot exceed one day (or such lesser period prescribed by regulation). It remains to be seen whether teachers will choose to impose a suspension or refer the matter to the principal. Clearly, a referral will be made if the alleged infraction would justify a suspension longer than one day.

From a procedural fairness perspective, a teacher's decision whether to suspend or refer is important because if a referral is made to the principal and a suspension of longer than one day is imposed, the pupil then has a right to a "review" and an appeal. Pupils who have been suspended for only one day are excluded from the "review" process and the appeal process. They have no formal route of appeal and their only recourse is to apply for judicial review. Because a suspension of any length is a mark against a pupil's academic record, boards may wish to provide a method of appealing a one-day suspension even though this is not required by the legislation.

A teacher may also recommend that his or her imposition of a mandatory suspension should be extended by the principal. The principal must then make a decision as to whether or not to impose an extension, and must satisfy him or herself that appropriate grounds exist. It appears that no extension is possible without the suspending teacher's recommendation. If a teacher imposes a suspension but does *not* recommend an extension, may the principal nevertheless impose a suspension (or other disciplinary measure) in addition to the teacher's suspension? Arguably, the inability to extend a teacher's suspension does not remove the principal's statutory authority to impose a suspension on his or her own initiative. The statutory purpose of enabling teachers to impose short suspensions, and thus deal quickly and effectively with a disciplinary problem, should be interpreted in a way that is compatible with the principals' overall authority to impose order and discipline in the school.

(ii) Discretionary Suspension

A principal may suspend a pupil if the pupil engages in an activity that board policy states is a ground for discretionary suspension. A pupil may be suspended from one or more classes, or one or more school-related activities, or from the school entirely and from all school-related activities. The maximum duration of a suspension is 20 days, although this may be varied by regulation. The minimum duration of a discretionary suspension may be prescribed by board policy. Teachers have the power to suspend a pupil if the pupil is observed engaging in an activity for which suspension is discretionary, but the suspension cannot be for longer than the minimum period set by board policy. Alternatively, a teacher may refer the matter to the principal. As with mandatory suspensions, if the teacher believes a longer suspension is required, he or she may recommend an extension of the suspension to the principal. Written notice of any discretionary or mandatory suspension must be given to the pupil and his/her parent or guardian (if the pupil is a minor).

(iii) Suspension Review

A suspension "review" may be requested by a parent or guardian (or adult pupil), or such other person as specified by board policy. A review is conducted by a person specified in board policy and in accordance with requirements established by board policy. Following a review, the parent/guardian, adult pupil or other person specified in board policy may appeal a decision to suspend to the school board. There is no review of a suspension of one day or less, and a decision to suspend for up to one day cannot be appealed to the board. The purpose of a "review" is unclear on the face of the legislation. It appears to be intended as an opportunity for a senior administrator of the board to give the suspension another "look" and possibly to mediate a solution with the pupil and parents. It enables informal discussion without the greater formality and expense of an appeal. It is an opportunity to clarify expectations in respect of the pupil's behaviour. All participants should clarify at the outset of a review whether their comments or admissions are off the record and without prejudice.

(iv) Suspension Appeal

A suspension appeal must be conducted according to the "requirements" established by board policy. The school board shall "hear and determine" the appeal and for that purpose has the powers and duties set out in board policy. The board's decision is "final". The powers and duties may be delegated to a committee of the board.

(v) Additional Parties to Suspension Review or Appeal

Board policy may allow another "person" to seek a review or to appeal a suspension decision. The right to be a party to a proceeding is obviously important. Possibilities include the school principal, children's aid society, non-custodial parent, and a pupil who is under the age of 18.

Expulsion

(i) Mandatory Expulsion

Expulsion is mandatory where a pupil commits any of the following infractions while at school or engaged in a school-related activity:

- possessing a weapon, including possessing a firearm
- using a weapon to cause or to threaten bodily harm to another person
- committing physical assault on another person that causes bodily harm requiring treatment by a medical practitioner
- committing sexual assault
- trafficking in weapons or in illegal drugs
- committing robbery
- giving alcohol to a minor
- engaging in another activity that, under a policy of the board, is one for which expulsion is mandatory.

Ontario Regulation 37/01 is another "mitigating factor" regulation, and it states that a mandatory expulsion is *not* mandatory if:

(a) the pupil does not have the ability to control his or her behaviour
(b) the pupil does not have the ability to understand the foreseeable consequences of his or her behaviour or
(c) the pupil's continuing presence in the school does not create an unacceptable risk to the safety or well-being of any person.

The minimum duration of a mandatory expulsion is 21 school days. As noted above, a principal is required to suspend a pupil where the principal believes the pupil has committed an infraction for which expulsion is mandatory. Upon suspending the pupil, the principal must either: (1) refer the matter to the board or (2) conduct an "inquiry" into the conduct of the pupil in order to determine if an infraction calling for mandatory expulsion has been committed. A principal's inquiry must be conducted in accordance with board policy, and the principal has the powers and duties specified in the policy.

Following an inquiry, a principal who is satisfied that an infraction has been committed may either: (1) impose a "limited expulsion" or (2) refer the matter to the board for a determination. If an expulsion matter is referred to the board by the principal, the board (or committee of the board) must hold an expulsion hearing, and for that purpose, has the powers and duties specified by board policy. An expulsion hearing must be conducted according to the requirements of board policy.

Following a hearing, if the board is satisfied that the pupil has committed an infraction for which expulsion is mandatory, it must impose either (1) a limited expulsion, or (2) a full expulsion. In a *full* expulsion, the pupil is not entitled to attend any school in the province or to engage in school-related activities of any school in the province until he or she meets such requirements as may be established by regulation for returning to school.

The duration of a *limited* expulsion (which can be imposed either by a principal or a board) cannot exceed the later of one year from the date the principal suspended the pupil, and (2) the date on which the pupil meets such requirements as may be established by the board for returning to school after being expelled. Presumably, if the pupil never meets the requirements, the result could be that he or she is expelled indefinitely without the benefit of a hearing by the board—a result surely not intended. Care must be taken to avoid unreasonable conditions or those that conflict with the pupil's rights under another statute such as the *Health Care Consent Act*.

Under a limited expulsion, a pupil is not entitled to attend the school he or she was attending when the infraction was committed and is not entitled to engage in school-related activities of that school. It is thus an expulsion from a specific school, not from all of the board's schools (unless, of course, the board only has one school). A limited or full expulsion must be imposed within 20 days of the time the principal first suspended the pupil, unless the parties agree to an extension. Written notice of the expulsion must be given to the pupil and parent or guardian if the pupil is a minor. As with mandatory suspensions, a board must give serious consideration as to whether it will add to the statutory list of infractions that result in mandatory expulsion.

(ii) Discretionary Expulsion

A board may, by policy, designate activities for which expulsion is discretionary. Under subsection 310(3), if a principal believes that a pupil has engaged in an activity for which expulsion is discretionary, he or she *may* suspend the pupil and then most of the provisions of section 309 dealing with mandatory expulsion apply with necessary modifications to the discretionary expulsion. If the principal does not initially suspend the pupil, the expulsion process cannot be initiated.

(iii) Appeal of Expulsion Decision

A parent or guardian (or the pupil if an adult), or such other person specified in board policy, may appeal a decision to expel a pupil. The appeal to the school board must be conducted according to requirements in board policy. An appeal of a principal's expulsion decision is made to the board (or committee of the board), and its decision is final. An appeal of a board's expulsion decision is made to the "Child and Family Services Review Board", the "entity" designated by regulation, whose decisions are "final".

Procedural Fairness

Principals and school boards have a duty of procedural fairness when they are considering whether to suspend or expel a pupil. It is well established that the duty of procedural fairness varies according to the matter before the decision-maker and according to the potential gravity of the consequences to the individual, although it is not always easy to determine in any particular situation what that duty entails. Although not required to hold a formal hearing preceding a suspension, or during an "inquiry" preceding a decision to impose a limited expulsion, a principal owes a duty of fairness toward a pupil who is being investigated to: (1) advise the pupil as to the possibility that he or she may face suspension or expulsion and as to the nature of the allegations; (2) permit the pupil to respond to the allegations; and (3) make a decision based on the facts. If a pupil presents a continuing danger or disruption to the school, the United States jurisprudence indicates that a principal may suspend the pupil without providing notice or an opportunity to be heard, provided that the opportunity is offered as quickly as possible after the fact.

However, a school board is required to conduct a hearing to determine whether to expel a pupil. A board is also required to conduct a hearing of an appeal of a suspension or principal-imposed limited expulsion. The *Statutory Powers Procedure Act* applies to school board expulsion hearings and appeals. Under that Act, a party has the right to be represented by counsel, to call witnesses, to cross-examine witnesses, to a record of the proceeding, and to receive a written statement of the reasons for the decision. A board has considerable latitude as to how an "inquiry", "review" or "hearing" will be conducted, and it may prescribe its own "powers and duties" in respect of hearings. However, a board does not have the express statutory power to make policies and guidelines that conflict with the *Statutory Powers Procedure Act*. Stringent procedural protection is required because of the profound impact that a suspension or expulsion may have on a pupil.

A pupil's right to procedural fairness includes the right to know the school rules, i.e. what behaviour is subject to punishment. A board is required to state in policy those infractions that may result in a discretionary suspension or discretionary expulsion. It must also state in policy what additional infraction, over and above the statutory infractions, will result in mandatory suspension or mandatory expulsion. A school's "Code of Conduct" is therefore a critically important document. The United States law clearly shows that failure to state and publish a rule may enable a pupil to successfully challenge a suspension or expulsion that tries to enforce the rule. Moreover, because pupils have a right to know the school rules, it is reasonable to expect a board to determine, as a matter of policy, the general circumstances in which Ontario Regulations 37/01 and 106/01 will be applied. As previously indicated, these regulations permit a board to exercise its discretion on certain grounds *not* to suspend or expel even where a mandatory infraction has been committed. However, such a policy must not be applied in a manner that fetters the exercise of discretion when deciding individual cases.

The courts will find a duty of fairness even where the *Education Act* pro-
visions do not apply, for example in private schools. See, for e.g., *Burke v.
Yeshiva Beit Yitzchak of Hamilton* (1996), [1996] O.J. No. 937, 1996
CarswellOnt 920, 90 O.A.C. 81 (Ont. Div. Ct.), *D. (C.) (Litigation
Guardian of) v. Ridley College* (1996), 1996 CarswellOnt 3962, 140
D.L.R. (4th) 696, 44 Admin. L.R. (2d) 108 (Ont. Gen. Div.), and
Gianfrancesco v. Junior Academy Inc. (2001), 2001 CarswellOnt 2383,
[2001] O.J. No. 2730 (Ont. S.C.J.), additional reasons at (2001), 2001
CarswellOnt 4536, [2001] O.J. No. 5107 (Ont. S.C.J.), affirmed (2003),
2003 CarswellOnt 1160, 169 O.A.C. 169 (Ont. Div. Ct.).

Unlike the other two cases, *Gianfrancesco* did not involve an application
for judicial review, but rather an action in contract for damages for failure
to exercise due process in an expulsion. The Court dealt with the issue of
"whether or not a private school must comply with the requirement for
procedural fairness when it decides to expel a pupil for behaviour which
contravenes a zero tolerance policy with respect to violence as recommended by the Ontario Schools Code of Conduct." MacDonald J. correctly
took issue with the finding in *Burke* that a private school is required to
comply with the *Education Act* in respect of suspension or expulsion of
pupils. However, MacDonald J. did agree that the "drastic punishment of
expulsion can only be imposed after adequate notice is provided to the parents, who should be given an opportunity to be heard." MacDonald J. con-
cluded that: "the principle of procedural fairness can be imported into the
realm of disciplinary matters involving private schools by virtue of the
contract of instruction that exists between the school and the pupil's parents." The Court found that, although a hearing need not be a formal oral
hearing, the pupil and parents should have been afforded notice and the
opportunity to be heard before the expulsion decision was made.

(c) Corporal Punishment: When Can Corrective Force be Used?

If a teacher is charged with assaulting a student, section 43 of the *Criminal
Code* (Canada) provides a defence if the teacher's action was "by way of
correction" and did not exceed what is reasonable in the circumstances.
Section 43 states:

Every school teacher, parent or person standing in the place of a parent is justified in using
force by way of correction toward a pupil or child, as the case may be, if the force does not
exceed what is reasonable in the circumstances.

The Ontario Court of Appeal, as well as the court below, found that the section does not contravene the *Charter*. In *Canadian Foundation for Children, Youth & the Law v. Canada (Attorney General)* (2002), 2002 CarswellOnt 32, 207 D.L.R. (4th) 632, 161 C.C.C. (3d) 178, 48 C.R. (5th) 218, 154 O.A.C. 144, 23 R.F.L. (5th) 101, 57 O.R. (3d) 511, 90 C.R.R. (2d) 223 (Ont. C.A.), leave to appeal allowed (2002), 2002 CarswellOnt 3410, 2002 CarswellOnt 3411, [2002] S.C.C.A. No. 113, 96 C.R.R. (2d) 376 (note), 172 O.A.C. 400 (note), 302 N.R. 199 (note) (S.C.C.), Goudge J.A., in the appellate court, observed at paragraph 49:

> The force [applied by the parent, surrogate parent or teacher] must be reasonable in the circumstances which will inevitably include consideration of the age and character of the child, the circumstances of the punishment, its gravity, the misconduct of the child giving rise to it, the likely effect of the punishment on the child and whether the child suffered any injuries. Finally, the person applying the force must intend it for "correction" and the child being "corrected" must be capable of learning from the correction. Hence s. 43 infringes the child's security of the person only to the extent of decriminalizing the limited application of force to the child in circumstances where the risk of physical harm is modest.

An appeal to the Supreme Court of Canada was dismissed (*Canadian Foundation for Children, Youth & the Law v. Canada (Attorney General)*, 2004 CarswellOnt 252, 2004 CarswellOnt 253, 2004 SCC 4 (S.C.C.)). The issue before the Court was the constitutionality of allowing children's parents and teachers to use minor corrective force in some circumstances without facing criminal sanction. The *Criminal Code* (R.S.C. 1985, c. C-46, s. 265) prohibits intentional, non-consensual application of force to another person. However, section 43 of the Code excludes from this crime reasonable physical correction of children by their parents and teachers.

The majority of the Court rejected the position of the applicant Foundation that section 43 violates that *Charter*. The Foundation's position was that the section: (1) violates section 7 of the *Canadian Charter of Rights and Freedoms* because it fails to give procedural protections to children, does not further the best interests of the child, and is both overbroad and vague; (2) violates section 12 of the *Charter* because it constitutes cruel and unusual punishment or treatment; and (3) violates section 15(1) of the *Charter* because it denies children the legal protection against assaults that is accorded to adults.

The Court held that section 43 does not exempt from criminal sanction conduct that causes harm or raises a reasonable prospect of harm. The section can be invoked only in cases of non-consensual application of force that results neither in harm nor in the prospect of bodily harm. This limits its operation to the mildest forms of assault. The Court stated that: "People must know that if their conduct raises an apprehension of bodily harm they cannot rely on s. 43. Similarly, police officers and judges must know that the defence cannot be raised in such circumstances."

The court decision (per McLachlin C.J.) contains the following summary at paragraphs 38 and 40:

> Contemporary social consensus is that, while teachers may sometimes use corrective force to remove children from classrooms or secure compliance with instructions, the use of corporal punishment by teachers is not acceptable. Many school boards forbid the use of corporal punishment, and some provinces and territories have legislatively prohibited its use by teachers: see, e.g., *Schools Act, 1997*, S.N.L. 1997, c. S-12.2, s. 42; *School Act*, R.S.B.C. 1996, c. 412, s. 76(3); *Education Act*, S.N.B. 1997, c. E-1.12, s. 23; *School Act*, R.S.P.E.I. 1988, c. S-2.1, s. 73; *Education Act*, S.N.W.T. 1995, c. 28, s. 34(3); *Education Act*, S.Y. 1989-90, c. 25, s. 36....

> ...Generally, s. 43 exempts from criminal sanction only minor corrective force of a transitory and trifling nature. On the basis of current expert consensus, it does not apply to corporal punishment of children under two or teenagers. Degrading, inhuman or harmful conduct is not protected. Discipline by the use of objects or blows or slaps to the head is unreasonable. Teachers may reasonably apply force to remove a child from a classroom or secure compliance with instructions, but not merely as corporal punishment. Coupled with the requirement that the conduct be corrective, which rules out conduct stemming from the caregiver's frustration, loss of temper or abusive personality, a consistent picture emerges of the area covered by s. 43. It is wrong for law enforcement officers or judges to apply their own subjective views of what is "reasonable under the circumstances"; the test is objective. The question must be considered in context and in light of all the circumstances of the case. The gravity of the precipitating event is not relevant.

A school board is expressly authorized in the *Education Act* (s. 171(1)[18]) to pay part or all of the legal costs of a teacher, officer or other employee in successfully defending any proceeding brought against him or her . . . for assault in respect of disciplinary action taken in the course of duty".

(d) When Can a Student be Searched?

The *Canadian Charter of Rights and Freedoms* (s. 8) states that "Everyone has the right to be secure against unreasonable search or seizure". The Ontario Court of Appeal, in *R. v. G. (J.M.)* (1986), 17 O.A.C. 107, 56 O.R. (2d) 705, 54 C.R. (3d) 380, 29 C.C.C. (3d) 455, 33 D.L.R. (4th) 277, 25 C.R.R. 366, 1986 CarswellOnt 138 (Ont. C.A.), leave to appeal refused (1987), 54 C.R. (3d) 380n, 29 C.C.C. (3d) 455n, 33 D.L.R. (4th) 277n, 28 C.R.R. 206n, 76 N.R. 78n, 59 O.R. (2d) 286n, 21 O.A.C. 239n (S.C.C.), stated that a principal may search a student in carrying out the duty to maintain order and discipline in the school. In this case, after receiving a report that a student was seen with drugs, and after inviting him to the office, the school principal removed some tin foil from the student's pant cuff; it was later discovered to contain marijuana.

A search must not be conducted for arbitrary reasons: there must be reasonable grounds. Was the search reasonably justified at its inception, and was the scope of the search reasonable in view of the objectives of the search? Was the search excessively intrusive in light of the age and sex of the student and the nature of the infraction?

The Court of Appeal in *G. (J.M.)* spoke strongly in support of the power and duty of the school principal to maintain discipline. It noted that the principal in fact has a duty to carry out his or her own investigation until he or she knows the nature and extent of the suspected offence: "It is often neither feasible nor desirable that the principal should require prior authority before searching his or her student and seizing contraband." When it becomes apparent that an offence may have been committed, the police should be notified. The requirement that a search must be conducted on reasonable grounds also applies to students' purses and knapsacks.

On November 26, 1998, the Supreme Court of Canada released its decision in *R. v. M. (M.R.)* (1998), 1998 CarswellNS 346, 1998 CarswellNS 347 (S.C.C.), a case on appeal from the Court of Appeal for Nova Scotia. In this case, the accused junior high school student was suspected of drug dealing. He was searched by the vice-principal. A bag of marijuana was found in one of the student's socks. A plain-clothed RCMP officer was present during the search but said and did nothing during the search. The trial judge had found that the vice-principal had been acting as an agent of the police, that the search violated the student's rights under the Charter, and that the evidence should therefore be excluded at trial. The Court of Appeal allowed the Crown's appeal and the student took the issue to the Supreme Court of Canada.

The Supreme Court of Canada (Major J. dissenting) found that there was no violation of the accused's rights. The Court said:

1. A student's reasonable expectation of privacy is diminished at school because the student knows that teachers and school authorities are responsible for providing a safe school environment and maintaining order and discipline in the school. Students know that this responsibility may require searches of students and their personal effects, and the seizure of prohibited items.

2. To require a search warrant would be impractical and unworkable in a school environment. Teachers and principals must be able to react quickly. They must have the power to search students.

3. A search may be made if there are reasonable grounds to believe that a school rule has been or is being violated and that evidence will be found in the location or on

the person of the student searched. All the circumstances surrounding a search must be taken into account in determining if the search was reasonable. Reasonable grounds for a search can be based on information received from a credible student, information from more than one student, the teacher's own observations, or any combination of these, all taken in the context of the circumstances existing at the school.

4. The permissible extent of the search depends on the gravity of the suspected infraction.

5. The search itself must be carried out in a sensitive and minimally intrusive manner.

6. On the facts of this case, the vice-principal was not acting as an agent of the police. The officer was at all times completely passive (until the evidence was handed over to him and an arrest was made). Teachers and school authorities have the authority to maintain order and discipline under the Nova Scotia *Education Act*.

(Ontario's *Education Act* has similar provisions in ss. 264 and 265.)

The Court also found that the student has not been "detained" (in the school's office) within the meaning of section 10(b) of the *Charter*. It also clarified that its ruling only applies to elementary and secondary school pupils, and that no consideration was given to searches made in a post-secondary setting.

It is sometimes necessary to search a student's locker or desk. When this need arises, an issue can arise as to who "owns" the property that is to be searched. If the school owns the property, then it does not need permission to search it. If the student owns or "rents" the property, and has not been informed that it is subject to search at any time, then a search should only be carried out on reasonable, not arbitrary, grounds, as part of the duty to maintain discipline. It is recommended that students be informed that their lockers are school property and could be searched by school staff at any time. It is advisable that the student be present at the locker during the search, along with a staff member as a witness. This will help to avoid allegations that school staff planted something in the locker, and will help establish in court the "continuity of possession" of the locker contents. It should be noted that, once the police are involved, they are governed by all the rules and laws that govern search and seizure by police. They are not clothed by the school principal's special status in respect of student discipline.

8.5 Reporting Child Abuse

(a) What is the Duty to Report Abuse?

The responsibility to report child abuse is found in the *Child and Family Services Act* (*CFSA*). The Act covers children who are under the age of 16. The duty to report applies to a person who has "reasonable grounds to suspect" one of the matters as described in paragraphs 1 to 13 of subsection 72(1) of the *CFSA*. A report is made directly to a "Society", e.g. Children's Aid Society or Catholic Children's Aid Society. The duty to report is upon the person who has the suspicion of abuse. The legislation specifically states that the person cannot rely upon any other person to make the report on his or her behalf (s. 72(3)). Moreover, the duty to report is on-going. If the Society does not respond, or if there are reasonable grounds to suspect that the abuse is continuing, then the person must continue to report his or her suspicion.

Teachers, principals and other school professionals such as social workers are among those professionals who may be found guilty of an offence if (1) they fail to report a suspicion, and (2) the information upon which the suspicion was based was obtained in the course of their professional or official duties. "Reasonable suspicion" does not mean "reasonable belief". Bowers, Knox and Zuker, in their seminal book, *Sexual Misconduct in Education: Prevention, Reporting and Discipline* (Markham: Butterworths, 2003) observe that:

> A suspicion can be based on conjecture, on speculation, on third-party reports, consistent rumours, gossip and observations of inappropriate student or staff behaviour. A suspicion does not require proof or independently verifiable evidence as would a reasonable belief.

It is important to note that no action for making a report can be instituted against a person who acts under section 72 unless the person acts maliciously or without reasonable grounds for the suspicion. The reporting requirement applies even though the information reported may be confidential or privileged. The confidentiality of the Ontario Student Record is therefore not an obstacle to making a report under section 72 of the *CFSA*.

Section 72 of the *CFSA* states as follows:

(1) Duty to report child in need of protection—Despite the provisions of any other Act, if a person, including a person who performs professional or official duties with respect to children, has reasonable grounds to suspect one of the following, the person shall forthwith report the suspicion and the information on which it is based to a society:

1.   The child has suffered physical harm, inflicted by the person having charge of the child or caused by or resulting from that person's,
       i.   failure to adequately care for, provide for, supervise or protect the child, or
       ii.   pattern of neglect in caring for, providing for, supervising or protecting the child.

2.   There is a risk that the child is likely to suffer physical harm inflicted by the person having charge of the child or caused by or resulting from that person's,
       i.   failure to adequately care for, provide for, supervise or protect the child, or
       ii.   pattern of neglect in caring for, providing for, supervising or protecting the child.

3.   The child has been sexually molested or sexually exploited, by the person having charge of the child or by another person where the person having charge of the child knows or should know of the possibility of sexual molestation or sexual exploitation and fails to protect the child.

4.   There is a risk that the child is likely to be sexually molested or sexually exploited as described in paragraph 3.

5.   The child requires medical treatment to cure, prevent or alleviate physical harm or suffering and the child's parent or the person having charge of the child does not provide, or refuses or is unavailable or unable to consent to, the treatment.

6.   The child has suffered emotional harm, demonstrated by serious,
       i.   anxiety,
       ii.   depression,
       iii. withdrawal,
       iv.   self-destructive or aggressive behaviour, or
       v.   delayed development,

      and there are reasonable grounds to believe that the emotional harm suffered by the child results from the actions, failure to act or pattern of neglect on the part of the child's parent or the person having charge of the child.

7.   The child has suffered emotional harm of the kind described in subparagraph i, ii, iii, iv or v of paragraph 6 and the child's parent or the person having charge of the child does not provide, or refuses or is unavailable or unable to consent to, services or treatment to remedy or alleviate the harm.

8.   There is a risk that the child is likely to suffer emotional harm of the kind described in subparagraph i, ii, iii, iv or v of paragraph 6 resulting from the actions, failure to act or pattern of neglect on the part of the child's parent or the person having charge of the child.

9.   There is a risk that the child is likely to suffer emotional harm of the kind described in subparagraph i, ii, iii, iv or v of paragraph 6 and that the child's parent or the person having charge of the child does not provide, or refuses or is unavailable or unable to consent to, services or treatment to prevent the harm.

10.   The child suffers from a mental, emotional or developmental condition that, if not remedied, could seriously impair the child's development and the child's parent

or the person having charge of the child does not provide, or refuses or is unavailable or unable to consent to, treatment to remedy or alleviate the condition.

11.   The child has been abandoned, the child's parent has died or is unavailable to exercise his or her custodial rights over the child and has not made adequate provision for the child's care and custody, or the child is in a residential placement and the parent refuses or is unable or unwilling to resume the child's care and custody.

12.   The child is less than 12 years old and has killed or seriously injured another person or caused serious damage to another person's property, services or treatment are necessary to prevent a recurrence and the child's parent or the person having charge of the child does not provide, or refuses or is unavailable or unable to consent to, those services or treatment.

13.   The child is less than 12 years old and has on more than one occasion injured another person or caused loss or damage to another person's property, with the encouragement of the person having charge of the child or because of that person's failure or inability to supervise the child adequately.

(2) **Ongoing duty to report**—A person who has additional reasonable grounds to suspect one of the matters set out in subsection (1) shall make a further report under subsection (1) even if he or she has made previous reports with respect to the same child.

(3) **Person must report directly**—A person who has a duty to report a matter under subsection (1) or (2) shall make the report directly to the society and shall not rely on any other person to report on his or her behalf. 1999, c. 2, s. 22(1).

(4) **Offence**—A person referred to in subsection (5) is guilty of an offence if,

(a)   he or she contravenes subsection (1) or (2) by not reporting a suspicion; and
(b)   the information on which it was based was obtained in the course of his or her professional or official duties. 1999, c. 2, s. 22(2).

(5) **Same**—Subsection (4) applies to every person who performs professional or official duties with respect to children including,

(a)   a health care professional, including a physician, nurse, dentist, pharmacist and psychologist;
(b)   a teacher, school principal, social worker, family counsellor, priest, rabbi, member of the clergy, operator or employee of a day nursery and youth and recreation worker;
(c)   a peace officer and a coroner;
(d)   a solicitor; and
(e)   a service provider and an employee of a service provider.

(6) **Same**—In clause (5)(b),

"youth and recreation worker" does not include a volunteer.

(6.1) **Same**—A director, officer or employee of a corporation who authorizes, permits or concurs in a contravention of an offence under subsection (4) by an employee of the corporation is guilty of an offence.

(6.2) Same—A person convicted of an offence under subsection (4) or (6.1) is liable to a fine of not more than $1,000.

(7) Section overrides privilege—This section applies although the information reported may be confidential or privileged, and no action for making the report shall be instituted against a person who acts in accordance with this section unless the person acts maliciously or without reasonable grounds for the suspicion. R.S.O. 1990, c. C.11, s. 72(7); 1999, c. 2, s. 22(4).

(8) Exception: solicitor client privilege—Nothing in this section abrogates any privilege that may exist between a solicitor and his or her client. R.S.O. 1990, c. C.11, s. 72(8).

Members of the Ontario College of Teachers should note that the Professional Misconduct regulation (O. Reg. 437/97) under the *Ontario College of Teachers Act, 1996*, states that professional misconduct includes "failing to comply with the member's duties under the Child and Family Services Act."

8.6 *YOUTH CRIMINAL JUSTICE ACT*

The *Youth Criminal Justice Act* (*YCJA*) was proclaimed in force effective April 1, 2003, and replaced the *Young Offenders Act*. The *YCJA* applies to young persons.

"Young person" is defined in the Act as:

a person who is or, in the absence of evidence to the contrary, appears to be twelve years old or older, but less than eighteen years old and, if the context requires, includes any person who is charged under this Act with having committed an offence while he or she was a young person or who is found guilty of an offence under this Act.

(a) Guiding Principles of the Act

Section 3 of *YCJA* sets out a comprehensive set of "principles" that are to govern youth criminal justice:

3. (1) The following principles apply in this Act:

    (a)   the youth criminal justice system is intended to
        (i)   prevent crime by addressing the circumstances underlying a young person's offending behaviour,
        (ii)   rehabilitate young persons who commit offences and reintegrate them into society, and
        (iii) ensure that a young person is subject to meaningful consequences for his or her offence
        in order to promote the long-term protection of the public;

    (b)   the criminal justice system for young persons must be separate from that of adults and emphasize the following:

        (i)   rehabilitation and reintegration,

        (ii)   fair and proportionate accountability that is consistent with the greater dependency of young persons and their reduced level of maturity,

        (iii)   enhanced procedural protection to ensure that young persons are treated fairly and that their rights, including their right to privacy, are protected,

        (iv)   timely intervention that reinforces the link between the offending behaviour and its consequences, and

        (v)   the promptness and speed with which persons responsible for enforcing this Act must act, given young persons' perception of time;

    (c)   within the limits of fair and proportionate accountability, the measures taken against young persons who commit offences should

        (i)   reinforce respect for societal values,

        (ii)   encourage the repair of harm done to victims and the community,

        (iii)   be meaningful for the individual young person given his or her needs and level of development and, where appropriate, involve the parents, the extended family, the community and social or other agencies in the young person's rehabilitation and reintegration, and

        (iv)   respect gender, ethnic, cultural and linguistic differences and respond to the needs of aboriginal young persons and of young persons with special requirements; and

    (d)   special considerations apply in respect of proceedings against young persons and, in particular,

        (i)   young persons have rights and freedoms in their own right, such as a right to be heard in the course of and to participate in the processes, other than the decision to prosecute, that lead to decisions that affect them, and young persons have special guarantees of their rights and freedoms,

        (ii)   victims should be treated with courtesy, compassion and respect for their dignity and privacy and should suffer the minimum degree of inconvenience as a result of their involvement with the youth criminal justice system,

        (iii)   victims should be provided with information about the proceedings and given an opportunity to participate and be heard, and

        (iv)   parents should be informed of measures or proceedings involving their children and encouraged to support them in addressing their offending behaviour.

A significant change in the new Act is that the process for transferring certain young persons to "adult court" has been eliminated. Instead, if the youth court has determined whether or not the young person is guilty of the offence, it may impose an adult sentence under certain circumstances as set out in sections 61 to 81 of the *YCJA*. The young person must have been found guilty of an offence for which an adult could receive a sentence of more than two years and he or she must have been at least 14 years old at the time the offence was committed. With respect to certain very serious offences (e.g. murder) or for repeat serious violent offenders, there is a presumption that an adult sentence will follow a finding of guilt. In any situation where no presumption applies, the Crown must apply to the Court if it wishes an adult sentence to be considered.

(b) Restrictions on Publication of Identity

The *YCJA* protects from publication (1) the identity of young persons who are in trouble with the law (i.e. being "dealt with under the Act"—under investigation, arrested, charged, convicted, discharged, etc.) or (2) any information that would identify the young person. The Act also prohibits the publication of the identity of children or young persons who are *victims* of, or *witnesses* in connection with, an offence committed or alleged to have been committed by a young person.

Section 110(1) and 111(1) of the *YCJA* state:

110. **(1)** Subject to this section, no person shall publish the name of a young person, or any other information related to a young person, if it would identify the young person as a young person dealt with under this Act.

111. **(1)** Subject to this section, no person shall publish the name of a child or young person, or any other information related to a child or a young person, if it would identify the child or young person as having been a victim of, or as having appeared as a witness in connection with, an offence committed or alleged to have been committed by a young person.

The non-publication is intended to maximize the chances of rehabilitation for young persons. (*Dagenais v. Canadian Broadcasting Corp.*, 1994 CarswellOnt 112, 1994 CarswellOnt 1168, [1994] S.C.J. No. 104, 34 C.R. (4th) 269, 20 O.R. (3d) 816 (note), [1994] 3 S.C.R. 835, 120 D.L.R. (4th) 12, 175 N.R. 1, 94 C.C.C. (3d) 289, 76 O.A.C. 81, 25 C.R.R. (2d) 1 (S.C.C.); and *N. (F.), Re*, 2000 CarswellNfld 213, 2000 CarswellNfld 214, [2000] S.C.J. No. 34, 2000 SCC 35, 146 C.C.C. (3d) 1, 188 D.L.R. (4th) 1, 35 C.R. (5th) 1, [2000] 1 S.C.R. 880, 191 Nfld. & P.E.I.R. 181, 577 A.P.R. 181 (S.C.C.).)

There are exceptions to the general rule against publication. The first exception permits publication of the names of young persons who have received an adult sentence. Another exception applies where the young person is convicted of a "presumptive" offence and received a youth sentence although an adult sentence was sought. Here the youth court judge must exercise his or her discretion to allow publication. A third exception occurs where publication is made in "the course of the administration of justice" and where the purpose of the disclosure is not to make the information known in the community. An *ex parte* court order must be obtained to allow disclosure where the police are pursuing a young person who is a suspect (s. 110(2)(c)). A fourth exception allows authorities to seek public assistance in apprehending a suspect or a young person who is unlawfully at large, if the young person is dangerous. A fifth exception applies where the young person wants his or her name publicized and the court agrees. In addition, young persons who have attained the age of 18 may publicize identifying information about themselves if they are not in custody.

Section 111 of the Act contains exceptions to the general prohibition against publication of the identity of a victim or witness. A victim or witness may choose to be identified upon attaining the age of 18, or earlier with parental consent, or where the victim or witness is deceased, upon parental request. A court may also permit disclosure where it is satisfied that it would not be contrary to the young person's interest or the public interest. It should be noted that disclosure of a victim or witness does not mean that the identity of the "young person" can be disclosed.

(c) Sharing Information with Schools

The *YCJA* sets out stringent provisions about who may *keep* records on young persons and who has a right of access to any such record (s. 114 to s. 119). Disclosure to *any* person is permitted under section 119(1)(s) if deemed by a youth court to have a valid interest in the record provided disclosure is desirable in the interest of the proper administration of justice.

Section 125 allows the authorities to disclose information in a record to a school engaged in the supervision or care of a young person. Section 125 states:

125. (1) A peace officer may disclose to any person any information in a record kept under section 114 (court records) or 115 (police records) that it is necessary to disclose in the conduct of the investigation of an offence.

. . .

(6) The provincial director, a youth worker, the Attorney General, a peace officer or any other person engaged in the provision of services to young persons may disclose to any professional or other person engaged in the supervision or care of a young person—including a representative of any school board or school or any other educational or training institution—any information contained in a record kept under sections 114 to 116 if the disclosure is necessary

    (a)   to ensure compliance by the young person with an authorization under section 91 or an order of the youth justice court;

    (b)   to ensure the safety of staff, students or other persons; or

    (c)   to facilitate the rehabilitation of the young person.

(7) A person to whom information is disclosed under subsection (6) shall

    (a)   keep the information separate from any other record of the young person to whom the information relates;

    (b)   ensure that no other person has access to the information except if authorized under this Act, or if necessary for the purposes of subsection (6); and

(c)   destroy their copy of the record when the information is no longer required for the purpose for which it was disclosed.

(d) The Right to Legal Counsel

A young person has the right to have a lawyer without delay at any stage of the proceedings, including arrest or detention, before the person makes a voluntary statement, during consideration of extrajudicial sanctions, and at a hearing. A young person is guaranteed access to counsel under the Act, regardless of whether he or she is qualified for legal aid (although provinces may determine rules for recovery of the costs of counsel). A "hearing" includes pre-trial detention, trial, sentencing, and various other hearings and reviews held under the Act (s. 25(3), *YCJA*). The right to counsel belongs to the young person, not a parent or guardian, and the right may be waived.

(e) Making a Voluntary Statement

There are strict requirements for taking voluntary statements from a young person by "a peace officer or other person who is, in law, a person in authority." To begin with, section 146 of the Act requires that a person taking the statement must caution the young person that he or she has the right to consult counsel and a parent (or if the parent is absent, an adult relative or if the parent or relative is absent, another appropriate adult). Indeed, any statement must be made in the presence of counsel, a parent, or other appropriate adult unless the young person declines this right.

In order for a statement to be admissible in court, the person taking a statement from a young person must, before the statement is taken, clearly inform the young person that he or she is under no obligation to make a statement, that any statement made may be used as evidence against the young person, that the young person has the right and reasonable opportunity to consult counsel and a parent, and that any statement is to be made in the presence of counsel, a parent, or other adult unless the young person desires otherwise (s. 146(2)(b)).

The requirement to explain the above rights to the young person does not apply to oral statements if they are made spontaneously by the young person to a peace officer or other person in authority before the person has had a reasonable opportunity to make the explanation to the young person.

The courts have generally taken a narrow approach as to who is, in law, a "person in authority". Although parents and teachers may be regarded by a young person as having a position of authority, they would not normally be a person in authority under the Act. The test is whether there is a realistic expectation that they are associated with the investigation. The question depends on the extent to which the young person believed the person could influence or control the proceedings against him or her. "A parent, doctor, teacher or employer all may be found to be a person in authority if the circumstances warrant, but their status, or the mere fact that they may wield some personal authority over the accused, is not sufficient to establish them as persons in authority for the purposes of the confessions rule." (per Cory J. in *R. v. Hodgson*, 1998 CarswellOnt 3417, 1998 CarswellOnt 3418, [1998] S.C.J. No. 66, (*sub nom. R. v. M.C.H.*) 230 N.R. 1, 127 C.C.C. (3d) 449, 163 D.L.R. (4th) 577, 18 C.R. (5th) 135, (*sub nom. R. v. M.C.H.*) 113 O.A.C. 97, [1998] 2 S.C.R. 449 (S.C.C.) at para. 35). See also *R. v. B. (A.)* (1986), 1986 CarswellOnt 100, 13 O.A.C. 68, 50 C.R. (3d) 247, 26 C.C.C. (3d) 17 (Ont. C.A.), leave to appeal refused 26 C.C.C. (3d) 17n, [1986] 1 S.C.R. v, 50 C.R. (3d) xxv (S.C.C.); *R. v. H. (C.)* (1995), [1995] O.J. No. 932, 1995 CarswellOnt 4179 (Ont. Prov. Div.); *R. v. H.* (1985), 1985 CarswellAlta 291, 43 Alta. L.R. (2d) 250 (Alta. Prov. Ct.); *R. v. R. (F.)* (November 10, 1988), Garfinkel Prov. J. (Man. Prov. Ct.)

(f) Extrajudicial Measures

The *Youth Criminal Justice Act* is guided by the fundamental principle that extrajudicial measures are often the most appropriate and effective way to address youth crime. The idea, then, is to keep young persons out of court altogether. There is a presumption that a first-time, non-violent offender will be dealt with outside the court process, although the measures are not limited to those who have not previously committed an offence. Section 6 of the Act requires a police officer, before charging a young person, to consider whether it would be sufficient to:

- take no further action
- warn the young person
- give the young person a formal caution (where a province has established such a program)
- with the consent of the young person, refer him or her to a community program or agency that may assist him or her not to commit offences.

The Act also allows the Crown attorney to use certain extrajudicial measures, namely a caution (where such a program is implemented by the province) or refer the young person to an extrajudicial sanctions (formally alternative measures) program (if one exists). Section 10 imposes restrictions on the use of extrajudicial sanctions (as opposed to "measures"), including a requirement for the consent of the young person.

The Crown may decide not to proceed with the charge. The Crown may also refer the young person to a community program or agency.

The police, Crown, a youth court judge, a justice of the peace, or a youth worker may convene or cause to be convened a "conference" under section 19 of the Act to obtain advice on appropriate extrajudicial measures. A conference is "a group of persons who are convened to give information in accordance with section 19". That group may include, for example, the young person, the parents of the young person, the victim, a police officer, a teacher, a guidance counsellor, a social worker, a coach, a youth worker and others who are familiar with the young person, community agencies, and professionals with relevant expertise. A conference may be a professional case conference, but it may also be a restorative justice mechanism that provides advice on ways to repair the harm done to the victim. A conference can be called to assist with any decision that has to be made under the *YCJA*.

(g) Parental Involvement

A key emphasis in the *YCJA* is the need for parental involvement. Parents are required to be kept informed at every stage of the involvement of their child in proceedings, including at arrest and detention, upon issuance of a summons or appearance notice, upon release on an undertaking or recognizance, or upon issuance of a ticket. If a parent is not available, an appropriate adult relative may be given notice. (s. 26(4), (5)) If a parent does not attend court with the young person, the court may order the parent's attendance if it is of the opinion that it is necessary or in the best interests of the young person (s. 27, *YCJA*).

(h) Sentencing

The *YCJA* contains a broad range of sentencing options, including some that did not exist in the *Young Offenders Act*. Sentences are either custodial or non-custodial. Non-custodial options are:

* reprimand—a formal rebuke or scolding by the judge in court
* absolute discharge
* conditional discharge

- fine up to $1,000
- compensation to another person for loss, damage or injury
- restitution of property to the person who owned it at the time of the offence
- reimbursement of an innocent purchaser of property
- compensation by way of personal service (up to 240 hours and completed within 12 months) for a loss, damage or injury, or alternatively, compensation in kind
- community service (up to 240 hours and completed within 12 months)
- order of prohibition, seizure or forfeiture that is authorized under federal legislation (e.g. prohibition against owning a firearm)
- probation with conditions, for up to two years; the range of mandatory and optional conditions is found in section 55 of the *YCJA*—the conditions may include attending school
- intensive support and supervision program order (where the program is implemented by the province)
- attendance order, requiring the young person to attend a program at specified times (up to 240 hours within a six-month period) where the program has been implemented by the province
- deferred custody and supervision order—the sentence is served in the community but, if conditions are breached, this may result in the young person serving the remainder of the sentence in custody and supervision
- custody and supervision order—all custody orders must include a period of supervision in the community under conditions; supervision conditions may include a requirement to attend school. The length of custody and supervision depends on the offence. Over the course of the custody portion of a sentence, a young person may seek a reintegration leave for the purpose of rehabilitation and preparation for eventual reintegration back into the community. The purpose of the leave can include, for example, attending school, and
- intensive rehabilitative custody and supervision order, intended for serious violent offenders, under the criteria set out in section 42(7) of the Act.

(i) What are the Requirements for Admitting a Young Person's Statement in Court?

In order for a young person's oral or written statement to be admissible in court, certain conditions must be met, as discussed in paragraph (e), above. Because statements to peace officers and persons in authority are inadmissible in evidence unless the above-noted statutory precautions are taken, it is important that teachers and principals be aware of the requirements. A principal or teacher can be a person in authority for the purposes of section 56. In *R. v. H.* (1985), 43 Alta. L.R. (2d) 250, 1985 CarswellAlta 291 (Alta. Prov. Ct.), the Court stated:

> The test is whether the accused believed that the person he dealt with had some degree of power over him and whether he thought that person could either make good his promise or carry out his threats. It is reasonable to presume that a 13-year-old boy would believe that his teacher would exercise power over him and could make good her promises.

In this case, as a result of statements to the teacher, the young person and his accomplices were interrogated by the school principal and futher implicated themselves. They were not informed of their rights. On the facts of this particular case, the court said the principal "became inextricably involved in the administration of justice by doing the work of the police themselves. The evidence he provided the police became the evidence in this case; there was no need for the police to attempt to obtain the statement from the accused; the principal had done their work for them."

In *R. v. R. (F.)* (November 10, 1988), Garfinkel Prov. J. (Man. Prov. Ct.), the Court ruled that a teacher was a person in authority:

> She ought not to have embarked upon an investigation. This was not a situation of maintaining school discipline. This was an investigation of a crime. When a crime is being investigated Charter rights, principles of fundamental justice, principles of Y.O.A. and legal procedures come into play. The police could have been called upon discovery of the theft. The actions of the young person should have been described to them and they should have conducted the investigation.

The test of whether or not a person is a "person in authority" is a subjective one: how would the young person view the teacher or principal? The courts do not question the legality, or desirability, of letting principals and teachers exercise their disciplinary role over young persons. There is a point, however, at which school discipline turns into investigation of a crime. At that point, the police should be called in.

8.7 Alphabetical List of Duties and Responsibilities Respecting School Administration

ABSENCE OF PUPIL

Parents must give the principal the reasons for their child's absence from school. A pupil has a duty to attend school regularly and punctually. The parent may request of the principal that the pupil be temporarily absent (s. 23, Reg. 298).

ABSENCE OF TEACHER

A teacher must notify the person designated by the board if he or she is to be absent from school, and the reason for the absence (s. 264, Act).

ADVERTISEMENTS/ANNOUNCEMENTS

No advertisements or announcements are permitted in a school without the consent of the board, except announcements of school activities (s. 24, Reg. 298).

BUILDINGS AND GROUNDS

The principal has responsibility for the condition and appearance of the school building and grounds and must inspect the school premises weekly and report repairs that are required (s. 265, Act; s. 11, Reg. 298).

CANVASSING (See Fund-raising)

CARE OF TEACHING MATERIALS AND BOARD PROPERTY

The principal has responsibility for the care of all teaching materials and other school property, and must provide for the instruction of pupils in the care of the school premises. Pupils have a duty to "show respect" for school property.

The principal must inform the board if a parent does not comply with a request to compensate the board for damage, destruction, loss or misappropriation of school property by a pupil (s. 265, Act; s. 11 and 23, Reg. 298).

CLEANLINESS

The principal has responsibility for the cleanliness, temperature and ventilation of the school (s. 265, Act).

COMMUNICABLE DISEASE

The principal must refuse admission to the school of any person he or she believes is infected with or exposed to a communicable disease. The principal must report to the board and Medical Officer of Health when he or she has reason to suspect the existence of any communicable disease in the school (s. 265, Act).

COMMUNITY

The principal has a duty to promote and maintain close co-operation with the residents, industry, business and other groups and agencies in the community. Teachers have a duty to assist in this respect (s. 11 and 20, Reg. 298). The principal is to serve on the school council (Ministry Guidelines for School Councils; O. Reg. 612/00).

CONFLICT OF INTEREST

No teacher, supervisory officer or other employee of a board or of the Ministry shall, for compensation of any kind other than his or her salary as such employee, promote, offer for sale or sell, directly or indirectly, any book or other teaching or learning materials, equipment, furniture, stationery or other article to any board, provincial school or teachers' college, or to any pupil enrolled therein. The penalty for contravening this provision is a fine or not more than $1,000. It is also an offence to employ or compensate a person who contravenes this provision of the *Education Act*. The conflict provision does not apply to an employee in respect of a book or other teaching materials of which the employee is an author where the only compensation that he or she receives is a fee or royalty (s. 217, Act).

CONTINUING EDUCATION

The principal of a day school is the principal of continuing education at the school unless another person is appointed to be principal of the continuing education classes (s. 2, Reg. 285).

COOPERATION AMONG STAFF

The principal has a duty to develop co-operation and co-ordination of effort among staff in the school. Teachers have a duty to assist the principal in this respect (ss. 264 and 265, Act; s. 20, Reg. 298).

COURSES OF STUDY

The principal is to retain on file outlines of all courses of study taught in the school. Teachers must prepare and submit teaching plans and outlines as required.

DISCIPLINE

The principal has the duty to maintain proper order and discipline in the school. He or she must report any neglect of duty or infraction of the school rules by a pupil to the pupil's parent. A teacher has the duty to co-operate with the principal and other teachers to establish and maintain consistent disciplinary practices in the school. A teacher must maintain, under the direction of the principal, proper order and discipline in the classroom and while on duty in the school and on the school grounds. The principal must report to the appropriate supervisory officer and the Minister respecting discipline in the school (ss. 264 and 265, Act; ss. 11, 20, Reg. 298).

A pupil has a duty to exercise self-discipline and to accept such discipline as would be exercised by a kind, firm and judicious parent. A pupil is responsible to the principal for his or her conduct at the school, on school activities and on the school bus (s. 23, Reg. 298).

EMERGENCY PROCEDURES

In addition to mandatory Fire Drills, the principal must hold at least one emergency drill during the school year if the board so decides. This includes night school and summer school. Every person in the school must participate in the drill (s. 6, Reg. 298).

EVALUATION OF TEACHERS

The principal has a duty to conduct performance appraisals of members of the teaching staff. If performance appraisal is not required by board policy or a collective agreement, the principal is to report to the board or supervisory officer on the effectiveness of the members of the teaching staff, with a copy to the teacher of any part of the report that mentions the teacher (s. 11, Reg. 298).

The principal shall recommend to the board the demotion or dismissal of a teacher whose work or attitude is unsatisfactory but only after warning the teacher in writing, giving the teacher assistance, and allowing the teacher a reasonable time to improve. The principal also has the duty to recommend to the board the appointment and promotion of teachers (s. 11, Reg. 298).

In 2001, the *Quality in the Classroom Act, 2001*, amended the *Education Act* by, among other things, setting standards for the appraisal of teachers' classroom performance and requiring school administrators to review teacher performance on a regular basis. Teachers are required to be evaluated on a three-year cycle and must have two evaluations in the year in which they are being evaluated (s. 277.28). Teachers new to the profession and teachers new to their employing board must be evaluated two times in each of the first two years with the board (s. 277.29). A principal may conduct additional evaluations if he or she considers it advisable in light of the circumstances relating to the teacher's performance (s. 277.30).

Section 277.35 of the Act sets out what is to happen if a teacher has received an initial unsatisfactory rating. In essence, the Act ensures that the teacher is given a full understanding of why he or she received the rating and what must be done to improve (s. 277.36(2). Within 60 days of the initial unsatisfactory rating, the principal must conduct a second evaluation. If the second evaluation is unsatisfactory, the principal must place the teacher under review and provide the teacher with complete information about the evaluation results, the areas that are in need of improvement, what must be done to improve, and a written improvement plan. After a second unsatisfactory appraisal, the principal and supervisory officer may recommend terminating the teacher's employment. Alternatively, the principal may conduct a third appraisal. When a recommendation for termination is made, the teacher must be suspended with pay or reassigned to other appropriate duties. The school board must make a decision on the termination within 60 days of receiving the recommendation (s. 277.39(2)), and must notify the Ontario College of Teachers of the termination.

Ontario Regulation 99/02 sets out the standards and method for performance appraisal, and requires, for example, that teachers receive notice of their forthcoming evaluation and an opportunity to discuss the results of the evaluation with the principal. The regulation also prescribes the rating system to be used and the areas of competency to be appraised. The general areas of competency are listed in s. 277.31(2). A board may provide for additional areas of competency and may develop its own standards, methods, processes timelines, and steps that add to those set in the Act and regulations. Boards are required to develop an annual parent survey seeking input from parents about their child's teacher. The board must also provide a pupil survey to seek input from senior division students about their teachers. Section 277.32 of the Act and section 5 of the regulation govern how the results of the surveys may be used.

EXAMINATIONS

Subject to the approval of the appropriate supervisory officer, the principal shall hold the examinations that the principal considers necessary for the promotion of pupils or for any other purpose. A teacher is responsible for the evaluation of the progress of pupils in the subjects assigned to the teacher. A pupil has a duty to take tests and examinations. Board policy may permit exemptions from writing final examinations where at least one other set of examinations has been held. Teaching staff are to be in the school during regular school hours on examination days and are to be accessible to pupils, unless the board otherwise directs (s. 265, Act; s. 20, Reg. 298).

A board may schedule up to 10 examination days on its school calendars. It may alter the date of an examination date without Ministry approval, but must notify parents and the Ministry of the alteration as far in advance as possible (Reg. 304 and s. 11(7.1), Act).

A pupil has a duty to take a test administered by the school on behalf of the Education Quality and Accountability Office. The Office decides the criteria for exempting pupils from its tests (s. 4, *Education Quality and Accountability Act, 1996*).

FIELD TRIPS AND OUT-OF-SCHOOL ACTIVITIES — CHECKLIST

If a teacher is responsible for organizing a field trip or out-of-school activity, the teacher should:

*   obtain permission of principal and appropriate supervisory officer
*   obtain permission of authorities at the location of the field trip or out-of-school activity and where applicable, inform local police or the Ministry of Natural Resources of the itinerary (e.g. trip in a Provincial Park)
*   obtain permission or consent of parent or guardian, in writing, for their child to participate, including the legal release form required by the school board; inform parents and guardians in writing of all pertinent details relating to the trip or activity, including the locale, facts

about transportation arrangements, time of departure and return, supervision arrangements, rules of student conduct, need for funds
- compile a list of phone numbers to contact parents or guardians if the return trip is delayed or if there is a medical emergency
- medical considerations:
    - one or more supervisors should be trained in first aid
    - supervisors must be aware of any medical or allergy considerations on file with the school that pertain to students on the trip or activity
    - supervisors must be aware of the medical facilities closest to the location of the trip or activity
    - consents to treatment must have been obtained in respect of emergency administration of medical services
- comply with the board's policy as to what ratio between supervisors and pupils is required
- discuss rules of conduct and safety with the pupils
- ensure that the facilities, if any, are adequately insured and that the proposed activity is within the board's own insurance coverage
- comply with the board's policy on private transportation of students, where applicable. If a van is being used to transport pupils, the driver must have the appropriate driver's licence classification, depending on the number of pupils being transported.

FIRE DRILL

A fire safety plan which is acceptable to the Chief Fire Official must be prepared. Schematic diagrams must be prepared showing the type, location and operation of all fire emergency systems. Staff must be instructed in fire emergency procedures as described in the fire safety plan, which must be distributed to all staff and posted on each floor of the school. Evacuation fire drills must be conducted three times in each of the fall and spring school terms. All persons present in the school must participate in the drill (s. 6, Reg. 298).

FLYING THE FLAG

Every school must fly both the National Flag of Canada and the Provincial Flag of Ontario on such occasions as the board directs, and every school must display in the school the National Flag and the Provincial Flag (s. 5, Reg. 298).

FUND-RAISING

A pupil must ensure that any canvassing or fund-raising activity on school property by the pupil is carried on only with the consent of the board (s. 25, Reg. 298).

No principal, vice-principal or teacher, without the approval of the board, shall authorize any canvassing or fund-raising activity that involves the participation of one or more pupils attending the school.

Ministry Policy on Canvassing and Fund-Raising:

- safety of pupils should receive prime consideration
- pupils in the primary division should not participate
- parent/guardian must provide written consent for pupil to participate
- pupils must be properly supervised
- purposes of the canvassing or fund-raising must be clearly explained and must be consistent with values related to the goals of education
- number and extent of such activities must be considered
- parents, pupils and community must be aware of the activities and their purposes
- proper financial procedures must be in place.

HEALTH OF PUPILS

The principal is responsible for the health and comfort of the pupils in the school. The principal must promptly report to the board and medical officer of health the unsanitary condition of the school building or school grounds. A teacher has a duty to ensure that all reasonable safety procedures are carried out in courses and activities for which the teacher is responsible (s. 265, Act; s. 20, Reg. 298).

HOME INSTRUCTION

The principal may arrange home instruction for a pupil where there is medical evidence that the pupil cannot attend school and the principal is satisfied that home instruction is required. The approval of the appropriate supervisory officer is required (s. 11, Reg. 298). Home instruction is delivered by a school board. It is not "home schooling", in which a child is excused from attending school because he or she is receiving satisfactory instruction at home.

IMMUNIZATION

The Medical Officer of Health may order that a pupil be suspended or excluded from school if the pupil is not immunized as required by the *Immunization of School Pupils Act*. A pupil may obtain a medical exemption from immunization, or may file a statement of conscience or religious belief claiming an exemption.

LANGUAGE OF INSTRUCTION

A teacher must use the English language in instruction in English-language schools, and in communication with pupils in regard to discipline and management of pupils, except where this is impractical because the pupil does not understand English or when teaching another language. In French-language schools or classes, the French language must be used by teachers, subject to the same exceptions (s. 264, Act).

MAINTENANCE

A principal shall report any lack of attention on the part of the building maintenance staff of the school (s. 11, Reg. 298).

MORALS

A teacher has a duty to inculcate by precept and example respect for religion and the principles of Judaeo-Christian morality and the highest regard for truth, justice, loyalty, love of country, humanity, benevolence, sobriety, industry, frugality, purity, temperance and all other virtues (s. 264, Reg. 298).

OPENING EXERCISES

Section 304 of the Act provides that every school board must hold opening or closing exercises in accordance with the regulations and that the exercises must include the singing of "O Canada" and may include a recitation of a pledge of citizenship in the form set out in the regulations.

Regulation 298, section 4, provides that every *public* elementary and secondary school shall hold opening or closing exercises. These exercises may include "God Save the Queen". An opening or closing exercise may include the following types of readings that impart social, moral or spiritual values and that are representative of Ontario's multicultural society:

(1)   scriptural writings, including prayers
(2)   secular writings.

Opening or closing exercises may include a period of silence.

No pupil in a public elementary or secondary school shall be required to take part in any opening or closing exercises where a parent or guardian of the pupil, or the pupil where the pupil is an adult, applies to the principal of the school that the pupil attends for exemption therefrom (s. 4, Reg. 298; Ministry Policy Memorandum 108).

PROBATIONARY PERIOD FOR TEACHERS

The probationary period, if any, for teachers when they first become employed by a board shall not exceed two years (s. 261 Act). Probationary teachers' contracts, that were prescribed by Regulation 310, cease to have effect on August 31, 1998 (*Education Quality Improvement Act, 1997*).

PROFESSIONAL ACTIVITY DAYS

The number of professional activity days in a school calendar may not exceed four days. Teachers have a duty to participate in professional activity days as designated by the board (s. 11(7.1) and s. 264, Act).

PROMOTION OF STUDENTS

The principal has a duty to promote such pupils as he or she considers proper, subject to revision by the appropriate supervisory officer. Pupils are to receive a statement of their promotion (s. 265).

PROPERTY OF THE SCHOOL

A teacher has a duty to deliver the register, the school key and other school property in his or her possession on demand, or when his or her agreement with the board has expired, or when his or her employment has ceased for any reason. By refusing to deliver school property to the board on demand, the teacher forfeits any claim against the board (s. 264, Act).

PUPIL RECORDS

It is the duty of a principal to:

- collect information for inclusion in a record in respect of each pupil enrolled in the school
- establish, maintain, retain, transfer, and dispose of a record of each pupil in compliance with the criteria established by the board
- ensure that materials in the Ontario Student Record comply with the policies of the OSR Guideline and the criteria established by the board
- ensure the security of the Ontario Student Record of the pupils
- ensure that all persons specified by a board to perform clerical functions with respect to the establishment and maintenance of the OSR are aware of the confidentiality provisions of the *Education Act* and the *Municipal Freedom of Information and Protection of Privacy Act* (see OSR Guideline and s. 265, Act).

RECEPTION OF PUPILS

It is a duty of a teacher, unless otherwise assigned by the principal, to be present in the classroom or teaching area and to ensure that the classroom or teaching area is ready for the reception of pupils at least fifteen minutes before the commencement of classes in the school in the morning and, where applicable, five minutes before the commencement of classes in the school in the afternoon (s. 20, Reg. 298).

REGISTER

It is an offence for a teacher to keep a false register. The maximum fine is $200 (s. 213, Act). The principal has a duty to register pupils and to ensure that the attendance of pupils at the school is recorded (s. 265, Act).

RELIGIOUS EDUCATION

Subject to the regulations, a pupil (in the public school system) shall be allowed to receive such religious instruction as the pupil's parent/guardian desires, or where an adult, as the pupil desires. A pupil in the public school system cannot be required to read or study in or from a religious book, or join in an exercise of devotion or religion if this is objected to by his or her parent or guardian or the (adult) pupil (s. 51, Act).

The regulations prohibit indoctrinational religious instruction in public schools. Ministry policy permits public school boards to provide education *about* religion. The board cannot give primacy to or indoctrination in a particular faith. In public elementary schools, programs of education about religion are limited to 60 minutes per week. A public board may permit its facilities to be used by external groups before or after the school day for the purpose of religious exercises or instruction. However, these religious activities are not to be under board auspices (s. 29, Reg. 298 and Ministry Policy Memorandum 112).

A Roman Catholic school board may establish and maintain programs and courses of study in religious education for its pupils in all schools under its jurisdiction (s. 52, Act).

REMEMBRANCE DAY

A Remembrance Day service shall be held in every school on the 11th day of November, or when the 11th day of November is a Saturday or Sunday, on the Friday preceding the 11th day of November. A service need not be held where the school participates in a service of remembrance at a cenotaph or other location in the community (s. 9, Reg. 298).

REPORTS

The principal has a duty to prepare such reports for the board as are required by the board. The principal's reports and recommendations to a board are sent through the appropriate supervisory officer. The principal shall give the Ministry and appropriate supervisory officer information on discipline in the school, the condition of school premises, the progress of pupils and other matters affecting the interests of the school. The principal shall give the Minister or designate, upon request, information concerning the instructional program, operation of the school, and administration of the school. He or she must inform the board of such a request (s. 265, Act; s. 11, Reg. 298).

RESTITUTION

The principal has a duty to report to the board that the parent of a pupil has not compensated the board after being requested to do so, for any damage to or destruction, loss or misappropriation of school property by a pupil (s. 11, Reg. 298).

SEXUAL MISCONDUCT—REPORTING

A school board that terminates the employment of a member of the Ontario College of Teachers or imposes restrictions on the member's duties for reasons of professional misconduct must file with the Registrar of the College, within 30 days, a written report setting out the reasons. If the member resigns his or her employment before his or her employment could be terminated or restrictions imposed, the board must nevertheless file a written report setting out the reasons why it intended to act. Similarly, if a member resigns during the course of an investigation by the board of allegations that, if proven, would have caused the board to terminate employment or impose restrictions, then the board must file a written report with the Registrar setting out the nature of the allegations being investigated. When a report is filed with the Registrar, the Registrar must report back to the board respecting the action, if any, taken in response to the board's report (s. 43.2, *Ontario College of Teachers Act*).

A board must make a written report to the College when a member who is or has been in its employ (1) has been charged with or convicted of an offence under the *Criminal Code* (Canada) involving sexual misconduct and minors or that, in the opinion of the board, indicates that students may be at risk of harm or injury; or (2) when the member has engaged in conduct or taken action that, in the opinion of the board, should be reviewed by a committee of the College. Such a report must be made even if the board becomes aware that the charge was withdrawn, the member was discharged following a preliminary inquiry, the charge was stayed, or the member was acquitted (s. 43.3, *Ontario College of Teachers Act*).

SMOKING

No smoking is permitted in a school or a day nursery. There is an exception for aboriginal persons if the use of tobacco is for traditional aboriginal cultural or spiritual purposes (ss. 9 and 13, *Tobacco Control Act*).

SUPERVISION OF PUPILS

The principal must make provision for the supervision of pupils while the school buildings and playgrounds are open to the pupils, and for the supervision and conducting of any authorized school activity. A teacher shall carry out the supervisory duties assigned to him or her by the principal (ss. 11 and 20, Reg. 298).

SUPPLIES

The principal shall inform the board if a pupil, or the parent of a pupil who is a minor, fails (after reasonable notice) to provide the supplies required by the pupil for a course of study (s. 11(9), Reg. 298).

SUPPORT STAFF (PROFESSIONAL).

Psychiatrists, psychologists, social workers, and other professional support staff employed by the board are subject to the administrative authority of the principal while in the principal's school (s. 26, Reg. 298).

TESTING of INTELLIGENCE or PERSONALITY

The principal must obtain the written permission of the parent or adult pupil where it is proposed to administer a test of intelligence or personality to a pupil (s. 11, Reg. 298).

TEXTBOOKS

The principal has a duty to ensure that all textbooks used are approved by the board and, where applicable, the Minister (s. 265, Act). The principal, in consultation with the teachers concerned, must select from the list of the textbooks approved by the Minister the textbooks for the use of pupils in the school, and the selection is subject to the approval of the board. Where no textbook for a course of study is included in the list of textbooks approved by the Minister, the principal must, in consultation with the teachers concerned, where they consider a textbook to be required, select a suitable textbook. Subject to the approval of the board, the selected textbook may be used in the school. In making the selection, the principals and teachers are to give preference to books that have been written by Canadian authors and edited, printed and bound in Canada (s. 7, Reg. 298).

The board is to provide textbooks to pupils without charge (s. 7, Reg. 298).

A teacher has a duty to use only approved textbooks (s. 264, Act).

TIMETABLE

The principal has a duty to prepare a timetable, conduct the school according to the timetable, and make the timetable accessible to pupils, teachers, and supervisory officers. A teacher must conduct his or her class in accordance with a timetable (s. 264 and 265, Act).

VICE-PRINCIPAL

Although each school must have a principal, there is no statutory requirement for a board to appoint a vice-principal for a school. The principal has the power to assign duties to the vice-principal and the vice-principal has the duty to perform those duties. In the absence of the principal, the vice-principal is in charge of the school and shall perform the duties of the principal (ss. 11 and 12, Reg. 298).

APPENDIX A

Ministry of Education **Ontario**	Issued under the authority of the Deputy Minister of Education	**Policy/Program Memorandum No. 108***

Date of Issue:
January 12, 1989

Effective:
Until revoked or modified

Subject: OPENING OR CLOSING EXERCISES IN PUBLIC
ELEMENTARY AND SECONDARY SCHOOLS

Application: Chairpersons of Boards of Education
Directors of Education of Boards of Education
Principals of Public Elementary and Secondary Schools

I. Background

The decision of the Ontario Court of Appeal, dated September 23, 1988, struck down subsection 28(1) of Regulation 262 concerning religious exercises in public elementary schools. This subsection, and the decision of the Court relating to it, did not apply to schools operated by separate school boards.

The spirit of the decision of the Court of Appeal was essentially that one religion must not be given a position of primacy and that the content of opening or closing exercises must reflect the multicultural realities and traditions of Ontario society.

Subsequent to the Court ruling, an interim policy, dated September 28, 1988, was established, whereby opening or closing exercises were made optional for school boards. In schools where such exercises were to be held, however, "O Canada" and content that reflected the spirit of the ruling of the Court of Appeal were required.

This interim policy was intended to remain in effect only until policy considerations were finalized and amendments to Regulation 262 were adopted.

II. Amendments to Regulation 262

A copy of the amendments to Regulation 262 relating to opening or closing exercises accompanies this memorandum. The amendments provide for a new section 4. Subsections 28(1), (2), and (3), and subsections 29(1), (2), and (3), as well as other references to "religious exercises" in sections 28 and 29, are deleted.

The following points summarize the content of the new section 4.

1. All public elementary and secondary schools in Ontario must be opened or closed each day with the national anthem. "God Save the Queen" may be included.

---

* Ministry of Education and Training, Policy/Program Memorandum No. 108: Opening or Closing Exercises in Public Elementary and Secondary Schools, issued January 12, 1989. © Queen's Printer for Ontario, 1989. Reproduced with permission.

2. The inclusion of any content beyond "O Canada" in opening or closing exercises is to be optional for public school boards.

3. Where public school boards resolve to include, in the opening or closing exercises in their schools, anything in addition to the content set out in item 1 above, it must be composed of either or both of the following:

   (a) one or more readings that impart social, moral, or spiritual values and that are representative of our multicultural society. Readings may be chosen from both scriptural writings, including prayers, and secular writings;

   (b) a period of silence.

4. Parents who object to part or all of the exercises may apply to the principal to have their children exempted. Pupils who are adults may also exercise such a right.

III. Implementation

When implementing the amendments listed above, school boards should take particular note of the following:

1. Purposes

The purposes of opening or closing exercises are patriotic and educational. Such exercises are intended to nurture allegiance to Canada and to contribute to the social, moral, and spiritual development of the pupils.

Contributing to the social, moral, and spiritual development of pupils includes reinforcing the positive societal values that, in general, Canadians hold and regard as essential to the well-being of our society. These values transcend cultures and faiths, reinforce democratic rights and responsibilities, and are based on a fundamental belief in the worth of all persons.

2. Readings

Readings selected for opening or closing exercises must fulfil educational purposes.

Since the social, moral, and spiritual development of Canadians has roots in many religious and philosophical traditions, readings must be drawn from a variety of scriptural and secular sources representative of our multicultural society. Prayers, including the "Lord's Prayer", may be included, but only as readings.

The collective recitation of a specific reading from a particular religious tradition can no longer be permitted, as such a practice is not in accordance with the Canadian Charter of Rights and Freedoms.

3. Period of Silence

A period of silence is intended to be used for such activities as personal reflection or individual silent prayer.

[Please Note: Regulation 262 is now Regulation 298.]

APPENDIX B

Ontario	Ministry of Education	Issued under the authority of the Deputy Minister of Education	**Policy/Program Memorandum No. 112***

Date of Issue: December 6, 1990

Effective: January 1, 1991

Subject: EDUCATION ABOUT RELIGION IN THE PUBLIC ELEMENTARY AND SECONDARY SCHOOLS

Application: Chairpersons of Boards of Education
Directors of Education of Boards of Education
Principals of Public Elementary and Secondary Schools

I. Background

On January 30, 1990, the Ontario Court of Appeal unanimously struck down subsection 28(4) of Regulation 262 concerning religious education in the public elementary schools. The court ruled that the subsection infringed on the freedom of conscience and religion guaranteed by section 2(a) of the Canadian Charter of Rights and Freedoms. Neither the subsection nor the court decision applied to schools operated by the Roman Catholic Separate school boards.

Section 29 of Regulation 262, regarding provision of religious instruction by clergy or designates in the public secondary schools, was not before the court, and the court's ruling did not apply expressly to that section. However, subsequent advice by legal counsel indicates that the principles outlined in the decision make section 29 equally untenable.

In its decision, the court made it very clear that subsection 28(4) of the regulation was invalid because it permitted the teaching of a single religious tradition as if it were the exclusive means through which to develop moral thinking and behaviour. The court also ruled that education designed to teach about religion and to foster moral values without indoctrination in a particular religious faith would not contravene the Charter.

In distinguishing between religious indoctrination and education about religion, the court made the following statement:

> While this is an easy test to state, the line between indoctrination and education, in some instances, can be difficult to draw. With this in mind, it may be of assistance to refer to the following more detailed statement of the distinction:
>
> — The school may sponsor the *study* of religion, but may not sponsor the *practice* of religion.
> — The school may *expose* students to all religious views, but may not *impose* any particular view.

---

* Ministry of Education and Training, Policy/Program Memorandum No. 112: Education About Religion in the Public Elementary and Secondary Schools, issued December 6, 1990. © Queen's Printer for Ontario, 1990. Reproduced with permission.

— The school's approach to religion is one of *instruction*, not one of *indoctrination*.
— The function of the school is to *educate* about all religions, not to *convert* to any one religion.
— The school's approach is *academic*, not *devotional*.
— The school should *study* what all people believe, but should not *teach* a student what to believe.
— The school should strive for student *awareness* of all religions, but should not press for student *acceptance* of any one religion.
— The school should seek to *inform* the student about various beliefs, but should not seek to *conform* him or her to any one belief.

Subsequent to the court's ruling, an interim policy for public elementary schools, dated February 28, 1990, was established, whereby boards were permitted to provide programs in education about religion in the time previously used during the school day, as long as these programs were in accordance with the court's ruling. Boards of education were also advised that they could continue to provide space outside the school day, as they do for various community-related activities, if parents requested that their children be taught religion by clergy or designates. This interim policy for elementary schools was intended to remain in effect only until policy considerations related to the public elementary and secondary schools were finalized.

II. Permanent Policy

The Ministry of Education will amend sections 28 and 29 of Regulation 262 to reflect the following permanent policy, which will apply to public elementary and secondary schools:

1. Boards of education may provide programs in education about religion in Grades 1 to 8 during the school day for up to 60 minutes per week.

2. Boards of education may continue to provide optional credit courses in World Religions in secondary schools, as specified in the curriculum guideline entitled *History and Contemporary Studies, Part C: Senior Division, Grades 11 and 12, 1987*. The program described in the guideline meets the court's definition of permissible education about religion.

3. Schools and programs, including programs in education about religion, under the jurisdiction of boards of education must meet both of the following conditions:
   a) They must not be indoctrinational.
   b) They must not give primacy to any particular religious faith.

4. Boards of education may continue to provide space before the beginning or after the close of the instructional program of the school day for indoctrinational religious education. Given the provisions for equality of treatment in the Canadian Charter of Rights and Freedoms, boards choosing this option must make space available on an equitable basis to all religious groups.

This policy will come into effect on January 1, 1991.

III. Purpose

The purpose of programs in education about religion is to enable students to acquire knowledge and awareness of a variety of the religious traditions that have shaped and continue to shape our world. The programs enable individuals to understand, appreciate, and respect various types of religious beliefs, attitudes, and behaviour.

The purpose of these programs is *not* to instil the beliefs of any particular religion. It is the prerogative of individual pupils and their families to decide which religious beliefs they should hold. Indoctrinational religious education has no place in the curriculum or programs of public elementary and secondary schools of the province.

IV. Content

Since the world's religions are many and varied, a particular program in education about religion cannot be expected to include every one of them. As a minimum, programs in any grade should include a balanced consideration of world religions that have continuing significance for the world's people.

Both content and method should be appropriate to the ages and levels of maturity of the pupils. In developing programs of education about religion, consideration may be given to various organizational frameworks.

V. Resources

The Ministry of Education will develop a resource document to assist boards of education in developing programs in education about religion for elementary schools.

Programs for the secondary schools will continue to be developed in accordance with *History and Contemporary Studies, Part C: Senior Division, Grades 11 and 12, 1987.*

VI. Context

This permanent policy and the forthcoming amendments to Regulation 262 are to be understood within the context of the long-established vision of the public elementary and secondary schools as places where people of diverse backgrounds can learn and grow together. The public schools are open and accessible to all on an equal basis and founded upon the positive societal values which, in general, Canadians hold and regard as essential to the well-being of our society. These values transcend cultures and faiths, reinforce democratic rights and responsibilities, and are founded on a fundamental belief in the worth of all persons.

[Please Note: Regulation 262 is now Regulation 298.]

APPENDIX C

Ministry of	Issued under the authority	**Policy/Program**
Education	of the Deputy	**Memorandum**
and Training	Minister	**No. 121***
Ontario	of Education	

| Date of Issue: | Effective: |
| October 11, 1994 | Until revoked or modified |

Subject: SUSPENSION AND DISMISSAL OF SUPERVISORY OFFICERS

Application: Chairpersons of School Boards
         Directors of Education
         Supervisory Officers

I. BACKGROUND

The Education Act provides that a supervisory officer may be suspended or dismissed by a school board, in accordance with the regulations, for neglect of duty, misconduct, or inefficiency. Regulation 309 contains provisions concerning the procedures for suspending and dismissing supervisory officers. Those provisions have been changed in a recent amendment, Ontario Regulation 162/93.

II. AMENDMENTS

The Education Act has not been amended with respect to the suspension or dismissal of supervisory officers. However, sections 8 to 15 of Regulation 309 were revoked by Ontario Regulation 162/93, and the following was substituted as section 8:

   (1) A board shall not suspend or dismiss a supervisory officer without first giving the supervisory officer reasonable information about the reasons for the suspension or dismissal and an opportunity to make submissions to the board.
   (2) A supervisory officer who wishes to make submissions to the board may make them orally or in writing.

III. PROCEDURAL FAIRNESS AND SUFFICIENCY OF EVIDENCE

To be sustainable, the suspension or dismissal of a supervisory officer must meet the following two requirements: (a) the process through which the board arrives at its decision must be fair; and (b) there must be sufficient evidence of neglect of duty, misconduct, or inefficiency to support the board's decision. Before suspending or dismissing a supervisory officer, a board must carefully consider all relevant facts and arguments. The Education Act and Regulation 309, as amended, do not permit boards to suspend or dismiss supervisory officers in a summary or an arbitrary manner. Boards should therefore be aware of the following procedural requirements:

---

* Ministry of Education and Training, Policy/Program Memorandum No. 121: Suspension and Dismissal of Supervisory Officers, issued October 11, 1994. © Queen's Printer for Ontario, 1994. Reproduced with permission.

a) *Notice and Disclosure.* The board must inform the supervisory officer in writing why it is considering his or her suspension or dismissal, and the board must provide the supervisory officer with a complete disclosure of all the information that it intends to consider in making its decision. The supervisory officer must have a reasonable period of time in which to consult legal counsel and to prepare oral or written submissions.

b) *Opportunity to Be Heard.* Prior to making its decision, the board must provide the supervisory officer with a genuine opportunity to be heard. That is, the board must give the supervisory officer an opportunity to respond to the allegations against him or her and to present any facts or arguments that may have a bearing on the matter. Legal counsel or another representative should be permitted to make submissions on behalf of the supervisory officer.

Although Regulation 309, as amended, does not require a formal hearing to be held, a hearing may be the best way to ensure fairness in some circumstances.

c) *Reasons for the Suspension or Dismissal.* Subsection 287(2) of the Education Act requires the board to provide the reasons in writing to the Minister and to the supervisory officer for its decision to suspend or dismiss the supervisory officer.

IV. CONTRACT OF EMPLOYMENT

A board and a supervisory officer may enter into a written individual contract of employment. The contract could contain a job description, as well as provisions concerning the board's performance appraisal process, salary and benefits, and other matters mutually agreed upon.

V. REDUNDANCY IN SUPERVISORY OFFICER POSITIONS

Section 7 of Regulation 309, which deals with redundancy in supervisory officer positions, was not affected by the amendments in Ontario Regulation 162/93. Since section 7 remains unchanged, its provisions are not discussed in this memorandum. Boards that are restructuring their organization are advised to review the requirements given in section 7.

APPENDIX D

Ontario Student Record (OSR) Guideline*

Contents

* Ministry of Education, Ontario Student Record (OSR) Guideline, issued December 1989, revised March 2000. © Queen's Printer for Ontario, 1989. Reproduced with permission. Page numbering in the Contents reflects the page numbers in this publication, not in the Guidelines.

INTRODUCTION

The Ontario Student Record (OSR) is the record of a student's educational progress through schools in Ontario. The Education Act requires that the principal of a school collect information "for inclusion in a record in respect of each pupil enrolled in the school and to establish, maintain, retain, transfer and dispose of the record". The act also regulates access to an OSR and states that the OSR is "privileged for the information and use of supervisory officers and the principal and teachers of the school for the improvement of instruction" of the student. Each student and the parent(s)[1] of a student who is not an adult (that is, a student who is under the age of eighteen) must be made aware of the purpose and content of, and have access to, all of the information contained in the OSR.

This guideline sets out the policies of the Ministry of Education with regard to the establishment, maintenance, use, retention, transfer, and disposal of the OSR. It replaces the *Ontario Student Record (OSR): Guideline, 1989.*

This guideline will be revised as needed. Each page of the guideline is dated, and replacement pages will be provided with a revision date.

The contents of this guideline have been reviewed for compliance with the provincial Freedom of Information and Protection of Privacy Act and the Municipal Freedom of Information and Protection of Privacy Act. When implementing the policies contained in this guideline or set by the school board,[2] school staff must take into consideration the requirements of the relevant freedom of information legislation.

The OSR folder, Ontario Student Transcript, documentation file folder, and office index card are available from those vendors that are listed on the ministry's website, at http://www.edu.gov.on.ca. Samples of these OSR components are contained in appendices A, C, D, and E, respectively, to this guideline.

Other forms needed for the OSR are available on the ministry's website. Samples are provided in appendices F, G, H, I, and J to this guideline. School boards and schools may wish to download and print these forms themselves, or they may have them printed by vendors of their choice. In either case, no changes of any kind may be made to the forms.

For instructions for obtaining the provincial report cards and for samples, boards and schools should refer to the *Guide to the Provincial Report Card, Grades 1-8* and the *Guide to the Provincial Report Card, Grades 9-12.* The provincial report cards are also available on the ministry's website.

1. ESTABLISHMENT OF THE OSR

An OSR will be established for each student who enrols in a school operated by a school board or the Ministry of Education.[3] Each student and the parent(s) of a student who is not an adult must be informed of the purpose and content of the OSR at the time of enrolment.

The OSR is an ongoing record and will be transferred, under the conditions outlined in section 6 of this guideline, if the student transfers to another school in Ontario.

Any part or parts, of the OSR my be microrecorded or recorded and stored electronically in a matter that permits the printing of a clear and legible reproduction. Provision should be made to retain original documents when it is important to keep an original signature or initial on a document. Any miscrorecording, electronic file, reproduction, or facsimile of an OSR is subject to the security and access requirements applicable to the original OSR.

---

1 Throughout this document, *parent(s)* is used to refer to both parent(s) and guardian(s).

2 The terms *school board* and *board* refer to district school boards and school authorities.

3 Schools operated by the ministry are Provincial Schools and Demonstration Schools.

If an OSR folder is lost or inadvertently destroyed, a new OSR folder will be created. Previous information can be obtained from the current office index card and, if applicable, from the card(s) at the previous school(s). A notation will be made in the margin on the front of the new OSR folder that gives the date on which the new folder was created and the reason.

The following schools in Ontario may choose to establish and maintain an OSR for their students:

- private schools
- schools operated by Indian and Northern Affairs, Canada, in First Nation communities (referred to as federal schools in this document)
- First Nation schools operated by Native education authorities

All schools that establish and maintain an OSR for their students must do so in accordance with this guideline.

2. RESPONSIBILITY FOR THE OSR

School boards are responsible for ensuring compliance with the policies set out in this guideline. Boards will specify those persons responsible for performing clerical functions with respect to the establishment and maintenance of the OSR. Boards will also develop policies for determining:

- the types of information beyond those specified in this guideline that could be considered to be conducive to the improvement of the instruction of the student;
- the uses of the information and materials contained in the OSR beyond those specified in this guideline (see section 3.4);
- the relevance of the materials in the OSR, with a view to removing those no longer considered to be conducive to the improvement of the instruction of the student (see section 9);
- the times other than those specified in this guideline at which it could be considered appropriate to issue report cards (see section 3.2.3.1);
- the types of information beyond those required by this guideline that could be added to the office index card (see section 3.5).

In addition, boards will develop procedures to be followed to ensure:

- the security of the information contained in the OSR, whether it is maintained electronically or in hard copy, during both the period of use and the period of retention and storage;
- the regular review of the OSR for the removal of any material that is no longer considered to be conducive to the improvement of the instruction of the student;
- the storage of the OSR for the period specified in the retention schedule (see section 8);
- the complete and confidential disposal of material removed from the OSR.

Boards will ensure that all persons that they assign to perform clerical functions with respect to the establishment and maintenance of the OSR are aware of the confidentiality provisions in the Education Act and the relevant freedom of information and protection of privacy legislation.

It is the duty of the principal of a school to:

- establish, maintain, retain, transfer, and dispose of a record for each student enrolled in the school in compliance with this guideline and the policies estab-

lished by the board;
- ensure that the materials in the OSR are collected and stored in accordance with the policies in this guideline and the policies established by the board;
- ensure the security of the OSR;
- ensure that all persons specified by a board to perform clerical, functions with respect to the establishment and maintenance of the OSR are aware of the confidentiality provisions in the Education Act and the relevant freedom of information and protection of privacy legislation.

3. COMPONENTS OF THE OSR

An OSR will consist of the following components:

- an OSR folder in Form 1A or Form 1
- report cards
- an Ontario Student Transcript where applicable
- a documentation file, where applicable
- an office index card
- additional information identified as being conducive to the improvement of the instruction of the student

3.1 The OSR Folder

Principals must establish an OSR folder, Form 1A (see appendix A), for students enrolling in school for the first time after September 1, 1985. For students attending school who enrolled in school before that date, the OSR folder Form 1 must be adjusted to correspond to Form 1A (see appendix B). The folder will contain the parts set out below in sections 3.1.1 to 3.1.7.

3.1.1 Biographical data: Part A

The following information will be provided:

- the student's full name and date of birth (The principal will indicate the method of verification on the folder—e.g. birth certificate, baptismal certificate, passport—and will initial and ate the folder
- a student number assigned by the school or the school board, where applicable
- a Ministry Identification Number (MIN) or Ontario Education Number (OEN) assigned by the ministry, where applicable

3.1.2 Schools attended: Part B

The following information will be provided:

- the name of each school that the student has attended
- the name of the board, the name of the Native education authority, or the name of the person who operated the private or federal school
- the date of entry and the date of the last day of attendance in each grade
- the name of a teacher contact

Where the student is transferring to a school from an educational institution that was not required to maintain an OSR Part B may include any information that will complete the record of schools previously amended.

3.1.3 Retirement from an Ontario school: Part C of Form 1A or Part J and K of Form 1

The following information will be provided on retirement: see also section 7

- the date of retirement
- the student's address at retirement
- the student's destination at retirement with respect to further education or employment

3.1.4 Names of parent(s): Part D

The following information will be provided:

- the first name of the student's parent(s) or the first name and surname of the student's parent(s) when the surname of the latter differs from that of the student
- if applicable, the date of death of the parent(s) of a student opposite the name of the deceased

3.1.5 Special health information: Part E

A summary of a student's special health conditions will be included when such conditions are disclosed to the principal. Entries in Part E will be dated and kept current.

3.1.6 Photographs and information on school activities: Parts F and G of Form 1A or Parts F, G, and I of Form 1

The information may be inserted if it satisfies the policies on inclusion set out by the board (see section 2).

3.1.7 Additional information: Part H

The following information will be provided, if applicable:

- the date on which the student enters a Supervised Alternative Learning for Excused Pupils (SALEP) program (Regulation 308), as well as the SALEP committee report, which is to be inserted in the OSR documentation file (see section 3, 4)

3.2 Report Cards

3.2.1 The Provincial Report Card, Grades 1-8

3.2.1.1 Use and completion

All school boards will use the Provincial Report Card, Grades 1-8, in all their elementary schools at least three times a year.

A completed Provincial Report Card, Grades 1-8 (all three pages), or an exact copy of it, will be filed in the OSR folder for each student who has been enrolled in the school for more than six weeks from the commencement of the reporting period:

- at the time of his or her transfer to another school; or
- at the time of his or her retirement from school; or
- at the end of each of three reporting periods the first to occur during the fall.

The Provincial Report Card, Grades 1-8, or an exact copy of it, will be forwarded to the parent(s) of a student who is not an adult or to the student if he or she is an adult.

3.2.1.2 Content

See the *Guide to the Provincial Report Card, Grades 1-8* for available versions and information about the content.

3.2.1.3 Quality of paper

The paper used to produce the report card must be suitable for long-term storage.

3.2.1.4 Electronic format

School boards may use an electronic format of the Provincial Report Card, Grades 1-8, to facilitate completion and use. However, a completed Provincial Report Card, Grades 1-8, or an exact copy of the report card, must be filed in the OSR as a hard copy.

3.2.2 The Provincial Report Card, Grades 9-12

3.2.2.1 Use and completion

Beginning with the 1999-2000 school year, boards will use the Provincial Report Card, Grades 9-12, for students in Grade 9 in all their secondary schools. Boards will use the Provincial Report Card, Grades 9-12, for students in Grade 9 and 10 in the 2000-2001 school year; for student sin Grades 9, 10, and 11 in the 2000-2001 school year; and for students in Grades 9 to 12 in the 2002-3 school year and thereafter.

A completed Provincial Report Card, Grades 9-12 (all three pages), or an exact copy of it, will be filed in the OSR folder for each student who has been enrolled in the school for more than six weeks from the commencement of the reporting period:

- at the time of his or her transfer to another school; or
- at the time of his or her retirement from school; or
- two times in each semester for semestered schools, the first to occur during the fall, or
- at the end of each of three reporting periods, the first to occur during the fall, for non-semestered schools.

The Provincial Report Card, Grades 9-12, or an exact copy of it, will be forwarded to the parent(s) of a student who is not an adult or to the student if he or she is an adult.

3.2.2.2 Content

See the *Guide to the Provincial Report Card, Grades 9-12* for available versions and information about the content.

3.2.2.3 Quality of paper

See section 3.2.1.3.

3.2.2.4 Ele ctronic format

School boards may use an electronic format of the Provincial Report Card, Grades 9-12, to facilitate completion and use. However, a completed Provincial Report Card, Grades

9-12, or an exact copy of the report card, must be filed in the OSR as a hard copy.

3.2.3 Board report cards

3.2.3.1 Use and completion

Boards may develop and use their own report cards for students in Junior Kindergarten and Kindergarten. They will use their own report cards fro students in Grades 10, 11, and 12 until required to use the Provincial Report Card, Grades 9-12, as indicated in section 3.2.2.1. In addition, they may use their own report cards for students with an Individual Education Plan (IEP), as indicated in the *Guide to the Provincial Report Card, Grades 1-8* and the *Guide to the Provincial Report Card, Grades 9-12* under "IEP".

Boards that have more reporting periods than those stipulated in sections 3.2.1.1 and 3.2.2.1 may use board-developed reports at such times.

A report card will be completed and filed in the OSR folder for each student who has been enrolled in the school for more than six weeks from the commencement of the reporting period:

- at the time of his or her transfer to another school; or
- at the time of his or her retirement from school; or
- at the end of the school year; or
- at the end of each semester, if the school is organized on a semester plan; or
- at such other times that the board may stipulate.

The report card or an exact copy of it will be forwarded to the parent(s) of a student who is not an adult or to the student if he or she is an adult.

3.2.3.2 Content

For those grades where there is no provincial report card, and under the conditions indicated in section 3.2.3.1, a school board will approve, for use in its schools, report cards that will include the following:

- the full name of the student, as recorded on the OSR folder
- the name and address of the school and any other particulars that may be required to identify the school
- the name of the principal
- the signature of the teacher
- the signature of the principal
- the record of attendance of the student at school
- the date the report card is issued
- for all courses taken, the student's level of achievement (indicated by an anecdotal description, a percentage grade, or a letter grade) or a statement that there has been insufficient time to assess the achievement of the student
- the grade in which the student is placed or to which he or she is promoted
- for each secondary school course, the title and common course code of the course
- for each secondary school course taken for credit, the value of the credit(s) assigned to the course (expressed as a whole number or a number with up to two decimal places), or for a course for which a credit is not given, the words 'non-credit course'
- space for comment by the parent(s) of a student who is not an adult or the student if he or she is an adult
- the following statement to parents and students:

To parents and Students

This copy of the report card should be retained for reference. The original or an exact copy has been placed in the student's Ontario student Record (OSR) folder and will be retained for five (5) years after the student leaves school.

3.2.3.3 Quality of paper

See section 3.2.1.3.

3.3 The Ontario Student Transcript (OST)

The requirements for the OST are outlined in the *Ontario Student Transcript OST): Manual, 1999.* Beginning with the 1999-2000 school year, the OST will be a cumulative and continuous record of a student's successful completion of Grade 9 and 10 courses, successful and unsuccessful attempts at completing Grade 11 and 12 courses and Ontario Academic Courses, and completion of other diploma requirements. The OST is part of the OSR. When it is maintained as a hard copy, it should be filed in the OSR folder. When it is maintained electronically, a hard copy must be produced and maintained in accordance with the *Ontario Student Transcript (OST): Manual, 1999.* For a sample of the OST form, see appendix C to this guideline.

3.4 The Documentation File

When a documentation file is required, it will be kept in the OSR folder. A documentation file will be established when the following information is required:

- verification of a custody order
- verification of a change of surname (see section 10)
- a written request to be named by repute (see section 10.1)
- the statement of decision of an Identification, Placement, and Review Committee (IPRC); the recommendation of an appeal board and the decision of the school board regarding identification and/or placement, where applicable; and a tribunal's decision regarding identification and/or placement, where applicable
- an Individual Education Plan (IEP) for a student receiving special education programs and services
- educational, psychological, and health assessments
- an Intensive Support Amount (ISA) status form
- the report of a Supervised Alternative Learning for Excused Pupils (SALEP) committee
- letters of request for a correction to, or a deletion from, the record where the request has not been granted (see section 9)
- other reports and/or information identified in accordance with the policies established by the school board (see section 2)
- a Violent Incident Form (see appendix)[4]

A sample documentation file folder is provider in appendix D.

---

4 See the ministry's publication *Violence-Free Schools Policy, 1994.* Part Two, Section V. "Record Keeping of Violent Incidents Leading to Suspension Expulsion and of Reports to the Police", pp. 39-40, for details on the keeping of records on violent incidents.

When a report is requested from a professional, paraprofessional, or other relevant person, that person should be advised that the report will be filed in the OSR and will be subject to the access provisions governing the OSR.

As with other material included in an OSR, these reports should only be included if, in the principal's opinion, they are conducive to the improvement of the instruction of the student.

3.5 The Office Index Card

The office index card provides the school with immediate access to information about a student. It will remain at the school during the period in which the student is enrolled at the school. The card is not filed in the OSR folder and is not transferred with the OSR when the student transfers from the school. A sample office index card is provided in appendix E.

The office index card will record the following information:

- the full name of the student, as recorded on the OSR folder
- the number assigned to the student by the school or school board, where applicable
- a Ministry Identification Number (MIN) or Ontario Education Number (OEN) assigned by the ministry, where applicable
- the gender of the student
- the student's date of birth (year, month, day)
- the name(s) of the student's parent(s)
- if applicable, the name(s) of the individual(s) who has (have) custody of the student
- the student's current address and home telephone number, as well as an emergency number if one has been provided
- the dates (year, month, day) on which the student enrols in the school, transfers from the school, and/or retires from school
- the name and address of the school to which the student transfers and the date on which the OSR is transferred
- the student's address on the date of transfer or retirement
- the name and address or some other means of identification of the school from which the student is transferring or retiring
- other information that is identified in accordance with the policies established by the school board (see section 2)

When a student transfers to another school, or to a private, federal, or First Nation school or retires from school, the office index card will be stored at the sending school or at a central record office provided by the board.

3.6 Student Record of Accumulated Instruction in French as a Second Language in Elementary School

An individual record of accumulated instruction in French as a second language will be established and maintained for each student enrolled in an elementary school. The record will be kept on a card that is identical to the one in appendix F, and will include all of the information required for each entry. An entry will be made on the record:

- at the end of a school year, semester, or summer course; and
- when a student transfers to another school, including a private, federal, or First Nation school; and
- when a student retires from school.

If a student has had previous instruction in French but no record is available, the entries on the card must be started at least from the date of enrolment in an Ontario school. A note will be made on the first lines of the instruction card indicating what is known about a student's previous instruction in French as a second language and in other subjects taught in French. If the number of accumulated hours must be estimated, an annotation must indicate that the figure is approximate.

4. ACCESS TO THE OSR

Access to an OSR means the right of those persons authorized by the Education Act or other legislation to examine the contents of the OSR. In addition, municipal and provincial freedom of information legislation permits persons who have the right to have access to personal information to receive copies of the information. This provision applies during both the period of use of the OSR and the period of retention and storage.

Both the Municipal Freedom of Information and Protection of Privacy Act, which applies to schools operated by school boards, and the Freedom of Information and Protection of Privacy Act, which applies to Provincial and Demonstration Schools, prohibit institutions from releasing personal information in their custody or under their control to anyone other than the person to whom the information relates, except in certain circumstances. These circumstances are defined in the legislation, and it is up to the head of an institution to decide whether or not to grant access to personal information in such circumstances. School boards should therefore consult with their freedom of information coordinators to determine whether they should develop policies on access to OSRs. Any such policies must be developed in accordance with the legislation.

Boards should develop their own consent forms, which they must use where the consent of the parent(s) or adult student is required for the release of information from the OSR. It is not acceptable to use Form 14 for this purpose; Form 14 should only be used for the release of clinical records under the Mental Health Act.

4.1 Students

Every student has the right to have access to his or her OSR.

4.2 Parents

The parents of a student have the right to have access to the student's OSR until the student becomes an adult (age eighteen). Under both the Children's Law Reform Act and the Divorce Act, 1985, the legal right of a non-custodial parent to have access to a child includes the right to make inquiries and to be given information concerning the child's health, education, and welfare.

4.3 Educational Personnel

Under the Education Act, only supervisory officers and the principal and teachers of the school have access to the OSR for the purpose of improving the instruction of the student. As noted above, additional access may be permitted under municipal and provincial freedom of information legislation, under specified and limited circumstances.

4.4 Ministry and School Boards

The Education Act permits the compiling and delivery of information contained in an OSR if it is required by the Minister of Education or the school board. In instances where ministry staff members are seeking to collect information from OSRs, students who are adults and parents of students who are not adults will be notified.

4.5 Courts and Law Enforcement Agencies

Subsection 266(2) of the Education Act states that the OSR will not be produced in the course of any legal proceedings. There may be occasions, however, when access to the OSR of current students or former students will be sought. In such cases, boards should obtain legal advice from their lawyers in order to deal with such issues as the following:

- whether the Education Act in fact prevents the production of the OSR
- whether the OSR in question is relevant to the proceedings
- if the OSR is relevant to the proceedings, whether a copy, rather than the original, may be submitted to the court

All of these issues are relevant in both civil and criminal cases see sections 4.5.1 and 4.5.2.

Both the municipal and provincial freedom of information acts permit disclosure of personal information for the purposes of law enforcement. The conditions for disclosure and the definition of 'law enforcement' are contained in the legislation. School boards should consult with their freedom of information coordinators and their legal counsel to determine whether they should develop policies on the disclosure of personal information in an OSR to courts and law enforcement agencies.

In court proceedings, subject to an appeal, the judge's order must be followed. If a principal receives a court order requiring the release of an OSR, the principal should contact the board's legal counsel. Although court orders must be followed the principal should obtain legal advice about the issues listed above.

4.5.1 Civil suits

A principal may be served with a subpoena requiring that he or she appear in court on a particular date and bring part or all of an OSR. If a principal receives a subpoena, he or she must comply with it, but should obtain legal advice from the board's legal counsel about the issues in section 4.5 above.

As a general rule, the principal should go to court with both the original OSR and a complete and exact photocopy of it, and should propose to the judge that the photocopy be submitted instead of the original. The principal should also inform the judge that the subpoena is inconsistent with subsection 266(2) of the Education Act. The principal must, however, relinquish the documents if ordered to do so by the judge.

4.5.2 Cases involving the Criminal Code

The Criminal Code is federal legislation where there is a conflict between it and provincial legislation, it takes precedence. Therefore, if a principal is served with a search warrant under the Criminal Code requiring the surrender of an OSR to the police, or is served with a subpoena requiring his or her appearance at court with the OSR, he or she is obliged to comply with the search warrant or the subpoena. In both cases, the principal should obtain legal advice from the board's legal counsel about any relevant issues, including those on page 15 in section 4.5. The principal should also inform the relevant authority (i.e., the police or the judge that the use of any part(s) of the OSR as evidence in court proceedings is inconsistent with subsection 266(2) of the Education Act. The principal should present the police or the judge with both the original OSR and a complete and exact photocopy of it, and should propose that the photocopy by submitted instead of the original.

4.5.3 Provisions under the Child and Family Services Act

Under the Child and Family Services Act, R.S.O. 1990, c. C.11, it is possible for a court to order a principal of a school to produce a student's OSR for inspection and copying. A court may make such an order if it is satisfied that (a) a record contains information that may be relevant to a consideration of whether a child is suffering abuse or likely to suffer abuse, and (b) the person in control of the record has refused to permit a Children's Aid Society director to inspect it. If a principal receives a court order under the Child and Family Services Act, he or she should seek legal advice about how to comply with it.

5. USE AND MAINTENANCE OF THE OSR

Information from an OSR may be used to assist in the preparation of a report required under the Education Act or the regulations made under it. Information from an OSR may also be used in the preparation of a report for an application for further education or an application for employment, if a written request for such a report is made by an adult student, a former student, or the parent(s) of a student.

The freedom of information legislation sets out criteria for the use of personal information. The purposes for which personal information in a student's OSR is being used must be consistent with the policies in this guideline and with school board policies. Students who are adults and parents of students who are not adults should be informed of the uses of personal information at the time that that information is collected for inclusion in an OSR.

The contents of the OSR should be reviewed on a regular basis according to the policies established by the school board to ensure that they remain conducive to the improvement of the instruction of the student. Any such review must comply with the provisions of section 9 of this guideline.

6. TRANSFER OF THE OSR

The transfer of the OSR means the transfer of all parts of the OSR other than the office index card (see section 3.5 for information on the index card. Subject to the conditions outlined below, the original OSR is transferable only to schools in Ontario.

When a student transfers to another school in Ontario, the receiving school must be sent written notification of the student's transfer (see form in appendix G) indicating that the student's OSR will be sent upon receipt of an official written request (see form in appendix H or I). When a student transfers to another school outside Ontario, only a copy of the student's OSR may be sent upon receipt of an official written request from the receiving school. See sections 6.1 to 6.3.

If the original OSR is being transferred between schools operated by the same school board, it may be transferred by a delivery service provided by the board.

If the original OSR is being transferred to a school in another board, to a private, federal, or First Nation school, or to a Provincial or Demonstration School, it must be transferred by Priority Post or an equivalent delivery method that is approved by the board and that maintains confidentiality and guarantees prompt delivery.

If some or all of the information in the OSR has been microrecorded or stored electronically and if the receiving school is capable of receiving this information in microrecorded form or electronically in such a way that the OSR can be effectively reproduced or viewed, the information may be transmitted to the receiving school either as a microrecording or by electronic transmission in advance of the paper parts of the OSR.

If a school is transmitting OSR information electronically or by means of facsimile, arrangements must be made to ensure the secure and confidential transfer of the information.

6.1 Transfer to a School in another Board or to a Provincial or Demonstration School in Ontario

Before a principal transfers an original OSR to a school operated by another school board in Ontario or to a Provincial or Demonstration School in Ontario, the principal must receive a written request for the information from the principal of the receiving school. A sample form for indicating this official request for information is provided in appendix H.

6.2 Transfer to a Private, Federal or First Nation School in Ontario

Before a principal transfers an original OSR to an inspected private school, a non-inspected private school, or a federal or First Nation school in Ontario, the principal must have received:

- a written request for the information from the receiving school in which the school agrees to accept responsibility for the OSR and to maintain retain, transfer, and dispose of the OSR in accordance with this guideline (see appendix I); and
- a written statement indicating consent to the transfer, which is signed by the parent(s) of the student if he or she is not an adult, or by the student if he or she is an adult.

6.3 Transfer to an Education Institution Outside Ontario

An original OSR may not be transferred outside Ontario. Only an exact copy of the OSR may be sent to the principal of an educational institution outside Ontario after the principal who is responsible for the OSR has received:

- a written request for the information from the principal of the education institution outside Ontario; and
- a written statement indicating consent to the transfer, which is signed by the parent(s) of the student if he or she is not an adult, or by the student if he or she is an adult.

7. RETIREMENT OF A STUDENT

A student retires from school when he or she ceases to be enrolled in school. A student is not considered to have retired if he or she (a) withdraws for a temporary period with the written consent of the principal, or (b) transfers to another school in Ontario.

When a student retires from the school that maintained an OSR for the student, the principal will give the following to the parent's of the student if he or she is not an adult, or to the student if he or she is an adult:

- an up-to-date copy of the student's OST, if applicable
- the information and materials stored in the OSR folder that are not required to be retained under the retention schedule provided in section 8

8. RETENTION, STORAGE, AND DESTRUCTION OF INFORMATION IN THE OSR

Regulations under freedom of information legislation require that personal information that has been used by an institution be retained by the institution for at least one year after use, unless the individual to whom the information relates consents in writing to its earlier disposal. Therefore, any personal information placed in an OSR should be retained by the school for at least one year after use, unless the principal receives written consent to its earlier disposal.

The following components of the OSR will be retained for five years after a student retires from school:

- report cards
- the documentation file, where applicable
- additional information that is identified by the school board as appropriate for retention.

The following components of the OSR will be retained for fifty-five years after a student retires from school:

- the OSR folder
- the OST
- the office index card

The destruction of all or any part of the OSR when its retention is no longer required under this guideline will be effected under conditions that ensure the complete and confidential disposal of the record.

9. CORRECTION OR REMOVAL OF INFORMATION IN THE OSR

If certain information or material in an OSR folder is determined, according to the board's policies, to be no longer conducive to the improvement of the instruction of the student, the principal will have the information or material removed from the OSR folder. Such information will be given to the parent(s) of a student who is not an adult or to the student if the student is an adult, or it will be destroyed (see section 8).

If the parent(s) or adult student is (are) of the opinion that the information contained in the student's OSR is inaccurately recorded or that it is not conducive to the improvement of the instruction of the student, the parent(s) or adult student may request in writing that the principal correct the alleged inaccuracy or remove the information from the record. If the principal complies with the request, the material will be corrected or will be removed from the file and destroyed or returned to the parent(s) or the adult student, and no record of the request will be retained in the OSR.

If the principal complies with the request, the parent(s) or the adult student, may request, the parent(s) or the adult student may request in writing that the principal refer the request to the appropriate supervisory officer. The supervisory officer will either (a) require that the principal comply with the request, or (b) submit the OSR and request to a person designated by the Minister of Education. If the supervisory officer requires that the principal comply with the request, no record of the request will be retain in the OSR. If the supervisory officer submits the request to a person designed by the Minister, that person will hold a hearing, which the principal and the person(s) who made the request will attend. After the hearing, the person designated by the Minister will make a decision on the matter. This decision will be final and binding. If the person designated by the Minister requires that the principal comply with the request, no record of the request will be retained in the OSR. If the person designated by the Minister denies the request, the original request, including the date on which it was made, and the statement of this final decision will be retained in the documentation file.

Freedom of information legislation also permits persons to request that recorded personal information be corrected.

Every principal will ensure that no OSR discloses (a) the contravention or alleged contravention by a student of any statute or regulation to which the Young Offenders Act or Part

V-A of the Provincial Offences Act applies, or (b) the disposition of any proceedings brought under those statutes or regulations. If an entry in an OSR does disclose such information, the principal of the school in which the student is enrolled will ensure that the entry is altered appropriately or deleted from the OSR.

10. CHANGE OF SURNAME

10.1 Change by Repute

When a principal receives a written request from an adult student or the parent(s) of a student who is not an adult that the student be identified by a surname other than the legal surname of the student and when (a) the student is known by a surname other than his or her legal surname, (b) the surname is a name obtained by repute, and (c) the use of the surname is the student's best interests, the principal will record the requested surname in Part A of the OSR folder in addition to the legal surname of the student, and the requested surname will be used henceforth. In this case, the legal surname will be enclosed in brackets. The written request will be stored in the documentation file (see sections 3.4).

10.2 Change by Marriage

When a principal receives a document that establishes that a student for whom the principal maintains an OSR has had his or her surname changed by marriage, the principal will file the document, a copy of the document, or a verification of his or her knowledge of the document in the documentation file, and will change the surname of the student on all current and future components of the OSR.

10.3 Change by Law

When a principal receives a document that establishes that a student for whom the principal maintains an OSR has has his or her surname changed in accordance with the law of the province, state, or country in which the document was made, the principal will file the document, a copy of the document, or a verification of his or her knowledge of the document in the documentation file, and, on request, will change the surname of the student on all components of the OSR so that the record will appear as if originally established in the new surname.

11. CONTINUING EDUCATION RECORDS

For each student enrolled in a school board continuing education course or program for the purpose of achieving an Ontario secondary school credit or credits, the principal of the continuing education course or program will establish an office index card, which will contain the following information:

- the full name of the student:
- the number assigned to the student by the school or school board, where applicable
- a Ministry Identification Number (MIN) or Ontario Education Number (OEN) assigned by the ministry where applicable
- the gender of the student
- the student's date of birth (year, month, day) and the source used to verify the date
- if applicable, the name(s) of the individual(s), who has (have) custody of the student and for whom verification of the custody order is included in the documentation file

- the student's current address and home telephone number, as well as an emergency number if one has been provided
- the dates (year, month, day) on which the student enroles in the program, transfers from the program, and/or retires from the program
- the name and address of the school to which the student transfers and the date
- the student's address on the the date of transfer or retirement
- the name and address or some other means of identification of the continuing education program from which the student is transferring or retiring
- other information that is identified in accordance with the policies established by the school board (see section 2)

The OST will be maintained by the principal of the continuing education program. If, however, the student is also enrolled in a day school program, the principal of the continuing education program will forward information on credits earned to the principal of the day school program for inclusion in the student's OST.

Appendices

Samples of folders and forms are provided on the following pages. For information on obtaining these materials, see page 3 of this guideline.

[Editor's note: Appendices are not included in this publication.]

APPENDIX E

Rules of Procedure

for Hearings Conducted under the *Education Act* by the Child and Family Services Review Board

Preamble

The purpose of these Rules is to ensure that procedural fairness and the rules of natural justice are observed in the proceedings before the Child and Family Services Review Board. The Rules are also intended to provide an efficient, effective, expeditious and accessible process to those involved in hearings before the CFSRB. Where an issue arises which is not covered by these Rules, it shall be resolved in a manner consistent with the Rules, the purpose of the Rules, the *SPPA* and the *Act* under which the issue arises.

General

1. These Rules are made pursuant to s. 25.1 of the *Statutory Powers Procedure Act (SPPA)*. The Rules apply to proceedings under the *Education Act*.

2. The Board may exercise any of its powers under these Rules on its own initiative or at the request of a party.

3. The Board may control its own processes, and may issue practice directions as it sees fit.

4. The Board may waive application of or vary any of the Rules at any time, subject to considerations of procedural fairness, and consistent with the *SPPA*.

5. The Rules may be amended by the Board from time to time. All such amendments shall be made available to the public in both English and French.

6. No proceeding is invalid by reason only of a defect or other irregularity in form. Substantial compliance with a form, notice or document required under the *SPPA*, the Board's enabling legislation or these Rules is sufficient to establish the validity of the form, notice or document.

Definitions

7. For the purposes of these Rules:

    a. 'Party' means a party as defined under the *Education Act* and the *Child and Family Services Act* and Regulations thereunder;

    b. 'holiday' means any Saturday, Sunday, Easter Monday, November 11, or statutory holiday. Where a holiday falls on a Saturday or Sunday, the Monday immediately following shall be deemed to be a holiday;

c. in the computation of time under these Rules or in an order of the Board,

    (i) where there is a reference to a number of days between two events, they shall be counted excluding the day on which the first event happens, and including the day on which the second event happens, even if they are described as clear days, or the words 'at least' are used;

    (ii) where the time for doing an act under these Rules expires on a holiday, the act may be done on the next day that is not a holiday;

    (iii) where a document would be deemed to be received or service would be deemed to be effective on a holiday, it shall be deemed to be received, or served effective, on the next day that is not a holiday;

    (iv) where a period of less than seven days is prescribed, holidays shall not be counted;

    (v) a document received by the Board after 4:00 pm shall be deemed to have been received on the next day which is not a holiday.

d. 'service' means the delivery of documentation to any person or to the person's lawyer or agent, or to the Board.

e. 'document' includes, but is not limited to writing, a sound recording, videotape, file, photograph, chart, 'graph, map, plan, survey, book of account, notice and information recorded or stored by means of any device.

f. 'hearing' includes:

    (i) an oral hearing, where parties and witnesses give evidence and submissions in person before the Board;

    (ii) a written hearing, where evidence and submissions are tendered by way of the exchange of documents in writing; and

    (iii) an electronic hearing, where evidence and submissions are given by parties and/or witnesses through teleconferencing or video conferencing.

g. 'Board' is the Child and Family Services Review Board, and includes a single member of the Board sitting in a pre-hearing or a panel of one or more members of the board sitting in a hearing.

Commencement of an Appeal

8. An appeal of a school board's decision to expel a student shall be commenced by filing with the Board an Application to Appeal a Decision to Expel a Student, form CFSRB-1-2001 within 60 days of the decision appealed from.

Notice of a Hearing

9. (1) Once the Board has received the written Application to Appeal a Decision to Expel a Student, form CFSRB-1-2001, it shall, as soon as practicable, serve upon the parties to the proceeding, the child if he or she is not a party, and any other person or entity the Board considers necessary in order to properly dispose of the appeal, a copy of the following documents:

(i)   the completed Application to Appeal a Decision to Expel a Student, form CFSRB-1-2001;
(ii)   the completed Notice of Hearing, form CFSRB-2-2001;
(iii)   a letter from the Board explaining the process of the hearing and pre-hearing, form CFSRB-3-2001;
(iv)   a blank Statement of Issues, form CFSRB-4-2001;
(v)   a blank List of Witnesses and Evidence, form CFSRB-5-2001;
(vi)   a blank Notice of Withdrawal, form CFSRB-6-2001;
(vii)   a blank Notice of Motion, form CFSRB-7-2001; and
(viii) a blank Affidavit in Support of Motion, form CFSRB-8-2001.

(2) Where a party is added at a later stage in the appeal process, the Board shall serve upon him or her the documents referred to in subsection (1) above.

(3) The Board may include any additional information beyond that referred to in subsection (2) above, as it deems necessary for the proper conduct of the hearing.

Service and Filing

10. "Service" means the delivery of documentation to any person or to the person's lawyer or agent, or to the Board.

11 Service is deemed to be delivered:

a. by regular, registered or certified mail on the fifth day after the day of mailing;
b. by fax on the same day of the transmission;
c. by overnight courier, on the second day after the document was given to the courier by the party serving; or
d. as directed by the Board to the last known address of the intended recipient. Where the person to whom the notice is to be given establishes in good faith that through absence, accident, illness or other causes beyond the person's control, he or she did not receive the notice until a later date or at all, the Board may make such ruling regarding the service of the person as it deems appropriate in the circumstances.

12. Documents delivered after 4:00 p.m. shall be deemed to have been served on the next day that is not a holiday.

13. Documents may be filed with the Board by any of the methods of delivery set out in Rule 11.

14. Documents filed by fax shall be filed by 4:00 p.m. and shall not exceed sixteen (16) pages, inclusive of cover sheet, except with leave of the Board.

15. The Board may require confirmation under oath of delivery of any documents under these Rules.

16. A person who serves or files a document shall include with it a statement of the person's address, telephone number, and the name of the proceeding to which the document relates.

Confidentiality of Information

17. Proceedings before the Board shall not be open to the public unless the Board specifically directs otherwise.

18. No public release shall be made of any document of the Board's or that is filed with the Board if it has the effect of identifying a student or the student's parent or foster parent or a member of the student's family.

Motions

19. A party who wishes to bring a motion before the Board for determination before the hearing shall file with the Board a Notice of Motion in form CSFRB-7-2001 and an affidavit in support of motion, in form CFSRB-8-2001, setting out the grounds for the motion, the evidence to be relied upon, and the relief sought.

20. On receipt of a Notice of Motion under Rule 19, the Board will forthwith serve the other parties with the following documents:

(i)   the Notice of Motion;
(ii)   the Affidavit in Support of Motion;
(iii) any other materials which the Board has received from the party bringing the motion;
(iv)   a letter, in form CFSRB-12-2001, setting out the process to be followed in replying to the motion, including time limits for the filing of reply materials; and
(v)   a blank Affidavit in Reply, form CFSRB-14-2001.

21. Forthwith upon receipt of any reply materials filed within the time limits set out by the Board, the Board shall serve the other parties with the reply materials and a letter in form CFSRB-13-2001.

22. The board may make a ruling on the motion in writing prior to the hearing, or orally and/or in writing at the time of the hearing.

23. Upon making a ruling on the motion, the Board shall forthwith notify all parties of the ruling.

24. The Board may consider a motion raised during the hearing of the appeal, whether such hearing is held orally, in writing, or electronically.

Evidence

25. The Board may direct, at a pre-hearing, a motion, or a hearing, in what form evidence shall be tendered before it.

Pre-Hearing Conferences

26. The Board may direct the parties and their counsel or agents to attend one or more pre-hearing conferences for the purpose of considering any matter, including:

   a. Identification of parties and other interested persons and the scope of their participation at the hearing;
   b. Issues relating to disclosure and the exchange of information;
   c. Identification and simplification of issues;
   d. Identification of preliminary motions to be raised;
   e. Procedural issues, including the dates by which any steps in the proceeding are to be taken or begun, the estimated duration of the hearing, and the date the hearing will begin;
   f. Identification of facts or evidence that may be agreed upon;
   g. The method by which evidence shall be adduced;
   h. Settlement of any or all of the issues;
   i. Any other matter that may assist in the just and most expeditious disposition of the proceeding.

27. Pre-hearings shall be conducted by a single member of the Board by teleconference, unless otherwise directed by the Board. The Board member hearing the pre-hearing shall not participate in the panel hearing the appeal, except with the consent of all parties.

28. The Board shall give notice of the pre-hearing conference to the parties and any other interested persons whose presence the Board feels is necessary for the proper disposition of the appeal, by way of a Notice of Hearing, in form CFSRB-2-2001.

29. During the pre-hearing conference, the member may make such rulings as he or she deems necessary for the proper disposition of the appeal, and the panel conducting the hearing shall be bound by such rulings unless the parties and the panel agree otherwise.

30. The member may decline to rule on any issue raised at a pre-hearing, and may instead direct that the issue be disposed of by the panel at the hearing. The member may recess or adjourn the pre-hearing from time to time, and may thereafter reconvene the pre-hearing.

31. Any rulings made by the member at a pre-hearing shall be recorded in writing in the Pre-Hearing Endorsement Sheet, form CFSRB-10-2001. The Board shall serve a copy of the Pre-Hearing Endorsement Sheet on all parties to the proceedings and such other persons as the member may direct as soon as practicable after the pre-hearing.

32. If settlement of any issue is discussed at a pre-hearing conference:

a. Statements made at the pre-hearing conference may not be communicated to the hearing panel;

b. The Board member who presides at the pre-hearing conference shall not preside at the hearing of the proceeding unless all parties consent in writing or on the record, unless prohibited by statute;

c. An agreement to settle any or all of the issues binds the parties to the agreement but is subject to approval by the Board, the hearing panel, or such other panel of the Board as is assigned to consider the settlement.

Disclosure

33. At any time in a proceeding, the Board may order any party to provide to any other party and to the Board such particulars, information, or documents as the Board considers necessary to enable the other party or the Board to obtain a full and satisfactory understanding of the issues in the proceeding.

34. The Board may at any stage of the proceeding order:

a. A party to disclose to any other party, by a time determined by the Board, the existence of all documents and things that the party intends to refer to or enter as evidence at the hearing;

b. A party to make available for inspection by any other party at a time determined by the Board all documents and things that the party will produce or enter as evidence at the hearing, and permit the inspecting party to make copies of the documents;

c. A party to deliver to any other party, by a time determined by the Board, copies of all documents that the party will produce or enter as evidence at the hearing.

35. If a party fails to comply with the provisions of Rules 33 or 34, the party may not refer to the document or thing in evidence at the hearing without the consent of the Board, which may be on such terms and conditions as the Board considers just.

36. If the good character, propriety of conduct, or competence of a party is an issue in the proceeding, the party making such allegations shall disclose to the party against whom the allegations are made all evidence in the party's possession or control relevant to the allegations, including:

a. All witness statements and transcripts or notes of witness interviews or, if these do not exist, statements of evidence that each witness is expected to give;

b. All documents and other things;

c. All experts' reports.

Hearings

37. The Board may hold hearings orally, in writing (by exchange of documents), or electronically (by tele-conference or video-conference).

38. In deciding the format of a hearing, the Board will consider:

a.   Whether it is a fair and accessible process for the parties;
b.   The costs and efficiency of the process;
c.   The potential for a more expeditious resolution;
d.   The convenience of the parties;
e.   Consistency with the fulfilment of the Board's mandate;
f.   Whether facts or evidence may be agreed upon;
g.   The estimated duration of the hearing;
h.   Whether the issues for hearing are predominantly legal issues; and
i.   Whether oral testimony is likely to be needed.

39.   The board may hold a combination of written, oral and/or electronic hearings in a single proceeding.

40.   The board will generally consider holding a hearing in writing where the issues raised are solely questions of law or where cross examination of evidence is not required.

41.   A party to a proceeding may object to a hearing being held in writing, and in that case shall provide the Board and the other parties with a statement giving reasons for the objection within ten (10) days of receiving the Notice of Hearing.

42.   Where a party objects to a hearing being conducted in writing, the Board may:

a.   Accept the objection, cancel the written hearing, and schedule either an oral or electronic hearing; or
b.   Reject the objection without inviting responses from the other parties and proceed with the written hearing; or
c.   Provide all parties with notice of an opportunity to respond to the objection, in which case the Board shall provide directions for the form and timing of responses and for reply, if any, allowing at least ten (10) days for response and for reply, and after considering such submissions, may make a ruling on the form of the hearing.

43.   The Board shall not hold a written hearing if a party satisfies it that there is good reason for not doing so.

44.   The Board may hold an electronic hearing to determine:

a.   Any matters pertaining to procedural issues; or
b.   Any other matter, including the merits of the case.

45.   The Board will not generally hold a hearing by teleconference if credibility of one or more witnesses will be in issue.

46.   The Board may impose any conditions regarding the electronic hearing that it considers appropriate.

47.   Upon receipt of a notice of an electronic hearing that will deal with issues other than procedural matters, a party may object to holding the hearing in that format, in which case Rule 42 applies *mutatis mutandis.*

48. The Board shall not hold an electronic hearing if a party satisfies it that an electronic hearing is likely to cause significant prejudice to the party.

49. A hearing will generally be heard by a panel of three (3) Board members assigned by the Chair of the Board.

50. Where a hearing has been commenced and one or two members of the panel are not able to proceed with the hearing for any reason, the remaining member or members may complete the hearing and rule on all issues. A hearing may be adjourned from time to time as deemed necessary by the panel.

Costs

51. At the conclusion of a hearing, the Board may, in its discretion, make an award of costs to be paid by one or more parties to one or more parties.

52. In exercising its discretion under Rule 51, the Board shall consider the following:

   a.   Whether the conduct of a party has been unreasonable, frivolous or vexatious; or
   b.   Whether the party has acted in bad faith.

53. In making an order for costs, the Board shall fix the amount of costs to be awarded, based upon the submissions of the parties.

Decisions

54. The Board shall provide each party, or the party's counsel or agent, with a copy of the Board's decision on the appeal within 10 days after completing the hearing. Written reasons for the decision shall be provided to each party, or the party's counsel or agent, as soon as practicable after a decision on the appeal is made.

Amendments to a Decision

55. The Board may at any time correct a typographical error, error of calculation, mis-statement, ambiguity, technical error or other similar error made in its decision or order without prior notice to the parties.

Legislation and Regulations

Regulations under the *Education Act*

REGULATION 285

under the Education Act

R.R.O. 1990, Reg. 285, as am. O. Reg. 96/95, O. Reg. 97/96, O. Reg. 71/03

CONTINUING EDUCATION

Part I

1. (1) The following classes or courses provided by a board other than as part of the day school program on an instructional day as defined in Regulation 304 of Revised Regulations of Ontario, 1990 (School Year and School Holidays) are continuing education courses or classes for the purpose of paragraph 31 of subsection 171(1) of the Act and the regulations:

1. A class or course that is designed to develop or to improve the basic literacy and numeracy skills of adults to a level that does not exceed the grade 8 level of competency.
2. A class or course in English or French for adults whose first language learned and still understood is neither English nor French and that is not a class in which a pupil may earn a credit in English or French as a second language.
3. A class or course in citizenship and, where necessary, in language instruction in the English or the French language for persons admitted to Canada as permanent residents under the *Immigration and Refugee Protection Act* (Canada).
4. A class or course in driver education in which a pupil may not earn a credit.
5. A class or course in the primary or junior division or in the first two years of the intermediate division in which a language other than English or French is the subject of instruction.
6. A class or course in which a pupil may earn a credit.
7. A class for the purpose of extending the knowledge of adults, for the purpose of improving the skills of adults, for the specific interest of adults or for the enhancement of the knowledge or skills of elementary or secondary school pupils beyond that expected or required of the pupils as part of the regular program in an elementary or secondary school,
     i. for which the board charges registration fees to persons taking the class and the fees are not calculated in accordance with the regulations, or
     ii. in which the work required for its successful completion is not acceptable to the Minister as partial fulfilment of the requirements for a diploma granted by the Minister.

(1.1) A continuing education course or class referred to in subsection (1) may be provided by a board at any time of the day or evening.

(2) The following classes or courses provided by a board between the hours of 8.00 a.m. and 5.00 p.m. that start after the completion of one school year and that end before the next following school year are continuing education classes or courses for the purposes of paragraph 31 of subsection 171(1) of the Act and the regulations:

1. A class or course for remedial purposes for pupils who are enrolled in an elementary school operated by the board and that is,
    i. a class or course that the board is required or authorized to provide during the school day to pupils enrolled in elementary schools and, in the school year immediately preceding commencement of the class or course, was a class or course that was provided to its elementary school pupils, and
    ii. approved by the Minister.
2. A class or course that is for trainable retarded pupils who are enrolled in an elementary school or school or class for trainable retarded pupils operated by the board.
3. A class or course in which a pupil may earn a credit. O. Reg. 97/96, s. 1; 71/03, s. 1.

2. (1) Subject to subsection (2) and Part II, a board that establishes continuing education courses or classes shall determine the courses to be given in each of its continuing education classes, the number of times that each continuing education course or class is held per week, the length of time per session of each continuing education course or class and the dates and the time of the day or evening upon which each continuing education course or class is given.

(2) An elementary school board may offer continuing education courses and classes only in courses of study that the board is authorized or required to provide in its day school program in the primary and junior divisions and the intermediate division.

(3) An elementary school board may, subject to Part II, offer as a subject a language other than English or French in the primary and junior divisions and in the first two years of the intermediate division in its continuing education courses and classes.

(4) The principal of a school shall be the principal of the continuing education courses and classes in the school unless the board appoints as principal thereof another person who holds the appropriate principal's qualifications set out in section 9 of Regulation 298 of Revised Regulations of Ontario, 1990 (Operation of Schools — General).

(5) A school site that was used for school purposes and a school site that is used as a school during the school year may be used for a continuing education course or class.

(6) Two or more boards may jointly establish continuing education courses and classes in a school or schools operated by one or more of the boards concerned and determine where such courses and classes shall be conducted.

3. (1) A valid certificate of qualification or a letter of standing is required to be held by a person,

(a) who provides the classroom teaching in a continuing education course or class referred to in paragraph 6 of subsection 1(1) or in subsection 1(b); or
(b) who is employed in respect of the development or co-ordination of the program of which a continuing education course or class referred to in clause (a) is a part.

(2) A board may employ a person who is not a teacher to provide instruction in a continuing education course or class, other than a continuing education course or class referred to in paragraph 6 of subsection 1(1) or in subsection 1(2), if the person holds qualifications acceptable to the board for such employment.

Part II

4. In this Part,

"board", other than in section 6, means a board of education, public school board, Roman Catholic separate school board or Protestant separate school board, The Metropolitan Toronto French-Language School Council and the public sector and the Roman Catholic sector of The Ottawa-Carleton French-language School Board;

"commencement date" means the last school day of the month of January or September, as the case requires;

"parent" includes guardian;

"program" means a program of instruction in a continuing education course or class referred to in paragraph 5 of subsection 1(1);

"qualified person", in respect of a board, means a person who is enrolled or is eligible to be enrolled in an elementary school, a kindergarten or a junior kindergarten operated by the board, and who is not enrolled or is not eligible to be enrolled in a secondary school operated by the board, but if the board does not operate a secondary school, does not include a person who is enrolled or is eligible to be enrolled in the last two years of the intermediate division.

5. (1) If a board is not providing a program and receives from parents written requests on behalf of twenty-five or more qualified persons of the board for the establishment of a program, the board shall establish the program requested.

(2) If a board is providing one or more programs and the board receives from parents written requests on behalf of twenty-five or more qualified persons of the board for the establishment of a program that the board is not providing, the board shall establish the program requested.

(3) Despite subsections (1) and (2), a board may enter into an agreement with another board for the other board to provide the program requested.

(4) A program established under this section shall start not later than the commencement date that first occurs ninety days or more after the date of the request.

(5) A board that establishes a program under this section shall provide a class or course in the program for all qualified persons of the board who wish to attend if at least ten qualified persons of the board attend the first scheduled class or course of the program.

(6) A program provided by a board shall be provided throughout the school year in which the program was established so long as a person attends the class or course in the program.

(7) If a board, other than a Roman Catholic separate school board or the Roman Catholic sector of The Ottawa-Carleton French-language School Board, establishes a program under this section, it shall admit to a class or course in the program a qualified person in respect of another board that is not a Roman Catholic separate school board or the Roman Catholic sector of The Ottawa-Carleton French-language School Board.

(8) If a Roman Catholic separate school board establishes a program under this sec-

tion, it shall admit to a class or course in the program a qualified person in respect of another Roman Catholic separate school board or the Roman Catholic sector of The Ottawa-Carleton French-language School Board.

(9) If the Roman Catholic sector of The Ottawa-Carleton French-language School Board establishes a program under this section, it shall admit to a class or course in the program a qualified person in respect of a Roman Catholic separate school board.

(10) A board may admit to a class or course in a program a person who is enrolled or eligible to be enrolled in an elementary school, a kindergarten or a junior kindergarten operated by a board and the person is not enrolled or eligible to be enrolled in a secondary school operated by a board, despite the fact that the board is not required to admit the person under this section.

6. (1) In this section,

"board" means the Conseil des écoles publiques d'Ottawa-Carleton, the Conseil des écoles catholiques de langue fran»aise de la région d'Ottawa-Carleton, the Conseil des écoles séparées Catholiques de langue fran»aise de Prescott-Rusell and The Metropolitan Toronto French-Language School Council;

"French-speaking person" means a child of a person who has the right under subsection 23(1) or (2), without regard to subsection 23(3), of the *Canadian Charter of Rights and Freedoms* to have his or her children receive their primary and secondary school instruction in the French language in Ontario.

(2) Despite section 5, a board shall not admit to a program that it operates or provides for another board a person who is not a French-speaking person.

(3) Subsection (2) does not apply to a person who is enrolled in an elementary school, a kindergarten or a junior kindergarten operated by the board or another board. O. Reg. 96/95, s. 1.

7. (1) Subject to subsections (2) and (3), a qualified person of a board may attend one or more programs provided in one or more languages by one or more boards.

(2) The maximum period in each week during the school year that a qualified person of a board may attend a program in any one language is two and one-half hours.

(3) The maximum period during a day that falls after the completion of one school year and before the commencement of the next following school year that a qualified person of a board may attend a program in any one language is two and one-half hours.

8. A board that provides a program before the end of the instructional program of a school day may do so only in a school site that is used for school purposes by the board during the school day.

9. (1) A board that provides a program following the end of the instructional program of a school day or on a day that is not a school day may provide a class or course in the program in a place that is not a school site.

(2) If a board conducts a class or course in a program in a place that is not used as a school site during the school day, the time that the class begins shall be not earlier than the time at which the instructional program of the board ends.

(3) A board that conducts a class or course in a program in a place that is not used as a school site during the school day shall allow an interval of time between the end of the instructional program and the beginning of the class sufficient to permit pupils enrolled in the instructional program to travel to the place in which the class is being conducted.

10. (1) A board may discontinue a program at the end of the school year if the number of qualified persons of the board enrolled in courses or classes provided under the program is fewer than twenty-five at the conclusion of the school year in which the program is provided.

(2) A board that proposes to discontinue a program shall advise any person who participated in the program to the end of the school year that the program will be discontinued and that the program may be re-established in accordance with this Part.

REGULATION 298

under the Education Act

R.R.O. 1990, Reg. 298, as am. O. Reg. 339/91 (Fr. version); 242/92; 95/96; 425/98; 436/00; 613/00; 492/01; 209/03

OPERATION OF SCHOOLS — GENERAL

1. In this Regulation,

"business studies" means the courses in general studies that are developed from curriculum guidelines listed under the heading "Business Studies" in Appendix B to OSIS;

"division" means the primary division, the junior division, the intermediate division or the senior division;

"French as a second language" includes programs for English speaking pupils in which French is the language of instruction;

"general studies" means the courses developed from curriculm guidelines that are issued by the Minister for the intermediate division and senior division and listed under a heading other than "Technological Studies" in Appendix B to OSIS;

"OSIS" means the circular entitled "Ontario Schools Intermediate and Senior Divisions Program and Diploma Requirements" issued by the Minister including any document issued by the Minister in accordance with paragraphs 1, 2, 3, 4 and 25 of subsection 8(1) of the Act;

"parent" includes guardian;

"technological studies" means the courses developed from curriculum guidelines that are issued by the Minister for the intermediate division and senior division and listed under the heading "Technological Studies" in Appendix B to OSIS.

ACCOMMODATION

2. (1) A board shall file with the Ministry plans for the erection of, addition to, or alteration of a school building together with details of the site thereof.

(2) It is a condition of the payment of a legislative grant in respect of capital cost that the plans and details referred to in subsection (1) be approved by the Minister.

DAILY SESSIONS

3. (1) The length of the instructional program of each school day for pupils of compulsory school age shall be not less than five hours a day excluding recesses or scheduled intervals between classes.

(2) The instructional program on a school day shall begin not earlier than 8 a.m. and end not later than 5 p.m. except with the approval of the Minister.

(3) Despite subsection (1), a board may reduce the length of the instructional program

on each school day to less than five hours a day for an exceptional pupil in a special education program.

(4) Every board may establish the length of the instructional program on each school day for pupils in junior kindergarten and kindergarten.

(5) Each pupil and each teacher shall have a scheduled interval for a lunch break.

(5.1) A pupil's interval for a lunch break shall be not less than forty consecutive minutes and need not coincide with the scheduled interval for the lunch break of any other pupil or any teacher.

(5.2) A teacher's interval for a lunch break shall be not less than forty consecutive minutes and need not coincide with the scheduled interval for the lunch break of any other teacher or any pupil.

(6) In the intermediate division and the senior division, a principal may, subject to the approval of the board, provide for recesses or intervals for pupils between periods.

(7) Every board shall determine the period of time during each school day when its school buildings and playgrounds shall be open to its pupils, but in every case the buildings and the playgrounds shall be open to pupils during the period beginning fifteen minutes before classes begin for the day and ending fifteen minutes after classes end for the day.

(8) There shall be a morning recess and an afternoon recess, each of which shall be not less than ten minutes and not more than fifteen minutes in length, for pupils in the primary and junior divisions. O. Reg. 492/01, s. 1

OPENING OR CLOSING EXERCISES

4. (1) This section applies with respect to opening and closing exercises in public elementary schools and in public secondary schools.

(2) The opening or closing exercises may include the singing of God Save the Queen and may also include the following types of readings that impart social, moral or spiritual values and that are representative of Ontario's multicultural society:

1. Scriptural writings including prayers.

2. Secular writings.

(3) The opening or closing exercises may include a period of silence.

(4) In the following circumstances, a pupil is not required to participate in the opening or closing exercises described in this section:

1. In the case of a pupil who is less than 18 years old, if the pupil's parent or guardian applies to the principal of the school for an exemption from the exercises.

2. In the case of a pupil who is at least 18 years old, if the pupil applies to the principal for an exemption from the exercises. O. Reg. 436/00, s. 1

FLAG

5. (1) Every school shall fly both the National Flag of Canada and the Provincial Flag of Ontario on such occasions as the board directs.

(2) Every school shall display in the school the National Flag of Canada and the Provincial Flag of Ontario.

EMERGENCY PROCEDURES

6. (1) In addition to the drills established under the fire safety plan required under Regulation 454 of Revised Regulations of Ontario, 1990 (Fire Code), every board may provide for the holding of drills in respect of emergencies other than those occasioned by fire.

(2) Every principal, including the principal of an evening class or classes or of a class or classes conducted outside the school year, shall hold at least one emergency drill in the period during which the instruction is given.

(3) When a fire or emergency drill is held in a school building, every person in the building shall take part in the fire or emergency drill.

TEXTBOOKS

7. (1) The principal of a school, in consultation with the teachers concerned, shall select from the list of the textbooks approved by the Minister the textbooks for the use of pupils of the school, and the selection shall be subject to the approval of the board.

(2) Where no textbook for a course of study is included in the list of the textbooks approved by the Minister the principal of a school, in consultation with the teachers concerned, shall, where they consider a textbook to be required, select a suitable textbook and, subject to the approval of the board, such textbook may be introduced for use in the school.

(3) In the selection of textbooks under subsection (2), preference shall be given to books that have been written by Canadian authors and edited, printed and bound in Canada.

(4) Every board shall provide without charge for the use of each pupil enrolled in a day school operated by the board such textbook selected under subsections (1) and (2) as related to the courses in which the pupil is enrolled.

ELEMENTARY SCHOOL BOARDS

8. (1) Where the area of jurisdiction of a district school area board, a Roman Catholic separate school board, other than a Roman Catholic school board, or a Protestant separate school board is not within a secondary school district, the board shall provide instruction that would enable its resident pupils to obtain sixteen credits towards a secondary school graduation diploma or an Ontario secondary school diploma.

(2) A board referred to in subsection (1) that offers courses of instruction during July or August or both in any year may provide instruction that would enable its resident pupils to obtain two credits in addition to the sixteen credits referred to in subsection (1).

(3) Where a board referred to in subsection (1) provides,

    (a) daily transportation for its resident pupils; or

    (b) reimbursement for board and lodging and for transportation once a week to and from the places of residence of its resident pupils,

that it considers necessary to enable its resident pupils to attend a school operated by another board, the other board may provide such instruction as would enable such resident pupils to obtain the number of credits referred to in subsections (1) and (2).

(4) A Roman Catholic separate school board, other than a Roman Catholic school board, or a Protestant separate school board that has jurisdiction in a secondary school district may provide instruction for its resident pupils that would enable the pupils to obtain up to eighteen credits towards a secondary school graduation diploma or an Ontario secondary school diploma.

QUALIFICATIONS FOR PRINCIPALS AND VICE-PRINCIPALS

9. (1) The principal and vice-principal of a school having an enrolment greater than 125 shall each be a teacher who,

    (a) holds or is deemed to hold, under Regulation 297 of Revised Regulations of Ontario, 1990, principal's qualifications; or

    (b) holds a principal's certificate that is a qualification to be principal or vice-principal, as the case may be, in the type of school identified on the certificate, or is deemed under section 47 of Regulation 297 of Revised Regulations of Ontario, 1990 to hold such a certificate,

and, in the case of a school,

    (c) in which English is the language of instruction; or

    (d) that is established under Part XII of the Act and in which French is the language of instruction,

shall each be a person who is eligible to teach in such school under subsection 19(11), (12) or (13), as the case may be.

(2) Despite subsection (1), where a teacher who does not hold the degree of Bachelor of Arts or Bachelor of Science from an Ontario university or a degree that the Minister considers equivalent thereto was, prior to the 1st day of September, 1961, employed by a board as principal or vice-principal of an elementary school that had an enrolment of 300 or more pupils, the teacher shall be deemed to be qualified as principal or vice-principal, as the case may be, of any elementary school operated by that board or its successor board.

(3) Despite subsection (1), where a teacher who does not hold the qualifications referred to in subsection (1),

    (a) was employed by a board prior to the 1st day of September, 1972 as principal of an elementary school that had an enrolment of 300 or more pupils and is employed by such board as principal of an elementary school on the 8th day of September, 1978;

    (b) was employed by a board on the 1st day of September, 1978 as vice-principal of an elementary school that had an enrolment on the last school day in April, 1978 of 300 or more pupils; or

    (c) was employed by a board on the 1st day of September, 1978 as principal or vice-principal of an elementary school that had an enrolment on the last school day in April, 1978 that was greater than 125 and less than 300,

such teacher shall be deemed to be qualified as principal or vice-principal, as the case may be, of any elementary school operated by that board or its successor board.

(4) A board may appoint a person who holds the qualifications required by subsection (1) as a supervising principal to supervise the administration of two or more elementary schools operated by the board and such person shall be subject to the authority of the appropriate supervisory officer.

(5) A supervising principal may be principal of only one school.

(6) Despite subsection (1), a teacher who, before the 1st day of September, 1970, held the necessary qualifications as principal of a secondary school continues to be qualified as principal or vice-principal of a secondary school.

10. (1) The principal and vice-principal of a school for trainable retarded pupils having an enrolment greater than 100 or of a school in which there are classes for trainable retarded pupils and the enrolment in such classes is greater than 100 shall each be a teacher who,

- (a) holds or is deemed to hold, under Regulation 297 of Revised Regulations of Ontario, 1990, principal's qualifications, or holds a certificate referred to in section 46 of such Regulation or is deemed to hold such certificate under section 47 thereof; and
- (b) holds an additional qualification in special education as recorded on the teacher's Ontario Teacher's Qualifications Record Card.

(2) The principal of an elementary or secondary school that includes one or more classes for trainable retarded pupils shall be the principal of such classes, and the vice-principal of such a school shall be the vice-principal of such classes except where a vice-principal is appointed to be in charge of such classes exclusively.

(3) Despite subsection (1), where a teacher who does not hold the qualifications referred to in subsection (1) was, on the 1st day of September, 1978 employed by a board as principal or vice-principal of a school for trainable retarded pupils that had an enrolment greater than 100 or of a school in which there were classes for trainable retarded pupils and the enrolment in such classes was greater than 100, the teacher shall be deemed to be qualified as principal or vice-principal, as the case may be, of a school for trainable retarded pupils or of a school in which there are classes for trainable retarded pupils the enrolment in which is greater than 100 that is operated by that board or its successor board.

DUTIES OF PRINCIPALS

11. (1) The principal of a school, subject to the authority of the appropriate supervisory officer, is in charge of,

- (a) the instruction and the discipline of pupils in the school; and
- (b) the organization and management of the school.

(2) Where two or more schools operated by a board jointly occupy or use in common

a school building or school grounds, the board shall designate which principal has authority over those parts of the building or grounds that the schools occupy or use in common.

(3) In addition to the duties under the Act and those assigned by the board, the principal of a school shall, except where the principal has arranged otherwise under subsection 26(3),

(a) supervise the instruction in the school and advise and assist any teacher in co-operation with the teacher in charge of an organization unit or program;

(b) assign duties to vice-principals and to teachers in charge of organizational units or programs;

(c) retain on file up-to-date copies of outlines of all courses of study that are taught in the school;

(d) upon request, make outlines of courses of study available for examination to a resident pupil of the board and to the parent of the pupil, where the pupil is a minor;

(e) provide for the supervision of pupils during the period of time during each school day when the school buildings and playgrounds are open to pupils;

(f) provide for the supervision of and the conducting of any school activity authorized by the board;

(g) where performance appraisals of members of the teaching staff are required under a collective agreement or a policy of the board, notwithstanding anything to the contrary in such collective agreement or board policy, conduct performance appraisals of members of the teaching staff;

(h) subject to the provisions of the policy of the board or the provisions of a collective agreement, as the case may be, in respect of reporting requirements for performance appraisals, report thereon in writing to the board or the supervisory officer on request and give to each teacher so appraised a copy of the performance appraisal of the teacher;

(i) where the performance appraisals of members of the teaching staff are not required by board policy or under a collective agreement, report to the board or to the supervisory officer in writing on request on the effectiveness of members of the teaching staff and give to a teacher referred to in any such report a copy of the portion of the report that refers to the teacher;

(j) make recommendations to the board with respect to,
   (i) the appointment and promotion of teachers, and
   (ii) the demotion or dismissal of teachers whose work or attitude is unsatisfactory;

(k) provide for instruction of pupils in the care of the school premises;

(l) inspect the school premises at least weekly and report forthwith to the board,
   (i) any repairs to the school that are required, in the opinion of the principal,
   (ii) any lack of attention on the part of the building maintenance staff of the school, and
   (iii) where a parent of a pupil has been requested to compensate the board for damage to or destruction, loss or misappropriation of school property by the pupil and the parent has not done so, that the parent of the pupil has not compensated the board;

(m) where it is proposed to administer a test of intelligence or personality to a pupil, inform the pupil and the parent of the pupil of the test and obtain the prior written permission for the test from the pupil or from the parent of the pupil, where the pupil is a minor;

(n) report promptly any neglect of duty or infraction of the school rules by a pupil to the parent or guardian of the pupil;

(o) promote and maintain close co-operation with residents, industry, business and other groups and agencies of the community;

(p) provide to the Minister or to a person designated by the Minister any information that may be required concerning the instructional program, operation or administration of the school and inform the appropriate supervisory officer of the request;

(q) assign suitable quarters for pupils to eat lunch.

(4) A principal shall only make a recommendation to the board under subclause (3)(j)(ii) after warning the teacher in writing, giving the teacher assistance and allowing the teacher a reasonable time to improve.

(5) A principal of a school,

(a) in which there is a French-language instructional unit as defined in section 309 of the Act, who does not hold qualifications to teach in the French-language as required by subsection 19(12) or is qualified to teach in such unit only under subsection 19(13); or

(b) in which there is an English-language instructional unit as mentioned in subsection 325(1) of the Act, who does not hold qualifications to teach in the English language as required by subsection 19(11) or is qualified to teach in each unit only under subsection 19(13),

shall notify the appropriate supervisory officer in writing of the impracticability of the duty placed on the principal, having regard to the qualifications of the principal, to supervise the instruction, to conduct performance appraisals and to assist and advise the teachers referred to in the notice.

(6) Where arrangements are made under subsection 26(3), the principal is relieved from compliance with clauses (3)(a), (g), (h) and (i) to the extent that such duties are performed by another qualified person or persons.

(7) The other qualified person or persons who perform the duties shall be responsible to the board for the performance of such duties.

(8) The outlines of the courses of study mentioned in clause (3)(c) shall be written and provided,

(a) in the French language in the case of courses of study provided in a French-language instructional unit operated under Part XII of the Act; and

(b) in both the English and French languages in the case of a course of study in a program established in the school under paragraph 25 of subsection 8(1) of the Act.

(9) Where, after reasonable notice by the principal, a pupil who is an adult, or the parent of a pupil who is a minor, fails to provide the supplies required by the pupil for a course of study, the principal shall promptly notify the board.

(10) A principal shall transmit reports and recommendations to the board through the appropriate supervisory officer.

(11) A principal, subject to the approval of the appropriate supervisory officer, may arrange for home instruction to be provided for a pupil where,

(a) medical evidence that the pupil cannot attend school is provided to the principal; and

(b) the principal is satisfied that home instruction is required.

(12) The principal of a school shall provide for the prompt distribution to each member of the school council of any materials received by the principal from the Ministry that are identified by the Ministry as being for distribution to the members of school councils.

(12.1) The principal shall post any materials distributed to members of the school council under subsection (12) in the school in a location that is accessible to parents.

(13) In each school year, the principal of a school shall make the names of the members of the school council known to the parents of the pupils enrolled in the school, by publishing those names in a school newsletter or by such other means as is likely to bring the names to the attention of the parents.

(14) The principal shall meet the requirements of subsection (13) in each school year not later than 30 days following the election of parent members of the school council.

(15) The principal of a school shall promptly provide the names of the members of the school council to a supporter of the board that governs the school or to a parent of a pupil enrolled in the school, on the request of the supporter or the parent. O. Reg. 425/98, s. 1.

(16) The principal of a school shall attend every meeting of the school council, unless he or she is unable to do so by reason of illness or other cause beyond his or her control.

(17) The principal of a school shall act as a resource person to the school council and shall assist the council in obtaining information relevant to the functions of the council, including information relating to relevant legislation, regulations and policies.

(18) The principal of a school shall consider each recommendation made to the principal by the school council and shall advise the council of the action taken in response to the recommendation.

(19) In addition to his or her other obligations to solicit the views of the school council under the Act and the regulations, the principal of a school shall solicit the views of the school council with respect to the following matters:

1. The establishment or amendment of school policies and guidelines that relate to pupil achievement or to the accountability of the education system to parents, including,

    i.   a local code of conduct established under subsection 303(1) or (2) of the Act governing the behaviour of all persons in the school, and

    ii. school policies or guidelines related to policies and guidelines established by the board under subsection 302(5) of the Act respecting appropriate dress for pupils in schools within the board's jurisdiction.

2. The development of implementation plans for new education initiatives that relate to pupil achievement or to the accountability of the education system to parents, including,

    i.   implementation plans for a local code of conduct established under subsection 303(1) or (2) of the Act governing the behaviour of all persons in the school, and

      ii.   implementation plans for school policies or guidelines related to policies and guidelines established by the board under subsection 302(5) of the Act respecting appropriate dress for pupils in schools within the board's jurisdiction.

   3.   School action plans for improvement, based on the Education Quality and Accountability Office's reports on the results of tests of pupils, and the communication of those plans to the public.

(20) Subsection (19) does not limit the matters on which the principal of a school may solicit the views of the school council. O. Reg. 425/98, s. 1; 613/00, s. 1

VICE-PRINCIPALS

12. (1) A board may appoint one or more vice-principals for a school.

(2) A vice-principal shall perform such duties as are assigned to the vice-principal by the principal.

(3) In the absence of the principal of a school, a vice-principal, where a vice-principal has been appointed for the school, shall be in charge of the school and shall perform the duties of the principal.

PRINCIPALS, VICE-PRINCIPALS AND TEACHERS IN CHARGE OF SCHOOLS AND CLASSES ESTABLISHED UNDER PART XII OF THE ACT

13. (1) Where, under section 289 of the Act, more than two classes where French is the language of instruction are established in an elementary school that is not a French-language elementary school, the board that operates the school shall appoint one of the teachers of such classes or a teacher who holds the qualifications required to teach such classes to be responsible to the principal for the program of education in such classes.

(2) Where the enrolment in classes established under section 291 of the Act in a secondary school that is not a French-language secondary school is more than seventy-five but not more than 200 pupils, the board that operates the school shall appoint one of the teachers of such classes or a teacher who holds the qualifications required to teach such classes to be responsible to the principal for the program of education in such classes.

(3) Where, in a secondary school, the enrolment in the classes referred to in subsection (2) is more than 200 pupils, the board shall appoint for such school a vice-principal who is qualified to teach in such classes and who shall be responsible to the principal for the program of education in such classes.

(4) Notwithstanding subsections (1), (2) and (3), where a teacher who does not hold the qualifications referred to in such subsections was, on the 8th day of September, 1978, employed by the board as a teacher or vice-principal, as the case may be, to carry out the responsibility referred to in such subsections, the teacher shall be deemed to be qualified for such position in any elementary or secondary school, as the case may be, operated by that board or its successor board.

(5) Subsections (1) to (4) apply with the necessary modifications to schools or classes for English-speaking pupils established under sections 289 and 301 of the Act.

TEACHERS IN CHARGE OF ORGANIZATIONAL UNITS

14. (1) The organization of a secondary school may be by departments or other organizational units.

(2) The organization of an elementary school may be by divisions or other organizational units.

(3) A board may appoint for each organizational unit of an elementary or secondary school a teacher to direct and supervise, subject to the authority of the principal of the school, such organizational unit.

(4) A teacher appointed under subsection (3) may be appointed to direct and supervise more than one organizational unit. O. Reg. 95/96, s. 1.

15. [Revoked O. Reg. 95/96, s. 1]

DUTIES OF TEACHERS IN CHARGE OF ORGANIZATIONAL UNITS

16. [Revoked O. Reg. 95/96, s. 1]

SUBJECT AND PROGRAM SUPERVISION AND CO-ORDINATION

17. (1) A board may, in respect of one or more subjects or programs in the schools under its jurisdiction, appoint a teacher to supervise or co-ordinate the subjects or programs or to act as a consultant for the teachers of the subjects or programs.

(2) A teacher appointed under subsection (1) shall hold specialist or honour specialist qualifications, if such are available, in one or more of the subjects or programs in respect of which the teacher is appointed.

(3) Despite subsection (1), a teacher who, on the 8th day of September, 1978, was employed by a board to supervise or co-ordinate a subject or program in its schools or to act as a consultant shall be deemed to be qualified for such position in the schools operated by that board or its successor board.

18. (1) Subject to the authority of the appropriate supervisory officer, a teacher appointed in a subject or program under section 17 shall assist teachers in that subject or program in maintaining proper standards and improving methods of instruction.

(2) A teacher appointed under section 17 in performing duties in a school is subject to the authority of the principal of that school.

QUALIFICATIONS OF TEACHERS

19. (1) A teacher in a school shall, subject to subsection (2), be a person who holds or is deemed under Regulation 297 of Revised Regulations of Ontario, 1990 to hold an Ontario Teacher's Certificate and shall, subject to subsections (4), (5), (11) and (12), be assigned or appointed to teach according to a qualification recorded on the teacher's Ontario Teacher's Qualifications Record Card or the record of qualification in respect of such teacher held by the Ministry.

(2) A teacher who does not hold and is not deemed under Regulation 297 of Revised Regulations of Ontario, 1990 to hold an Ontario Teacher's Certificate but who,

(a) holds Temporary Letter of Standing or a Provisional Letter of Standing or a Permanent Letter of Standing; or

(b) holds a certificate or Letter of Standing referred to in subsection 26(3) or 27(1) of Regulation 297 of Revised Regulations of Ontario, 1990,

may teach in a school in a subject or program for which the Letter of Standing or certificate is valid or in which the teacher has received professional education as indicated on the Temporary Letter of Standing or Provisional Letter of Standing.

(3) A person who does not hold any of the qualifications referred to in subsection (2) but who holds a Letter of Eligibility issued under section 12 or 13 of Regulation 297 of Revised Regulations of Ontario, 1990 may be employed by a board as an occasional teacher only,

(a) in classes where English is the language of instruction if the Letter of Eligibility is in Form 5 to Regulation 297 of Revised Regulations of Ontario, 1990; or

(b) in classes where French is the language of instruction if the Letter of Eligibility is in Form 5a to Regulation 297 of Revised Regulations of Ontario, 1990.

(4) Subject to subsections (6), (11), (12), (14) and (15), and with due regard for the safety and welfare of the pupils and the provision of the best possible program, a teacher whose Ontario Teacher's Qualifications Record Card, or the record of qualification in respect of such teacher held by the Ministry, indicates qualification in the primary division, the junior division, the intermediate division in general studies or the senior division in general studies may, by mutual agreement of the teacher and the principal of a school and with the approval of the appropriate supervisory officer, be assigned or appointed to teach in a division or a subject in general studies for which no qualification is recorded on the teacher's Ontario Teacher's Qualifications Record Card or the record of qualification in respect of such teacher held by the Ministry.

(5) Subject to subsections (11), (12) and (15), and with due regard for the safety and welfare of the pupils and the provisions of the best possible program, a teacher whose Ontario Teacher's Qualifications Record Card, or the record of qualification in respect of such teacher held by the Ministry, has entries indicating qualifications in technological studies, may by mutual agreement of the teacher and the principal of a school, with the approval of the appropriate supervisory officer, be assigned or appointed to teach a subject in technological studies for which no qualification is recorded on the Ontario Teacher's Qualifications Record Card or the record of qualification in respect of such teacher held by the Ministry.

(6) Subject to subsections (7), (8), (9) and (10), a teacher who does not hold an acceptable university degree as defined in the definition of "acceptable university degree" in section 1 of Regulation 297 of Revised Regulations of Ontario, 1990 shall not be assigned or appointed to teach general studies in a secondary school, except that where the teacher is qualified to teach in the primary division, the junior division and the intermediate division of an elementary school and,

(a) on the 30th day of June, 1981 was teaching in a secondary school; or

(b) on or before the 2nd day of October, 1981 was assigned or appointed to teach general studies in a secondary school, and on the 30th day of June, 1982 was teaching in a secondary school,

the teacher may be assigned or appointed to teach general studies to pupils enrolled in a modified or basic level course by that board or its successor board.

(7) Despite subsection (1), a teacher who holds,

(a) a commercial-vocational qualification; or
(b) technological studies qualifications in any one or more of clerical practice, merchandising or warehousing,

may be assigned or appointed to teach the courses in business studies equivalent to the courses in business studies shown on the teacher's Ontario Teacher's Qualifications Record Card or the record of qualification in respect of the teacher held by the Ministry.

(8) A teacher who holds qualifications in technological studies in sewing and dressmaking, or textiles and clothing, or home economics may be assigned or appointed to teach in a secondary school the clothing portion of the family studies course.

(9) A teacher who holds qualifications in technological studies in food and nutrition or home economics may be assigned or appointed to teach in a secondary school the food and nutrition portion of the family studies course.

(10) A teacher who holds qualifications in technological studies in vocational art, instrumental music or vocal music may be assigned or appointed to teach art, instrumental music or vocal music, as the case may be, in general studies in a secondary school.

(11) A teacher who has not received basic teacher education in the English language or who is not otherwise qualified under the regulations for such assignment or appointment shall not be assigned or appointed to teach in classes where English is the language of instruction.

(12) A teacher who has not received basic teacher education in the French language or who is not otherwise qualified under the regulations for such assignment or appointment shall not be assigned or appointed to teach in schools or classes established under Part XII of the Act where French is the language of instruction.

(13) Despite subsections (11) and (12), a teacher who holds qualifications to teach in the intermediate division and the senior division may be assigned or appointed to teach in either or both of such divisions in classes where English or French is the language of instruction.

(14) No teacher shall,

(a) be assigned, or appointed to teach, in any of grades 9, 10, 11, 12 and 13 in any one school year for more than the time required for two courses that are recognized for credit in art, business studies, guidance including counselling, family studies, instrumental music, vocal music or physical education; or
(b) be placed in charge of,
    (i) a school library program,
    (ii) a guidance program, or
    (iii) special education; or
(c) be assigned or appointed to teach,

    (i)   French as a second language,

    (ii) English as a second language,

    (iii) design and technology,

    (iv) subject to subsections (5) and (15), technological studies,

    (v) in a special education class,

    (vi) in a class for deaf, hard of hearing, blind or limited vision pupils, or

    (vii) as a resource or withdrawal teacher in special education programs,

unless,

    (d) the teacher's Ontario Teacher's Qualifications Record Card or the record of qualification in respect of such teacher held by the Ministry indicates qualifications in the subject or program to which the teacher is to be assigned or appointed or placed in charge; or

    (e) the teacher is qualified for such assignment, appointment or placement under subsections (2) or (16) or deemed to be qualified therefor under subsection (17).

(15) On or after the 1st day of September, 1982, no teacher shall be assigned or appointed to teach courses in the senior division in technological studies at the General or Advanced levels unless the teacher's Ontario Teacher's Qualifications Record Card or the record of qualification in respect of such teacher held by the Ministry indicates advanced level qualifications in the area of technological studies to which the teacher is to be assigned or appointed.

(16) A teacher in a school or class for trainable retarded pupils shall,

    (a) have an entry on the teacher's Ontario Teacher's Qualifications Record Card or on the record of qualification in respect of such teacher held by the Ministry, indicating qualifications in the area of teaching the trainable retarded; or

    (b) hold one of the following:
        1. Elementary Certificate in Teaching Trainable Retarded Children.
        2. Intermediate Certificate in Teaching Trainable Retarded Children.
        3. Certificate as Teacher of the Trainable Retarded.
        4. Provisional or Permanent Letter of Standing valid for the teaching of the trainable retarded.

(17) A teacher who, on the 8th day of September, 1978, was employed by a board to teach,

    (a) French as a second language or English as a second language in an elementary school or a secondary school; or

    (b) industrial arts in an elementary school,

and is not qualified for such position under subsection (14), shall be deemed to be qualified for such position in the elementary school or the secondary schools, as the case may be, that are operated by that board or its successor board.

(18) Where a teacher's Ontario Teacher's Qualifications Record Card or record of qualification has entries indicating qualifications both in technological studies and in guidance, the teacher may be assigned or appointed to teach guidance and counselling in general studies in a secondary school.

(19) The provision of subsection (14) that no teacher shall be assigned or appointed to

teach in a special education class or program unless the teacher holds qualifications in special education does not apply to the teaching of classes in general studies or technological studies in what was formerly designated a special vocational or occupational program until the 1st day of September, 1985.

(20) A teacher may be assigned or appointed to teach those courses that are equivalent to those courses that appear on the teacher's Ontario Teacher's Qualifications Record Card or the record of qualification in respect of the teacher held by the Ministry. O. Reg. 243/92, s. 1.

DUTIES OF TEACHERS

20. In addition to the duties assigned to the teacher under the Act and by the board, a teacher shall,

(a) be responsible for effective instruction, training and evaluation of the progress of pupils in the subjects assigned to the teacher and for the management of the class or classes, and report to the principal on the progress of pupils on request;

(b) carry out the supervisory duties and instructional program assigned to the teacher by the principal and supply such information related thereto as the principal may require;

(c) where the board has appointed teachers under section 14 or 17, co-operate fully with such teachers and with the principal in all matters related to the instruction of pupils;

(d) unless otherwise assigned by the principal, be present in the classroom or teaching area and ensure that the classroom or teaching area is ready for the reception of pupils at least fifteen minutes before the commencement of classes in the school in the morning and, where applicable, five minutes before the commencement of classes in the school in the afternoon;

(e) assist the principal in maintaining close co-operation with the community;

(f) prepare for use in the teacher's class or classes such teaching plans and outlines as are required by the principal and the appropriate supervisory officer and submit the plans and outlines to the principal or the appropriate supervisory officer, as the case may be, on request;

(g) ensure that all reasonable safety procedures are carried out in courses and activities for which the teacher is responsible;

(h) co-operate with the principal and other teachers to establish and maintain consistent disciplinary practices in the school.

(i) ensure that report cards are fully and properly completed and processed in accordance with the guides known in English as Guide to the Provincial Report Card, Grades 1-8 and Guide to the Provincial Report Card, Grades 9-12, and in French as Guide d'utilisation du bulletin scolaire de l'Ontario de la 1ere a la 8e; annee and Guide du bulletin scolaire de l'Ontario de la 9e a la 12e; annee, as the case may be, both available electronically through a link in the document known in English as Ontario School Record (OSR) Guideline, 2000 and in French as Dossier scolaire de l'Ontario: Guide, 2000, online at www.edu.gov.on.ca/eng/document/curricul/osr/osr.html or www.edu.gov.on.ca/fre/document/curricul/osr/osrf.html;

(j) co-operate and assist in the administration of tests under the *Education Quality and Accountability Office Act, 1996*;

(k) participate in regular meetings with pupils' parents or guardians;

(l) perform duties as assigned by the principal in relation to co-operative placements of pupils; and

(m) perform duties normally associated with the graduation of pupils. O. Reg. 95/96, s. 2; 209/03, s. 1.

21. (1) Where no teacher is available, a board may appoint, subject to section 22, a person who is not a teacher or a temporary teacher.

(2) A person appointed under subsection (1) shall be eighteen years of age or older and the holder of an Ontario secondary school diploma, a secondary school graduation diploma or a secondary school honour graduation diploma.

(3) An appointment under this section is valid for ten school days commencing with the day on which the person is appointed.

22. (1) A board shall not appoint a person whose teaching certificate is cancelled or under suspension to teach under section 21 or in accordance with a Letter of Permission.

(2) A person whose teaching certificate is cancelled or under suspension ceases to hold teacher's qualifications during the period of cancellation or suspension and shall not be appointed as a teacher.

23. (1) A pupil shall,

(a) be diligent in attempting to master such studies as are part of the program in which the pupil is enrolled;
(b) exercise self-discipline;
(c) accept such discipline as would be exercised by a kind, firm and judicious parent;
(d) attend classes punctually and regularly;
(e) be courteous to fellow pupils and obedient and courteous to teachers;
(f) be clean in person and habits;
(g) take such tests and examinations as are required by or under the Act or as may be directed by the Minister; and
(h) show respect for school property.

(2) When a pupil returns to school after an absence, a parent of the pupil, or the pupil where the pupil is an adult, shall give the reason for the absence orally or in writing as the principal requires.

(3) A pupil may be excused by the principal from attendance at school temporarily at any time at the written request of a parent of the pupil or the pupil where the pupil is an adult.

(4) Every pupil is responsible for his or her conduct to the principal of the school that the pupil attends,

(a) on the school premises;
(b) on out-of-school activities that are part of the school program; and

(c)   while travelling on a school bus that is owned by a board or on a bus or school bus that is under contract to a board.

ADVERTISEMENTS AND ANNOUNCEMENTS

24. (1) No advertisement or announcement shall be placed in a school or on school property or distributed or announced to the pupils on school property without the consent of the board that operates the school except announcements of school activities.

(2) Subsection (1) does not apply to anything posted in the school in accordance with the regulations. O. Reg. 613/00, s. 2

CANVASSING AND FUND-RAISING

25. (1) It is the duty of a pupil to ensure that any canvassing or fund-raising activity on school property by the pupil is carried on only with the consent of the board that operates the school.

(2) No principal, vice-principal or teacher, without the prior approval of the board that operates the school at which they are employed, shall authorize any canvassing or fund-raising activity that involves the participation of one or more pupils attending the school.

SUPERVISION

26. (1) The appropriate supervisory officer, in addition to the duties under the Act, may, during a visit to a school, assume any of the authority and responsibility of the principal of the school.

(2) Psychiatrists, psychologists, social workers and other professional support staff employed by a board shall perform, under the administrative supervision of the appropriate supervisory officer, such duties as are determined by the board and, where such persons are performing their duties in a school, they shall be subject to the administrative authority of the principal of that school.

(3) A supervisory officer who is notified under subsection 11(5), shall forthwith notify the French-language education council or section, English-language education council or section or majority language section of the board, as the case requires, and arrange for,

(a)   the provision of supervision of instruction;
(b)   assistance and advice to the teachers in respect of whom the supervisory officer was given notice under subsection 11(5); and
(c)   the conducting of performance appraisals, where appropriate, of the teachers in respect of whom the supervisory officer was given notice under subsection 11(5),

in the language in which the instruction is provided.

RELIGION IN SCHOOLS

27. Sections 28 and 29 do not apply to a separate school board or to the Roman Catholic sector of The Ottawa-Carleton French-Language School Board.

28. (1) A board may provide in grades one to eight and in its secondary schools an optional program of education about religion.

(2) A program of education about religion shall,

(a) promote respect for the freedom of conscience and religion guaranteed by the *Canadian Charter of Rights and Freedoms*; and
(b) provide for the study of different religions and religious beliefs in Canada and the world, without giving primacy to, and without indoctrination in, any particular religion or religious belief.

(3) A program of education about religion shall not exceed sixty minutes of instruction per week in an elementary school.

29. (1) Subject to subsections (2) and (3), a board shall not permit any person to conduct religious exercises or to provide instruction that includes indoctrination in a particular religion or religious belief in a school.

(2) A board may enter into an agreement with a separate school board or the Roman Catholic sector of The Ottawa-Carleton French-Language School Board that permits the separate school board or the Roman Catholic sector to use space and facilities to conduct religious exercises or provide religious instruction for the purposes of the separate school board or the Roman Catholic sector.

(3) A board may permit a person to conduct religious exercises or to provide instruction that includes indoctrination in a particular religion or religious belief in a school if,

(a) the exercises are not conducted or the instruction is not provided by or under the auspices of the board;
(b) the exercises are conducted or the instruction is provided on a school day at a time that is before or after the school's instructional program, or on a day that is not a school day;
(c) no person is required by the board to attend the exercises or instruction; and
(d) the board provides space for the exercises or instruction on the same basis as it provides space for other community activities.

(4) A board that permits religious exercises or instruction under subsection (3) shall consider on an equitable basis all requests to conduct religious exercises or to provide instruction under subsection (3).

SPECIAL EDUCATION PROGRAMS AND SERVICES

30. A hearing-handicapped child who has attained the age of two years may be admitted to a special education program for the hearing-handicapped.

31. The maximum enrolment in a special education class shall depend upon the extent of the exceptionalities of the pupils in the class and the special education services that are available to the teacher, but in no case shall the enrolment in a self-contained class exceed,

(a) in a class for pupils who are emotionally disturbed or socially maladjusted, for pupils who have severe learning disabilities, or for pupils who are younger than compulsory school age and have impaired hearing, eight pupils;
(b) in a class for pupils who are blind, for pupils who are deaf, for pupils who are trainable retarded, or for pupils with speech and language disorders, ten pupils;
(c) in a class for pupils who are hard of hearing, for pupils with limited vision, or for pupils with orthopaedic or other physical handicaps, twelve pupils;

- (d) in a class for pupils who are educable retarded children, twelve pupils in the primary division and sixteen pupils in the junior and intermediate divisions;
- (e) in an elementary school class for pupils who are gifted, twenty-five pupils;
- (f) in a class for aphasic or autistic pupils, or for pupils with multiple handicaps for whom no one handicap is dominant, six pupils; and
- (g) on and after the 1st day of September, 1982, in a class for exceptional pupils consisting of pupils with different exceptionalities, sixteen pupils.

REGULATION 304

under the Education Act

R.R.O. 1990, Reg. 304, as am. O. Reg. 91/98

SCHOOL YEAR CALENDAR
[As am. O. Reg. 91/98, s. 1]

1. (1) In this Regulation,

"instructional day" means a school day that is designated as an instructional day on a school calendar and upon which day an instructional program that may include examinations is provided for each pupil whose program is governed by such calendar;

"professional activity" includes evaluation of the progress of pupils, consultation with parents, the counselling of pupils, curriculum and program evaluation and development, professional development of teachers and attendance at educational conferences;

"professional activity day" means a school day that is designated as a day for professional activities on a school calendar;

"school day" means a day that is within a school year and is not a school holiday;

"school year" means the period prescribed as such by or approved as such under this Regulation.

(2) A board may designate half a school day an instructional program and the remainder of the day for professional activities, but such a day constitutes a half-day in determining the number of instructional days in the school year.

2. (1) Subject to section 5, the school year shall commence on or after the 1st day of September and end on or before the 30th day of June.

(2) [Revoked O. Reg. 91/98, s. 2(2)]

(3) [Revoked O. Reg. 91/98, s. 2(4)]

(3.1) Subject to section 5, every school year after the 1997-1998 school year shall include a minimum of 194 school days of which up to 4 days may be designated by the board as professional activity days and the remaining school days shall be instructional days.

(4) Subject to section 5, the following are school holidays:

1. Every Saturday and Sunday.
2. When the school is open during July, Canada Day.
3. Labour Day.
4. A day appointed by the Governor General or the Lieutenant Governor as a public holiday or for Thanksgiving.
5. A Christmas vacation consisting of fourteen consecutive days commencing on the Monday next following the Friday preceding the 21st day of December, but when the 21st day of December is a Thursday or a Friday, commencing on the Monday next following.

6. Five consecutive days commencing on the Monday next following the Friday preceding the 14th day of March.
7. Good Friday.
8. Easter Monday.
9. Victoria Day. O. Reg. 91/98, s. 2.

3. (1) [Revoked O. Reg. 91/98, s. 3(2)]

(2) [Revoked O. Reg. 91/98, s. 3(4)]

(3) Where a school has a policy of granting exemptions to pupils from the writing of examinations, such exemptions may be granted only from the final examinations in a course and only where at least one other set of examinations has been held.

(3.1) With respect to every school year after the 1997-1998 school year, a board may designate up to 10 instructional days as examination days.

(4) The teaching staff shall be in school during regular school hours on examination days and accessible to pupils, unless the board directs otherwise. O. Reg. 91/98, s. 3.

4. (1) In each year every board shall, except in respect of a school or class for which the board has submitted a proposed school calendar under section 5, prepare, adopt and submit to the Minister on or before the 1st day of May in respect of the school year next following, the school calendar or school calendars to be followed in the schools under its jurisdiction, and each such school calendar shall,

(a) state the school or schools in which the calendar is to be followed;
(b) conform to section 2; and
(c) identify each day of the school year as an instructional day, a professional activity day or a school holiday.

(2) In preparing a school calendar under subsection (1), the board shall ensure that some of the professional activity days are designated for the purposes of curriculum development, implementation and review.

(3) A school calendar submitted under subsection (1) shall be accompanied by a general outline of the activities to be conducted on the professional activity days identified on the calendar.

5. (1) For one or more schools under its jurisdiction a board may designate a school year and school holidays that are different from those prescribed in section 2 and, where a board does so, the board shall submit to the Minister on or before the first day of March a proposed school calendar for the school year next following in respect of such school or schools, identifying thereon each day of the school year as an instructional day, a professional activity day or a school holiday, and the board may, upon approval thereof by the Minister, implement such school calendar.

(2) Where the Minister informs a board that he or she does not approve the school calendar submitted under subsection (1), the board may amend its proposed school calendar and submit to the Minister a revised school calendar and, upon approval thereof by the Minister, the board may implement the revised school calendar.

(3) Where a board has submitted a proposed school calendar under subsection (1) and the Minister has not approved on or before the 15th day of April such calendar or a revision

thereof submitted under subsection (2), the board shall, on or before the 1st day of May, prepare, adopt and submit to the Minister a school calendar in accordance with section 4.

6. (1) Where, in the opinion of the board it is desirable to alter the date of a professional activity day or an examination day on a school calendar that has been submitted under section 4 or subsection 5(3) or approved and implemented under subsection 5(1) or (2), the board may alter the school calendar.

(2) Where, the board alters a school calendar under subsection (1), the board shall notify the parents concerned and the Minister of the altered date as far in advance as possible.

(3) The prior approval of the Minister is required for changes other than to the date of a professional activity day or an examination day.

(4) Where,

(a) a school or class is closed for a temporary period because of failure of transportation arrangements, inclement weather, fire, flood, a breakdown of the school heating plant or a similar emergency, or a school is closed under the *Health Act and Promotion Act* or the *Education Act*; and
(b) the school calendar is not altered under subsection (1),

the day on which the school or class is closed remains an instructional day or a professional activity day, as the case may be, as designated on the school calendar applicable to such school or class.

7. (1) Every board shall publish annually its school calendar or school calendars and ensure that copies thereof are available at the beginning of the school year for the information of parents and pupils.

(2) A school calendar or school calendars published under subsection (1) shall, in addition to the information required to be listed under subsection 4(1), indicate in a general manner the activities to be conducted on professional activity days.

8. In each year, every board shall undertake an annual evaluation of the activities of the professional activity days of the previous year and retain such evaluations on file.

9. (1) A Remembrance Day service shall be held in every school on the 11th day of November or, when the 11th day of November is a Saturday or a Sunday, on the Friday preceding the 11th day of November.

(2) Subsection (1) does not apply where the school participates in a service of remembrance at a cenotaph or other location in the community.

REGULATION 309

under the Education Act

R.R.O. 1990, Reg. 309, as am. O. Reg. 665/92; 162/93; 182/97

SUPERVISORY OFFICERS

PART I

QUALIFICATIONS OF SUPERVISORY OFFICERS

1. (1) In this Part,

"acceptable university degree" means a degree from an Ontario university or post-secondary institution that is an ordinary member of the Association of Universities and Colleges of Canada or a degree that is equivalent thereto from a university other than such Ontario university or post-secondary institution;

"architect" means a person who is an architect within the meaning of the *Architects Act*;

"certified general accountant" means a member of the Certified General Accountants Association of Ontario;

"certified management accountant" means a registered or certified member of The Society of Management Accountants of Ontario;

"chartered accountant" means a member of The Institute of Chartered Accountants of Ontario;

"lawyer" means a member of the Law Society of Upper Canada;

"Principal's Certificate" means a permanent principal's certificate;

"professional engineer" means a person who is a professional engineer within the meaning of the *Professional Engineers Act*;

"program in school board management" means two compulsory graduate courses approved by the Minister that are offered by a university, one of which is a course in school board finance and the other in school board administration, and four optional graduate courses approved by the Minister that are offered by a university in education, public administration or political science;

"university" means,

   (a) an Ontario university or post-secondary institution that is an ordinary member of the Association of Universities and Colleges of Canada,
   (b) a Canadian university in a province other than Ontario that is an ordinary member of the Association of Universities and Colleges of Canada,
   (c) a university in the United States that is recognized by,
      (i) Middle States Association of Colleges and Schools,
      (ii) New England Association of Schools and Colleges,
      (iii) North Central Association of Colleges and Schools,

     (iv) Northwest Association of Colleges and Schools,

     (v) Southern Association of Colleges and Schools,

     (vi) Western Association of Schools and Colleges, or

  (d) a university that is located in a country other than Canada or the United States and that is a member of the association of Commonwealth Universities or the International Association of Universities.

(2) A person who holds or who under this Regulation is deemed to hold a Supervisory Officer's Certificate is, subject to subsection 6(1), qualified as a supervisory officer for the purposes of the Act and this Regulation.

(3) A person referred to in subsection 3(4) who is employed by a board is qualified as a business supervisory officer for the purposes of the Act and this Regulation for the period during which the person is employed by the board in a position referred to in that subsection.

(4) For the purposes of this Regulation, a person who is the holder of a Master's degree that is an acceptable university degree and who successfully completes a graduate course, either as part of or in addition to the courses necessary to obtain the degree, in each of school board finance and school board administration at a university shall be deemed to have completed a program in school board management.

(5) For the purposes of this Regulation, a person who is the holder of an acceptable university degree and who is a certified general accountant, a certified management accountant or a chartered accountant shall be deemed to be a person who has completed the four optional graduate courses as part of a program in school board management. O. Reg. 665/92, s. 1.

2. The Minister shall issue a Supervisory Officer's Certificate to a person if the person applies for it and the Ontario College of Teachers certifies that the person meets the qualifications of a Supervisory Officer. O. Reg. 665/92, s. 2, *part*; O. Reg. 182/97, s. 1.

2.1 (1) On application, the Minister shall issue a Business Supervisory Officer's Certificate to a person who meets the following qualifications:

1. The person has at least seven years of successful experience in business administration, including at least three years in a managerial role relevant to the role of business supervisory officer.
2. The person holds an acceptable university degree.
3. The person,
     i. holds a master's degree from a university, or
     ii. is qualified to practise as an architect, certified general account, certified management accountant, chartered accountant, lawyer or professional engineer, or is qualified to practise in another professional capacity that, in the opinion of the Minister, provides experience appropriate for the position of business supervisory officer.
4. The person has successfully completed a program in school board management.
5. The person has successfully completed the business supervisory officer's qualifications program described in section 2.2 within five years after starting the program.

(2) A person shall be deemed to meet the qualifications set out in paragraphs 1 to 4 of subsection (1) if, not later than the 31st day of December, 1977, the person obtains the qual-

ifications that were required of a candidate for a Business Supervisory Officer's Certificate under subsection 2(3) of this Regulation as it read immediately before the 6th day of November, 1992. O. Reg. 665/92, s. 2, *part.*

2.2 The business supervisory officer's qualifications program referred to in section 2.1 shall have the following features:

1. The program shall be provided by an organization or institution that has entered into a contract with the Minister to provide the instruction and arrange for the practical experience referred to in paragraphs 3 and 4.
2. No person shall be admitted to the program unless the person has submitted proof to the organization or institution that provides the program that the person meets the qualifications set out in paragraphs 1 to 4 of subsection 2.1(1).
3. The program shall consist of,
   i. four instructional modules, each consisting of at least fifty hours of instruction, and
   ii. one module consisting of at least fifty hours of practical experience in the workplace.
4. The instructional modules shall provide instruction that, in the opinion of the Minister, is relevant to the position of business supervisory officer, in the following subject areas:
   i. Statutes, regulations and government policies affecting education in Ontario.
   ii. Curriculum guidelines and other reference material pertaining to elementary and secondary education in Ontario.
   iii. Theories and practices of supervision, administration and business organization. O. Reg. 665/92, s. 2, *part*; O. Reg. 182/97, s. 2.

3. (1) A supervisory officer responsible for the development, implementation, operation and supervision of educational programs in schools shall,

(a) hold a Supervisory Officer's Certificate; or
(b) be a person who is deemed to hold a Supervisory Officer's Certificate under section 4.

(2) A senior business official who,

(a) reports to a director of education;
(b) reports to an assistant director of education or associate director of education; or
(c) is employed by a board that has an enrolment of more than 600 pupils and that does not employ a director of education,

shall, subject to subsections (4) and (5), be a person who holds, or who under this Regulation is deemed to hold, a Business Supervisory Officer's Certificate.

(3) A business official who,

(a) is assigned one or more of the duties of a supervisory officer;
(b) reports to a senior business official referred to in subsection (2); and
(c) has been appointed to a position designated by a board as superintendent, assistant superintendent, comptroller, assistant comptroller, business administrator or assistant business administrator or to a position that the board considers equivalent thereto and that has been approved by the Minister,

shall, subject to subsection (4), be a person who holds, or who under this Regulation is deemed to hold, a Business Supervisory Officer's Certificate.

(4) A board may appoint a person who does not hold or who under this Regulation is not deemed to hold a Business Supervisory Officer's Certificate as a senior business official referred to in subsection (2) or as a business official referred to in subsection (3) for a term of not more than two years if the person,

    (a) holds an acceptable university degree or is qualified to practise as an architect, certified general accountant, certified management accountant, chartered accountant, lawyer or professional engineer, or in another professional capacity that, in the opinion of the Minister, provides experience appropriate for the position of business supervisory officer; and

    (b) has entered into an agreement in writing with the Board that sets out that the person will endeavour to obtain a Business Supervisory Officer's Certificate within the term of the appointment. O. Reg. 665/92, s. 3(2).

(5) Despite subsection (4), a board may employ a person appointed under that subsection for an additional period of not more than two years if the person continues to make progress towards obtaining a Business Supervisory Officer's Certificate.

(6) A person who was appointed under subsection (4) before the 6th day of November, 1992 may, by agreement with the board, amend the agreement under clause (4)(b) to be consistent with the new requirements of that clause. O. Reg. 655/92, s. 3(3).

4. A person who, prior to the 1st day of July, 1974,

    (a) held an Elementary School Inspector's Certificate, a Public School Inspector's Certificate, a Secondary School Principal's Certificate, or a Secondary School Principal's Certificate, Type A; or

    (b) served as a provincial inspector of secondary schools or a municipal inspector of secondary schools,

is deemed to hold a Supervisory Officer's Certificate.

5. (1) A person who was in the employ of a board on the 31st day of August, 1975, in a position referred to in subsection 3(2) or (3), is deemed to hold a Supervisory Officer's Certificate.

(2) A person employed in the Ministry on the 31st day of August, 1975, in a position that the Minister considers similar to one of those referred to in subsection 3(2) or (3) is deemed to hold a Supervisory Officer's Certificate.

6. (1) A person who,

    (a) holds a Supervisory Officer's Certificate and was not required, at the time the certificate was obtained, to have seven years of successful teaching experience;

    (b) is deemed to hold a Supervisory Officer's Certificate under section 5; or

    (c) holds a Business Supervisory Officer's Certificate,

is qualified as a supervisory officer under this Regulation for business administration purposes only.

(2) A supervisory officer other than a supervisory officer referred to in subsection (1) who, on the 30th day of September, 1986, was performing the duties,

(a) of a senior business official referred to in clause 3(2)(c) and who reports as referred to in clauses 3(2)(a) and (b); or

(b) of a business official referred to in clause 3(3)(c) who reports to a senior business official referred to in subsection 3(2),

is deemed to hold a Business Supervisory Officer's Certificate. O. Reg. 665/92, s. 4.

PART II

TRANSFER AND DISMISSAL

7. (1) In this section, "redundant" in respect of the position of a supervisory officer means no longer required to be filled by reason of,

(a) the implementation by a board of a long range organizational plan of operation in respect of schools or of supervisory services that eliminates the position or merges it with another position;

(b) a reduction in the number of classes or in the business functions of the board for which supervision is required; or

(c) a change in duties or requirements placed upon boards by or under any Act that renders a supervisory service unnecessary or reduces the need for such service.

(2) Where a board declares the position of a supervisory officer redundant, the board shall,

(a) give the supervisory officer at least three months' notice in writing that the position has been declared redundant;

(b) transfer the supervisory officer to a position for which he is qualified, with supervisory and administrative responsibilities as similar as possible to those of his previous position; and

(c) pay the supervisory officer for at least one year following the date of the transfer with no reduction in his or her rate of salary.

8. (1) A board shall not suspend or dismiss a supervisory officer without first giving the supervisory officer reasonable information about the reasons for the suspension or dismissal and an opportunity to make submissions to the board.

(2) A supervisory officer who wishes to make submissions to the board may make them orally or in writing. O. Reg. 162/93, s. 1.

9.-15. [Revoked O. Reg. 162/93, s. 1.]

REGULATION 461/97
PUPIL REPRESENTATION ON BOARDS

O. Reg. 461/97

1. (1) Every board shall develop and implement a policy providing for the representation of the interests of pupils on the board.

(2) The policy shall be in accordance with this regulation and with any policies and guidelines issued by the Minister under paragraph 3.5 of subsection 8(1) of the Act.

2. (1) Each board shall have one pupil representative or such greater number of pupil representatives as is specified in the policy.

(2) A pupil representative must be in the last two years of the intermediate division or in the senior division at the time that he or she is elected or appointed.

3. (1) The policy shall specify whether the pupil representatives are to be chosen by peer election or by appointment and shall specify the procedures to be followed for the purpose.

(2) The procedures specified under subsection (1) shall ensure that the elections or appointments occur not later than June 30 in each school year, to take effect with respect to the following school year.

(3) The policy shall provide for,

(a) the type and extent of participation by pupil representatives;
(b) disqualification of pupil representatives;
(c) the filling of vacancies;
(d) the term of office of pupil representatives.

(4) With respect to the type and extent of participation by pupil representatives, the policy shall provide that, subject to subsections 55(3) and (5) of the Act, pupil representatives have at least the same opportunity for participation at meetings of the board and at meetings of committees of the board as a board member has.

4. (1) The policy may provide for reimbursement of pupil representatives for all or part of their out-of-pocket expenses reasonably incurred in connection with carrying out the responsibilities of pupil representatives.

(2) Where reimbursement of expenses is provided for under subsection (1), it shall be according to the same policies as govern the reimbursement of board members for such expenses.

5. This Regulation comes into force on the day section 30 of the *Education Quality Improvement Act, 1997* comes into force.

REGULATION 463/97
ELECTRONIC MEETINGS

O. Reg. 463/97

1. Subject to any conditions or limitations provided for under the Act or under this regulation, a member of a district school board who participates in a meeting through electronic means in accordance with this regulation shall be deemed to be present at the meeting for the purposes of every Act.

2. (1) Every district school board shall develop and implement a policy providing for the use of electronic means for the holding of meetings of a district school board and meetings of a committee of a district school board, including a committee of the whole board.

(2) The policy shall be in accordance with this regulation and with any policies established and guidelines issued by the Minister under paragraph 3.6 of subsection 8(1) of the Act.

3. (1) The policy shall provide for the following:

1. At the request of any board member or pupil representative, the board shall provide the member or representative with electronic means for participating in one or more meetings of the board or of a committee of the board, including a committee of the whole board.
2. The electronic means required by paragraph 1 shall permit the member or representative to hear and be heard by all other participants in the meeting.
3. The electronic means shall be provided in such a way that the rules governing conflict of interest of members are complied with.

(2) The policy shall ensure that pupil representatives who are participating through electronic means do not participate in any proceedings that are closed to the public in accordance with the Act.

4. (1) Subsection (2) applies in respect of meetings of the board or of a committee of the board, including a committee of the whole board, that are open to the public.

(2) Every board shall determine, in accordance with any policies established and guidelines issued under paragraph 3.6 of subsection 8(1) of the Act, whether electronic means should be provided at one or more locations within the area of jurisdiction of the board, to permit participation by members of the public in meetings or classes of meetings.

(3) Where the board determines that electronic means should be provided under this section, the board's policy shall,

(a) provide for the extent and manner of participation by members of the public through electronic means; and
(b) ensure that members of the public who are participating through electronic means do not participate in any proceedings that are closed to the public in accordance with the Act.

5. (1) The policy shall require that, at every meeting of the board or of a committee of the whole board, the following persons be physically present in the meeting room of the board:

1. The chair of the board or his or her designate.
2. At least one additional member of the board.
3. The director of education of the board or his or her designate.

(2) The policy shall require that, at every meeting of a committee of the board, except a committee of the whole board, the following persons be physically present in the meeting room of the committee:

1. The chair of the committee or his or her designate.
2. The director of education of the board or his or her designate.

(3) Despite paragraph 1 of subsection 3(1), the policy shall include provisions permitting the board to refuse to provide a member with electronic means of participation in a meeting of the board, a meeting of a committee of the whole board or a meeting of any other committee of the board, where to do so is necessary to ensure compliance with this section.

6. (1) The meeting room of the board or of a committee of the board, as the case may be, shall be open to permit physical attendance by members of the public at every meeting of the board or of the committee of the board.

(2) For the purposes of subsection (1), the meeting room of a committee of the whole board is the meeting room of the board.

(3) Subsection (1) does not apply where a meeting is closed to the public in accordance with the Act.

7. This Regulation comes into force on the day section 107 of the *Education Quality Improvement Act, 1997* comes into force.

REGULATION 90/98
PRINCIPALS AND VICE-PRINCIPALS —
REDUNDANCY AND REASSIGNMENT

O. Reg. 90/98

1. (1) This Regulation applies when a board declares the position of a principal or vice-principal to be redundant.

(2) This Regulation applies when any of the following positions is declared to be redundant:

1. Principal or vice-principal of continuing education courses and classes that are offered for credit during the day on instructional days.
2. Principal or vice-principal who administers the board's program of continuing education courses and classes that are offered for credit.

(3) This Regulation does not apply when the position of principal or vice-principal of continuing education courses and classes that is not described in subsection (2) is declared to be redundant.

(4) A position is redundant if the board decides that the position is no longer required because of,

(a) the implementation of a restructuring plan that eliminates the position or merges it with another position;
(b) a reduction in the number of classes or schools of the board; or
(c) a change in the board's duties under any Act.

2. (1) The board shall give the affected principal or vice-principal notice in writing that his or her position is declared to be redundant.

(2) The notice must be given at least 90 days before the date on which the position becomes redundant.

(3) The notice must specify the date on which the position becomes redundant.

(4) The board may rescind the notice at any time.

(5) A notice given under this section is not notice of the termination of the principal's or vice-principal's permanent teacher's contract or probationary teacher's contract.

(6) Subsection (5) is revoked on September 1, 1998.

3. (1) The board shall assign the principal or vice-principal to another position for which he or she is qualified.

(2) The principal or vice-principal may be assigned to a position in a teachers' bargaining unit if the position is vacant after the procedures under the applicable collective agreement for filling it have been exhausted.

(3) The assignment take effect on the date on which the principal's or vice-principal's

position becomes redundant, or on such other date as the board and the principal or vice-principle may agree upon.

4. (1) The following rule applies if the principal or vice-principal is employed by a district school board and is assigned to a position in which he or she is employed, other than as a principal or vice-principal, to teach:

1. For the purpose of determining his or her seniority under the applicable collective agreement, his or her length of service when he or she begins work in the new position is the sum of,
   i. the length of his or her service before January 1, 1998 while employed by the district school board or a predecessor board to teach, and
   ii. the length of his or her service after December 31, 1997 while employed, other than as a principal or vice-principal, by the district school board or a predecessor board to teach.

(2) The following rule applies if the principal or vice-principal is employed by a school authority and is assigned to a position in which he or she is employed, other than as a principal or vice-principal, to teach:

1. For the purpose of determining his or her seniority under the applicable collective agreement, his or her length of service when he or she begins work in the new position is the sum of,
   i. the length of his or her service before January 1, 1998 while employed by the school authority to teach, and
   ii. the length of his or her service after December 31, 1997 while employed, other than as a principal or vice-principal, by the school authority to teach.

(3) The following rule applies if the principal or vice-principal is assigned to a position other than one described in subsection (1) or (2):

1. For one year after he or she begins work in the new position, he or she is entitled to be paid the salary that he or she would have been paid as principal or vice-principal.

5. On August 31, 2001, section 4 is revoked and the following substituted:

4. (1) The following rule applies if the principal or vice-principal is assigned to a position other than one described in subsecton (2):

1. For one year after he or she begins work in the new position, he or she is entitled to be paid the salary that he or she would have been paid as principal or vice-principal.

(2) Subsection (1) does not apply if the principal or vice-principal is assigned to a position in which he or she is employed, other than as a principal or vice-principal, to teach.

6. This Regulation comes into force on April 1, 1998.

REGULATION 181/98
IDENTIFICATION AND PLACEMENT OF
EXCEPTIONAL PUPILS

O. Reg. 181/98, as am. 137/01

PART I

GENERAL

1. (1) In this Regulation,

"committee" means a special education identification, placement and review committee established under Part II and includes a committee established under Regulation 305 of the Revised Regulations of Ontario, 1990;

"designated representative" means,

    (a) in relation to a board that has a director of education, the director of education of the board, and

    (b) in relation to a board that does not have a director of education, the secretary or equivalent of the board;

"parent" includes a guardian;

"special education appeal board" means a special education appeal board established under Part VI.

(2) In this Regulation, a reference to the category and definition of an exceptionality is a reference to the category and definition of the exceptionality as established under subsection 8(3) of the Act.

2. Where the time limited by this Regulation for doing anything expires or falls on a school holiday within the meaning of Regulation 304 of the Revised Regulations of Ontario, 1990, the time so limited extends to and the thing may be done on the next day following that is not a school holiday.

3. (1) Subject to subsection (2), mail shall be deemed to have been received by the person to whom it was sent on the fifth day after the day on which it was mailed.

(2) If the fifth day is a school holiday within the meaning of Regulation 304 of the Revised Regulations of Ontario, 1990, the mail shall be deemed to have been received by the person to whom it was sent on the first day after the fifth day that is not a school holiday.

4. A person or body required by this Regulation to communicate in writing to a parent or pupil shall, at the request of the parent or pupil, use a braille, large print or audio-cassette format for the communication.

5. (1) A parent of a pupil and, where the pupil is 16 years of age or older, the pupil, are entitled,

(a) to be present at and participate in all committee discussions about the pupil; and

(7) In developing a transition plan under subsection (4), the principal shall consult with such community agencies and post-secondary educational institutions as he or she considers appropriate.

(8) Within 30 school days after placement of the pupil in the program, the principal shall ensure that the plan is completed and a copy of it sent to a parent of the pupil and, where the pupil is 16 years of age or older, the pupil. O. Reg. 137/01, s. 1.

7. (1) Subsection (2) applies when,

(a) a board implements a change in placement under section 25;
(b) a board implements a change in placement under section 31 following an appeal to a special education appeal board in respect of a committee decision under Part V;
(c) a board implements a change in placement in accordance with a decision of the Special Education Tribunal following an appeal to the Special Education Tribunal in respect of a committee decision under Part V;
(d) an existing placement is confirmed in a statement of decision under Part V and a parent of the pupil consents in writing to the decision or the time period provided in section 31 for filing a notice of appeal from the decision expires without a notice of appeal being filed;
(e) an existing placement is confirmed in a decision under subsection 30(1) and a parent consents in writing to the decision or the time period provided in section 31 expires without an appeal being commenced;
(f) an existing placement is confirmed in a decision under subsection 30(1), an appeal from the decision is made under section 57 of the Act to the Special Education Tribunal and the appeal is dismissed or abandoned; or
(g) an existing placement is confirmed in an order of the Special Education Tribunal granting an appeal under section 57 of the Act.

(2) The board shall promptly notify the principal of the school at which the special education program is to be provided of the need to review the pupil's individual education plan to determine whether it needs to be updated.

(3) In reviewing the plan, the principal shall,

(a) consult with the parent and, where the pupil is 16 years of age or older, the pupil; and
(b) take into consideration any recommendations of the committee or the Special Education Tribunal, as the case may be, regarding special education programs or special education services.

(4) Where an individual education plan does not include a plan for transition to appropriate post-secondary school activities and the pupil has attained the age of 14 or will attain the age of 14 within the school year, the principal shall ensure that a transition plan is developed and included in the individual education plan.

(5) Subsection (4) does not apply in respect of a pupil identified as exceptional solely on the basis of giftedness.

(6) In reviewing an individual education plan that includes a transition plan or in developing a transition plan under subsection (4), the principal shall consult with such com-

munity agencies and post-secondary educational institutions as he or she considers appropriate.

(7) Within 30 school days of an implementation of a change in placement or, where the placement is confirmed, within 30 school days of receiving the notice under subsection (1), the principal shall ensure that,

(a) the plan has been reviewed and updated as appropriate;
(b) a transition plan has been added to the individual education plan where required by subsection (4); and
(c) a copy of the individual education plan has been sent to a parent of the pupil and, where the pupil is 16 years of age or older, the pupil. O. Reg. 137/01, s. 2.

8. The principal shall ensure that.the individual education plan for a pupil is included in the record kept in respect of the pupil under clause 265(d) of the Act, unless a parent of the pupil has objected in writing.

9. (1) In accordance with requirements under the *Education Act*, no pupil is to be denied an education program pending a meeting or decision under this Regulation.

(2) Where an education program is provided to a pupil pending a meeting or decision under this Regulation,

(a) the program must be appropriate to the pupil's apparent strengths and needs;
(b) the placement for the program must be consistent with the principles underlying section 17; and
(c) appropriate education services must be provided to meet the pupil's apparent needs.

PART II

ESTABLISHMENT OF COMMITTEES AND COMMITTEE PROCEDURES

10. Each board shall, in accordance with section 11, establish one or more committees for the identification and placement of exceptional pupils, determine the jurisdiction of each committee and establish the manner of selecting the chair of each committee.

11. (1) A board shall appoint three or more persons to each committee that it establishes.

(2) The board shall appoint, as one of the members of each committee,

(a) a principal employed by the board;
(b) a supervisory officer employed by the board under Part XI of the Act; or
(c) a supervisory officer whose services are used by the board under Part XI of the Act.

(3) A principal or supervisory officer appointed under subsection (2) may designate a person to act in his or her place as a member of the committee without the approval of the board.

(4) Only a person who is eligible to be appointed to the committee under subsection (2) may be designated to act on the committee under subsection (3).

(5) No member of the board may be appointed to a committee under subsection (2) or designated to act on the committee under subsection (3).

12. (1) A board may establish procedures for committees in addition to those set out in this Regulation.

(2) Committee decisions made under this Regulation must be consistent with the board's special education plan.

PART III

PARENTS' GUIDE

13. (1) Each board shall prepare a guide for the use and information of parents and pupils that,

(a) explains the function of a committee on a referral under Part IV and on a review under Part V;

(b) outlines the procedures set out in this Regulation or established under section 12 that a committee must follow in identifying a pupil as exceptional and in deciding the pupil's placement;

(c) explains the committee's duty to describe pupils' strengths and needs and to include, in its statements of decision, the categories and definitions of any exceptionalities it identifies;

(d) explains the function of a special education appeal board under Part VI and the right of parents to appeal committee decisions to it;

(e) lists the parent organizations that are, to the best of the board's knowledge, local associations of the board, within the meaning of Ontario Regulation 464/97;

(f) includes the names, addresses and telephone numbers of the provincial and demonstration schools in Ontario;

(g) indicates the extent to which the board provides special education programs and special education services and the extent to which it purchases those programs and services from another board;

(h) explains that no committee placement decision can be implemented unless,

(i) a parent has consented to the decision, or

(ii) the time limit for filing a notice of appeal in respect of the decision has expired and no such notice has been filed.

(2) The board shall. ensure that copies of the guide are available at each school in the board's jurisdiction and at the board's head office and shall provide a copy to the appropriate district office of the Ministry.

(3) The board shall, at the request of a parent or pupil, provide the parent or pupil with a guide in a braille, large print or audio-cassette format.

PART IV

REFERRAL OF PUPILS TO COMMITTEES

14. (1) The principal of the school at which a pupil is enrolled,

(a) may on written notice to a parent of the pupil; and

(b)   shall at the written request of a parent of the pupil,

refer the pupil to a committee established by the board, for a decision as to whether the pupil should be identified as an exceptional pupil and, if so, what the placement of the pupil should be.

(2) Where a decision is made that a pupil is to leave a demonstration school and enter a school of a board, the superintendent of the demonstration school shall so notify the designated representative of the board.

(3) On receiving the notice under subsection (2), the designated representative of the board shall ensure that the pupil is referred to a committee established by the board, for a decision as to what the placement of the pupil should be.

(4) The superintendent of the demonstration school acting under subsection (2) and the designated representative of the board acting under subsection (3) shall use their best efforts to ensure that the committee meets as soon as possible after the decision is made to move the pupil from the demonstration school to the school of the board.

(5) Where more than one committee has been established by the board, the referral under subsection (1) or (3) shall be to the committee that the principal or the designated representative, as the case may be, considers to be the most appropriate for the pupil, having regard to the jurisdiction of the committees.

(6) Within 15 days of giving a notice under clause (1)(a) or receiving a request under clause (1)(b), the principal shall provide the parent with,

(a)   a copy of the guide prepared under section 13;
(b)   a written statement of approximately when the principal expects that a committee will meet for the first time to discuss the pupil; and
(c)   in the case of a request under clause (1)(b), a written acknowledgement of the request.

(7) Within 15 days of receiving a notification under subsection (2), the designated representative shall provide the parent with,

(a)   a copy of the notification under subsection (2);
(b)   a copy of the guide prepared under section 13; and
(c)   a written statement of approximately when the designated representative expects that a committee will meet for the first time to discuss the pupil.

15. (1) A committee that has received a referral under section 14 shall obtain and consider an educational assessment of the pupil.

(2) Subject to the *Health Care Consent Act, 1996*, the committee shall also obtain and consider a health assessment of the pupil by a qualified medical practitioner if the committee determines that the assessment is required to enable it to make a correct identification or placement decision.

(3) Subject to the *Health Care Consent Act, 1996*, the committee shall also obtain and consider a psychological assessment of the pupil if the committee determines that the assessment is required to enable it to make a correct identification or placement decision.

(4) Where the committee determines that it would be useful to do so and the pupil is

less than 16 years of age, the committee shall, with the consent of a parent, interview the pupil.

(5) A parent of the pupil has a right to be present at the interview.

(6) The committee shall also consider any information about the pupil submitted to it by a parent of the pupil and, where the pupil is 16 years of age or older, the pupil.

(7) In addition to complying with this section, the committee shall consider any information submitted to it that it considers relevant.

(8) As soon as possible after the chair of the committee obtains any information relating to the pupil, the chair shall provide the information to,

(a) a parent of the pupil; and
(b) the pupil, where the pupil is 16 years of age or older.

(9) Subsection (8) does not apply to oral information submitted at a meeting that the committee holds in respect of the pupil in accordance with this Regulation.

16. (1) The committee may discuss any proposal for special education services or special education programs and shall do so at the request of a parent or a pupil who is 16 years of age or older.

(2) The committee may make recommendations regarding special education programs and special education services.

(3) The committee may recommend that an exceptional pupil who is 21 years of age or older remain in a secondary day school program.

(4) Despite subsections (1) to (3), the committee shall not make decisions about special education services or special education programs.

(5) Despite subsection (4), a recommendation of a committee under subsection (3) is effective for the purposes of subsection 49.2(7) of the Act.

(6) A recommendation under this section is not a decision for the purposes of subsection 26(1).

17. (1) When making a placement decision on a referral under section 14, the committee shall, before considering the option of placement in a special education class, consider whether placement in a regular class, with appropriate special education services,

(a) would meet the pupil's needs; and
(b) is consistent with parental preferences.

(2) If, after considering all of the information obtained by it or submitted to it under section 15 that it considers relevant, the committee is satisfied that placement in a regular class would meet the pupil's needs and is consistent with parental preferences, the committee shall decide in favour of placement in a regular class.

18. (1) As soon as possible after making its decisions on a referral under section 14, the chair of the committee shall send a written statement of decision to,

(a) a parent of the pupil;

(b) the pupil, where the pupil is 16 years of age or older;

(c) the principal who made the referral, where the referral was made by a principal; and

(d) the designated representative of the board that established the committee.

(2) In the case of a referral by a principal under subsection 14(1), the statement of decision shall,

(a) state whether the committee has identified the pupil as an exceptional pupil;

(b) where the committee has identified the pupil as an exceptional pupil, include,
   (i)   the committee's description of the pupil's strengths and needs,
   (ii) the categories and definitions of any exceptionalities identified by the committee,
   (iii) the committee's placement decision, and
   (iv) the committee's recommendation under subsection 16(2), if any; and

(c) where the committee has decided that the pupil should be placed in a special education class, state the reasons for that decision.

(3) In the case of a referral by a designated representative under subsection 14(3), the statement of decision shall,

(a) include,
   (i)   the committee's description of the pupil's strengths and needs,
   (ii) the categories and definitions of any exceptionalities identified by the committee,
   (iii) the committee's placement decision, and
   (iv) the committee's recommendation under subsection 16(2), if any; and

(b) where the committee has decided that the pupil should be placed in a special education class, state the reasons for that decision.

19. (1) A parent who receives a statement of decision under section 18 may, by written notice delivered to the person specified in subsection (2) within 15 days of receipt of the statement of decision, request a meeting with the committee.

(2) The notice under subsection (1) shall be delivered to the principal in the case of a referral under subsection 14(1) and to the designated representative in the case of a referral under subsection 14(3).

(3) On receiving the request, the principal or designated representative, as the case may be, shall arrange for the committee to meet as soon as possible with the parent and, where the pupil is 16 years of age or older and wishes to attend, the pupil, to discuss the statement of decision.

(4) As soon as possible following a meeting under this section, the chair of the committee shall send a written notice to each of the persons described in subsection 18(1), stating whether any changes in its decisions were made as a result of the meeting.

(5) If changes in the committee's decisions were made as a result of the meeting, the notice under subsection (4) shall be accompanied by a revised statement of decision, together with written reasons for the changes.

20. (1) A board shall implement a placement decision made by a committee under this Part when one of the following two events occurs:

1. A parent of the pupil consents in writing to the placement.
2. The time period provided in subsection 26(2) for filing a notice of appeal from the decision expires without a notice of appeal being filed.

(2) The board shall implement a placement decision made by a committee under this Part as soon as possible after an event described in paragraph 1 or 2 of subsection (1) occurs.

(3) A board that, without the written consent of a parent of the pupil, implements a placement decision made by a committee under this Part shall give written notice of the implementation to a parent of the pupil.

PART V

COMMITTEE REVIEWS

21. (1) The principal of the school at which a pupil's special education program is being provided,

(a) may on written notice to a parent of the pupil;

(b) shall at the written request of a parent of the pupil; and

(c) shall, at the written request of the designated representative of the board that is providing the special education program to the pupil,

refer the pupil to a committee established by the board that is providing the special education program to the pupil, for a review of the identification or placement of the pupil.

(2) A request by a parent under clause (1)(b) may be made at any time after a placement has been in effect for three months but may not be made more often than once in every three month period.

(3) Subject to subsection (4), the designated representative shall make a request under clause (1)(c) when in his or her opinion it is necessary to do so in order to ensure that a review in respect of the pupil is held under this Part at least once in each school year.

(4) Subsection (3) does not apply where,

(a) a committee proceeding with respect to the pupil was held under Part IV during the school year; or

(b) a parent of the pupil gives a written notice dispensing with the annual review to the principal of the school at which the special education program is being provided.

(5) Within 15 days of giving a notice under clause (1)(a) or receiving a request under clause (1)(b) or (c), the principal shall provide the parent with a written statement of the approximate time when the review meeting will take place.

22. (1) Where more than one committee has been established by a board, the principal of the school at which the special education program is provided shall determine which of the committees most appropriate for the pupil, having regard to the jurisdiction of the committees.

(2) Where one board purchases a special education program from another board, the

board that is providing the special education program to the pupil shall invite the purchasing board to select a representative who may,

    (a) be present at and participate in all committee discussions about the pupil; and

    (b) be present when the committee's identification and placement decisions are made.

23. (1) Sections 15 and 16 apply with necessary modifications to a committee engaged in a review under this Part.

(2) With the written permission of a parent of the pupil, a committee conducting a review under this Part shall consider the pupil's progress with reference to the pupil's individual education plan.

(3) As soon as possible after a committee engaged in a review under this Part decides that it is satisfied with the identification and placement of a pupil, the chair of the committee shall send a written statement of decision confirming the identification and placement to,

    (a) a parent of the pupil;

    (b) the pupil, where the pupil is 16 years of age or older;

    (c) the principal of the school at which the pupil's special education program is being provided;

    (d) the designated representative of the board that is providing the special education program to the pupil; and

    (e) in the circumstances described in subsection 22(2), the designated representative of the board that is purchasing the special education program.

(4) As soon as possible after a committee engaged in a review under this Part decides that the identification or placement or both should be changed, the chair of the committee shall send a written statement of decision to the persons described in subsection (3).

(5) A statement of decision under subsection (4) shall state,

    (a) the reasons for the committee's decision that the pupil's identification or placement or both should be changed;

    (b) whether the committee considers that the pupil should continue to be identified as an exceptional pupil;

    (c) where the committee considers that the pupil should continue to be identified as an exceptional pupil,

        (i) the committee's placement decision,

        (ii) the committee's description of the pupil's strengths and needs, and

        (iii) the categories and definitions of any exceptionalities identified by the committee; and

    (d) where the committee considers that the pupil should be placed in a special education class, the reasons for that decision.

(6) Section 17 applies with necessary modifications where a committee is considering the option of placing a pupil in a special education class and the pupil is not already in such a placement.

24. (1) A parent who receives a confirmation under subsection 23(3) or a statement of decision under subsection 23(4) may request a meeting with the committee by written notice, delivered within 15 days of receiving the confirmation or statement of decision, to the principal of the school at which the pupil's special education program is being provided.

(2) On receiving the request for a meeting, the principal shall arrange for the committee to meet as soon as possible with the parent and, where the pupil is 16 years of age or older and wishes to attend, the pupil, to discuss the statement of decision.

(3) As soon as possible following a meeting under this section, the chair of the committee shall send a written notice to each of the persons described in subsection 23(3), stating whether any changes in its decisions were made as a result of the meeting.

(4) If changes in the committee's decisions were made as a result of the meeting, the notice under subsection (3) shall be accompanied by a revised statement of decision, together with written reasons for the changes.

25. (1) A board shall implement a change in placement as a result of a decision made by a committee under this Part when one of the following two events occurs:

    1. A parent of the pupil consents in writing to the placement.
    2. The time period provided in subsection 26(3) for filing a notice of appeal from the decision expires without a notice of appeal being filed.

(2) The board shall implement a change in placement as a result of a decision made by a committee under this Part as soon as possible after an event described in paragraph 1 or 2 of subsection (1) occurs.

(3) A board that, without the written consent of a parent of the pupil, implements a change in placement as a result of a decision made by a committee under this Part shall give written notice of the implementation to a parent of the pupil.

PART VI

APPEALS FROM COMMITTEE DECISIONS

26. (1) A parent of a pupil may, by filing a notice of appeal in accordance with subsection (2) or (3), require a hearing by a special education appeal board in respect of,

    (a) a committee decision under Part IV or V that the pupil is an exceptional pupil;
    (b) a committee decision under Part IV or V that the pupil is not an exceptional pupil; or
    (c) a committee decision under Part IV or V on placement of the pupil.

(2) A notice of appeal in respect of a committee decision under Part IV shall be filed with the secretary of the board,

    (a) if no meeting is held under section 19, within 30 days of receipt of the statement of decision under section 18 by the parent who is seeking to appeal; or
    (b) if a meeting is held under section 19, within 15 days of receipt of the notice under subsection 19(4) by the parent who is seeking to appeal.

(3) A notice of appeal in respect of a committee decision under Part V shall be filed with the secretary of the board,

    (a) if no meeting is held under section 24, within 30 days of receipt of the confirmation under subsection 23(3) or the statement of decision under subsection 23(4) by the parent who is seeking to appeal; or

(b) if a meeting is held under section 24, within 15 days of receipt of the notice under subsection 24(3) by the parent who is seeking to appeal.

(4) A notice of appeal shall indicate which of the decisions referred to in subsection (1) the parent disagrees with and shall include a statement that sets out the nature of the disagreement.

(5) The special education appeal board shall not reject or refuse to deal with an appeal by reason of any actual or alleged deficiency in the statement referred to in subsection (4) or by reason of the failure of the parent, in the opinion of the special education appeal board, to accurately indicate in the notice of appeal the subject of the disagreement.

27. (1) The special education appeal board shall be composed of,

(a) one member selected by the board in which the pupil is placed;

(b) one member selected by a parent of the pupil; and

(c) a chair, selected jointly by the members selected under clauses (a) and (b) or, where those members cannot agree, by the appropriate district manager of the Ministry.

(2) Selections under clauses (1)(a) and (b) shall be made within 15 days of receipt of the notice of appeal by the secretary of the board.

(3) The selection of a chair under clause (1)(c) shall be made within 15 days of the last selection under clause (1)(a) and (b).

(4) No member or employee of the board providing or purchasing the special education program and no employee of the Ministry may be selected under subsection (1).

(5) No person who has had any prior involvement with the matter under appeal may be selected under subsection (1).

(6) The chair of the committee the decision of which is being appealed shall provide the special education appeal board with the record of the committee proceeding, including the statement of decision and any reports, assessments or other documents considered by the committee.

(7) The board shall provide the special education appeal board with the secretarial and administrative services it requires and shall, in accordance with the rules and policies that apply to members of the board under section 191.2 of the Act, pay the travelling and other expenses incurred by the members of the special education appeal board while engaged in their duties.

28. (1) The chair of the special education appeal board shall arrange for a meeting of the members of the special education appeal board to discuss the matters under appeal and shall give notice of the meeting, in accordance with subsection 5(5), to a parent of the pupil and, where the pupil is 16 years of age or older, the pupil.

(2) The meeting shall be arranged to take place at a convenient place and at a time that is no more than 30 days after the day on which the chair is selected and shall be conducted in an informal manner.

(3) Despite subsection (2), with the written consent of the parents of the pupil and the

designated representative of the board, the meeting may be scheduled for a time that is more than 30 days after the day on which the chair is selected.

(4) Any person who in the opinion of the chair of the special education appeal board may be able to contribute information with respect to the matters under appeal shall be invited to attend the meeting.

(5) Where the pupil's special education program is being purchased by one board from another board, the chair shall invite the purchasing board to select a representative who may be present at and participate in all discussions about the pupil at the meeting held by the special education appeal board under section 28.

(6) Where the special education appeal board is satisfied that the opinions, views and information that bear on the appeal have been sufficiently presented to it, the special education appeal board shall end the meeting and, within three days of ending the meeting, shall,

    (a) agree with the committee and recommend that its decisions be implemented; or

    (b) disagree with the committee and make a recommendation to the board about the pupil's identification, placement or both.

29. (1) The special education appeal board shall send a written statement of its recommendations under section 28 to,

    (a) a parent of the pupil;

    (b) where the pupil is 16 years of age or older, the pupil;

    (c) the chair of the committee;

    (d) the principal of the school in which the pupil is placed;

    (e) the designated representative of the board in which the pupil is placed; and

    (f) in the circumstances described in subsection 28(5), the designated representative of the board that is purchasing the special education program.

(2) The written statement shall be accompanied by written reasons for the recommendations.

30. (1) Within 30 days of receiving the special education appeal board's written statement, the board shall consider the special education appeal board's recommendations, shall decide what action to take with respect to the pupil and shall give notice in writing of the decision to each of the persons described in subsection 29(1).

(2) In deciding what action to take with respect to a pupil, the board is not limited to the actions that the special education appeal board recommended or could have recommended.

(3) Notice to a parent under subsection (1) shall include an explanation of the further right of appeal provided by section 57 of the Act.

31. (1) The board shall implement a decision under subsection 30(1) when one of the following events occurs:

    1. A parent of the pupil consents in writing to the decision.

    2. Thirty days have elapsed from receipt of the notice under subsection 30(1) by a parent of the pupil and no appeal has been commenced in respect of the decision under section 57 of the Act.

3. An appeal under section 57 of the Act from the decision is dismissed or abandoned.

(2) In accordance with an agreement between the board and a parent or the pupil, the board may change a decision made by it under section 30,

(a) while an appeal under section 57 of the Act is pending; or
(b) before the end of the period referred to in paragraph 2 of subsection (1).

(3) Where the board changes a decision under subsection (2), the board shall give notice in writing of the change in decision to each of the persons described in subsection 29(1).

(4) Subsections 30(2) and (3) apply with necessary modifications in respect of a change in decision under subsection (2).

PART VII

TRANSITIONAL PROVISIONS

Interpretation

32. In this Part,

"old regulation" means Regulation 305 of the Revised Regulation of Ontario, 1990.

Committees Established Before September 1, 1998

33. (1) Where a matter was referred to a committee under section 2 of the old Regulation, the matter shall be dealt with on and after September 1, 1998 as if it had been referred to a committee under Part IV of this Regulation and, for the purpose, the provisions of this Regulation apply to the committee proceeding and to all related proceedings, including appeals, with appropriate modifications.

(2) Where a matter was referred to a committee under section 8 of the old Regulation, the matter shall be dealt with on and after September 1, 1998 as if it had been referred to a committee under Part V of this Regulation and, for the purpose, the provisions of this Regulation, apply to the committee proceeding and to all related proceedings, including appeals, with appropriate modifications.

(3) The modifications required by subsections (1) and (2) are such modifications as the person or body exercising a power or meeting a requirement under this Regulation considers appropriate having regard to the stage to which the matter has proceeded.

Parents' Guide

34. Until December 31, 1998, a board may meet the requirements of subsection 13(2) and clauses 14(6)(a) and 14(7)(b) using copies of a guide prepared under section 2 of the old regulation.

Individual Education Plans

35. Subsections 7(2) to (7) apply with necessary modifications if, as a result of a decision of a committee, a special education appeal board or the Special Education Tribunal,

(a) an existing placement of an exceptional pupil who does not yet have an individual education plan is confirmed; or

(b) a board implements a change in placement of an exceptional pupil who does not yet have an individual education plan.

Appeals Filed Before September 1, 1998

36. (1) This section applies if a notice of appeal is given under section 4 of the old regulation before September 1, 1998 but the appeal is not finally determined before that date.

(2) If three people are appointed before September 1, 1998 under section 7 of the old regulation to form an appeal board to hear the appeal, the appeal shall be held in accordance with the old regulation as it read immediately before it was revoked.

(3) If three people are not appointed before September 1, 1998 under section 7 of the old regulation to form an appeal board to hear the appeal, the appeal shall be held in accordance with this Regulation.

(4) For the purposes of subsection (3),

(a) the notice given under section 4 of the old regulation shall be deemed to be a notice properly given under section 26 of this Regulation; and

(b) selections under clauses 27(1)(a) and (b) shall be made on or before September 15, 1998 rather than within the times specified in subsections 27(2) and (3).

37. (1) This section applies where an appeal is held in accordance with the old regulation as a result of the application of subsection 36(2) of this Regulation.

(2) If the board receives the report of the appeal decision under subsection 7(10) of the old regulation before September 1, 1998, subsection 7(11) of the old regulation applies as it read immediately before it was revoked.

(3) If the board does not receive the report of the appeal decision under subsection 7(10) of the old regulation before September 1, 1998, sections 30 and 31 of this Regulation apply as if the report of the appeal decision given under subsection 7(10) of the old regulation were a statement given under section 29 of this Regulation.

PART VIII

REVOCATION

38. Regulation 305 of the Revised Regulations of Ontario, 1990 and Ontario Regulation 663/91 are revoked.

PART IX

COMMENCEMENT

39. (1) This Regulation, except subsection 13(3), comes into force on September 1, 1998.

(2) Subsection 13(3) comes into force on January 1, 1999.

REGULATION 435/00
OPENING OR CLOSING EXERCISES

under the Education Act

O. Reg. 435/00

APPLICATION

1. The requirements set out in this Regulation apply with respect to the opening and closing exercises referred to in section 304 of the Act.

PLEDGE OF CITIZENSHIP

2. (1) The principal may decide whether the opening or closing exercises at a school will include the recitation of the pledge of citizenship.

(2) The principal's decision about reciting the pledge of citizenship must be consistent with the policies and guidelines, if any, established by the board.

(3) Before making his or her decision about reciting the pledge of citizenship, the principal shall consult the school council.

(4) The principal shall review his or her decision about reciting the pledge of citizenship at the beginning of each school year and must consult with the school council.

3. The following is the pledge of citizenship:

I affirm that I will be faithful and bear true allegiance to Her Majesty Queen Elizabeth the Second, Queen of Canada, and to her heirs and successors, and that I will faithfully observe the laws of Canada and fulfill my duties as a Canadian citizen.

EXEMPTIONS

4. A pupil is not required to sing *O Canada* or recite the pledge of citizenship in the following circumstances:

1. In the case of a pupil who is less than 18 years old, if the pupil's parent or guardian applies to the principal to be exempted from doing so.

2. n the case of a pupil who is at least 18 years old, if the pupil applies to the principal to be exempted from doing so.

REGULATION 474/00
ACCESS TO SCHOOL PREMISES

under the Education Act

O. Reg. 474/00

1. This Regulation governs access to school premises under section 305 of the Act.

2. (1) The following persons are permitted to be on school premises on any day and at any time:

1. A person enrolled as a pupil in the school.

2. A parent or guardian of such a pupil.

3. A person employed or retained by the board.

4. A person who is otherwise on the premises for a lawful purpose.

(2) A person who is invited to attend an event, a class or a meeting on school premises is permitted to be on the premises for that purpose.

(3) A person who is invited onto school premises for a particular purpose by the principal, a vice-principal or another person authorized by board policy to do so is permitted to be on the premises for that purpose.

(4) Subsection (1), (2) or (3) does not entitle a person to have access to all areas of the school premises.

(5) Subsection (1) does not restrict the right of the board to lock the school premises when the premises are not being used for a purpose authorized by the board.

3. (1) A person is not permitted to remain on school premises if his or her presence is detrimental to the safety or well-being of a person on the premises, in the judgment of the principal, a vice-principal or another person authorized by the board to make such a determination.

(2) A person is not permitted to remain on school premises if a policy of the board requires the person to report his or her presence on the premises in a specified manner and the person fails to do so.

REGULATION 612/00
SCHOOL COUNCILS

under the Education Act

O. Reg. 612/00

INTERPRETATION

1. (1) In this Regulation,

"meeting" does not include a training session or other event where a school council does not discuss or decide matters that it has authority to decide; (*"réunion"*)

"parent" includes a guardian as defined in section 1 of the Act; (*"père ou mère"*)

"parent member" means a member of a school council who is elected to the council in accordance with section 4 or who fills a vacancy created when a parent member ceases to hold office. (*"père ou mère membre"*)

(2) In the case of a school that is established primarily for adults, a reference in this Regulation to a parent or to a parent of a pupil shall be deemed, with necessary modifications, to be a reference to a pupil who is enrolled in the school.

PURPOSE

2. (1) The purpose of school councils is, through the active participation of parents, to improve pupil achievement and to enhance the accountability of the education system to parents.

(2) A school council's primary means of achieving its purpose is by making recommendations in accordance with this Regulation to the principal of the school and the board that established the council.

COMPOSITION

3. (1) A school council for a school shall be composed of the following people:

1. The number of parent members determined under subsection (2).

2. The principal of the school.

3. One teacher who is employed at the school, other than the principal or vice-principal, elected in accordance with section 5.

4. One person who is employed at the school, other than the principal, vice-principal or any other teacher, elected in accordance with section 5.

5. In the case of a school with one or more secondary school grades,

    i.   one pupil enrolled in the school who is appointed by the student council, if the school has a student council, or

ii.   one pupil enrolled in the school who is elected in accordance with section 5, if the school does not have a student council.

6.   In the case of a school with no secondary school grades, one pupil enrolled in the school who is appointed by the principal of the school, if the principal determines, after consulting the other members of the school council, that the council should include a pupil.

7.   Subject to subsection (3), one community representative appointed by the other members of the council.

8.   One person appointed by an association that is a member of the Ontario Federation of Home and School Associations, the Ontario Association of Parents in Catholic Education or Parent Partenaires en Education, if the association that is a member of the Ontario Federation of Home and School Associations, the Ontario Association of Parents in Catholic Education or Parent Partenaires en Education is established in respect of the school.

(2) For the purposes of paragraph 1 of subsection (1), the number of parent members shall be determined as follows:

1.   If the school council has a by-law that specifies the number of parent members, the number specified in the by-law.

2.   If the school council does not have a by-law that specifies the number of parent members, the number specified by the board that established the council.

(3) A school council may specify by by-law that the council shall include two or more community representatives, appointed by the other members of the council.

(4) In specifying numbers under subsections (2) and (3), the board or the school council, as the case may be, shall ensure that parent members constitute a majority of the members of the school council.

(5) A person who is employed by the board that established a school council cannot be appointed as a community representative on the council unless,

(a)   he or she is not employed at the school; and

(b)   the other members of the school council are informed of the person's employment before the appointment.

(6) A member of a board cannot be a member of a school council established by the board.

(7) Paragraphs 5 and 6 of subsection (1) do not apply in respect of a school that is established primarily for adults.

ELECTION OF PARENT MEMBERS

4. (1) A person is qualified to be a parent member of a school council if he or she is a parent of a pupil who is enrolled in the school.

(2) Despite subsection (1), a person is not qualified to be a parent member of a school council if,

(a)   he or she is employed at the school; or

(b)   he or she is not employed at the school but is employed elsewhere by the board that established the council, unless he or she takes reasonable steps to inform people qualified to vote in the election of parent members of that employment.

(3) A person is qualified to vote in an election of parent members of a school council if he or she is a parent of a pupil who is enrolled in the school.

(4) An election of parent members of a school council shall be held during the first 30 days of each school year, on a date that is fixed by the chair or co-chairs of the school council after consulting with the principal of the school.

(5) Despite subsection (4), if a new school is established, the first election of parent members to the school council shall be held during the first 30 days of the school year, on a date that is fixed by the board that established the school council.

(6) The principal of a school shall, at least 14 days before the date of the election of parent members, on behalf of the school council, give written notice of the date, time and location of the election to every parent of a pupil who, on the date the notice is given, is enrolled in the school.

(7) The notice required by subsection (6) may be given by,

(a)   giving the notice to the parent's child for delivery to his or her parent; and

(b)   posting the notice in the school in a location that is accessible to parents.

(8) The election of parent members shall be by secret ballot.

OTHER ELECTIONS

5. (1) The elections of members of school councils referred to in paragraph 3, paragraph 4 and subparagraph 5 ii of subsection 3(1) shall be held during the first 30 days of each school year.

(2) A person is qualified to vote in an election of a member of a school council referred to in paragraph 3 of subsection 3(1) if he or she is a teacher, other than the principal or vice-principal, who is employed at the school.

(3) A person is qualified to vote in an election of a member of a school council referred to in paragraph 4 of subsection 3(1) if he or she is a person, other than the principal, vice-principal or any other teacher, who is employed at the school.

(4) A person is qualified to vote in an election of a member of a school council referred to in subparagraph 5 ii of subsection 3(1) if he or she is a pupil enrolled in the school.

TERM OF OFFICE

6. (1) A person elected or appointed as a member of a school council holds office from the later of,

(a)   the date he or she is elected or appointed; and

(b)   the date of the first meeting of the school council after the elections held under sections 4 and 5 in the school year,

until the date of the first meeting of the school council after the elections held under sections 4 and 5 in the next school year.

(2) A member of a school council may be re-elected or reappointed, unless otherwise provided by the by-laws of the council.

VACANCIES

7. (1) A vacancy in the membership of a school council shall be filled by election or appointment in accordance with the by-laws of the council.

(2) If an election is held to fill a vacancy in the membership of a school council, section 4 or 5, as the case may be, applies, with necessary modifications, to the election.

(3) A vacancy in the membership of a school council does not prevent the council from exercising its authority.

OFFICERS

8. (1) A school council shall have a chair or, if the by-laws of the council so provide, two co-chairs.

(2) A chair or co-chair of a school council must be a parent member of the council, and shall be elected by the members of the council.

(3) A person who is employed by the board that established the council cannot be the chair or co-chair of the council.

(4) A school council may have such other officers as are provided for in the by-laws of the council.

(5) Subject to subsections (2) and (3), vacancies in the office of chair, co-chair or any other officer of a school council shall be filled in accordance with the by-laws of the council.

COLLECTION OF INFORMATION

9. (1) The Ministry may, for the purpose of consulting and communicating directly with members of school councils, collect the names, mailing addresses, telephone numbers and e-mail addresses of the chair or co-chairs of a school council and of the other members of the council.

(2) The Ministry may disclose information collected under subsection (1) to the Ontario Parent Council, which may use the information for the purpose of consulting and communicating directly with members of school councils.

MINISTRY POWERS AND DUTIES

10. (1) As part of its accountability to parents, the Ministry shall report annually to members of school councils on education in the province.

(2) The Ministry may,

(a) make other reports to members of school councils; and

(b) provide information to members of school councils respecting the roles and responsibilities of school councils.

REMUNERATION

11. (1) A person shall not receive any remuneration for serving as a member or officer of a school council.

(2) Every board shall establish policies respecting the reimbursement of members and officers of school councils established by the board.

(3) The board that established a school council shall reimburse members and officers of the council, in accordance with the policies referred to in subsection (2), for expenses they incur as members or officers of the council.

MEETINGS

12. (1) A school council shall meet at least four times during the school year.

(2) A school council shall meet within the first 35 days of the school year, after the elections held under sections 4 and 5, on a date fixed by the principal of the school.

(3) A meeting of a school council cannot be held unless,

(a) a majority of the current members of the council are present at the meeting; and

(b) a majority of the members of the council who are present at the meeting are parent members.

(4) All meetings of a school council shall be open to the public.

(5) A school council is entitled to hold its meetings at the school.

(6) All meetings of a school council shall be held at a location that is accessible to the public.

(7) The principal of a school shall, on behalf of the school council, give written notice of the dates, times and locations of the meetings of the council to every parent of a pupil who, on the date the notice is given, is enrolled in the school.

(8) The notice required by subsection (7) may be given by,

(a) giving the notice to the parent's child for delivery to his or her parent; and

(b) posting the notice in the school in a location that is accessible to parents.

COMMITTEES

13. (1) A school council may, in accordance with its by-laws, establish committees to make recommendations to the council.

(2) Every committee of a school council must include at least one parent member of the council.

(3) A committee of a school council may include persons who are not members of the council.

(4) Subsections 12(4) to (8) apply, with necessary modifications, to committees of school councils.

VOTING

14. (1) Subject to subsection (3), each member of a school council is entitled to one vote in votes taken by the council.

(2) Subject to subsection (3), each member of a committee of a school council is entitled to one vote in votes taken by the committee.

(3) The principal of the school is not entitled to vote in votes taken by the school council or by a committee of the school council.

BY-LAWS

15. (1) A school council may make by-laws governing the conduct of its affairs.

(2) Every school council shall make the following by-laws:

1. A by-law that governs election procedures and the filling of vacancies in the membership of the school council.

2. A by-law that establishes rules respecting participation in school council proceedings in cases of conflict of interest.

3. A by-law that, in accordance with any applicable policies established by the board that established the council, establishes a conflict resolution process for internal school council disputes.

MINUTES AND FINANCIAL RECORDS

16. (1) A school council shall keep minutes of all of its meetings and records of all of its financial transactions.

(2) The minutes and records shall be available at the school for examination without charge by any person.

(3) Subsections (1) and (2) do not apply to minutes and records that are more than four years old.

INCORPORATION

17. A school council shall not be incorporated.

PRINCIPAL

18. (1) The principal of a school may delegate any of his or her powers or duties as a member of the school council, including any powers or duties under this Regulation, to a vice-principal of the school.

(2) In addition to his or her duties under this Regulation, the principal of a school shall perform the duties relating to school councils that are imposed on the principal by *Regulation 298* of the *Revised Regulations of Ontario, 1990* (Operation of Schools—General).

CONSULTATION BY BOARD

19. (1) In addition to its other obligations to solicit the views of school councils under the Act, every board shall solicit the views of the school councils established by the board with respect to the following matters:

1. The establishment or amendment of board policies and guidelines that relate to pupil achievement or to the accountability of the education system to parents, including,

    i.   policies and guidelines established under subsection 302(1) of the Act with respect to the conduct of persons in schools within the board's jurisdiction,

    ii. policies and guidelines established under subsection 302(5) of the Act respecting appropriate dress for pupils in schools within the board's jurisdiction,

    iii. policies and guidelines respecting the allocation of funding by the board to school councils,

    iv. policies and guidelines respecting the fundraising activities of school councils,

    v.   policies and guidelines respecting conflict resolution processes for internal school council disputes, and

    vi. policies and guidelines respecting reimbursement by the board of expenses incurred by members and officers of school councils.

2. The development of implementation plans for new education initiatives that relate to pupil achievement or to the accountability of the education system to parents, including,

    i.   implementation plans for policies and guidelines established under subsection 302(1) of the Act with respect to the conduct of persons in schools within the board's jurisdiction, and

    ii. implementation plans for policies and guidelines established under subsection 302(5) of the Act respecting appropriate dress for pupils in schools within the board's jurisdiction.

3.   Board action plans for improvement, based on the Education Quality and Accountability Office's reports on the results of tests of pupils, and the communication of those plans to the public.

4.   The process and criteria applicable to the selection and placement of principals and vice-principals.

(2) Subsection (1) does not limit the matters on which a board may solicit the views of school councils.

ADVISORY AUTHORITY OF SCHOOL COUNCILS

20. A school council may make recommendations to the principal of the school or to the board that established the council on any matter.

DUTY OF BOARD TO RESPOND

21. The board that established a school council shall consider each recommendation made to the board by the council and shall advise the council of the action taken in response to the recommendation.

FUNDRAISING

22. (1) Subject to subsection (2), a school council may engage in fundraising activities.

(2) A school council shall not engage in fundraising activities unless,

(a)   the activities are conducted in accordance with any applicable policies established by the board; and

(b)   the activities are to raise funds for a purpose approved by the board or authorized by any applicable polices established by the board.

(3) A school council shall ensure that the funds raised by it are used in accordance with any applicable policies established by the board.

CONSULTATION WITH PARENTS

23. A school council shall consult with parents of pupils enrolled in the school about matters under consideration by the council.

ANNUAL REPORT

24. (1) Every school council shall annually submit a written report on its activities to the principal of the school and to the board that established the council.

(2) If the school council engages in fundraising activities, the annual report shall include a report on those activities.

(3) The principal shall, on behalf of the school council, give a copy of the report to every parent of a pupil who, on the date the copy is given, is enrolled in the school.

(4) Subsection (3) may be complied with by,

(a)   giving the report to the parent's child for delivery to his or her parent; and

(b)   posting the report in the school in a location that is accessible to parents.

TRANSITION

25. Every school council established by a board before this Regulation comes into force is continued.

26. (1) Sections 3, 4 and 5 do not apply until September 1, 2001.

(2) Until the date of the first meeting of a school council after the first election held under section 4 after September 1, 2001, the references in subsection 8(2), clause 12(3)(b) and subsection 13(2) to a parent member shall be deemed to be references to a member of the school council who is a parent of a pupil enrolled in the school.

REGULATION 521/01
COLLECTION OF PERSONAL INFORMATION

under the Education Act

O. Reg. 521/01, as am. O. Reg. 170/02; 49/03; 322/03

1. (1) **Definitions**—In this Regulation,

"criminal background check" means, in respect of a board, a document concerning an individual,

    (a) that was prepared by a police force or service from national data on the Canadian Police Information Centre database within six months before the day the board collects the document, and

    (b) that contains information concerning the individual's personal criminal history; (*"relevé des antécédents criminels"*)

"offence declaration" means, in respect of a board, a written declaration signed by an individual, listing all of the individual's convictions for offences under the *Criminal Code* (Canada) up to the date of the declaration,

    (a) that are not included in a criminal background check collected by the Ontario College of Teachers after December 31, 1998 or in the last criminal background check collected by the board under this Regulation, and

    (b) for which a pardon under section 4.1 of the *Criminal Records Act* (Canada) has not been issued or granted; (*"déclaration d'infraction"*)

"personal criminal history" means, in respect of an individual, information on criminal offences of which the individual has been convicted under the *Criminal Code* (Canada) and for which a pardon under section 4.1 of the *Criminal Records Act* (Canada) has not been issued or granted to the individual; (*"antécédents criminels"*)

"service provider" means an individual who comes into direct contact with pupils on a regular basis,

    (a) at a school site of a board in the normal course of,

        (i) providing goods or services under contract with the board,

        (ii) carrying out his or her employment functions as an employee of a person who provides goods or services under contract with the board, or

        (iii) providing services to a person who provides goods or services under contract with the board, or

    (b) at a school under the jurisdiction of the Minister in the normal course of,

        (i) providing goods or services under contract with the Minister,

        (ii) carrying out his or her employment functions as an employee of a person who provides goods or services under contract with the Minister, or

(iii)   providing services to a person who provides goods or services under contract with the Minister. (*"fournisseur de services"*)

(2) An individual who would be a service provider under this Regulation only by reason of being a school bus driver, a driving instructor or both is not a service provider for the purposes of this Regulation while he or she satisfies the requirements set out by the Ministry of Transportation applicable to school bus drivers or driving instructors, as the case may be. O. Reg. 49/03, s. 1

2. Personal information to be collected by the board — (1) For the purposes of ensuring the safety of pupils, every board shall collect a personal criminal history of every individual who is,

(a)   an employee of the board; or

(b)   a service provider at a school site of the board.

(2) The board shall collect a personal criminal history of an individual described in subsection (1) at the following times and in the following manner:

1.   If the individual commences employment after March 31, 2002, the board shall collect a criminal background check in respect of the individual before the day the individual commences employment with the board and an offence declaration from the individual by September 1 of each year in which the individual is employed by the board after that day.

2.   If the individual first becomes a service provider in respect of the board after December 31, 2003, the board shall collect a criminal background check in respect of the individual before the individual first becomes a service provider at a school site of the board and an offence declaration from the individual by September 1 of each year in which the individual is a service provider at a school site of the board after that day.

3.   If the individual became a member of the Ontario College of Teachers after December 31, 1998 and commenced employment with the board before April 1, 2002, the board shall collect an offence declaration from the individual by September 1 of each year in which the individual is employed by the board after that day, commencing in 2002.

4.   If the individual commenced employment with the board before April 1, 2002 and is not an individual described in paragraph 3, the board shall collect,

   i.   a criminal background check in respect of the individual by July 31, 2003 if the individual is employed by the board at any time in 2003 after July 31, and

   ii.   an offence declaration from the individual by September 1 of each year in which the individual is employed by the board after that day, commencing in 2004.

4.1   If the individual became a service provider in respect of the board before December 31, 2003, the board shall collect,

   i.   a criminal background check in respect of the individual by December 31,

2003 if the individual is a service provider at a school site of the board after that day, and

    ii.   an offence declaration from the individual by September 1 of each year in which the individual is a service provider at a school site of the board after that day, commencing in 2004.

5.   If an employee transfers to a different school site of the board after March 31, 2002, the board shall collect an offence declaration from the employee before the transfer.

6.   If an individual is a service provider in respect of the board at one or more school sites and, after December 31, 2003, becomes a service provider at a different school site of the board, the board shall collect an offence declaration from the individual before the individual becomes a service provider at that school site. O. Reg. 170/02, s. 1; 322/03, s. 1

3. Personal information to be collected by Minister — For the purposes of subsection 315(1) of the Act, the personal information that may be collected by the Minister to ensure the safety of pupils is the personal criminal history of an individual who is,

(a)   an employee of the Ministry who works at a school under the jurisdiction of the Minister; or

(b)   a service provider at a school under the jurisdiction of the Minister.

4. Commencement — This Regulation comes into force on the later of January 1, 2002 and the day it is filed.

REGULATION 99/02
TEACHER PERFORMANCE APPRAISAL

under the Education Act

O. Reg. 99/02 as am. O. Reg. 1/03

PART I — GENERAL
[Heading added O. Reg. 1/03, s. 1.]

1. Interpretation — (1) This Regulation applies to performance appraisals of teachers conducted under Part X.2 of the Act.

(2) References in this Regulation to a principal include references to a person other than a principal who conducts a performance appraisal of a teacher under Part X.2 of the Act.

(3) The interpretations and definitions in Part X.2 of the Act apply for the purposes of this Regulation.

2. Notice of evaluation year — Within 20 school days after a teacher commences teaching in a year that is scheduled as an evaluation year for the teacher, the appropriate principal shall notify the teacher that the year is an evaluation year.

3. Competencies and rating scale — (1) In conducting a performance appraisal, a principal shall evaluate the teacher's competencies, as set out in the Schedule.

(2) The principal shall assign one of the following overall performance ratings to a teacher, based on the results of the performance appraisal:

1. Exemplary.

2. Good.

3. Satisfactory.

4. Unsatisfactory.

4. Performance appraisal — (1) A performance appraisal of a teacher must satisfy the following requirements:

1. The teacher must be evaluated with respect to the areas of competency in section 3 and such other areas of competency as may be provided for by the appropriate board under subsection 277.32(1) of the Act.

2. The performance appraisal must include the steps listed in subsection (2).

3. The performance appraisal must be conducted in accordance with such guidelines as the Minister may issue and in accordance with such additional policies, rules, standards, methods, processes, timelines and steps as may be established by the appropriate board.

(2) A performance appraisal must include the following steps:

1.   A meeting between the principal and the teacher in preparation for a classroom observation of the teacher and to review the teacher's current learning plan.

2.   The completion by the principal and teacher of a pre-observation profile in a form approved by the Minister.

3.   A classroom observation to evaluate the teacher's competencies, including a determination by the principal of whether the teacher has the knowledge and is employing the practices described in the guidelines issued by the Minister under subsection 277.33(1) of the Act.

4.   A meeting between the principal and the teacher after the classroom observation,

    i.   to review the results of the classroom observation,

    ii.   to discuss other information relevant to the principal's evaluation of the teacher's competency, including parental input and pupil input concerning the teacher,

    iii.   to complete the post observation report, in a form approved by the Minister, and

    iv.   to finalize the teacher's learning plan for the current year.

5.   An opportunity for the teacher to review and respond to the principal in respect of the parental input, pupil input or both, within such period of time as the principal considers reasonable in the circumstances.

6.   Consideration by the principal of any response provided by the teacher under paragraph 5.

7.   Preparation by the principal of a summative report of the performance appraisal, in a form approved by the Minister, containing,

    i.   the principal's evaluation of the teacher,

    ii.   the principal's overall performance rating of the teacher, and

    iii.   the principal's explanation for the rating.

8.   Provision to the teacher of a copy of the summative report, signed by the principal, within 20 school days after the classroom observation.

9.   Signature by the teacher of a copy of the summative report, to acknowledge receipt by the teacher of a copy of the report.

10.   Provision to the appropriate board of a copy of the summative report, as signed by both the principal and the teacher, and the teacher's learning plan for the year.

(3) At the request of either the teacher or the principal, the teacher and principal shall meet to discuss the performance appraisal after the teacher receives a copy of the summative report.

(4) In this section,

"**classroom observation**" includes the observation of a teacher in his or her ordinary teaching environment if that environment is not a classroom.

5. Parental and pupil input — (1) Starting in the school year commencing in 2002, every board shall develop an annual written parent survey and pupil survey in consultation with the school councils and principals for the schools governed by the board, the special education advisory committee and those parents, pupils and teachers who are interested.

(2) A parent survey must ask for parental input on each teacher of each child of the parent and the parent's level of satisfaction with communication between the parent and the teacher about the child's learning and progress.

(3) A pupil survey must ask for input from each pupil who is in a grade 11 or 12 or OAC course in a school governed by the board, relating to,

    (a)   communication between the pupil and each of the pupil's teachers of a grade 11 or 12 or OAC course; and

    (b)   whether each of the teachers effectively promotes pupil learning.

(4) The responses given in a parent survey and a pupil survey,

    (a)   must not be used for any purpose other than a performance appraisal of a teacher referred to in the responses; and

    (b)   must not be disclosed to any person other than the principal, the appropriate supervisory officer and the appropriate board, except as permitted under this Regulation.

(5) The principal shall, on the request of a parent or pupil, remove all words and names that would identify the parent or pupil from a document that contains input from the parent or pupil, including a parent survey and a pupil survey, before the document or a copy of the document is provided to a teacher.

(6) The principal shall not disclose to a teacher any parental input or pupil input that relates to another teacher.

6. Performance appraisals if teaching only one semester — If a teacher is teaching in only one semester during a year that is scheduled as an evaluation year of the teacher, all performance appraisals of the teacher required during that evaluation year must be conducted in that semester.

7. Periods of time excluded from three-year cycle — (1) For the purposes of section 277.28 of the Act, the three-year cycle of a teacher employed by a board excludes the following periods of time:

    1.   A year during which the teacher does not teach at any time in a school governed by the board.

    2.   A period in a year in the three-year cycle that is scheduled as an evaluation year for the teacher if, throughout the period, the teacher is on an extended leave that has been approved by the board.

    3.   A period when the teacher is on secondment to a non-teaching position.

4.   A period when the teacher is on secondment to a teaching position outside the Ontario public education system.

(2) If a teacher is on an extended leave during all or part of a year that is scheduled as an evaluation year, any performance appraisal that would otherwise be carried out during that period must be conducted within 60 school days after the teacher returns from leave.

8. Rules, seconded teachers — (1) The following rules apply to every teacher who is seconded to a teaching position in the Ontario public education system during a three-year cycle:

1.   The year that is scheduled as an evaluation year for the teacher during the cycle does not change.

2.   The board from which the teacher is seconded must advise the board to which the teacher is seconded of the teacher's position in the teacher's three-year cycle.

3.   The board to which the teacher is seconded shall ensure that all performance appraisals of the teacher that are required during the period the teacher is on secondment to the board are carried out.

(2) If a performance appraisal carried out while a teacher is seconded to another board results in an unsatisfactory overall performance rating, the following rules apply:

1.   The secondment agreement terminates.

2.   The performance appraisal is deemed not to have been conducted except for the purposes of terminating the secondment agreement.

3.   The teacher's three-year cycle recommences on the termination of the secondment agreement and the first year in the cycle is an evaluation year for the teacher.

4.   The board to which the teacher returns shall ensure a performance appraisal of the teacher is conducted within 60 school days after the teacher's return.

9. Records — Every board shall retain each record made under Part X.2 of the Act for a period of at least six years from the date of the summative report of the performance appraisal to which the record relates.

PART II — PROVINCIAL SCHOOLS AND DEMONSTRATION SCHOOLS
[Heading added O. Reg. 1/03, s. 2.]

10. Provincial schools — (1) Part X.2 of the Act, Part I of this Regulation, the other regulations under Part X.2 of the Act, and the guidelines, rules and policies under Part X.2 of the Act, apply to schools established or continued under subsection 13(1), (2) or (4) of the Act and to schools operated by a ministry under the *Provincial Schools Negotiations Act*, subject to such modifications as the circumstances require, including the modifications set out in this section.

(2) If a teacher employed by a board is seconded to a school referred to in subsection (1), subsection (1) does not apply to the teacher unless Part X.2 of the Act applies to the board.

(3) Despite subsection 277.15(1) of the Act and subsection 1(3) of this Regulation, in Part X.2 of the Act, Part I of this Regulation, the other regulations under Part X.2 of the Act, and the guidelines, rules and policies under Part X.2 of the Act, unless the context requires otherwise,

(a) a reference to a board shall be deemed to be a reference to the Provincial Schools Authority;

(b) a reference to the designated bargaining agent for a teachers' bargaining unit shall be deemed to be a reference to the bargaining agent referred to in subsection 5(4) of the *Provincial Schools Negotiations Act*;

(c) a reference to a teacher shall be deemed to be a reference to a teacher as defined in section 1 of the *Provincial Schools Negotiations Act*, other than a continuing education teacher;

(d) a reference to a teachers' bargaining unit shall be deemed to be a reference to the bargaining unit referred to in subsection 5(2) of the *Provincial Schools Negotiations Act*;

(e) a reference to a director of education for a board shall be deemed to be a reference to the chair of the Provincial Schools Authority;

(f) a reference to a school council shall be deemed to be a reference to any body that acts in a capacity similar to a school council; and

(g) a reference to a special education advisory committee shall be deemed to be a reference to any body that acts in a capacity similar to a special education advisory committee.

(4) Subsections 277.15(2) and (3) and sections 277.24 to 277.27 of the Act have no application to the schools referred to in subsection (1).

(5) Despite subsections 277.29(1) and (2) of the Act, for the purposes of section 277.29 of the Act,

(a) a teacher shall be considered to be new to the Provincial Schools Authority during the 24-month period following his or her being hired as a teacher by the Authority, if the teacher was not employed by the Authority as a teacher immediately before being hired;

(b) a teacher shall be considered to be new to the profession during the 24-month period following his or her being hired by the Provincial Schools Authority or a board, if the teacher has never been,

(i) employed as a teacher by a board,

(ii) employed as a teacher by the Provincial Schools Authority, or

(iii) employed as a teacher in connection with a demonstration school established or continued under section 13 of the Act; and

(c) a teacher shall not be considered new to the Provincial Schools Authority if the teacher is seconded from a board to the Authority and is not new to the board within the meaning of subsection 277.29(1) of the Act.

(6) Subsection 5(1) of this Regulation permits, but does not require, the Provincial Schools Authority to develop an annual written parent survey with respect to schools operated under the *Provincial Schools Negotiations Act* by a person or body other than the Ministry.

(7) Subsections (3) to (6) apply only for the purposes of subsection (1). O. Reg. 1/03, s. 2

11. Demonstration schools — (1) Part X.2 of the Act, Part I of this Regulation, the other regulations under Part X.2 of the Act, and the guidelines, rules and policies under Part X.2 of the Act, apply to the demonstration schools established under clause 13(5)(a) of the Act, subject to such modifications as the circumstances require, including the modifications set out in this section.

(2) If a teacher employed by a board is seconded to a school referred to in subsection (1), subsection (1) does not apply to the teacher unless Part X.2 of the Act applies to the board.

(3) Despite subsection 277.15(1) of the Act and subsection 1(3) of this Regulation, in Part X.2 of the Act, Part I of this Regulation, the other regulations under Part X.2 of the Act, and the guidelines, rules and policies under Part X.2 of the Act, unless the context requires otherwise,

(a)   a reference to a board shall be deemed to be a reference to the Ministry;

(b)   a reference to a teacher employed by a board shall be deemed to be a reference to a teacher employed by a board and seconded to a school referred to in subsection (1);

(c)   a reference to a school council shall be deemed to be a reference to any body that acts in a capacity similar to a school council; and

(d)   a reference to a special education advisory committee shall be deemed to be a reference to the Learning Disabilities Association of Ontario.

(4) Clauses (3)(a) and (b) do not apply to the following provisions with respect to a teacher that is employed by a board and seconded to a school referred to in subsection (1):

1.   Subsections 277.28(1) and (3) of the Act.

2.   Section 277.29 of the Act.

3.   Sections 277.42, 277.43 and 277.44 of the Act.

4.   Section 2 of Ontario Regulation 98/02 (Teacher Learning Plans).

(5) Despite subsections 277.15(5) and (6) of the Act,

(a)   nothing in Part X.2 of the Act, or any regulation, guideline, policy or rule under that Part, shall be interpreted to limit rights otherwise available to the Ministry or a board relating to discipline of any teacher, including but not limited to rights relating to reassignment of duties, suspension or termination of the employment of the teacher, whether or not a performance appraisal process relating to the teacher is being conducted under that Part; and

(b) nothing in Part X.2 of the Act, or any regulation, guideline, policy or rule under it, shall be interpreted to limit the Ministry's ability or a board's ability to complete a performance appraisal of a teacher begun before that Part begins to apply to the Ministry, board or teacher, or to follow any process or take any action relating to that performance appraisal that the Ministry or board might have followed or taken but for that Part.

(6) Despite subsection 277.18(3) of the Act, in the circumstances described in clause 277.18(1)(b) of the Act, where no other supervisory officer employed by the Ministry is able to perform the duty and exercise the power in a timely way, because of absence or for some other reason, a supervisory officer employed by a board may, by arrangement between the Ministry and the board, perform the duty and exercise the power.

(7) Despite clauses 277.21(1)(b) and (4)(b) of the Act, the Lieutenant Governor in Council may make regulations in relation to Part X.2 of the Act establishing rules to apply where a board seconds a teacher to the Ministry, and the regulations may assign responsibilities under that Part between the seconding board and the Ministry.

(8) Sections 277.24 to 277.27 and 277.35 to 277.41 of the Act have no application to the schools referred to in subsection (1).

(9) Subsections (3) to (8) apply only for the purposes of subsection (1). O. Reg. 1/03, s. 2

SCHEDULE — TEACHER COMPENTENCIES

Commitment to pupils and pupil learning

Teachers:

(a) demonstrate commitment to the well-being and development of all pupils,

(b) are dedicated in their efforts to teach and support pupil learning and achievement,

(c) treat all pupils equitably and with respect,

(d) provide an environment for learning that encourages pupils to be problem-solvers, decision-makers, life-long learners and contributing members of a changing society,

Professional knowledge

Teachers:

(e) know their subject matter, the Ontario curriculum and education-related legislation,

(f) know a variety of effective teaching and assessment practices,

(g) know a variety of effective classroom management strategies,

(h) know how pupils learn and factors that influence pupil learning and achievement,

Teaching practice

Teachers:

    (i)   use their professional knowledge and understanding of pupils, curriculum, legislation, teaching practices and classroom management strategies to promote the learning and achievement of their pupils,

    (j)   communicate effectively with pupils, parents and colleagues,

    (k)   conduct ongoing assessment of their pupils' progress, evaluate their achievement and report results to pupils and parents regularly,

    (l)   adapt and refine their teaching practices through continuous learning and reflection, using a variety of sources and resources,

    (m)   use appropriate technology in their teaching practices and related professional responsibilities,

Leadership and community

Teachers:

    (n)   collaborate with other teachers and school colleagues to create and sustain learning communities in their classrooms and in their schools,

    (o)   work with other professionals, parents and members of the community to enhance pupil learning, pupil achievement and school programs,

Ongoing professional learning

Teachers:

    (p)   engage in ongoing professional learning and apply it to improve their teaching practices.

REGULATIONS UNDER THE *ONTARIO COLLEGE OF TEACHERS ACT, 1996*

REGULATION 72/97
GENERAL

O. Reg. 72/97 as am. O. Reg. 392/01

Employers' Obligation to Submit Fees

1. In sections 2 to 4,

"due date" means the date on which the annual membership fee is due in any year, as specified in the by-laws; ("date d'échéance")

"private school" has the same meaning as in subsection 1(1) of the *Education Act.* ("école privée)

2. (1) Where, on the due date in any year, a school board employs a member, the school board shall,

(a) deduct the amount of the annual membership fee payable in respect of the year by the member from the member's salary; and

(b) submit the amount of the fee to the College.

(2) Where, on the due date in any year, the Provincial Schools Authority employs a member and the Ministry of Education and Training is responsible for paying the member's salary, the Ministry of Education and Training shall,

(a) deduct the amount of the annual membership fee payable in respect of the year by the member from the member's salary; and

(b) submit the amount of the fee to the College.

(3) Where, on the due date in any year, a private school employs a member who contributes to the Ontario Teachers' Pension Plan, the private school shall,

(a) deduct the amount of the annual membership fee payable in respect of the year by the member from the member's salary; and

(b) submit the amount of the fee to the College.

(4) Subsection (3) applies only if the private school has received notice that the member contributes to the Ontario Teachers' Pension Plan.

(5) The amounts referred to in subsections (1) to (3) shall be submitted no later than 35 days after the due date.

(6) The amount may be submitted by cheque or by any other means approved by the Registrar.

(7) When submitting an amount under this section, the school board, the Ministry of Education and Training or the private school, as the case may be, shall provide the Registrar with sufficient information to identify the member on whose behalf the amount is submitted.

(8) The Registrar may issue directions respecting the content and form of the information to be provided under subsection (7).

3. At the written request, made before the due date, of a school board, the Ministry of Education and Training or a private school, as the case may be, the Registrar may extend the period specified in subsection 2(5), if the Registrar is of the opinion that the extension is warranted because of exceptional circumstances.

4. (1) A school board, the Ministry of Education and Training or a private school, as the case may be, shall pay interest on any amount in arrears, from the day the amount was required to be submitted under section 2 or, where applicable, section 3, to the day before the day on which the payment is made.

(2) The interest shall be calculated at the bank prime rate plus 4 per cent per year.

(3) In subsection (2),

"bank prime rate" means the prime rate quoted by the College's bank of record on the day the payment was due.

Quorum at Council Meetings

5. Sixteen members of the Council, at least four of whom shall be persons appointed to the Council under clause 4(2)(b) of the Act, constitute a quorum of the Council.

Disqualification of Council Members

6. (1) The Council shall disqualify an elected member of the Council from sitting on the Council if the member,

(a) is found by the Discipline Committee to be guilty of professional misconduct or to be incompetent;
(b) is found by the Fitness to Practise Committee to be incapacitated;
(c) fails, without cause, to attend three consecutive meetings of the Council;
(d) fails, without cause, to attend half the meetings of the Council in any 12-month period;
(e) fails, without cause, to attend three consecutive meetings of a committee of which he or she is a member;
(f) fails, without cause, to attend a hearing of a panel of a committee for which he or she has been selected; or
(g) fails or ceases to meet the criteria set out in the regulations for eligibility to be nominated for the position for which the member was elected, as those regulations read on the day the member was declared elected.

(2) An elected member of the Council who is disqualified from sitting on the Council ceases to be a member of the Council.

(3) An elected member of the Council who is the subject of a proceeding before the

Discipline Committee or the Fitness to Practise Committee as a result of a referral under section 26 or 29 of the Act is suspended from his or her office as member of the Council pending the outcome of the proceeding.

(4) A person who is suspended under subsection (3) from his or her office as member of the Council shall not participate in any meeting or other proceeding of the Council.

Vacancies on Council

7. (1) For the purposes of this Regulation, the seat of an elected member of the Council becomes vacant if the member dies, resigns or is disqualified from sitting on the Council.

(2) For the purposes of this Regulation, the resignation of an elected member of the Council is effective when received by the Registrar, the chair or the vice-chair.

8. (1) If the seat of the elected member of the Council becomes vacant not more than six months before the expiry of the member's term of office, the Council may leave the seat vacant or may fill the vacated position by appointment.

(2) If the Council chooses to fill the vacated position by appointment, it shall appoint the person who had the most votes of all the unsuccessful candidates for the position in the last Council election, not including those persons who, as of the date of the appointment,

(a) are not willing to fill the vacancy; or
(b) do not meet the criteria set out in the regulations for eligibility to be nominated for the position, as those regulations read on the day the member was declared elected.

(3) If no person can be appointed in accordance with subsection (2), the Council may fill the vacated position by appointing any person who, as of the date of the appointment, is willing to fill the vacancy and meets the criteria set out in the regulations for eligibility to be nominated for the position, as those regulations read on the day the member was declared elected.

(4) The Council shall make its determination under subsection (1) as soon as reasonably possible and, if the Council decides to fill the vacated position, the Council shall do so as soon as reasonably possible.

9. (1) If the seat of an elected member of the Council becomes vacant more than six months before the expiry of the member's term of office, the Council shall fill the vacated position by appointing the person who had the most votes of all the unsuccessful candidates for the position in the last Council election, not including the persons who, as of the date of the appointment,

(a) are not willing to fill the vacancy; or
(b) do not meet the criteria set out in the regulations for eligibility to be nominated for the position, as those regulations read on the day the member was declared elected.

(2) If no person can be appointed in accordance with subsection (1), the Council shall fill the vacated position by appointing any person who, as of the date of the appointment, is willing to fill the vacancy and meets the criteria set out in the regulations for eligibility to be nominated for the position, as those regulations read on the day the member was declared elected.

(3) The Council shall fill the vacated position as soon as reasonably possible.

10. Within 10 days of a vacancy to which section 8 or 9 applies arising, the Registrar shall,

(a) notify the members of the Council that the vacancy has arisen;

(b) provide the members of the Council with the information that they need in order to be able to fill the vacancy; and

(c) draw the attention of the Council to its obligation under section 8 or 9, as the case may be, to act expeditiously.

11. (1) If the seat of one or more elected Council members becomes vacant and no quorum of the Council remains in office, the Registrar shall hold an election for the vacant positions and, for the purpose, shall adapt the provisions of the regulation that governed the last election to the Council, as those provisions read on the last voting day in that election, as he or she considers appropriate.

(2) Where an election is required under this section, the Registrar shall,

(a) within 10 days of the requirement to hold an election arising under subsection (1), set a date or time period during which the voting will occur; and

(b) ensure that the election is held as soon as reasonably possible.

12. A person appointed under section 8 or 9 or elected under section 11 shall hold office until the former Council member's term would have expired.

Statutory Committees

13. In sections 14 to 18,

"statutory committee" means,

(a) the Executive Committee,

(b) the Investigation Committee,

(c) the Discipline Committee,

(d) the Registration Appeals Committee, and

(e) the Fitness to Practise Committee.

14. (1) Subject to subsections 25(1), 27(1) and 28(1) of the Act, the Council shall determine the number of members to be appointed by it to the Investigation Committee, the Discipline Committee and the Fitness to Practise Committee.

(2) The members of a statutory committee to be appointed by the Council shall be appointed as soon as reasonably possible.

(3) A person appointed to a statutory committee shall continue to be a member of the committee until the first meeting of the next Council.

(4) Subject to subsection 20(1), the Council shall appoint a chair for each statutory committee, from among the members appointed to the committee.

(5) Subject to subsection 20(2), a statutory committee shall elect a vice-chair from among its members.

(6) In the absence of the chair of a statutory committee, the vice-chair shall temporarily act as and have all the powers of the chair.

(7) In the absence of the chair of a statutory committee, the vice-chair shall temporarily act as and have all the powers of the chair.

(8) The chair of a statutory committee may vote at meetings of the committee.

15. (1) Subject to subsection (4), a quorum of the Investigation Committee, the Discipline Committee or the Fitness to Practise Committee is a majority of the number of positions on the committee, as determined under subsection 14(1), whether or not one or more of the positions is vacant.

(2) Subject to subsection (4), a quorum of the Registration Appeals Committee is three.

(3) Subject to subsection (4), a quorum of the Executive Committee if four.

(4) A quorum of a statutory committee is not constituted unless at least one of the members of the committee participating in the meeting is a person appointed to the Council under clause 4(2)(b) of the Act.

16. (1) The seat of a member of a statutory committee becomes vacant if the member dies, resigns from the committee, resigns from the Council or is disqualified from sitting on the Council.

(2) For the purposes of this Regulation, the resignation of a member of a statutory committee from the committee is effective when received by the Registrar or the chair of the committee.

(3) If the seat of a member of a statutory committee becomes vacant, the Executive Committee shall, as soon as reasonably possible, appoint a member of the Council to fill the vacancy.

(4) Subsection (3) does not apply to vacancies on the Executive Committee.

(5) If the seat of a member of the Executive Committee becomes vacant, the Council shall, as soon as reasonably possible, appoint one of its members to fill the vacancy.

(6) In filling a vacancy under this section, the Executive Committee or Council, as the case may be, shall ensure that the requirements of subsections 25(2), 27(2) and 28(2) of the Act and of section 19 and subsections 23(2) and (3) of this Regulation are complied with.

(7) Within 10 days of a vacancy to which subsection (3) or (5) applies arising, the Registrar shall,

(a) notify the members of the Executive Committee or Council, as the case may be, that the vacancy has arisen;
(b) provide the members of the Executive Committee or the Council, as the case may be, with the information that they need in order to be able to fill the vacancy; and
(c) draw the attention of the Executive Committee or the Council, as the case may be, to its obligation under this section to act expeditiously.

(8) A person appointed under this section shall hold office until the former committee member's term would have expired.

(9) A person who is suspended under subsection 6(3) from his or her office as mem-

ber of the Council is also suspended from his or her office as member of a statutory condition.

(10) A person who is suspended under subsection (9) from his or her office as member of a committee shall not participate in any meeting or other proceeding of the committee or of a panel of the committee.

17. (1) Each statutory committee shall meet at least once a year.

(2) Each statutory committee shall meet,

(a) when requested by its chair;
(b) when requested in writing signed by a sufficient number of members to constitute a quorum under section 15;
(c) when requested by the Council; or
(d) when requested by the Executive Committee.

18. (1) A meeting of a statutory committee may be held by any means that permit every person participating in the meeting to communicate with each other simultaneously.

(2) The chair of a statutory committee shall ensure that minutes are,

(a) taken at each meeting;
(b) reviewed and approved at the meeting following the one at which they are taken; and
(c) signed by the chair after approval.

(3) Subsections (1) and (2) apply with necessary modifications to a meeting of a panel of a statutory committee.

(4) This section does not apply to a hearing of a statutory committee or of a panel of a statutory committee.

Executive Committee

19. (1) The Council shall appoint the chairs of the following committees as members of the Executive Committee:

1. The Fitness to Practise Committee.
2. The Discipline Committee.
3. The Registration Appeals Committee.
4. The Investigation Committee.
5. The Standards of Practice and Education Committee.
6. The Finance Committee.
7. The Accreditation Committee.

(2) The Council shall also appoint the chair and vice-chair of the Council as members of the Executive Committee, where they are not appointed under subsection (1).

(3) The Council shall appoint additional members to the Executive Committee in accordance with the following rules, where applicable:

1. If all persons appointed under subsections (1) and (2) are members of the Council elected under clause 4(2)(a) of the Act, the Council shall appoint two additional

persons to the Executive Committee, both of whom shall be members of the Council appointed under clause 4(2)(b) of the Act.

2. If only one of the persons appointed under subsections (1) and (2) is a member of the Council appointed under clause 4(2)(b) of the Act, the Council shall appoint one additional person to the Executive Committee, who shall be a member of the Council appointed under clause 4(2)(b) of the Act.

3. If all the persons appointed under subsections (1) and (2) are members of the Council appointed under clause 4(2)(b) of the Act, the Council shall appoint two additional persons to the Executive Committee, both of whom shall be members of the Council elected under clause 4(2)(a) of the Act.

4. If only one of the persons appointed under subsections (1) and (2) is a member of the Council elected under clause 4(2)(a) of the Act, the Council shall appoint one additional person to the Executive Committee, who shall be a member of the Council elected under clause 4(2)(a) of the Act.

20. (1) The chair of the Council shall be the chair of the Executive Committee.

(2) The vice-chair of the Council shall be the vice-chair of the Executive Committee.

Roster of Eligible Panelists
[Heading added O. Reg. 392/01, s. 1.]

20.1 The appointment of a person by the Lieutenant Governor in Council under subsection 17(4) of the Act to a roster of eligible panelists for a Committee mentioned in paragraph 2, 3, 4 or 5 of subsection 15(1) of the Act is for the term specified in the appointment. O. Reg. 391/01, s. 1

Investigation Committee

21. (1) A complaint to be considered and investigated by the Investigation Committee under section 26 of the Act shall be considered and investigated by a panel of the Committee selected for the purpose in accordance with section 17 of the Act by the chair of the Committee.

(2) The chair of the Committee shall appoint as the chair of the panel a member of the panel who is a member of the Committee.

(3) If a panelist's term of appointment to the Committee or to the roster of eligible panelists for the Committee ends before the consideration and investigation of the complaint is completed or the panel's decision is given, the panelist's term is deemed to continue for the purpose of participation in the decision.

(4) A panel may exercise all the powers and carry out all the duties of the Committee with respect to the complaint before the panel. O. Reg. 392/01, s. 2

Discipline Committee

22. (1) A hearing on matters directed or referred to the Discipline Committee under section 26, 29 or 33 of the Act shall be conducted by a panel of the Committee selected for the purpose in accordance with section 17 of the Act by the chair of the Committee.

(2) The chair of the Committee shall appoint as the chair of the panel a member of the panel who is a member of the Committee.

(3) If a panelist's term of appointment to the Committee or to the roster of eligible panelists for the Committee ends before the hearing is completed or the panel's decision is given, the panelist's term is deemed to continue for the purpose of participation in the decision.

(4) A panel may exercise all the powers and carry out all the duties of the Committee with respect to the matter before the panel. O. Reg. 392/01, s. 3

Registration Appeals Committee

23. (1) The Council shall appoint five of its members to the Registration Appeals Committee.

(2) At least two of the members of the Registration Appeals Committee shall be persons appointed to the Council under clause 4(2)(b) of the Act.

(3) At least two of the members of the Registration Appeals Committee shall be persons elected to the Council under clause 4(2)(a) of the Act.

24. (1) A request for review under section 21 of the Act or an application for variation under section 22 of the Act shall be decided by a panel of the Registration Appeals Committee selected for the purpose in accordance with section 17 of the Act by the chair of the Committee.

(2) The chair of the Committee shall appoint as the chair of the panel a member of the panel who is a member of the Committee.

(3) If a panelist's term of appointment to the Committee or to the roster of eligible panelists for the Committee ends before the proceeding is completed or the panel's decision is given, the panelist's term is deemed to continue for the purpose of participation in the decision.

(4) A panel may exercise all the powers and carry out all the duties of the Committee with respect to the matter before the panel. O. Reg. 392/01, s. 4

Fitness to Practise Committee

25. (1) A hearing on matters directed or referred to the Fitness to Practise Committee under section 26, 29 or 33 of the Act shall be conducted by a panel of the Committee selected for the purpose in accordance with section 17 of the Act by the chair of the Committee.

(2) The chair of the Committee shall appoint as the chair of the panel a member of the panel who is a member of the Committee.

(3) If a panelist's term of appointment to the Committee or to the roster of eligible panelists for the Committee ends before the hearing is completed or the panel's decision is given, the panelist's term is deemed to continue for the purpose of participation in the decision.

(4) A panel may exercise all the powers and carry out all the duties of the Committee with respect to the matter before the panel. O. Reg. 392/01, s. 5

Designation for Purposes of Section 47 of the Act

26. The following persons or bodies are designated for the purposes of subsection 47(1) of the Act:

1. A private school, as defined in subsection 1(1) of the *Education Act*, in respect of which a current notice of intention has been filed under section 16 of that Act.
2. A college of applied arts and technology established under section 5 of the *Ministry of Colleges and Universities Act.*
3. An institution specified in the Schedule to the *University Foundations Act, 1992.*
4. The Ontario Teachers' Pension Plan Board.
5. The Ontario Teachers' Federation.
6. L'Association des enseignantes et des enseignants franco-ontariens.
7. The Elementary Teachers' Federation of Ontario.
8. The Ontario English Catholic Teachers' Association.
9. [Revoked O. Reg. 392/01, s. 6(2).]
10. The Ontario Secondary School Teachers' Federation.

O. Reg. 392/01, s. 6

REGULATION 184/97
TEACHERS QUALIFICATIONS

O. Reg. 184/97 as am. O. Reg. 505/00; 373/01; 50/04

DEFINITIONS

1. (1) In this Regulation,

"acceptable university degree" means a degree that is,

    (a) granted by an Ontario university that is an ordinary member of the Association of Universities and Colleges of Canada,

    (b) granted by a Canadian university in a province other than Ontario that is an ordinary member of the Association of Universities and Colleges of Canada, and is a degree that is considered by the College to be equivalent to a degree referred to in clause (a),

    (c) granted by a university in the United States that is recognized by,

        (i) Middle States Association of Colleges and Schools,

        (ii) New England Association of Schools and Colleges,

        (iii) North Central Association of Colleges and Schools,

        (iv) Northwest Association of Schools and Colleges,

        (v) Southern Associatin of Colleges and Schools, or

        (vi) Western Association of Schools and Colleges

        and is considered by the College to be equivalent to a degree referred to in clause (a), and

    (d) granted by a university that is located in a country other than Canada and the United States and that is considered by the College to be equivalent to a degree referred to in clause (a);

"appropriate supervisory officer" means, in respect of a teacher, the supervisory officer assigned by a board in accordance with the *Education Act* and the regulations under it or by the Minister to provide supervisory services in respect of the performance by the teacher of his or her duties under the *Education Act* and the regulations under it;

"approved program" means a program approved by the College;

"band" and "council of the band" have the same meaning as in the *Indian Act* (Canada);

"candidate" means a candidate for any qualifications granted in a Certificate of Qualification under this Regulation;

"certificate of qualification" means a certificate of qualification referred to in subsection (2);

"division" means the primary division, junior division, intermediate division or senior division, as defined in the *Education Act*;

"general studies" means the courses developed from curriculum guidelines that are issued by the Minister for the intermediate division and senior division and listed under a heading other than "Technological Studies" in Appendix B to OSIS;

"holds a degree" means, in respect of a candidate, that he or she has completed all the requirements for and has been approved for, the granting of a degree, regardless of whether or not the degree has been conferred;

"OSIS" means the circular entitled "Ontario Schools Intermediate and Senior Divisions Program and Diploma Requirements" issued by the Minister including any document issued by the Minister in accordance with paragraphs 1, 2, 3, 4 and 25 of subsection 8(1) of the *Education Act*;

"program of professional education" means a program approved by the College and conducted at a college, faculty or school of education in Ontario that includes,

    (a) a concentrated study of,
        (i) the primary and junior divisions, with or without a focus on the teaching of French as a second language,
       (ii) the junior division and one optional course from Schedule A that is in the intermediate division and a course related to grades 7 and 8 of the intermediate division,
      (iii) the intermediate and senior divisions including two optional courses from Schedule A, or
      (iv) technological studies, including a minimum of two optional courses from Schedule B at the basic level, or one optional course from Schedule B at the basic level and the other such course at the advanced level,
    (b) studies in education including learning and development throughout the primary, junior, intermediate and senior division,
    (c) teaching methods designed to meet the individual needs of pupils,
    (d) the acts and regulations respecting education,
    (e) a review of the curriculum guidelines issued by the Minister related to all of the divisions and a study of curriculum development, and
    (f) a minimum of 40 days of practical experience in schools or in other situations approved by the College for observation and practice teaching;

"technological qualifications" means, in respect of a candidate for a certificate of qualification, an interim certificate of qualification or a certificate of qualification (limited, restricted),

    (a) the holding of the secondary school graduation diploma or the successful completion of courses that are considered by the College to be the equivalent of such diploma,
    (b) proof of his or her competence in the area or areas of technological studies selected as options in the program of professional education, and
    (c) one of,
        (i) five years of wage-earning, business or industrial experience in the area or areas of technological studies selected as options in the program of professional education,
       (ii) a combination of education related to the area or areas of technological studies selected as options in the program of professional education beyond that referred to in clause (a) and business or industrial experience in the area or areas of technological studies selected as options in the program of technological studies that totals five years, including at least two years of wage-earning experience, no less than 16 months of which is continuous employment, or
      (iii) at least 3,700 hours of wage-earning experience and successful completion

of a post-secondary education program acceptable to the College that includes at least 24 months of academic studies, if the wage-earning experience and the education program are related to the area or areas of technological studies selected as options in the program of professional education;

"technological studies" means the courses developed from curriculum guidelines issued by the Minister and entitled "Broad-Based Technological Education, Grades 10, 11 and 12, 1995" and "Technological Studies, Intermediate and Senior Divisions, Part C: Ontario Academic Courses, 1987";

"university course" means a one-year university course beyond the Ontario Academic Credit level, or the equivalent of such one-year university course, where the course is part of a program leading to an acceptable university degree;

"university credit" means a unit of recognition in respect of the successful completion of a university course, such that 60 such university credits are required to complete a four-year university program leading to an acceptable university degree.

(2) The following shall be two classes of certificates of qualification and registration:

1. A certificate of registration, which shall set out the holder's membership relationship with the College.
2. A certificate of qualification, which shall set out the holder's qualifications for teaching.

PART I

BASIC QUALIFICATIONS

2. A candidate for the certificate of qualification shall submit to the dean of a college or faculty of education or the director of a school of education in Ontario,

(a) a certificate of birth or baptism, or other acceptable proof of the date and place of birth;

(b) in the case of a candidate who is a married woman who wishes to have her certificate issued in her married name, a certificate of marriage or other acceptable proof that she is the person referred to in the certificate or other document submitted under clause (a);

(c) a certificate of change of name where applicable;

(d) evidence satisfactory to such dean or director of his or her academic or technological qualifications;

(e) in the case of a person who was not born in Canada, the basis upon which the candidate is present in Canada;

(f) proof of freedom from active tuberculosis.

3. The Registrar may grant a certificate of qualification to a candidate, in the form provided in the by-laws of the College and indicating the areas of concentration the candidate has successfully completed, if,

(a) the dean of a college or faculty of education or the director of a school of education in Ontario reports to the Registrar that the candidate,

(i) has complied with section 2,

      (ii) holds an acceptable university degree or qualifications the College considers equivalent thereto, or technological qualifications, and

      (iii) has successfully completed a program of professional education; and

  (b) the candidate has passed the qualifying test under section 10.1 of the *Education Act*, unless the candidate is not required under that Act to pass the test before the certificate may be granted. O. Reg. 50/04, s. 1

4. (1) An entry on a certificate of qualification in respect of a program successfully completed in Canada shall indicate by the language in which the entry is recorded whether the program was taken in English or in French.

(2) An entry on a certificate of qualification in respect of a program successfully completed out of Canada shall indicate by the language in which the entry is recorded whether the qualification referred to is for teaching in schools and classes where English is the language of instruction or in French-language schools and classes established under Part XII of the *Education Act*.

(3) Despite section 14, qualifications valid in French-language schools and classes established under Part XII of the *Education Act* are valid in French-language classes where the teacher may otherwise be assigned or appointed to teach according to subsection 19(14) of Regulation 298 of the Revised Regulations of Ontario, 1990.

5. An entry on a certificate of qualification in respect of a program in International Languages shall specify which language was studied in the program.

6. (1) Where the dean of a college or faculty of education or the director of a school of education in Ontario reports to the Registrar that a candidate,

  (a) has complied with section 2;

  (b) is of native ancestry;

  (c) holds the requirements for a Secondary School Graduation Diploma or standing the College considers equivalent thereto; and

  (d) has successfully completed a program of professional education with concentration in the primary division and the junior division,

the Registrar may grant to the candidate a certificate of qualification in the form provided for in the by-laws of the College.

(2) The Registrar may grant to a candidate a certificate of qualification (limited) valid for one year for teaching in the primary division and junior division if the dean of a college or faculty of education or the director of a school of education in Ontario reports to the Registrar that the candidate meets the qualifications of clauses (1)(a) to (c) and has successfully completed the first session of a program of professional education with concentration in the primary division and the junior division.

(3) The certificate of qualification (limited) granted under subsection (2) shall be in the form provided for in the by-laws of the College.

(4) The Registrar may renew a candidate's certificate of qualification (limited) for one year for teaching in the primary division and junior division if the candidate submits to the Registrar evidence that the candidate,

  (a) holds a certificate of qualification (limited) granted under subsection (2) that has expired or is about to expire; and

(b) has an offer of a position as a teacher in the primary division or junior division from

    (i) a board,

    (ii) a private school,

    (iii) the Provincial Schools Authority established under section 2 of the *Provincial Schools Negotiations Act*,

    (iv) the Department of Indian Affairs and Northern Development of the Government of Canada, or

    (v) a council of a band or an education authority, if the council of the band or the education authority is authorized by the Crown in right of Canada to provide education for Indians.

7. (1) Where the dean of a college or faculty of education or the director of a school of education in Ontario at the time of making a report under section 3, 6, 8 or 11 is of the opinion from the information provided under section 2 by the candidate in respect of whom the report is to be made, that the candidate is not entitled under the laws of Canada to obtain employment as a teacher in Canada, the dean or director at the time of making the report shall so inform the Registrar.

(2) Where the Registrar is informed as set out in subsection (1), the Registrar may refuse to grant the certificate referred to in section 3 or 6 or in the subsection 11(2), as the case may be, or may withhold the certificate of qualification (limited) referred to in section 8 or it extension under subsection 11(1), until the candidate provides proof to the Registrar that the candidate is entitled under the laws of Canada to obtain employment as a teacher in Canada.

8. Where the dean of a college or faculty of education or the director of a school of education in Ontario reports to the Registrar that a candidate,

(a) has complied with section 2;

(b) holds an acceptable university degree or qualifications the College considers equivalent thereto or technological qualifications; and

(c) has successfully completed the first session of a program of professional education,

the Registrar may grant to the candidate a certificate of qualification (limited) in the form provided for in the by-laws of the College.

9. Where a person who is the holder of a certificate of qualification (limited) granted under section 8 that has expired, or is about to expire, submits to the Registrar evidence that he or she has an offer of a position as a teacher from,

(a) a board;

(b) a private school;

(c) the Provincial Schools Authority established under section 2 of the *Provincial Schools Negotiations Act*;

(d) the Department of Indian Affairs and Northern Development of the Government of Canada; or

(e) a council of a band or an education authority where such council of the band or education authority is authorized by the Crown in right of Canada to provide education for Indians,

the Registrar may renew the certificate of qualification (limited) for a period of one year.

10. For the purposes of section 11, a person who holds a Temporary Elementary School Certificate or a Temporary Secondary School Certificate is deemed to hold a certificate of qualification (limited) granted on the date of his or her Temporary Elementary School Certificate or his or her Temporary Secondary School Certificate.

11. (1) Where the dean of a college or faculty of education or the director of a school of education in Ontario reports to the Registrar that a person who holds a certificate of qualification (limited),

(a) has taught successfully for one school year in Ontario as certified by the appropriate supervisory officer; and
(b) has successfully completed the second session of a program of professional education where such second session is not the final session of the program,

the Registrar may extend the person's certificate of qualification (limited) for one year.

(2) Where the dean of a college or a faculty of education or the director of a school of education in Ontario reports to the Registrar that a candidate who holds a certificate of qualification (limited),

(a) has taught successfully in Ontario, as certified by the appropriate supervisory officer, for one school year after the granting of a certificate of qualification (limited) and after its extension where it was extended; and
(b) has successfully completed the final session of a program of professional education,

the Registrar may grant to the candidate a certificate of qualification in the form provided for in the by-laws of the College, indicating the areas of concentration successfully completed.

12. (1) An applicant for an interim certificate of qualification who completed a teacher education program outside Ontario shall submit to the Registrar with the application,

(a) the items required to be submitted under section 2;
(b) evidence of his or her academic or technological qualifications;
(c) his or her teaching certificate and a transcript of his or her teacher education program;
(d) a statement from the issuing authority that his or her teaching certificate has not been suspended or cancelled;
(e) where the candidate is not a Canadian citizen or a permanent resident of Canada, evidence that the candidate is entitled under the laws of Canada to obtain employment in Canada as a teacher; and
(f) such evidence as the Registrar may require of successful teaching experience in schools and programs similar to those for which the interim certificate of qualification applied for is valid.

13. (1) The Registrar may grant an interim certificate of qualification to an applicant under section 12 if the Registrar is satisfied that,

(a) the applicant has complied with section 12;
(b) the applicant has successfully completed a teacher education program acceptable to the College,
  (i) in a Canadian province other than Ontario or a Canadian territory, or
  (ii) outside Canada;
(c) the applicant holds the academic or technological qualifications required for a certificate of qualification; and

(d)   the applicant has passed the qualifying test under section 10.1 of the *Education Act*, unless the applicant is not required under that Act to pass that test before the certificate may be granted.

(2) An interim certificate of qualification granted under this section shall be in the form provided for in the by-laws and shall be valid for six years from the date of issue.

(3) Despite subsections (1) and (2), the following rules apply if an interim certificate of qualification referred to in this section was granted after March 14, 2002 and before the day section 13.2 comes into force to an applicant who is required to pass the qualifying test under section 10.1 of the *Education Act* but has not done so on or before the day section 13.2 comes into force:

1.   The certificate shall be deemed, as of the day section 13.2 comes into force, to be an interim certificate of qualification (provisional) referred to in that section, valid for one year from the day the interim certificate of qualification was granted.
2.   The interim certificate of qualification (provisional) referred to in paragraph 1 shall be deemed to have been granted on the day the interim certificate of qualification was granted. O. Reg. 505/00, s. 2; 50/04, s. 2

13.1 (1) The Registrar may grant an interim certificate of qualification (limited) to an applicant under section 12 if the Registrar is satisfied that,

(a)   the applicant has complied with section 12;
(b)   the applicant holds a valid teaching certificate for a Canadian province other than Ontario or for a Canadian territory;
(c)   the applicant does not have the academic or technological qualifications required for a certificate of qualification or has not successfully completed a teacher education program acceptable to the College; and
(d)   the applicant has passed the qualifying test under section 10.1 of the *Education Act*, unless the applicant is not required under that Act to pass that test before the certificate may be granted.

(2) The Registrar may impose conditions on an interim certificate of qualification (limited) relating to any of the following:

1.   Requiring the holder to obtain the academic or technological qualifications required for a certificate of qualification.
2.   Requiring the holder to complete successfully a program of professional education, as defined in subsection 1(1).
3.   Requiring the holder to obtain, while holding the interim certificate of qualification (limited), at least 10 months of successful teaching experience in Ontario and to have such experience certified by the appropriate supervisory officer.

(3) An interim certificate of qualification (limited) must be in the form provided for in the by-laws and is valid for an initial term of three years from the date it is granted.

(4) The Registrar may extend the period of validity of a person's interim certificate of qualification (limited) granted under subsection (1) for an additional term of three years if,

(a)   the person requests the extension before the end of the initial term of the certificate;
(b)   the person is a member in good standing of the College; and

(c) the Registrar is satisfied that the person has taken reasonable steps during the initial term of the certificate to meet approximately half of the conditions the Registrar has imposed on the certificate.

(5) If the Registrar has extended the period of validity of a person's interim certificate of qualification (limited) under subsection (4), the Registrar may extend its period of validity again for not more than three additional consecutive terms of one year each, if,

(a) the person requests the extension before the end of the most recent extended term of the certificate;
(b) the person is a member in good standing of the College; and
(c) the Registrar is satisfied that there are exceptional circumstances that have prevented the person from meeting all of the conditions the Registrar has imposed on the certificate.

(6) After the third extension under subsection (5) of the period of validity of an interim certificate of qualification (limited), the Registrar shall not extend its period of validity again.

(7) Despite subsections (1) to (6), the following rules apply if an interim certificate of qualification (limited) referred to in this section was granted after March 14, 2002 and before the day section 13.3 comes into force to an applicant who is required to pass the qualifying test under section 10.1 of the *Education Act* but has not done so on or before the day section 13.3 comes into force:

1. The certificate shall be deemed, as of the day section 13.3 comes into force, to be an interim certificate of qualification (limited, provisional) referred to in that section, valid for one year from the day the interim certificate of qualification (limited) was granted.
2. The interim certificate of qualification (limited, provisional) referred to in paragraph 1 shall be deemed to have been granted on the day the interim certificate of qualification (limited) was granted. O. Reg. 373/01, s. 1; 50/04, s. 3

13.2 (1) The Registrar may grant an interim certificate of qualification (provisional), valid for one year, to an applicant who is required to pass the qualifying test under section 10.1 of the *Education Act* but has not done so, if the Registrar is satisfied that the applicant has satisfied the requirements of clauses 13(1)(a) to (c).

(2) An interim certificate of qualification referred to in section 13 may be granted to the holder of an interim certificate of qualification (provisional) referred to in subsection (1) if the holder passes the qualifying test under section 10.1 of the *Education Act*,

(a) within the one-year period after the date the interim certificate of qualification (provisional) was granted; or
(b) within the one-year period referred to in subsection 13(3), in the case of a certificate that is deemed under that subsection to be an interim certificate of qualification (provisional).

(3) An interim certificate of qualification referred to in subsection (2) is valid for a period of six years from the date that the interim certificate of qualification (provisional) referred to in that subsection was granted or is deemed to have been granted. O. Reg. 50/04, s. 4

13.3 (1) The Registrar may grant an interim certificate of qualification (limited, provisional), valid for one year to an applicant who is required to pass the qualifying test under section 10.1 of the *Education Act* but has not done so, if the Registrar if satisfied that the applicant has satisfied the requirements of clauses 13.1(1)(a) to (c).

(2) An interim certificate of qualification (limited) referred to in section 13.1 may be granted to the holder of an interim certificate of qualification (limited, provisional) referred to in subsection (1) if the holder passes the qualifying test under section 10.1 of the *Education Act*,

(a) within the one-year period after the date the interim certificate of qualification (limited, provisional) was granted; or

(b) within the one-year period referred to in subsection 13.1(7), in the case of a certificate that is deemed under that subsection to be an interim certificate of qualification (limited, provisional).

(3) An interim certificate of qualification (limited) referred to in subsection (2) is valid for three years from the date the interim certificate of qualification (limited, provisional) referred to in that subsection was granted or is deemed to have been granted.

(4) The Registrar may impose any conditions on an interim certificate of qualification (limited, provisional) that the Registrar may impose on an interim certificate qualification (limited) under subsection (2) of section 13.1. O. Reg. 50/04, s. 4

14. Sections 12, 13, 14 and 15 of this Regulation, as they read on the day before Ontario Regulation 505/00 is filed, continue to apply with respect to every person to whom a letter of eligibility was issued before that day if it was still in effect under those sections on that day. O. Reg. 505/00, s. 2

15. [Revoked O. Reg. 505/00, s. 2.]

16. The Registrar may grant an interim certificate of qualification, in the form provided for in the by-laws that is valid for a period of one year from the date of issue to a person who,

(a) was the holder of a letter of standing that was issued under Parts I, II, and IV of Ontario Regulation 295/73 and that had the force of an Interim Certificate referred to in subsection 28(1); and

(b) is not the holder of a certificate of qualification or an interim certificate of qualification and who is offered a position as a teacher by,

(i) a board,

(ii) a private school,

(iii) the Provincial Schools Authority established under section 2 of the *Provincial Schools Negotiations Act,*

(iv) the Department of Indian Affairs and Northern Development of the Government of Canada, or

(v) a council of a band or an education authority, where such council of the band or education authority is authorized by the Crown in right of Canada to provide education for Indians.

17. (1) Where a person who holds an interim certificate of qualification granted under section 13 or 16, that is still valid or that has expired, submits to the Registrar evidence that the person had, while the person was the holder of the interim certificate of qualification, at least ten months of successful teaching experience in Ontario as certified by the appropriate supervisory officer, the Registrar may grant to the person a certificate of qualification in the form provided for in the by-laws, indicating the areas of concentration successfully completed.

(2) Where an interim certificate of qualification issued under section 13 or 16 expires, the person who is the holder of the interim certificate of qualification is not eligible for another interim certificate of qualification. O. Reg. 505/00, s. 3

17.1 The Registrar may grant to a person a certificate of qualification in the form provided for in the by-laws, indicating the areas of concentration successfully completed, if,

    (a) the person has been granted an interim certificate of qualification (limited) under section 13.1, regardless of whether the interim certificate of qualification (limited) is still valid or has expired; and

    (b) the Registrar is satisfied that, before the expiry of the person's interim certificate of qualification (limited), including any extensions of its period of validity, the person met all of the conditions the Registrar imposed on the interim certificate of qualification (limited). O. Reg. 373/01, s. 1

18. (1) Where a person who holds an interim certificate of qualification granted under section 13 or 16 that has expired or is about to expire, submits to the Registrar,

    (a) evidence that the person had while the person was the holder of the interim certificate of qualification fewer than 10 months of successful teaching experience in Ontario, as certified by the appropriate supervisory officer; and

    (b) evidence that the person has an offer of a position as a teacher from,

        (i) a board,

        (ii) a private school,

        (iii) the Provincial Schools Authority established under section 2 of the *Provincial Schools Negotiations Act*,

        (iv) the Department of Indian Affairs and Northern Development of the Government of Canada, or

        (v) a council of a band or an education authority established by two or more bands where such council of the band or education authority is authorized by the Crown in right of Canada to provide education for Indians.

the Registrar may, despite subsection 17(2), extend the period of validity of the interim certificate of qualification that has expired or is about to expire, as the case may be, for one year periods.

(2) Where the Registrar extends the period of validity of an interim certificate of qualification under subsection (1), the interim certificate of qualification issued to the person shall be altered to indicate the extended period of validity. O. Reg. 505/00, s. 4

18.1 If an interim certificate of qualification (provisional) referred to in subsection 13(3) or section 13.2 or an interim certificate of qualification (limited, provisional) referred to in subsection 13.1(7) or section 13.3 expires without the holder qualifying for an interim certificate of qualification or an interim certificate of qualification (limited), the holder of the certificate is not eligible for another interim certificate of qualification (provisional) or interim certificate of qualification (limited, provisional). O. Reg. 50/04, s. 4

19. (1) Where the dean of a college or faculty of education or the director of a school of education in Ontario reports to the Registrar that a candidate,

    (a) has complied with section 2;

    (b) is entitled under the laws of Canada to obtain employment in Canada as a teacher, if the candidate is not a Canadian citizen or a permanent resident of Canada;

    (c) is unable to undertake a program leading to the certificate of qualification by reason of impaired hearing;

    (d) holds an acceptable university degree or qualifications the College considers equivalent thereto; and

    (e) has successfully completed an approved program of teacher education for teaching the deaf,

the Registrar may grant to the candidate a certificate of qualification (restricted) that is in the form provided for in the by-laws and valid in Ontario for teaching the deaf.

(2) The Registrar may grant a certificate of qualification (limited, restricted) valid for one year for teaching the deaf to a candidate who has successfully completed an approved program of teacher education outside Ontario for teaching the deaf, if the candidate submits to the Registrar,

    (a) evidence that the candidate has complied with section 2;

    (b) evidence that the candidate is deaf or hard of hearing;

    (c) evidence that the candidate is a Canadian citizen or a permanent resident of Canada or is entitled under the laws of Canada to obtain employment in Canada as a teacher;

    (d) evidence that the candidate holds an acceptable university degree or qualifications that the College considers equivalent to an acceptable university degree; and

    (e) if the candidate is qualified to teach outside Ontario,

        (i) the candidate's teaching certificate and a transcript of the candidate's teacher education program, and

       (ii) a statement from the authority that issued the candidate's teaching certificate that the certificate has not been suspended or cancelled.

(3) The certificate of qualification (limited, restricted) granted under subsection (2) shall be in the form provided for in the by-laws.

(4) The Registrar may extend a certificate of qualification (limited, restricted) granted under subsection (2) for one-year periods.

(5) The Registrar may grant a certificate of qualification (restricted) for teaching the deaf to a person who holds a certificate of qualification (limited, restricted) granted under subsection (2) if the person submits to the Registrar evidence of at least one year of experience successfully teaching the deaf in Ontario since the granting of the certificate of qualification (limited, restricted), as certified by the appropriate supervisory officer.

(6) The certificate of qualification (restricted) granted under subsection (5) shall be in the form provided for in the by-laws.

20. Where the principal of a course leading to the additional qualification of Part I Special Education, or the dean of a college or faculty of education or the director of a school of education in Ontario, repots to the Registrar that a candidate,

    (a) holds one of,

        (i) a Diploma in Pre-School Education obtained at Ryerson Polytechnic University,

       (ii) a Diploma in Child Study obtained at the Institute of Child Study of the University of Toronto, or

      (iii) a Diploma in Early Childhood Education obtained at an Ontario college of applied arts and technology;

    (b) has complied with section 2;

    (c) has successfully completed the program for Part I Special Education including Part I of the Teaching Trainable Retarded option; and

    (d) is entitled under the laws of Canada to obtain employment in Canada as a teacher, if the candidate is not a Canadian citizen or a permanent resident of Canada,

the Registrar may grant to the candidate a certificate of qualification (limited, restricted), in the form provided for in the by-laws, that is valid for one year for teaching in schools or classes for the trainable retarded.

21. Where a person who is the holder of a certificate of qualification (limited, restricted) granted under section 20 that has expired, or is about to expire, submits to the Registrar evidence that he or she has an offer of a position as a teacher in schools or classes for the trainable retarded, the Registrar may renew the certificate of qualification (limited, restricted) for a period of one year.

22. Where the principal of a course leading to the additional qualification of Part II Special Education, or the dean of a college or faculty of education or the director of a school of education in Ontario reports to the Registrar that a candidate,

    (a) holds a certificate of qualification (limited, restricted) granted under section 20;

    (b) has taught successfully for one year in Ontario in a school or class for the trainable retarded as certified by the appropriate supervisory officer;

    (c) is entitled under the laws of Canada to obtain employment in Canada as a teacher, if the candidate is not a Canadian citizen or a permanent resident of Canada; and

    (d) has successfully completed the program for Part II Special Education including Part II of the Teaching Trainable Retarded option,

the Registrar may grant to the candidate a certificate of qualification (restricted), in the form provided for in the by-laws, that is valid for teaching in schools or classes for the trainable retarded.

23. (1) The Registrar may grant to a candidate a certificate of qualification (limited, restricted) valid for one year for the teaching of a Native language as a second language if the dean of a college or faculty of education or the director of a school of education in Ontario reports to the Registrar that the candidate,

    (a) has demonstrated an acceptable degree of fluency in the Algonquin or Iroquoian language;

    (b) has complied with section 2;

    (c) has successfully completed the first session of an approved program for Teacher of a Native Language as a Second Language; and

    (d) is entitled under the laws of Canada to obtain employment in Canada as a teacher, if the candidate is not a Canadian citizen or a permanent resident of Canada.

    (2) A certificate of qualification (limited, restricted) granted under subsection (1) shall be in the form provided for in the by-laws.

24. The Registrar may extend a candidate's certificate of qualification (limited, restricted) for one year for the teaching of a Native language as a second language if the dean of a college or faculty of education or the director of a school of education in Ontario reports to the Registrar that the candidate,

    (a) holds a certificate of qualification (limited, restricted) granted under section 23;

(b) has submitted evidence of at least one year of successful teaching experience in a Native language as a second language, as certified by,

    (i) the appropriate supervisory officer, where the successful teaching experience was in Ontario and was not in a school operated on an Indian reserve, or

    (ii) the appropriate supervisory official, where the successful teaching experience was outside Ontario or in a school operated on an Indian reserve in Ontario; and

(c) has successfully completed the second session of an approved program for Teacher of a Native Language as a Second Language after completing the experience referred to in clause (b).

25. (1) The Registrar may grant to a candidate a certificate of qualification (restricted) for the teaching of a Native language as a second language if the dean of a college or faculty of education or the director of a school of education in Ontario reports to the Registrar that the candidate,

(a) holds a certificate of qualification (limited, restricted) extended under section 24;

(b) has submitted evidence of at least one year of successful teaching experience in a Native language as a second language, following the completion of the teaching experience referred to in section 24, as certified by,

    (i) the appropriate supervisory officer, where the successful teaching experience was in Ontario and was not in a school operated on an Indian Reserve, or

    (ii) the appropriate supervisory official, where the successful teaching experience was outside Ontario or in a school operated on an Indian Reserve in Ontario; and

(c) has successfully completed the third session of an approved program for Teacher of a Native Language as a Second Language after completing the successful teaching experience referred to in clause (b).

(2) The certificate of qualification (restricted) granted under subsection (1) shall be in the form provided for in the by-laws.

26. (1) The Registrar may grant to a candidate a certificate of qualification (limited, restricted) valid for one year for teaching dance if the dean of a college or faculty of education or the director of a school of education in Ontario reports to the Registrar that the candidate,

(a) has complied with section 2;

(b) holds a Secondary School Graduation Diploma or has qualifications that the College considers to be equivalent to a Secondary School Graduation Diploma;

(c) has successfully completed, before August 31, 1995, the first session of the program in Dance referred to in Schedule D;

(d) is competent to perform in the areas of dance taught in elementary and secondary schools; and

(e) is entitled under the laws of Canada to obtain employment in Canada as a teacher, if the candidate is not a Canadian citizen or a permanent resident of Canada.

(2) A certificate of qualification (limited, restricted) granted under subsection (1) shall be in the form provided for in the by-laws.

(3) The Registrar may extend a candidate's certificate of qualification (limited, restricted) for one year for teaching dance if the dean of a college or faculty of education or the director of a school of education in Ontario reports to the Registrar that the candidate,

    (a) holds a certificate of qualification (limited, restricted) granted under subsection (1);

    (b) has submitted evidence of at least one year of experience successfully teaching dance in Ontario since the granting of the certificate of qualification (limited, restricted), as certified by the appropriate supervisory officer; and

    (c) has successfully completed, before August 31, 1996, the second session of the program in Dance referred to in Schedule D.

(4) The Registrar may grant a candidate a certificate of qualification (restricted) for teaching dance if the dean of a college or faculty of education or the director of a school of education in Ontario reports to the Registrar that the candidate,

    (a) holds a certificate of qualification (limited, restricted) granted under subsection (1);

    (b) has submitted evidence of at least one year of experience successfully teaching dance in Ontario following the experience referred to in clause (3)(b), as certified by the appropriate supervisory officer; and

    (c) has successfully completed, before August 31, 1997, the third session of the program in Dance referred to in Schedule D.

(5) The certificate of qualification (restricted) granted under subsection (4) shall be in the form provided for in the by-laws.

27. The Registrar may grant to a candidate a certificate of qualification in the form provided for in the by-laws if the candidate submits to the Registrar evidence that the candidate,

    (a) holds a valid certificate of qualification (restricted);

    (b) holds an acceptable university degree or qualifications that the College considers equivalent to an acceptable university degree; and

    (c) has successfully completed an approved program of teacher education leading to qualifications in two areas of concentration in the primary division, junior division, intermediate division or senior division.

28. (1) A person who holds one of the following certificates and who is,

    (a) a Canadian citizen; or

    (b) a British subject who was granted the certificate prior to September 1, 1973,

is deemed to hold the certificate of qualification:

    1. First Class Certificate valid in Secondary Schools.
    2. High School Specialist's Certificate.
    3. Interim Elementary School Teacher's Certificate.
    4. Interim Elementary School Teacher's Certificate, Standard 1, 2, 3 or 4.
    5. Interim Elementary School Teacher's Certificate, Standard 1, 2, 3 or 4 (French only).
    6. Interim First Class Certificate.
    7. Interim High School Assistant's Certificate.
    8. Interim High School Assistant's Certificate, Type A.
    9. Interim High School Assistant's Certificate, Type B.
    10. Interim Occupational Certificate, Type A (Practical Subjects).
    11. Interim Occupational Certificate, Type B (Practical Subjects).

12. Interim Primary School Specialist's Certificate.
13. Interim Second Class Certificate.
14. Interim Vocational Certificate, Type A.
15. Interim Vocational Certificate, Type B.
16. Occupational Specialist's Certificate (Practical Subjects).
17. Permanent Commercial—Vocational Certificate.
18. Permanent Elementary School Teacher's Certificate.
19. Permanent Elementary School Teacher's Certificate, Standard 1, 2, 3 or 4.
20. Permanent Elementary School Teacher's Certificate, Standard 1, 2, 3 or 4 (French only).
21. Permanent First Class Certificate.
22. Permanent High School Assistant's Certificate.
23. Permanent Occupational Certificate (Practical Subjects).
24. Permanent Primary School Specialist's Certificate.
25. Permanent Second Class Certificate.
26. Permanent Vocational Certificate.
27. Vocational Specialist's Certificate.

(2) The Registrar shall grant to a person referred to in subsection (1) a certificate of qualification in the form provided for in the by-laws.

(3) A person who holds an interim certificate referred to in subsection (1) continues to be qualified to teach in accordance with the certificate until the date to which the certificate is valid as shown thereon and the person may upon application be granted by the Registrar a certificate of qualification in the form provided for in the by-laws.

(4) Where a person who held a Letter of Standing granted before July 1, 1978 submits to the Registrar evidence of at least 10 months of successful teaching experience in Ontario, as certified by the appropriate supervisory officer, in a division or subject for which the Letter of Standing is valid, the Registrar may grant to the person a certificate of qualification in the form provided for in the by-laws.

29. (1) A person who holds one of the following certificates or Letters of Standing that was valid on July 1, 1978 but who was not qualified for an Ontario Teacher's Certificate under Regulation 297 of the Revised Regulations of Ontario, 1990, as it read on the day before this regulation comes into force holds a certificate of qualification (restricted) indicating qualifications to teach in the classes schools and subjects that were indicated on the person's certificate or letter of standing:

1. Elementary Certificate in Teaching Trainable Retarded Children.
2. Elementary Instrumental Music Certificate, Type A.
3. Elementary Instrumental Music Certificate, Type B.
4. Elementary Vocal Music Certificate, Type A.
5. Elementary Vocal Music Certificate, Type B.
6. Interim School Class Certificate (French only).
7. Interim Specialist Certificate in Instrumental Music.
8. Interim Specialist Certificate in Vocal Music.
9. Intermediate Certificate in Teaching Trainable Retarded Children.
10. Intermediate Industrial Arts Only Certificate.
11. Intermediate Instrumental Music Certificate, Type A.
12. Intermediate Instrumental Music Certificate, Type B.
13. Intermediate Vocal Music Certificate, Type A.
14. Intermediate Vocal Music Certificate, Type B.

15. Letter of Standing (renewable).
16. Permanent Letter of Standing (Renewable).
17. Permanent Second Class Certificate (French only).
18. Permanent Specialist Certificate in Instrumental Music.
19. Permanent Specialist Certificate in Vocal Music.
20. Specialist Certificate as Teacher of the Blind.
21. Specialist Certificates as Teacher of the Deaf.
22. Supervisor's Certificate in Instrumental Music.
23. Supervisor's Certificate in Vocal Music.
24. Teacher of the Trainable Retarded.
25. Temporary Certificate as Teacher of French to English-speaking Pupils in Elementary Schools.

(2) Where the dean of a college or faculty of education or the director of a school of education in Ontario reports to the Registrar that the candidate,

(a) has complied with section 2;
(b) is entitled under the laws of Canada to obtain employment in Canada as a teacher, if the candidate is not a Canadian citizen or a permanent resident of Canada;
(c) holds or is deemed to hold a certificate of qualification (restricted) referred to in subsection (1);
(d) holds an acceptable university degree or qualifications the College considers equivalent thereto, or technological qualifications or, in the case of a candidate for a certificate of qualification valid for teaching in French-language schools and classes established under Part XII of the *Education Act*, a Secondary School Honour Graduation Diploma; and
(e) has successfully completed approved programs with concentration in two divisions, the Registrar may grant to the candidate a certificate of qualification in the form provided for in the by-laws, indicating the areas of concentration successfully completed.

(3) A person who holds a Deferred Elementary School Teacher's Certificate or a Deferred First Class Certificate that was valid on July 1, 1978 remains qualified to teach in the schools and classes for which he or she is qualified by the certificate and, upon submission to the College of evidence of completion of the academic requirements for an Interim Elementary School Teacher's Certificate or an Interim First Class Certificate, as the case may be, in force at the time the deferred certificate was issued, the Registrar may grant to the person a certificate of qualification in the form provided for in the by-laws.

PART II

ADDITIONAL QUALIFICATIONS FOR TEACHERS

30. A session of a course leading to an additional qualification shall consist of a minimum of 125 hours of work that is approved by the Registrar.

31. Where the dean of a college or faculty of education or the director of a school of education in Ontario reports to the Registrar that a candidate,

(a) holds or has been recommended by the dean or the director for an interim certificate of qualification or certificate of qualification (restricted);
(b) holds an acceptable university degree or qualifications the College considers equivalent thereto; and

(c) has successfully completed an approved program leading to qualifications in an additional area of concentration in the primary division, the junior division, the intermediate division in general studies or the senior division in general studies, or has qualifications that the College considers equivalent to the successful completion of such a program,

the Registrar may have entered on the candidate's certificate of qualification such additional area of concentration.

32. (1) Subject to subsection (2), where the dean of a college or faculty of education in Ontario reports to the Registrar that a candidate,

(a) holds or has been recommended by the dean or the director for a certificate of qualification or an interim certificate of qualification;

(b) has successfully completed an approved program leading to additional qualifications in a subject listed in Schedule B, or has qualifications that the College considers equivalent to the successful completion of such a program.

(c) in the case of a candidate for a qualification listed in Schedule B at the advanced level, has produced evidence of,

    (i) twelve months of business or individual experience in the area of qualification,

    (ii) academic experience that the College considers equivalent to 12 months of business or industrial experience in the area of the qualification, or

    (iii) a combination of academic, business and industrial experience that the College considers equivalent to 12 months of business or industrial experience in the area of the qualification; and

(d) has demonstrated competence in the area referred to in clause (c),

the Registrar may have entered on the candidate's certificate of qualification the additional qualification in such subject.

(2) An additional qualification may not be entered under subsection (1) on the certificate of qualification in respect of such teacher, of a candidate whose areas of concentration in the program of professional education that qualified him or her for the certificate of qualification were not in technological studies unless the candidate meets the requirements of clause (c) of the definition of "technological qualifications" in subsection 1(1).

ONE-SESSION COURSES

33. Where the principal of a single-session course leading to a qualification listed in Schedule C or the dean of a college or faculty of education or the director of a school of education in Ontario reports to the Registrar that a candidate,

(a) holds or has been recommended by the dean or the director for a certificate of qualification or an interim certificate of qualification; and

(b) has successfully completed an approved program leading to additional qualifications in a subject listed in Schedule C, or has qualifications that the College considers equivalent to the successful completion of such a program,

the Registrar may have entered upon the candidate's certificate of qualification the additional qualification in such subject.

THREE-SESSION SPECIALIST COURSES

34. The Registrar may have entered on a candidate's certificate of qualification the Part I qualification in a subject listed in Schedule D if the principal of the first session of a three-session course leading to a specialist qualification in the subject, the dean of a college or faculty of education or the director of a school of education in Ontario reports to the Registrar that the candidate,

(a) holds a certificate of qualification or an interim certificate of qualification;

(b) has successfully completed an approved program leading to the Part I qualification; and

(c) has an entry on the candidate's certificate of qualification that shows,

    (i) qualification in the primary division, the junior division, the intermediate division in general studies or the senior division in general studies, in the case of Part I qualification other than Primary Education, Junior Education or Intermediate Education,

    (ii) an area of concentration for the corresponding division, in the case of a Part I qualification in Primary Education, Junior Education or Intermediate Education, or

    (iii) qualification in technological studies, in the case of a Part I qualification in one of the following:

1. Actualisation linguistique en français/Perfectionnement du français (ALF/PDF),
2. Computers in the Classroom.
3. Co-operative Education.
4. Design and Technology.
5. English as a Second Language.
6. Guidance.
7. Media.
8. Multiculturalism in Education.
9. Music—Instrumental.
10. Music—Vocal (Primary, Junior).
11. Music—Vocal (Intermediate, Senior).
12. Religious Education.
13. Special Education.
14. The Blind.
15. The Deaf.
16. The Deaf/Blind.
17. Visual Arts.

35. Where the principal of the second session of a three-session course or the dean of a college or faculty of education or the director of a school of education in Ontario reports to the Registrar that a candidate,

(a) holds or is deemed to hold a certificate of qualification or an interim certificate of qualification;

(b) has successfully completed the first session, or the equivalent thereof, of a course leading to an additional qualification in a subject listed in Schedule D;

(c) has submitted evidence of at least one year of successful teaching experience in Ontario certified by the appropriate supervisory officer or of at least one year of successful teaching experience outside Ontario certified by the appropriate supervisory official; and

(d) has successfully completed the approved program for the second session of the course after completing the experience referred to in clause (c), the Registrar may have entered upon the candidate's certificate of qualification the Part II qualification in such subject.

36. Where the principal of the third session of a three-session course or the dean of a college or faculty of education or the director of a school of education in Ontario reports to the Registrar that the candidate,

    (a) holds or is deemed to hold a certificate of qualification or an interim certificate of qualification;

    (b) has successfully completed the second session, or the equivalent thereof, of a course leading to an additional qualification in a subject listed in Schedule D;

    (c) submits evidence of at least two years of successful teaching experience, including at least one year of experience in Ontario in the subject referred to in clause (b), certified by the appropriate supervisory officer and, if some of the experience was outside Ontario, by the appropriate supervisory official; and

    (d) has successfully completed subsequent to the experience referred to in clause (c) the approved program for the third session of such course,

the Registrar may have entered upon the candidate's certificate of qualification the specialist qualification in such subject.

37. Where the dean of a college or faculty of education or the director of a school of education in Ontario reports to the Registrar that the candidate who does not hold a certificate of qualification,

    (a) holds a certificate of qualification (restricted) valid in Ontario for teaching the deaf only; and

    (b) has otherwise met the requirements of section 33, 34, 35, 36, 40, 46 or 47,

the Registrar may grant to the candidate the appropriate additional qualification.

38. (1) A teacher who holds or is deemed to hold a certificate of qualification and who, prior to October 1, 1978, began a Master of Education program that was approved by the Minister as leading to the Specialist Certificate in Guidance, may obtain the specialist qualification in Guidance by completing the requirements for such Certificate as they existed on June 30, 1978, and the Registrar shall, upon submission to the Registrar of evidence satisfactory to the Registrar of the completion of such requirements, have entered on such teacher's certificate of qualification the specialist qualifications in Guidance.

(2) A teacher who holds or is deemed to hold a certificate of qualification and who, prior to October 1, 1978, began a Master of Library Science program that was approved by the Minister as leading to the Specialist Certificate in Librarianship, may obtain the specialist qualification in Librarianship by completing the requirements for such Certificate as they existed on June 30, 1978, and the Registrar shall, upon submission to the Registrar of evidence satisfactory to the Registrar of the completion of such requirements, have entered on such teacher's certificate of qualification the specialist qualification in Librarianship.

39. A teacher who holds a special certificate in a subject listed in Schedule C, D or E, or a special certificate no longer issued, continues to be qualified in accordance with such certificate, and the Registrar shall have the additional qualification corresponding to such special certificate recorded on the teacher's certificate of qualification where the teacher holds or is granted a certificate of qualification.

ONE-SESSION HONOUR SPECIALIST COURSE

40. (1) Where the dean of a college or faculty of education in Ontario reports to the Registrar that a candidate for an Honour Specialist qualification in a subject or subjects listed in Schedule E,

(a) holds or is deemed to hold a certificate of qualification or an interim certificate of qualification and the candidate's certificate of qualification has an entry showing qualifications in the primary division, the junior division, the intermediate division in general studies or the senior division in general studies; and

(b) holds,

(i) a degree of Bachelor of Arts or Bachelor of Science from an Ontario university in a program,

(A) that requires four years of university study, or the equivalent thereof, to a total of at least 60 university credits, and

(B) in which the candidate has obtained at least second class or equivalent standing in the subject or subjects in which the candidate seeks an Honour Specialist qualification, including, in the case of two subjects, at least 42 university credits therein and not fewer than 18 university credits in each subject or, in the case of one subject, at least 27 university credits therein, or

(ii) qualifications the College considers equivalent to the qualifications referred to in subclause (i);

(c) submits evidence of at least two years of successful teaching experience, including at least one year of experience in Ontario in the subject or one or both of the subjects in which the Honours Specialist qualification is sought, certified by the appropriate supervisory officer and, if some of the experience was outside Ontario, by the appropriate supervisory official; and

(d) has successfully completed subsequent to the experience referred to in clause (c) the approved program for the Honour Specialist qualification in the subject or subjects referred to in sub-subclause (b)(i)(B),

the Registrar may have entered upon the candidate's certificate of qualification the Honour Specialist qualification in such subject or subjects referred to in sub-subclause (b)(i)(B).

(2) A university credit that has been used to meet the requirements for an Honour Specialist qualification established by clause (1)(b) shall not be used to meet the requirements for another Honour Specialist qualifications.

(3) For the purpose of clause (1)(b), a university credit in Anthropology, Psychology or Sociology shall be deemed to be a university credit in Individual and Society.

(4) Where the dean of a college or faculty of education in Ontario reports to the Registrar that a candidate for the Honour Technological Studies Specialist Qualification,

(a) holds or is deemed to hold a certificate of qualification or an interim certificate of qualification;

(b) has entries on his or her certificate of qualification indicating qualifications in at least,

(i) three of the subjects listed in Schedule B including at least one at both the basic and the advanced level, or

(ii) four of the subjects listed in Schedule B at the basic level and an entry indicating the Specialist qualification in one of the subjects in Schedule D listed in subclause 34(c)(iii);

(c) submits evidence of at least two years of successful teaching experience, including at least one year of experience in Ontario in technological studies, certified by the appropriate supervisory officer and, if some of the experience was outside Ontario, by the appropriate supervisory official;

(d) holds a Secondary School Honour Graduation Diploma or has successfully completed the equivalent of one year's full-time study in a program in respect of which a Secondary School Graduation Diploma or its equivalent is required for admission; and

(e) has successfully completed subsequent to the experience referred to in clause (c) the approved program for the Honour Technological Studies Specialist qualification,

the Registrar may have entered upon the candidate's certificate of qualification the Honour Technological Studies Specialist qualification.

(5) The entry on a candidate's certificate of qualification indicating that he or she has completed successfully the first session of a three-session course leading to the Specialist qualification in Design and Technology or Computer Studies — Computer Technology is deemed to be equivalent to one basic level entry for the purposes of clause (4)(b).

41. (1) Where a teacher who completed prior to September 1, 1979 the first session of a two-session course leading to an Interim Vocational Certificate, Type A or an Interim Occupational Certificate, Type A completes the requirements for such certificate as they existed on June 30, 1978, the Registrar may have entered on the teacher's certificate of qualification the appropriate qualification.

(2) Where a teacher who,

(a) held an Interim High School Assistant's Certificate, Type A on July 1, 1978; or

(b) completed at a college or faculty of education in Ontario prior to July 1, 1979 the requirements for such certificate as they existed immediately before July 1, 1978,

completes the requirements for the High School Specialist Certificate as they existed immediately before July 1, 1978, the Registrar may have entered on the teacher's certificate of qualification the appropriate Honours Specialist qualification.

42. A teacher who before May 20, 1997 held an Honour Specialist qualification in Latin or Greek shall be deemed to hold an Honour Specialist qualification in Classical Studies (Latin, Greek).

PRINCIPAL'S QUALIFICATIONS

43. (1) The Principal's Qualification Program shall consist of two one-session courses.

(2) A teacher holds principal's qualifications if the teacher's certificate of qualification has an entry for Part II of the Principal's Qualification Program.

44. An applicant for admission to the Principal's Qualification Program must,

(a) hold an acceptable university degree;

(b) hold a certificate of qualification or interim certificate of qualification;

(c) hold concentrations in three divisions including the intermediate division, as indicated on the applicant's certificate of qualification;

(d) provide evidence of at least five years of successful teaching experience in a school providing elementary or secondary education, as certified by the appropriate supervisory officer or, in the case of experience outside Ontario, by the appropriate supervisory official; and

(e) hold or provide evidence of one of the following:
   1. A Specialist or Honour Specialist qualification as indicated on the applicant's certificate of qualification and,
       (i) successful completion of at least half the number of courses required to qualify for a master's degree that is an acceptable university degree, or
       (ii) an additional Specialist or Honour Specialist qualification as indicated on the applicant's certificate of qualification.
   2. A master's degree or doctorate that is an acceptable university degree.
   3. Successful completion of such number of graduate university courses as is equivalent to the number of graduate university courses that are required to qualify for a master's degree that is an acceptable university degree.

45. If the principal of a course leading to qualifications in Part I of the Principal's Qualification Program reports to the Registrar that a candidate has met the admission requirements of section 44 and has successfully completed the course, the Registrar may have the Part I qualification entered on the candidate's certificate of qualification.

46. An applicant for admission to a course leading to qualifications in Part II of the Principal's Qualification Program must have an entry on his or her certificate of qualification showing qualifications in Part I of the program.

47. If the principal of a course leading to qualifications in Part II of the Principal's Qualification Program reports to the Registrar that a candidate has met the admission requirements of section 46 or 51 and has successfully completed the course, the Registrar may have the Part II qualifications entered on the candidate's certificate of qualification.

48. Where the principal of a Principal's Development Centre reports to the Registrar that a candidate,

(a) holds principal's qualifications;
(b) has two years of successful experience as a principal or vice-principal as certified by the appropriate supervisory officer; and
(c) has successfully completed the Course.

the Registrar may have entered on the candidate's certificate of qualification the Principal's Development Course qualification.

49. A teacher who holds a High School Principal's Certificate, an Elementary School Principal's Certificate, a Secondary School Principal's Certificate, Type B, a Secondary School Principal's Certificate, Type A, a Secondary School Principal's Certificate or a Vocation School Principal's Certificate, whether such certificate is an interim certificate or a permanent certificate, remains qualified within the limitations of the certificate except that the interim qualification will not lapse after the five-year period of validity and such qualification shall be shown on his or her certificate of qualification.

50. A teacher who holds an Elementary School Inspector's Certificate shall be deemed to hold an Elementary School Principal's Certificate.

51. Despite section 46, a teacher who holds or who is deemed to hold an interim or permanent Elementary School Principal's Certificate, or who holds an interim or permanent

Secondary School Principal's Certificate, Type B, an interim or permanent Vocational School Principal's Certificate, an interim Secondary School Principal's Certificate, or an interim Secondary School Principal's Certificate Type A, may be admitted to the course leading to qualifications in Part II of the Principal's Qualification Program.

52. (1) Where a teacher held an interim Elementary School Principal's Certificate, an interim Secondary School Principal's Certificate, Type B, or an interim Secondary School Principal's Certificate, Type A, on July 1, 1978 and completes the requirements for the permanent certificate that corresponds thereto as they existed immediately before July 1, 1978, the Registrar shall have entered on the teacher's certificate of qualification the appropriate qualification.

(2) A teacher who holds a permanent Secondary School Principal's Certificate, Type A or a permanent Secondary School Principal's Certificate is deemed to hold principal's qualifications.

PART IV

TEMPORARY LETTERS OF APPROVAL

53. (1) The Registrar may grant to a board a Temporary Letter of Approval for a period specified in the letter if the director of education or secretary of the board submits to the Registrar, in duplicate, an application in the form provided for in the by-laws certifying that,

(a) the board finds it necessary to assign or appoint a teacher to teach a subject or hold a position who does not hold the qualifications required by the regulations made under the *Education Act* for teaching the subject or holding the position; and

(b) the teacher in respect of whom the application is made,
   (i) holds a certificate of qualification, an interim certificate of qualification, a certificate of qualification (restricted), a certificate of qualification (limited), or a certificate of qualification (limited, restricted), and
   (ii) is considered competent to teach the subject or hold the position.

(2) The period for which a Temporary Letter of Approval is granted,

(a) shall not exceed one year; and

(b) shall not extend beyond the end of a school year unless the period begins after the end of a school year and ends before the beginning of the next school year.

PART V

QUALIFICATIONS OF SUPERVISORY OFFICERS

54. In this Part,

"acceptable university degree" means a degree from an Ontario university or post-secondary institution that is an ordinary member of the Association of Universities and Colleges of Canada or a degree that is equivalent thereto from a university other than such Ontario university or post-secondary institution;

"Principal's Certificate" means a permanent principal's certificate;

"university" means,

    (a) an Ontario university or post-secondary institution that is an ordinary member of the Association of Universities and Colleges of Canada,

    (b) a Canadian university in a province other than Ontario that is an ordinary member of the Association of Universities and Colleges of Canada,

    (c) a university in the United States that is recognized by,

        (i) Middle States Association of Colleges and Schools,

        (ii) New England Association of Schools and Colleges,

        (iii) North Central Association of Colleges and Schools,

        (iv) Northwest Association of Schools and Colleges,

        (v) Southern Association of Colleges and Schools,

        (vi) Western Association of Schools and Colleges, or

    (d) a university that is located in a country other than Canada or the United States and that is a member of the association of Commonwealth Universities or the International Association of Universities.

55. A person who meets the following qualifications shall have an entry recorded on his or her certificate of qualification or interim certificate of qualification indicating an additional qualification as a supervisory officer:

1. The person has at least seven years of successful teaching experience in a school providing elementary or secondary education.

2. The person holds a certificate of qualification or an interim certificate of qualification.

3. The person holds qualifications to teach in the intermediate division and at least two other divisions that are indicated on the person's certificate of qualification.

4. The person holds an acceptable university degree.

5. The person holds a master's degree from a university.

6. The person meets one or more of the following criteria:

    i. The person holds,

        A. an Elementary School Principal's Certificate,

        B. a Secondary School Principal's Certificate, Type A.

        C. a Secondary School Principal's Certificate, Type B, or

        D. a Secondary School Principal's Certificate.

    ii. The person holds a certificate of qualification indicating Part I and Part II Principal's Qualifications.

    iii. The person holds specialist or honours specialist qualifications in one or more subjects and has, in addition to the experience required by paragraph 1, at least two years of successful experience as a teacher appointed by a board under section 17 of Regulation 298 of the Revised Regulations of Ontario, 1990 to supervise or co-ordinate a subject or program or to act as a consultant for the teachers of a subject or program, as certified by the appropriate supervisory officer.

    iv. The person has, in addition to the experience required by paragraph 1, at least two years of experience,

        A. as an education officer employed by the Ministry of Education and Training, as certified by a district manager or branch director of the Ministry of Education and Training,

        B. as an employee outside Ontario in a position that is equivalent in the Registrar's opinion to the position of supervisory officer of a school board, as certified by a person acceptable to the Registrar, or

      C. as a program consultant seconded to the Ministry for French language, English language or Native language programs, as certified by a district manager or branch director of the Ministry of Education and Training.

    7. The person has successfully completed the supervisory officer's qualifications program described in section 56 within five years after starting the program.

56. The supervisory officer's qualifications programs referred to in section 55 shall have the following features:

    1. The program shall be provided by an organization or institution that has entered into a contract with the College to provide the instruction and arrange for the practical experience referred to in paragraphs 3 and 4.

    2. No person shall be admitted to the program unless the person has submitted proof to the organization or institution that provides the program that the person meets the qualifications set out in paragraphs 1 to 6 of section 55.

    3. The program shall consist of,

        i. four instructional modules, each consisting of at least 50 hours of instruction, and

       ii. one module consisting of at least 50 hours of practical experience in the workplace.

    4. The instructional modules shall provide instruction that, in the opinion of the Registrar, is relevant to the position of supervisory officer in the following subject areas:

        i. Statutes, regulations and government policies affecting education in Ontario.

       ii. Curriculum guidelines and other reference material pertaining to elementary and secondary education in Ontario.

      iii. Theories and practices of supervision, administration and business organization.

PART VI

REGISTRATION

57. A person may apply for a certificate of qualification and registration by submitting to the Registrar a completed application in the form prescribed by the by-laws together with the fee prescribed by the by-laws.

PART VII

TRANSITIONAL

58. The day prescribed for the purposes of subsection 62(1) of the Act is May 20, 1997.

59. For the purposes of subsection 62(2) of the Act, on and after May 20, 1997 any person holding a qualification referred to in one of the following paragraphs shall be deemed to have been granted by the Registrar and to hold the corresponding certificate of qualification under this Regulation containing the same terms, conditions or limitations:

    1. Regulation 297 of the Revised Regulations of Ontario, 1990.

    2. Ontario Teacher's Qualifications Record Cards.

    3. Any other records of qualification held by the Ministry of Education and Training.

60. Any person who is deemed under subsection 63(1) of the Act to have fulfilled the requirements for the issuance of a particular certificate of qualification shall be issued that certificate containing the same terms, conditions and limitations that would have applied to their qualifications referred to in paragraphs 1, 2 and 3 of section 59 before May 20, 1997.

Schedule A
INTERMEDIATE AND SENIOR DIVISION OPTIONS TAKEN IN ENGLISH OR FRENCH

Business Studies—Accounting
Business Studies—Data Processing
Business Studies—Marketing and Merchandising
Business Studies—Information Management
Classical Studies—Greek
Classical Studies—Latin
Computer Science
Dance
Design and Technology
Dramatic Art
Economics
English (First language)
English (Second language)—anglais
Environmental Science
Family Studies
French (Second language)
French (First language)—français
Geography
History
Individual and Society
International Languages
Law
Mathematics
Music—Instrumental
Music—Vocal
Native Language (Second language)
Native Studies
Politics
Physical and Health Education
Religious Education
Science—General
Science—Biology
Science—Chemistry
Science—Geology
Science—Physics
Visual Arts

Schedule B
TECHNOLOGICAL STUDIES OPTIONS TAKEN IN ENGLISH OR FRENCH

BASIC LEVEL	ADVANCED LEVEL
Communications Technology	Communications Technology

Construction Technology
Hospitality Services
Manufacturing Technology
Personal Services
Technological Design
Transportation Technology

Construction Technology
Hospitality Services
Manufacturing Technology
Personal Services
Technological Design
Transportation Technology

Schedule C
ONE-SESSION QUALIFICATIONS TAKEN IN ENGLISH OR FRENCH

Adult Education
Associate Teacher
Childhood Education
Childhood Education in Great Britain
Community School Development
Computer Studies—Computer Technology
Driver Education Instructor
Integrated Arts
Law
Preschool Deaf Education
Teaching Children with Language Difficulties — Aphasia
Teacher of Cree
Teacher of Mohawk
Teacher of Native Children
Teacher of Ojibway
Teaching Writing

Schedule D
THREE SESSION QUALIFICATIONS TAKEN IN ENGLISH OR FRENCH

Actualisation linguistic en français/Perfectionnement du français (ACF/PDF)
Business Studies—Accounting
Business Studies—Data Processing
Business Studies—Entrepreneurship Studies
Business Studies—Marketing and Merchandising
Business Studies—Information Management
Computer Studies—Computer Science
Computers in the Classroom
Co-operative Education
Dance
Design and Technology
Dramatic Arts
English as a Second Language
Environmental Science
Family Studies
French as a Second Language
Guidance
Intermediate Education
International Languages
Junior Education
Librarianship

Mathematics in Primary and Junior Education
Media
Multiculturalism in Education
Music—Instrumental
Music—Vocal (Primary, Junior)
Music—Vocal (Intermediate, Senior)
Native Language as a Second Language
Physical and Health Education (Primary, Junior)
Physical and Health Education (Intermediate, Senior)
Primary Education
Reading
Religious Education
Science in Primary and Junior Education
Special Education
The Blind
The Deaf
The Deaf/Blind
Visual Arts

Schedule E
HONOUR SPECIALIST QUALIFICATIONS TAKEN IN ENGLISH OR FRENCH

Biology
Business Studies
Chemistry
Classical Studies (Latin, Greek)
Computer Science
Contemporary Studies
Dance
Dramatic Arts
English (First language)
English (Second language) — anglais
Environmental Science
Family Studies
French (Second language)
French (First language) — français
Geography
Geology
History
International Languages
Mathematics
Music
Physical and Health Education
Physics
Religious Education
Science
Visual Arts

REGULATION 437/97
PROFESSIONAL MISCONDUCT

O. Reg. 437/97

1. The following acts are defined as professional misconduct for the purposes of subsection 30(2) of the Act:

1. Providing false information or documents to the College or any other person with respect to the member's professional qualifications.
2. Inappropriately using a term, title or designation indicating a specialization in the profession which is not specified on the member's certificate of qualification and registration.
3. Permitting, counselling or assisting any person who is not a member to represent himself or herself as a member of the College.
4. Using a name other than the member's name, as set out in the register, in the course of his or her professional duties.
5. Failing to maintain the standards of the profession.
6. Releasing or disclosing information about a student to a person other than the student or, if the student is a minor, the student's parent or guardian. The release or disclosure of information is not an act of professional misconduct if,
    i. the student (or if the student is a minor, the student's parent or guardian) consents to the release or disclosure, or
    ii. if the release or disclosure is required or allowed by law.
7. Abusing a student physically, sexually, verbally, psychologically or emotionally.
8. Practising or purporting to practise the profession while under the influence of any substance or while adversely affected by any dysfunction,
    i. which the member knows or ought to know impairs the member's ability to practise, and
    ii. in respect of which treatment has previously been recommended, ordered or prescribed but the member has failed to follow the treatment.
9. Contravening a term, condition or limitation imposed on the member's certificate of qualification and registration.
10. Failing to keep records as required by his or her professional duties.
11. Failing to supervise adequately a person who is under the professional supervision of the member.
12. Signing or issuing, in the member's professional capacity, a document that the member knows or ought to know contains a false, improper or misleading statement.
13. Falsifying a record relating to the member's professional responsibilities.
14. Failing to comply with the Act or the regulations or the by-laws.
15. Failing to comply with the *Education Act* or the regulations made under that Act, if the member is subject to that Act.
16. Contravening a law if the contravention is relevant to the member's suitability to hold a certificate of qualification and registration.
17. Contravening a law if the contravention has caused or may cause a student who is under the member's professional supervision to be put at or to remain at risk.
18. An act or omission that, having regard to all the circumstances, would reasonably be regarded by members as disgraceful, dishonourable or unprofessional.
19. Conduct unbecoming a member.
20. Failing to appear before a panel of the Investigation Committee to be cautioned or

admonished, if the Investigation Committee has required the member to appear under clause 26(5)(c) of the Act.

21. Failing to comply with an order of a panel of the Discipline Committee or an order of a panel of the Fitness to Practise Committee.

22. Failing to co-operate in a College investigation.

23. Failing to take reasonable steps to ensure that the requested information is provided in a complete and accurate manner if the member is required to provide information to the College under the Act and the regulations.

24. Failing to abide by a written undertaking given by the member to the College or by an agreement entered into by the member with the College.

25. Failing to respond adequately or within a reasonable time to a written inquiry from the College.

26. Practising the profession while the member is in a conflict of interest.

27. Failing to comply with the member's duties under the *Child and Family Services Act*.

2. A finding of incompetence, professional misconduct or a similar finding against a member by a governing authority of the teaching profession in a jurisdiction other than Ontario that is based on facts that would, in the opinion of the Discipline Committee, constitute professional misconduct as defined in section 1, is defined as professional misconduct for the purposes of subsection 30(2) of the Act.

CHILD AND FAMILY SERVICES ACT

R.S.O. 1990, c. C.11 [ss. 130, 131, 132(4), (5), 178, 179(1), (2)(a)-(c), (e)-(g), 180-182, 184-191 not in force at date of publication.] as am. S.O. 1992, c. 32, s. 3; 1993, c. 27, Sched.; 1994, c. 27, s. 43(2); 1996, c. 2, s. 62; 1999, c. 2 [ss. 2(3),11, 23(2), 27, 28, 30(2), (3), (5), 31, 33(2) not in force at date of publication.]; 1999, c. 6, s. 6; 1999, c. 12, Sched. E, s. 1 (Fr.); 1999, c. 12, Sched. G, s. 16; 2001, c. 13, s. 5; 2002, c. 17, Sched. F, s. 1; 2002, c. 18, Sched. D, s. 1

(Excerpts)

1. (1) **Paramount purpose.**—The paramount purpose of this Act is to promote the best interests, protection and well being of children.

(2) **Other purposes.**—The additional purposes of this Act, so long as they are consistent with the best interests, protection and well being of children, are:

1. To recognize that while parents may need help in caring for their children, that help should give support to the autonomy and integrity of the family unit and, wherever possible, be provided on the basis of mutual consent.

2. To recognize that the least disruptive course of action that is available and is appropriate in a particular case to help a child should be considered.

3. To recognize that children's services should be provided in a manner that,

   i. respects children's needs for continuity of care and for stable family relationships, and

   ii. takes into account physical and mental developmental differences among children.

4. To recognize that, wherever possible, services to children and their families should be provided in a manner that respects cultural, religious and regional differences.

5. To recognize that Indian and native people should be entitled to provide, wherever possible, their own child and family services, and that all services to Indian and native children and families should be provided in a manner that recognizes their culture, heritage and traditions and the concept of the extended family. 1999, c. 2, s. 1

Transitional Provision

Pursuant to 1999, c. 2, s. 37(5), section 1 of the Child and Family Services Act, as it read on the day before the March 31, 2000 proclamation of 1999, c. 2, s. 1, continues to apply to any proceeding under Part III, including a status review proceeding, commenced before that date.

On the day before the proclamation, s. 1 read as follows:

   1. Declaration of principles.—The purposes of this Act are,

(a)   *as a paramount objective, to promote the best interests, protection and well-being of children;*

(b)   *to recognize that while parents often need help in caring for their children, that help should give support to the autonomy and integrity of the family unit and, wherever possible, be provided on the basis of mutual consent;*

(c)   *to recognize that the least restrictive or disruptive course of action that is available and is appropriate in a particular case to help a child or family should be followed;*

(d)   *to recognize that children's services should be provided in a manner that,*

   (i)   *respects children's needs for continuity of care and for stable family relationships, and*

   (ii)   *takes into account physical and mental developmental differences among children;*

(e)   *to recognize that, wherever possible, services to children and their families should be provided in a manner that respects cultural, religious and regional differences; and*

(f)   *to recognize that Indian and native people should be entitled to provide, wherever possible, their own child and family services, and that all services to Indian and native children and families should be provided in a manner that recognizes their culture, heritage and traditions and the concept of the extended family.*

. . .

37. (1) **Definitions.**—In this Part,

"child" does not include a child as defined in subsection 3(1) who is actually or apparently sixteen years of age or older, unless the child is the subject of an order under this Part;

"child protection worker" means a Director, a local director or a person authorized by a Director or local director for the purposes of section 40 (commencing child protection proceedings);

"extended family", when used in reference to a child, means the persons to whom the child is related by blood, marriage or adoption;

"parent", when used in reference to a child, means each of,

   (a)   the child's mother,

   (b)   an individual described in one of paragraphs 1 to 6 of subsection 8(1) of the Children's Law Reform Act, unless it is proved on a balance of probabilities that he is not the child's natural father,

   (c)   the individual having lawful custody of the child,

(d) an individual who, during the twelve months before intervention under this Part, has demonstrated a settled intention to treat the child as a child of his or her family, or has acknowledged parentage of the child and provided for the child's support,

(e) an individual who, under a written agreement or a court order, is required to provide for the child, has custody of the child or has a right of access to the child, and

(f) an individual who has acknowledged parentage of the child in writing under section 12 of the Children's Law Reform Act, but does not include a foster parent;

"place of safety" means a foster home, a hospital, and a place or one of a class of places designated as such by a Director under subsection 17(2) of Part I (Flexible Services), but does not include,

(a) a place of secure custody as defined in Part IV (Young Offenders), or

(b) a place of secure temporary detention as defined in Part IV.

(2) **Child in need of protection.**—A child is in need of protection where,

(a) the child has suffered physical harm, inflicted by the person having charge of the child or caused by or resulting from that person's,

    (i) failure to adequately care for, provide for, supervise or protect the child, or

    (ii) pattern of neglect in caring for, providing for, supervising or protecting the child.

(b) there is a risk that the child is likely to suffer physical harm inflicted by the person having charge of the child or caused by or resulting from that person's,

    (i) failure to adequately care for, provide for, supervise or protect the child, or

    (ii) pattern of neglect in caring for, providing for, supervising or protecting the child.

(c) the child has been sexually molested or sexually exploited, by the person having charge of the child or by another person where the person having charge of the child knows or should know of the possibility of sexual molestation or sexual exploitation and fails to protect the child;

(d) there is a risk that the child is likely to be sexually molested or sexually exploited as described in clause (c).

(e) the child requires medical treatment to cure, prevent or alleviate physical harm or suffering and the child's parent or the person having charge of the child does not provide, or refuses or is unavailable or unable to consent to, the treatment;

(f) the child has suffered emotional harm, demonstrated by serious,

    (i) anxiety,

    (ii) depression,

(iii) withdrawal,

(iv) self-destructive or aggressive behaviour, or

(v) delayed development,

and there are reasonable grounds to believe that the emotional harm suffered by the child results from the actions, failure to act or pattern of neglect on the part of the child's parent or the person having charge of the child;

(f.1) the child has suffered emotional harm of the kind described in subclause (f)(i), (ii), (iii), (iv) or (v) and the child's parent or the person having charge of the child does not provide, or refuses or is unavailable or unable to consent to, services or treatment to remedy or alleviate the harm;

(g)   there is a risk that the child is likely to suffer emotional harm of the kind described in subclause (f)(i), (ii), (iii), (iv) or (v) resulting from the actions, failure to act or pattern of neglect on the part of the child's parent or the person having charge of the child;

(g.1) there is a risk that the child is likely to suffer emotional harm of the kind described in subclause (f)(i), (ii), (iii), (iv) or (v) and that the child's parent or the person having charge of the child does not provide, or refuses or is unavailable or unable to consent to, services or treatment to prevent the harm.

(h)   the child suffers from a mental, emotional or developmental condition that, if not remedied, could seriously impair the child's development and the child's parent or the person having charge of the child does not provide, or refuses or is unavailable or unable to consent to, treatment to remedy or alleviate the condition;

(i)   the child has been abandoned, the child's parent has died or is unavailable to exercise his or her custodial rights over the child and has not made adequate provision for the child's care and custody, or the child is in a residential placement and the parent refuses or is unable or unwilling to resume the child's care and custody;

(j)   the child is less than twelve years old and has killed or seriously injured another person or caused serious damage to another person's property, services or treatment are necessary to prevent a recurrence and the child's parent or the person having charge of the child does not provide, or refuses or is unavailable or unable to consent to, those services or treatment;

(k)   the child is less than twelve years old and has on more than one occasion injured another person or caused loss or damage to another person's property, with the encouragement of the person having charge of the child or because of that person's failure or inability to supervise the child adequately; or

(l)   the child's parent is unable to care for the child and the child is brought before the court with the parent's consent and, where the child is twelve years of age or older, with the child's consent, to be dealt with under this Part.

(3) **Best interests of child.**—Where a person is directed in this Part to make an order or determination in the best interests of a child, the person shall take into consideration those of the following circumstances of the case that he or she considers relevant:

1. The child's physical, mental and emotional needs, and the appropriate care or treatment to meet those needs.

2. The child's physical, mental and emotional level of development.

3. The child's cultural background.

4. The religious faith, if any, in which the child is being raised.

5. The importance for the child's development of a positive relationship with a parent and a secure place as a member of a family.

6. The child's relationships by blood or through an adoption order.

7. The importance of continuity in the child's care and the possible effect on the child of disruption of that continuity.

8. The merits of a plan for the child's care proposed by a society, including a proposal that the child be placed for adoption or adopted, compared with the merits of the child remaining with or returning to a parent.

9. The child's views and wishes, if they can be reasonably ascertained.

10. The effects on the child of delay in the disposition of the case.

11. The risk that the child may suffer harm through being removed from, kept away from, returned to or allowed to remain in the care of a parent.

12. The degree of risk, if any, that justified the finding that the child is in need of protection.

13. Any other relevant circumstance.

(4) **Where child an Indian or native person.**—Where a person is directed in this Part to make an order or determination in the best interests of a child and the child is an Indian or native person, the person shall take into consideration the importance, in recognition of the uniqueness of Indian and native culture, heritage and traditions, of preserving the child's cultural identity. 1999, c. 2, s. 9

Transitional Provision

Pursuant to 1999, c. 2, s. 37(5), section 37 of the Child and Family Services Act, as it read on the day before the March 31, 2000 proclamation of 1999, c. 2, s. 9, continues to apply to any proceeding under Part III, including a status review proceeding, commenced before that date.

On the day before the proclamation, section 37 read as follows:

37. (1) Definitions—Is this Part,

"child" does not include a child as defined in subsection 3(1) who is actually or apparently sixteen years of age or older, unless the child is the subject of an order under this Part;

"child protection worker" means a Director, a local director or a person authorized

by a Director or local director for the purposes of section 40 (commencing child protection proceedings);

"extended family", when used in reference to a child, means the persons to whom the child is related by blood, marriage or adoption;

"parent", when used in reference to a child, means each of,

(a)   the child's mother,

(b)   an individual described in one of paragraphs 1 to 6 of subsection 8(1) of the Children's Law Reform Act, unless it is proved on a balance of probabilities that he is not the child's natural father,

(c)   the individual having lawful custody of the child,

(d)   an individual who, during the twelve months before intervention under this Part, has demonstrated a settled intention to treat the child as a child of his or her family, or has acknowledged parentage of the child and provided for the child's support,

(e)   an individual who, under a written agreement or a court order, is required to provide for the child, has custody of the child or has a right of access to the child, and

(f)   an individual who has acknowledged parentage of the child in writing under section 12 of the Children's Law Reform Act, but does not include a foster parent;

"place of safety" means a foster home, a hospital and a place or one of a class of places designated as such by a Director under subsection 17(2) of Part I (Flexible Services), but does not include,

(a)   a place of secure custody as defined in Part IV (Young Offenders), or

(b)   a place of secure temporary detention as defined in Part IV.

(2) Child in need of protection-A child is in need of protection where,

(a)   the child has suffered physical harm inflicted by the person having charge of the child or caused by that person's failure to care and provide for or supervise and protect the child adequately;

(b)   there is a substantial risk that the child will suffer physical harm inflicted or caused as described in clause (a);

(c)   the child has been sexually molested or sexually exploited, by the person having charge of the child or by another person where the person having charge of the child knows or should know of the possibility of sexual molestation or sexual exploitation and fails to protect the child;

(d)   there is a substantial risk that the child will be sexually molested or sexually exploited as described in clause (c);

(e)   the child requires medical treatment to cure, prevent or alleviate physical harm or suffering and the child's parent or the person having charge of the child does not provide, or refuses or is unavailable or unable to consent to, the treatment;

(f)   the child has suffered emotional harm, demonstrated by severe,

    (i)   anxiety,

    (ii)   depression,

    (iii)   withdrawal, or

    (iv)   self-destructive or aggressive behaviour,

and the child's parent or the person having charge of the child does not provide, or refuses or is unavailable or unable to consent to, services or treatment to remedy or alleviate the harm;

(g)   there is a substantial risk that the child will suffer emotional harm of the kind described in clause (f), and the child's parent or the person having charge of the child does not provide, or refuses or is unavailable or unable to consent to, services or treatment to prevent the harm;

(h)   the child suffers from a mental, emotional or developmental condition that, if not remedied, could seriously impair the child's development and the child's parent or the person having charge of the child does not provide, or refuses or is unavailable or unable to consent to, treatment to remedy or alleviate the condition;

(i)   the child has been abandoned, the child's parent has died or is unavailable to exercise his or her custodial rights over the child and has not made adequate provision for the child's care and custody, or the child is in a residential placement and the parent refuses or is unable or unwilling to resume the child's care and custody;

(j)   the child is less than twelve years old and has killed or seriously injured another person or caused serious damage to another person's property, services or treatment are necessary to prevent a recurrence and the child's parent or the person having charge of the child does not provide, or refuses or is unavailable or unable to consent to, those services or treatment;

(k)   the child is less than twelve years old and has on more than one occasion injured another person or caused loss or damage to another person's property, with the encouragement of the person having charge of the child or because of that person's failure or inability to supervise the child adequately; or

(l)   the child's parent is unable to care for the child and the child is brought before the court with the parent's consent and, where the child is twelve years of age or older, with the child's consent, to be dealt with under this Part.

(3) Best interests of child-Where a person is directed in this Part to make an order or determination in the best interests of a child, the person shall take into consideration those of the following circumstances of the case that he or she considers relevant:

1. The child's physical, mental and emotional needs, and the appropriate care or treatment to meet those needs.

   The child's physical, mental and emotional level of development.

3. The child's cultural background.

4. The religious faith, if any, in which the child is being raised.

5. The importance for the child's development of a positive relationship with a parent and a secure place as a member of a family.

6. The child's relationships by blood or through an adoption order.

7. The importance of continuity in the child's care and the possible effect on the child of disruption of that continuity.

8. The merits of a plan for the child's care proposed by a society, including a proposal that the child be placed for adoption or adopted, compared with the merits of the child remaining with or returning to a parent.

9. The child's views and wishes, if they can be reasonably ascertained.

10. The effects on the child of delay in the disposition of the case.

11. The risk that the child may suffer harm through being removed from, kept away from, returned to or allowed to remain in the care of a parent.

12. The degree of risk, if any, that justified the finding that the child is in need of protection.

13. Any other relevant circumstance.

(4) Where child an Indian or native person—Where a person is directed in this Part to make an order or determination in the best interests of a child and the child is an Indian or native person, the person shall take into consideration the importance, in recognition of the uniqueness of Indian and native culture, heritage and traditions, of preserving the child's cultural identity.

. . .

57. (1) **Order where child in need of protection**.—Where the court finds that a child is in need of protection and is satisfied that intervention through a court order is necessary to protect the child in the future, the court shall make one of the following orders, in the child's best interests:

1. **Supervision order**—That the child be placed with or returned to a parent or another person, subject to the supervision of the society, for a specified period of at least three and not more than twelve months.

2.   Society wardship—That the child be made a ward of the society and be placed in its care and custody for a specified period not exceeding twelve months.

3.   Crown wardship—That the child be made a ward of the Crown, until the wardship is terminated under section 65 or expires under subsection 71(1), and be placed in the care of the society.

4.   Consecutive orders of society wardship and supervision—That the child be made a ward of the society under paragraph 2 for a specified period and then be returned to a parent or another person under paragraph 1, for a period or periods not exceeding an aggregate of twelve months.

(2) **Court to inquire.**—In determining which order to make under subsection (1), the court shall ask the parties what efforts the society or another agency or person made to assist the child before intervention under this Part.

(3) **Less disruptive alternatives preferred.**—The court shall not make an order removing the child from the care of the person who had charge of him or her immediately before intervention under this Part unless the court is satisfied that alternatives that are less disruptive to the child, including non-residential services and the assistance referred to in subsection (2), would be inadequate to protect the child.

(4) **Community placement to be considered.**—Where the court decides that it is necessary to remove the child from the care of the person who had charge of him or her immediately before intervention under this Part, the court shall, before making an order for society or Crown wardship under paragraph 2 or 3 of subsection (1), consider whether it is possible to place the child with a relative, neighbour or other member of the child's community or extended family under paragraph 1 of subsection (1) with the consent of the relative or other person.

(5) **Idem: where child an Indian or a native person.**—Where the child referred to in subsection (4) is an Indian or a native person, unless there is a substantial reason for placing the child elsewhere, the court shall place the child with,

(a)   a member of the child's extended family;

(b)   a member of the child's band or native community; or

(c)   another Indian or native family.

(6) [Repealed 1999, c. 2, s. 15(2).]

(7) **Idem.**—When the court has dispensed with notice to a person under subsection 39(7), the court shall not make an order for Crown wardship under paragraph 3 of subsection (1), or an order for society wardship under paragraph 2 of subsection (1) for a period exceeding thirty days, until a further hearing under subsection 47(1) has been held upon notice to that person.

(8) **Terms and conditions of supervision order.**—Where the court makes a supervision order under paragraph 1 of subsection (1), the court may impose reasonable terms and conditions relating to the child's care and supervision on,

(a)   the person with whom the child is placed or to whom the child is returned;

(b)   the supervising society;

(c)   the child; and

(d)   any other person who participated in the hearing.

(9) **Where no court order necessary**.—Where the court finds that a child is in need of protection but is not satisfied that a court order is necessary to protect the child in the future, the court shall order that the child remain with or be returned to the person who had charge of the child immediately before intervention under this Part. 1999, c. 2, s. 15

Transitional Provision

Pursuant to 1999, c. 2, s. 37(5), section 57 of the Child and Family Services Act, as it read on the day before the March 31, 2000 proclamation of 1999, c. 2, s. 15, continues to apply to any proceeding under Part III, including a status review proceeding, commenced before that date.

On the day before the proclamation, section 57 read as follows:

57. *(1) Order where child in need of protection—Where the court finds that a child is in need of protection and is satisfied that intervention through a court order is necessary to protect the child in the future, the court shall make one of the following orders, in the child's best interests:*

   1.   *Supervision order—That the child be placed with or returned to a parent or another person, subject to the supervision of the society, for a specified period of at least three and not more than twelve months.*

   2.   *Society wardship—That the child be made a ward of the society and be placed in its care and custody for a specified period not exceeding twelve months.*

   3.   *Crown wardship—That the child be made a ward of the Crown, until the wardship is terminated under section 65 or expires under subsection 71(1), and be placed in the care of the society.*

   4.   *Consecutive orders of society wardship and supervision—That the child be made a ward of the society under paragraph 2 for a specified period and then be returned to a parent or another person under paragraph 1, for a period or periods not exceeding an aggregate of twelve months.*

   (2) Court to inquire—In determining which order to make under subsection (1), the court shall ask the parties what efforts the society or another agency or person made to assist the child before intervention under this Part.

   (3) Less restrictive alternatives preferred—The court shall not make an order removing the child from the care of the person who had charge of him or her immediately before intervention under this Part unless the court is satisfied that less restrictive alternatives, including non-residential services and the assistance referred to in subsection (2),

   (a)   *have been attempted and have failed;*

(b)   have been refused by the person having charge of the child; or

(c)   would be inadequate to protect the child.

(4) Community placement to be considered—Where the court decides that it is necessary to remove the child from the care of the person who had charge of him or her immediately before intervention under this Part, the court shall, before making an order for society or Crown wardship under paragraph 2 or 3 of subsection (1), consider whether it is possible to place the child with a relative, neighbour or other member of the child's community or extended family under paragraph 1 of subsection (1) with the consent of the relative or other person.

(5) Idem: where child an Indian or a native person—Where the child referred to in subsection (4) is an Indian or a native person, unless there is a substantial reason for placing the child elsewhere, the court shall place the child with,

(a) a member of the child's extended family;

(b) a member of the child's band or native community; or

(c) another Indian or native family.

(6) Crown wardship order restricted—The court shall not make an order for Crown wardship under paragraph 3 of subsection (1) unless the court is satisfied that the circumstances justifying the order are unlikely to change within a reasonably foreseeable time not exceeding twenty-four months so that the child can be returned to the care of the person who had charge of him or her immediately before intervention under this Part.

(7) Idem—When the court has dispensed with notice to a person under subsection 39(7), the court shall not make an order for Crown wardship under paragraph 3 of subsection (1), or an order for society wardship under paragraph 2 of subsection (1) for a period exceeding thirty days, until a further hearing under subsection 47(1) has been held upon notice to that person.

(8) Terms and conditions of supervision order—Where the court makes a supervision order under paragraph 1 of subsection (1), the court may impose reasonable terms and conditions relating to the child's care and supervision on,

(a)   the person with whom the child is placed or to whom the child is returned;

(b)   the supervising society;

(c)   the child; and

(d)   any other person who participated in the hearing.

(9) Where no court order necessary—Where the court finds that a child is in need of protection but is not satisfied that a court order is necessary to protect the child in the future, the court shall order that the child remain with or be returned to the person who had charge of the child immediately before intervention under this Part.

. . .

72. (1) **Duty to report child in need of protection**.—Despite the provisions of any other Act, if a person, including a person who performs professional or official duties with respect to children, has reasonable grounds to suspect one of the following, the person shall forthwith report the suspicion and the information on which it is based to a society:

1.   The child has suffered physical harm, inflicted by the person having charge of the child or caused by or resulting from that person's,

    i.   failure to adequately care for, provide for, supervise or protect the child, or

    ii.   pattern of neglect in caring for, providing for, supervising or protecting the child.

2.   There is a risk that the child is likely to suffer physical harm inflicted by the person having charge of the child or caused by or resulting from that person's,

    i.   failure to adequately care for, provide for, supervise or protect the child, or

    ii.   pattern of neglect in caring for, providing for, supervising or protecting the child.

3.   The child has been sexually molested or sexually exploited, by the person having charge of the child or by another person where the person having charge of the child knows or should know of the possibility of sexual molestation or sexual exploitation and fails to protect the child.

4.   There is a risk that the child is likely to be sexually molested or sexually exploited as described in paragraph 3.

5.   The child requires medical treatment to cure, prevent or alleviate physical harm or suffering and the child's parent or the person having charge of the child does not provide, or refuses or is unavailable or unable to consent to, the treatment.

6.   The child has suffered emotional harm, demonstrated by serious,

    i.   anxiety,

    ii.   depression,

    iii.   withdrawal,

    iv.   self-destructive or aggressive behaviour, or

    v.   delayed development,

and there are reasonable grounds to believe that the emotional harm suffered by the child results from the actions, failure to act or pattern of neglect on the part of the child's parent or the person having charge of the child.

7.   The child has suffered emotional harm of the kind described in subparagraph i, ii, iii, iv or v of paragraph 6 and the child's parent or the person having charge of the child does not provide, or refuses or is unavailable or unable to consent to, services or treatment to remedy or alleviate the harm.

8. There is a risk that the child is likely to suffer emotional harm of the kind described in subparagraph i, ii, iii, iv or v of paragraph 6 resulting from the actions, failure to act or pattern of neglect on the part of the child's parent or the person having charge of the child.

9. There is a risk that the child is likely to suffer emotional harm of the kind described in subparagraph i, ii, iii, iv or v of paragraph 6 and that the child's parent or the person having charge of the child does not provide, or refuses or is unavailable or unable to consent to, services or treatment to prevent the harm.

10. The child suffers from a mental, emotional or developmental condition that, if not remedied, could seriously impair the child's development and the child's parent or the person having charge of the child does not provide, or refuses or is unavailable or unable to consent to, treatment to remedy or alleviate the condition.

11. The child has been abandoned, the child's parent has died or is unavailable to exercise his or her custodial rights over the child and has not made adequate provision for the child's care and custody, or the child is in a residential placement and the parent refuses or is unable or unwilling to resume the child's care and custody.

12. The child is less than 12 years old and has killed or seriously injured another person or caused serious damage to another person's property, services or treatment are necessary to prevent a recurrence and the child's parent or the person having charge of the child does not provide, or refuses or is unavailable or unable to consent to, those services or treatment.

13. The child is less than 12 years old and has on more than one occasion injured another person or caused loss or damage to another person's property, with the encouragement of the person having charge of the child or because of that person's failure or inability to supervise the child adequately.

(2) **Ongoing duty to report.**—A person who has additional reasonable grounds to suspect one of the matters set out in subsection (1) shall make a further report under subsection (1) even if he or she has made previous reports with respect to the same child.

(3) **Person must report directly.**—A person who has a duty to report a matter under subsection (1) or (2) shall make the report directly to the society and shall not rely on any other person to report on his or her behalf.

(4) **Offence.**—A person referred to in subsection (5) is guilty of an offence if,

(a) he or she contravenes subsection (1) or (2) by not reporting a suspicion; and

(b) the information on which it was based was obtained in the course of his or her professional or official duties.

(5) **Same.**—Subsection (4) applies to every person who performs professional or official duties with respect to children including,

(a) a health care professional, including a physician, nurse, dentist, pharmacist and psychologist;

(b) a teacher, school principal, social worker, family counsellor, priest, rabbi, member of the clergy, operator or employee of a day nursery and youth and recreation worker;

(c)   a peace officer and a coroner;

(d)   a solicitor; and

(e)   a service provider and an employee of a service provider.

(6) **Same.**—In clause (5)(b),

"youth and recreation worker" does not include a volunteer.

(6.1) **Same.**—A director, officer or employee of a corporation who authorizes, permits or concurs in a contravention of an offence under subsection (4) by an employee of the corporation is guilty of an offence.

(6.2) **Same.**—A person convicted of an offence under subsection (4) or (6.1) is liable to a fine of not more than $1,000.

(7) **Section overrides privilege.**—This section applies although the information reported may be confidential or privileged, and no action for making the report shall be instituted against a person who acts in accordance with this section unless the person acts maliciously or without reasonable grounds for the suspicion.

(8) **Exception: solicitor client privilege.**—Nothing in this section abrogates any privilege that may exist between a solicitor and his or her client. 1993, c. 27, Sched.; 1999, c. 2, s. 22

· · ·

74. (1) **Definition.**—In this section and sections 74.1 and 74.2,

"record" means recorded information, regardless of physical form or characteristics.

(2) **Motion or application, production of record.**—A Director or a society may at any time make a motion or an application for an order under subsection (3) or (3.1) for the production of a record or part of a record.

(3) **Order.**—Where the court is satisfied that a record or part of a record that is the subject of a motion referred to in subsection (2) contains information that may be relevant to a proceeding under this Part and that the person in possession or control of the record has refused to permit a Director or the society to inspect it, the court may order that the person in possession or control of the record produce it or a specified part of it for inspection and copying by the Director, by the society or by the court.

(3.1) **Same.**—Where the court is satisfied that a record or part of a record that is the subject of an application referred to in subsection (2) may be relevant to assessing compliance with one of the following and that the person in possession or control of the record has refused to permit a Director or the society to inspect it, the court may order that the person in possession or control of the record produce it or a specified part of it for inspection and copying by the Director, by the society or by the court:

1.   An order under clause 51(2)(b) or (c) that is subject to supervision.

2.   An order under clause 51(2)(c) or (d) with respect to access.

3.   A supervision order under section 57.

4.   An access order under section 58.

5.   An order under section 65 with respect to access or supervision.

6.   A restraining order under section 80.

(4) **Court may examine record.**—In considering whether to make an order under subsection (3) or (3.1), the court may examine the record.

(5) **Information confidential.**—No person who obtains information by means of an order made under subsection (3) or (3.1) shall disclose the information except,

(a)   as specified in the order; and

(b)   in testimony in a proceeding under this Part.

(6) **Application: solicitor client privilege excepted.**—Subject to subsection (7), this section applies despite any other Act, but nothing in this section abrogates any privilege that may exist between a solicitor and his or her client.

(7) **Matters to be considered by court.**—Where a motion or an application under subsection (2) concerns a record that is a clinical record within the meaning of section 35 of the Mental Health Act, subsection 35(6) (attending physician's statement, hearing) of that Act applies and the court shall give equal consideration to,

(a)   the matters to be considered under subsection 35(7) of that Act; and

(b)   the need to protect the child.

(8) **Same.**—Where a motion or an application under subsection (2) concerns a record that is a record of a mental disorder within the meaning of section 183, that section applies and the court shall give equal consideration to,

(a)   the matters to be considered under subsection 183(6); and

(b)   the need to protect the child. 1999, c. 2, s. 24

...

CONSTITUTION ACT, 1982

Schedule B to Canada Act 1982 (U.K)
as am. SI/84-102; SI/93-54

PART 1

CANADIAN CHARTER OF RIGHTS AND FREEDOMS

Whereas Canada is founded upon principles that recognize the supremacy of God and the rule of law.

Guarantee of Rights and Freedoms

1. Rights and freedoms in Canada.—The *Canadian Charter of Rights and Freedoms* guarantees the rights and freedoms set out in it subject only to such reasonable limits prescribed by law as can be demonstrably justified in a free and democratic society.

Fundamental Freedoms

2. Fundamental freedoms.—Everyone has the following fundamental freedoms:

(*a*) freedom of conscience and religion;
(*b*) freedom of thought, belief, opinion and expression, including freedom of the press and other media of communication;
(*c*) freedom of peaceful assembly; and
(*d*) freedom of association.

Democratic Rights

3. Democratic rights of citizens.—Every citizen of Canada has the right to vote in an election of members of the House of Commons or of a legislative assembly and to be qualified for membership therein.

4. (1) Maximum duration of legislative bodies.—No House of Commons and no legislative assembly shall continue for longer than five years from the date fixed for the return of the writs at a general election of its members.

(2) **Continuation in special circumstances.**—In time of real or apprehended war, invasion or insurrection, a House of Commons may be continued by Parliament and a legislative assembly may be continued by the legislature beyond five years if such continuation is not opposed by the votes of more than one-third of the members of the House of Commons or the legislative assembly, as the case may be.

5. Annual sitting of legislative bodies.—There shall be a sitting of Parliament and of each legislature at least once every twelve months.

6. (1) Mobility of citizens.—Every citizen of Canada has the right to enter, remain in and leave Canada.

(2) **Rights to move and gain livelihood.**—Every citizen of Canada and every person who has the status of a permanent resident of Canada has the right

(*a*) to move to and take up residence in any province; and

(*b*) to pursue the gaining of a livelihood in any province.

(3) **Limitation.**—The rights specified in subsection (2) are subject to

(*a*) any laws or practices of general application in force in a province other than those that discriminate among persons primarily on the basis of province of present or previous residence; and

(*b*) any laws providing for reasonable residency requirements as a qualification for the receipt of publicly provided social services.

(4) **Affirmative action programs.**—Subsections (2) and (3) do not preclude any law, program or activity that has as its object the amelioration in a province of conditions of individuals in that province who are socially or economically disadvantaged if the rate of employment in that province is below the rate of employment in Canada.

Legal Rights

7. Life, liberty and security of person.—Everyone has the right to life, liberty and security of the person and the right not to be deprived thereof except in accordance with the principles of fundamental justice.

8. Search or seizure.—Everyone has the right to be secure against unreasonable search or seizure.

9. Detention or imprisonment.—Everyone has the right not to be arbitrarily detained or imprisoned.

10. Arrest or detention.—Everyone has the right on arrest or detention

(*a*) to be informed promptly of the reasons therefor;

(*b*) to retain and instruct counsel without delay and to be informed of that right; and

(*c*) to have the validity of the detention determined by way of *habeas corpus* and to be released if the detention is not lawful.

11. Proceedings in criminal and penal matters.—Any person charged with an offence has the right

(*a*) to be informed without unreasonable delay of the specific offence;

(*b*) to be tried within a reasonable time;

(*c*) not to be compelled to be a witness in proceedings against that person in respect of the offence;

(*d*) to be presumed innocent until proven guilty according to law in a fair and public hearing by an independent and impartial tribunal;

(*e*) not to be denied reasonable bail without just cause;

(*f*) except in the case of an offence under military law tried before a military tribunal, to the benefit of trial by jury where the maximum punishment for the offence is imprisonment for five years or a more severe punishment;

(*g*) not to be found guilty on account of any act or omission unless, at the time of the act or omission, it constituted an offence under Canadian or international law or was criminal according to the general principles of law recognized by the community of nations;

(*h*) if finally acquitted of the offence, not to be tried for it again and, if finally found guilty and punished for the offence, not to be tried or punished for it again; and (*i*) if found guilty of the offence and if the punishment for the offence has been varied between the time of commission and the time of sentencing, to the benefit of the lesser punishment.

12. Treatment or punishment.—Everyone has the right not to be subjected to any cruel and unusual treatment or punishment.

13. Self-crimination.—A witness who testifies in any proceedings has the right not to have any incriminating evidence so given used to incriminate that witness in any other proceedings, except in a prosecution for perjury or for the giving of contradictory evidence.

14. Interpreter.—A party or witness in any proceedings who does not understand or speak the language in which the proceedings are conducted or who is deaf has the right to the assistance of an interpreter.

Equality Rights

15. (1) Equality before and under law and equal protection and benefit of law.—Every individual is equal before and under the law and has the right to the equal protection and equal benefit of the law without discrimination and, in particular, without discrimination based on race, national or ethnic origin, colour, religion, sex, age or mental or physical disability.

(2) **Affirmative action programs.**—Subsection (1) does not preclude any law, program or activity that has as its object the amelioration of conditions of disadvantaged individuals or groups including those that are disadvantaged because of race, national or ethnic origin, colour, religion, sex, age or mental or physical disability.

Official Languages of Canada

16. (1) Official languages of Canada.—English and French are the official languages of Canada and have equality of status and equal rights and privileges as to their use in all institutions of the Parliament and government of Canada.

(2) **Official languages of New Brunswick.**—English and French are the official languages of New Brunswick and have equality of status and equal rights and privileges as to their use in all institutions of the legislature and government of New Brunswick.

(3) **Advancement of status and use.**—Nothing in this Charter limits the authority of Parliament or a legislature to advance the equality of status or use of English and French.

16.1 (1) English and French linguistic communities in New Brunswick.—The English linguistic community and the French linguistic community in New Brunswick have equality of status and equal rights and privileges, including the right to distinct educational institutions and such distinct cultural institutions as are necessary for the preservation and promotion of those communities.

(2) **Role of the legislature and government of New Brunswick.**—The role of the legislature and government of New Brunswick to preserve and promote the status, rights and privileges referred to in subsection (1) is afirmed. SI/93-54, s. 1.

17. (1) Proceedings of Parliament.—Everyone has the right to use English or French in any debates and other proceedings of Parliament.

(2) **Proceedings of New Brunswick legislature.**—Everyone has the right to use English or French in any debates and other proceedings of the legislature of New Brunswick.

18. (1) **Parliamentary statutes and records.**—The statutes, records and journals of Parliament shall be printed and published in English and French and both language versions are equally authoritative.

(2) **New Brunswick statutes and records.**—The statutes, records and journals of the legislature of New Brunswick shall be printed and published in English and French and both language versions are equally authoritative.

19. (1) **Proceedings in courts established by Parliament.**—Either English or French may be used by any person in, or in any pleading in or process issuing from, any court established by Parliament.

(2) **Proceedings in New Brunswick courts.**—Either English or French may be used by any person in, or in any pleading in or process issuing from, any court of New Brunswick.

20. (1) **Communications by public with federal institutions.**—Any member of the public in Canada has the right to communicate with, and to receive available services from, any head or central office of an institution of the Parliament or government of Canada in English or French, and has the same right with respect to any other office of any such institution where

(*a*) there is a significant demand for communications with and services from that office in such language; or

(*b*) due to the nature of the office, it is reasonable that communications with and services from that office be available in both English and French.

(2) **Communications by public with New Brunswick institutions.**—Any member of the public in New Brunswick has the right to communicate with, and to receive available services from, any office of an institution of the legislature or government of New Brunswick in English or French.

21. Continuation of existing constitutional provisions.—Nothing in sections 16 to 20 abrogates or derogates from any right, privilege or obligation with respect to the English and French languages, or either of them, that exists or is continued by virtue of any other provision of the Constitution of Canada.

22. Rights and privileges preserved.—Nothing in sections 16 to 20 abrogates or derogates from any legal or customary right or privilege acquired or enjoyed either before or after the coming into force of this Charter with respect to any language that is not English or French.

Minority Language Educational Rights

23. (1) **Language of instruction.**—Citizens of Canada

(*a*) whose first language learned and still understood is that of the English or French linguistic minority population of the province in which they reside, or

(*b*) who have received their primary school instruction in Canada in English or French and reside in a province where the language in which they received that instruction is the language of the English or French linguistic minority population of the province, have the right to have their children receive primary and secondary school instruction in that language in that province.

(2) **Continuity of language instruction.**—Citizens of Canada of whom any child has received or is receiving primary or secondary school instruction in English or French in Canada, have the right to have all their children receive primary and secondary school instruction in the same language.

(3) **Application where numbers warrant.**—The right of citizens of Canada under subsections (1) and (2) to have their children receive primary and secondary school instruction in the language of the English or French linguistic minority population of a province

(*a*) applies wherever in the province the number of children of citizens who have such a right is sufficient to warrant the provision to them out of public funds of minority language instruction; and

(*b*) includes, where the number of those children so warrants, the right to have them receive that instruction in minority language educational facilities provided out of public funds.

Enforcement

24. (1) **Enforcement of guaranteed rights and freedoms.**—Anyone whose rights or freedoms, as guaranteed by this Charter, have been infringed or denied may apply to a court of competent jurisdiction to obtain such remedy as the court considers appropriate and just in the circumstances.

(2) **Exclusion of evidence bringing administration of justice into disrepute.**— Where, in proceedings under subsection (1), a court concludes that evidence was obtained in a manner that infringed or denied any rights or freedoms guaranteed by this Charter, the evidence shall be excluded if it is established that, having regard to all the circumstances, the admission of it in the proceedings would bring the administration of justice into disrepute.

General

25. Aboriginal rights and freedoms not affected by Charter.—The guarantee in this Charter of certain rights and freedoms shall not be construed so as to abrogate or derogate from any aboriginal treaty or other rights or freedoms that pertain to the aboriginal peoples of Canada including

(*a*) any rights or freedoms that have been recognized by the Royal Proclamation of October 7, 1963; and

(*b*) any rights or freedoms that now exist by way of land claims agreements or may be so acquired. SI/84-102, s. 1.

26. Other rights and freedoms not affected by Charter.—The guarantee in this Charter of certain rights and freedoms shall not be construed as denying the existence of any other rights or freedoms that exist in Canada.

27. Multicultural heritage.—This Charter shall be interpreted in a manner consistent with the preservation and enhancement of the multicultural heritage of Canadians.

28. Rights guaranteed equally to both sexes.—Notwithstanding anything in this Charter, the rights and freedoms referred to in it are guaranteed equally to male and female persons.

29. Rights respecting certain schools preserved.—Nothing in this Charter abrogates or derogates from any rights or privileges guaranteed by or under the Constitution of Canada in respect of denominational, separate or dissentient schools.

30. Application to territories and territorial authorities.—A reference in this Charter to a province or to the legislative assembly or legislature of a province shall be deemed to include a reference to the Yukon Territory and the Northwest Territories, or to the appropriate legislative authority thereof, as the case may be.

31. Legislative powers not extended.—Nothing in this Charter extends the legislative powers of any body or authority.

Application of Charter

32. (1) **Application of Charter.**—This Charter applies

(*a*) to the Parliament and government of Canada in respect of all matters within the authority of Parliament including all matters relating to the Yukon Territory and Northwest Territories; and

(*b*) to the legislature and government of each province in respect of all matters within the authority of the legislature of each province.

(2) **Exception.**—Notwithstanding subsection (1), section 15 shall not have effect until three years after this section comes into force.

33. (1) **Exception where express declaration.**—Parliament or the legislature of a province may expressly declare in an Act of Parliament or of the legislature, as the case may be, that the Act or a provision thereof shall operate notwithstanding a provision included in section 2 or sections 7 to 15 of this Charter.

(2) **Operation of exception.**—An Act or a provision of an Act in respect of which a declaration made under this section is in effect shall have such operation as it would have but for the provision of this Charter referred to in the declaration.

(3) **Five-year limitation.**—A declaration made under subsection (1) shall cease to have effect five years after it comes into force or on such earlier date as may be specified in the declaration.

(4) **Re-enactment.**—Parliament or a legislature of a province may re-enact a declaration made under subsection (1).

(5) **Five-year limitation.**—Subsection (3) applies in respect of a re-enactment made under subsection (4).

Citation

34. Citation.—This Part may be cited as the *Canadian Charter of Rights and Freedoms.*

EDUCATION ACT

R.S.O. 1990, c. E.2, as am. S.O. 1991, Vol. 2, c. 10 and 15; 1992, c. 15, ss. 85-89; c. 16; c. 17, ss. 1-3; c. 27, s. 59; c. 32, s. 9; 1993, c. 11, ss. 8-43; c. 23, s. 67; c. 26, ss. 44-45; c. 27, Schedule; c. 41; 1994, c. 1, s. 22; c. 17, ss. 48, 51; c. 23, s. 65 (not yet in force); 1996, c. 11, s. 29; c. 12, s. 64; c. 13, ss. 1-11; c. 13, s. 12; c. 32, s. 70; 1997, c. 3, ss. 2-10; c. 16, s. 5; c. 19, s. 33; c. 22, s. 1; c. 31; c. 32, s. 10; 2000, c. 11, ss. 17, 18; c. 12, ss. 2, 3; 2001, c. 14, Sched. A, ss. 7, 8; 2003, c. 2, s. 20(1)

(Excerpts)

. . . . .

Duties

264. (1) **Duties of teacher.**—It is the duty of a teacher and a temporary teacher,

(a) **teach.**—to teach diligently and faithfully the classes or subjects assigned to the teacher by the principal;

(b) **learning.**—to encourage the pupils in the pursuit of learning;

(c) **religion and morals.**—to inculcate by precept and example respect for religion and the principles of Judaeo-Christian morality and the highest regard for truth, justice, loyalty, love of country, humanity, benevolence, sobriety, industry, frugality, purity, temperance and all other virtues;

(d) **co-operation.**—to assist in developing co-operation and co-ordination of effort among the members of the staff of the school;

(e) **discipline.**—to maintain, under the direction of the principal, proper order and discipline in the teacher's classroom and while on duty in the school and on the school ground;

(f) **language of instruction.**—in instruction and in all communications with the pupils in regard to discipline and the management of the school,

    (i) to use the English language, except where it is impractical to do so by reason of the pupil not understanding English, and except in respect of instruction in a language other than English when such other language is being taught as one of the subjects in the course of study, or

    (ii) to use the French language in schools or classes in which French is the language of instruction except where it is impractical to do so by reason of the pupil not understanding French, and except in respect of instruction in a language other than French when such other language is being taught as one of the subjects in the course of study;

(g) **timetable.**—to conduct the teacher's class in accordance with a timetable which shall be accessible to pupils and to the principal and supervisory officers;

(h) **professional activity days.**—to participate in professional activity days as designated by the board under the regulations;

(i) **absence from school.**—to notify such person as is designated by the board if the teacher is to be absent from school and the reason therefor;

(j) **school property.**—to deliver the register, the school key and other school property in the teacher's possession to the board on demand, or when the teacher's agreement with the board has expired, or when for any reason the teacher's employment has ceased; and

(k) **textbooks.**—to use and permit to be used as a textbook in a class that he or she teachers in an elementary or a secondary school,

(i) in a subject area for which textbooks are approved by the Minister, only textbooks that are approved by the Minister, and

(ii) in all subject areas, only textbooks that are approved by the board.

(l) duties assigned to perform all duties assigned in accordance with this Act and the regulations.

(1.1) **Sign language.**—Despite clause (1)(f), a teacher or temporary teacher may use American Sign Language or Quebec Sign Language in accordance with the regulations.

(1.2) [Repealed 2001, c. 14, Sched. A, s. 7.]

(1.3) [Repealed 2001, c. 14, Sched. A, s. 7.]

(2) **Refusal to give up school property.**—A teacher who refuses, on demand or order of the board that operates the school concerned, to deliver to the board any school property in the teacher's possession forfeits any claim that the teacher may have against the board.

(3) **Teachers, conferences.**—Teachers may organize themselves for the purpose of conducting professional development conferences and seminars.

1993, c. 11, s. 36; 2000, c. 11, s. 17; 2001, c. 14, Sched. A, s. 7; 2003, c. 2, s. 20(1).

265. (1) Duties of principal.—It is the duty of a principal of a school, in addition to the principal's duties as a teacher,

(a) **discipline.**—to maintain proper order and discipline in the school;

(b) **co-operation.**—to develop co-operation and co-ordination of effort among the members of the staff of the school;

(c) **register pupils and record attendance.**—to register the pupils and to ensure that the attendance of pupils for every school day is recorded either in the register supplied by the Minister in accordance with the instructions contained therein or in such other manner as is approved by the Minister;

(d) **pupil records.**—in accordance with this Act, the regulations and the guidelines issued by the Minister, to collect information for inclusion in a record in respect of each pupil enrolled in the school and to establish, maintain, retain, transfer and dispose of the record;

(e) **timetable.**—to prepare a timetable. to conduct the school according to such timetable and the school year calendar or calendars applicable thereto, to make the calendar or calendars and the timetable accessible to the pupils, teachers and supervisory officers and to assign classes and subjects to the teachers;

(f) **examinations and reports.**—to hold, subject to the approval of the appropriate supervisory officer, such examinations as the principal considers necessary for the promotion of pupils or for any other purpose and report as required by the board the progress of the pupil to his or her parent or guardian where the pupil is a minor and otherwise to the pupil;

(g) **promote pupils.**—subject to revision by the appropriate supervisory officer, to promote such pupils as the principal considers proper and to issue to each such pupil a statement thereof;

(h) **textbooks.**—to ensure that all textbooks used by pupils are those approved by the board and, in the case of subject areas for which the Minister approves textbooks, those approved by the Minister;

(i) **reports.**—to furnish to the Ministry and to the appropriate supervisory officer any information that it may be in the principal's power to give respecting the condition of the school premises, the discipline of the school, the progress of the pupils and any other matter affecting the interests of the school, and to prepare such reports for the board as are required by the board;

(j) **care of pupils and property.**—to give assiduous attention to the health and comfort of the pupils, to the cleanliness, temperature and ventilation of the school, to the care of all teaching materials and other school property, and to the condition and appearance of the school buildings and grounds;

(k) **report to M.O.H.**—to report promptly to the board and to the medical officer of health when the principal has reason to suspect the existence of any communicable disease in the school, and of the unsanitary condition of any part of the school building or the school grounds;

(l) **persons with communicable diseases.**—to refuse admission to the school of any person who the principal believes is infected with or exposed to communicable diseases requiring an order under section 22 of the *Health Protection and Promotion Act* until furnished with a certificate of a medical officer of health or of a legally qualified medical practitioner approved by the medical officer of health that all danger from exposure to contact with such person has passed;

(m) **access to school or class.**—subject to an appeal to the board, to refuse to admit to the school or classroom a person whose presence in the school or classroom would in the principal's judgment be detrimental to the physical or mental well-being of the pupils; and

(n) **visitor's book.**—to maintain a visitor's book in the school when so determined by the board.

(2) **Co-instructional activities**.—In addition, it is the duty of a principal in accordance with the board plan to provide for co-instructional activities under subsection 170(1), to develop and implement a school plan providing for co-instructional activities.

(3) **School council**.—The principal shall consult the school council at least once in each school year respecting the school plan providing for co-instructional activities.

(4) [Repealed 2001, c. 14, Sched. A, s. 8.]

             1991, vol. 2, c. 10, s. 6; 2000, c. 11, s. 18; 2001, c. 14, Sched. A, s. 8.

·   ·   ·   ·   ·

286. (1) **Duties of supervisory officers.**—Subject to the policies and guidelines established under paragraph 3.4 of subsection 8(1) and subject to the regulations, a board or the Minister shall assign the following duties to its or the Minister's supervisory officer or officers,

(a) **assist teachers.**—to bring about improvement in the quality of education by assisting teachers in their practice;

(b) **co-operate with boards.**—to assist and co-operate with boards to the end that the schools may best serve the needs of the pupils;

(c) **visit schools.**—to visit schools and classrooms as the Minister may direct and, where the supervisory officer has been appointed by a board, as the board may direct;

(d) **prepare reports.**—to prepare a report of a visit to a school or classroom when required by the Minister and, where the supervisory officer has been appointed by a board, when required by the board and to give to a teacher referred to in any such report a copy of the portion of the report that refers to the teacher;

(e) **Acts and regulations.**—to ensure that the schools under his or her jurisdiction are conducted in accordance with this Act and the regulations;

(f) **annual report to Minister.**—to make a general annual report as to the performance of his or her duties and the condition of the schools in his or her area of jurisdiction when required by the Minister and, where the supervisory officer has been appointed by a board, when required by the board;

(g) **report to M.O.H.**—to report to the appropriate medical officer of health any case in which the school buildings or premises are found to be in an unsanitary condition;

(h) **report to the Minister.**—to furnish the Minister with information respecting any school in his or her area of jurisdiction whenever required to do so;

(i) **supervise business.**—to supervise the business functions of the board;

(j) **supervise buildings and property.**—to supervise the use and maintenance of the buildings and property of the board; and

(k) others to exercise such other powers and perform such other duties as may be prescribed by a regulation made, or a policy established, under Part XIII (Behaviour, Discipline and Safety).

(2) **Responsibility to Minister.**—Every supervisory officer appointed by the Minister is responsible to the Minister for the performance of his or her duties.

(3) **Responsibility to board.**—Every supervisory officer appointed by a board is responsible to the board through the chief executive officer for the performance of the duties assigned to the supervisory officer by the board.

(4) **Full-time position.**—Except as otherwise provided by this Act or the regulations, a supervisory officer shall not, without the approval of the Minister, hold any other office, have any other employment or follow any other profession or calling, during his or her tenure as a supervisory officer.

(5) **Access to books and records, etc.**—A provincial supervisory officer or a person designated by the Minister shall have access, as required by the Minister, to any school and to the books and records of a board or a school.

1997, c. 31, s. 126; 2000, c. 12, s. 2.

300. (1) **Definition.**—In this Part,

"school premises" means, with respect to a school, the school buildings and premises.

(2) **Interpretation.**—In this Part, where reference is made to a regulation or to a matter prescribed by regulation, it means a regulation to be made by the Minister under this Part.

2000, c. 12, s. 3

301. (1) **Provincial code of conduct.**—The Minister may establish a code of conduct governing the behaviour of all persons in schools.

(2) **Purposes.**—The following are the purposes of the code of conduct:

1. To ensure that all members of the school community, especially people in positions of authority, are treated with respect and dignity.
2. To promote responsible citizenship by encouraging appropriate participation in the civic life of the school community.

3. To maintain an environment where conflict and difference can be addressed in a manner characterized by respect and civility.

4. To encourage the use of non-violent means to resolve conflict.

5. To promote the safety of people in the schools.

6. To discourage the use of alcohol and illegal drugs.

(3) **Notice**.—Every board shall take such steps as the Minister directs to bring the code of conduct to the attention of pupils, parents and guardians of pupils and others who may be present in schools under the jurisdiction of the board.

(4) **Code is policy**.—The code of conduct is a policy of the Minister.

(5) **Policies and guidelines governing conduct**.—The Minister may establish additional policies and guidelines with respect to the conduct of persons in schools.

(6) **Same, governing discipline**.—The Minister may establish policies and guidelines with respect to disciplining pupils, specifying, for example, the circumstances in which a pupil is subject to discipline and the forms and the extent of discipline that may be imposed in particular circumstances.

(7) **Same, promoting safety**.—The Minister may establish policies and guidelines to promote the safety of pupils.

(8) **Different policies, etc.**—The Minister may establish different policies and guidelines under this section for different circumstances, for different locations and for different classes of persons.

(9) **Duty of boards**.—The Minister may require boards to comply with policies and guidelines established under this section.

(10) **Not regulations**.—Policies and guidelines established under this section are not regulations within the meaning of the Regulations Act.

2000, c. 12, s. 3

302. (1) **Boards' policies and guidelines governing conduct**.—Every board shall establish policies and guidelines with respect to the conduct of persons in schools within the board's jurisdiction and the policies and guidelines must address such matters and include such requirements as the Minister may specify.

(2) **Same, governing discipline**.—A board may establish policies and guidelines with respect to disciplining pupils, and the policies and guidelines must be consistent with this Part and with the policies and guidelines established by the Minister under section 301, and must address such matters and include such requirements as the Minister may specify.

(3) **Same, promoting safety**.—If required to do so by the Minister, a board shall establish policies and guidelines to promote the safety of pupils, and the policies and guidelines must be consistent with those established by the Minister under section 301 and must address such matters and include such requirements as the Minister may specify.

(4) **Same, governing access to school premises**.—A board may establish policies and guidelines governing access to school premises, and the policies and guidelines must be consistent with the regulations made under section 305 and must address such matters and include such requirements as the Minister may specify.

(5) **Same, governing appropriate dress.**—If required to do so by the Minister, a board shall establish policies and guidelines respecting appropriate dress for pupils in schools within the board's jurisdiction, and the policies and guidelines must address such matters and include such requirements as the Minister may specify.

(6) **Same, procedural matters.**—A board shall establish policies and guidelines governing a review or appeal of a decision to suspend a pupil and governing, with respect to expulsions, a principal's inquiry, an expulsion hearing and an appeal of a decision to expel a pupil, and the policies and guidelines must address such matters and include such requirements as the Minister may specify.

(7) **Different policies, etc.**—A board may establish different policies and guidelines under this section for different circumstances, for different locations and for different classes of persons.

(8) **Role of school councils.**—When establishing policies and guidelines under this section, a board shall consider the views of school councils with respect to the contents of the policies and guidelines.

(9) **Periodic review.**—The board shall periodically review its policies and guidelines established under this section and shall solicit the views of pupils, teachers, staff, volunteers working in the schools, parents and guardians, school councils and the public.

(10) **Not regulations.**—Policies and guidelines established under this section are not regulations within the meaning of the Regulations Act.

2000, c. 12, s. 3

303. (1) **Local codes of conduct.**—A board may direct the principal of a school to establish a local code of conduct governing the behaviour of all persons in the school, and the local code must be consistent with the provincial code established under subsection 301(1) and must address such matters and include such requirements as the board may specify.

(2) **Same, mandatory.**—A board shall direct a principal to establish a local code of conduct if the board is required to do so by the Minister, and the local code must address such matters and include such requirements as the Minister may specify.

(3) **Role of school council.**—When establishing or reviewing a local code of conduct, the principal shall consider the views of the school council with respect to its contents.

(4) **Not regulation.**—A local code of conduct is not a regulation within the meaning of the Regulations Act.

2000, c. 12, s. 3

304. (1) **Opening and closing exercises at schools.**—Every board shall ensure that opening or closing exercises are held in each school under the board's jurisdiction, in accordance with the requirements set out in the regulations.

(2) **Same.**—The opening or closing exercises must include the singing of O Canada and may include the recitation of a pledge of citizenship in the form set out in the regulations.

(3) **Exceptions.**—A pupil is not required to participate in the opening or closing exercises in such circumstances as are prescribed by regulation.

2000, c. 12, s. 3

305. (1) **Access to school premises.**—The Minister may make regulations governing access to school premises, specifying classes of persons who are permitted to be on school premises and specifying the days and times at which different classes of persons are prohibited from being on school premises.

(2) **Prohibition.**—No person shall enter or remain on school premises unless he or she is authorized by regulation to be there on that day or at that time.

(3) **Same, board policy.**—A person shall not enter or remain on school premises if he or she is prohibited under a board policy from being there on that day or at that time.

(4) **Direction to leave.**—The principal of a school may direct a person to leave the school premises if the principal believes that the person is prohibited by regulation or under a board policy from being there.

(5) **Offence.**—Every person who contravenes subsection (2) is guilty of an offence.

2000, c. 12, s. 3

306. (1) **Mandatory suspension of a pupil.**—It is mandatory that a pupil be suspended from his or her school and from engaging in all school-related activities if the pupil commits any of the following infractions while he or she is at school or is engaged in a school-related activity:

1. Uttering a threat to inflict serious bodily harm on another person.
2. Possessing alcohol or illegal drugs.
3. Being under the influence of alcohol.
4. Swearing at a teacher or at another person in a position of authority.
5. Committing an act of vandalism that causes extensive damage to school property at the pupil's school or to property located on the premises of the pupil's school.
6. Engaging in another activity that, under a policy of the board, is one for which a suspension is mandatory.

(2) **Duration of mandatory suspension.**—The minimum duration of a mandatory suspension is one school day and the maximum duration is 20 school days. The minimum and maximum duration may be varied by regulation, and different standards may be established for different circumstances or different classes of persons.

(3) **Duties of teachers.**—If a teacher observes a pupil committing an infraction that requires a mandatory suspension, the teacher shall suspend the pupil or refer the matter to the principal.

(4) **Duty to suspend, principal.**—The principal has a duty to suspend a pupil who commits an infraction requiring a mandatory suspension, unless a teacher has already suspended the pupil for the infraction.

(5) **Mitigating factors.**—Despite subsection (1), suspension of a pupil is not mandatory in such circumstances as may be prescribed by regulation.

(6) **Restriction on suspension by teacher.**—A teacher cannot suspend a pupil under this section for a period longer than the minimum duration required by subsection (2).

(7) **Referral to principal.**—If a teacher who suspends a pupil under this section is of the opinion that a longer suspension of the pupil is warranted, the teacher shall recommend to the principal that the suspension be extended.

(8) **Extension by principal.**—Upon receiving a recommendation from a teacher to extend the suspension imposed on a pupil by the teacher, the principal may extend the suspension up to the maximum duration permitted by subsection (2).

(9) **Factors affecting duration of suspension.**—In order to determine the duration of a mandatory suspension, the principal shall consider the pupil's history and such other factors as may be prescribed by regulation and the principal may consider such other matters as he or she considers appropriate.

(10) **Notice.**—The teacher or principal who suspends a pupil under this section shall ensure that written notice of the mandatory suspension is given promptly to the pupil and, if the pupil is a minor, to the pupil's parent or guardian.

(11) **Policies and guidelines.**—The Minister may issue policies and guidelines to boards to assist principals and teachers in interpreting and administering this section.

(12) **School-related activities.**—A pupil who is suspended is not considered to be engaged in school-related activities by virtue of using services, taking a course or participating in a program to assist such pupils.

(13) **Definition.**—In this section,

"mandatory suspension" means a suspension required by subsection (1).

(14) **Commencement.**—This section comes into force on a day to be named by proclamation of the Lieutenant Governor.

2000, c. 12, s. 3

307. (1) **Discretionary suspension of a pupil.**—A pupil may be suspended if he or she engages in an activity that, under a policy of the board, is an activity for which suspension is discretionary.

(2) **Same.**—A pupil may be suspended,

(a) from his or her school and from engaging in all school-related activities; or
(b) from one or more classes or one or more school-related activities or both.

(3) **Duration of discretionary suspension.**—The minimum duration of a discretionary suspension is as specified by the board policy that authorizes the suspension and the maximum duration is 20 school days. The maximum duration may be varied by regulation, and different standards may be established for different circumstances or different classes of persons.

(4) **Authority to suspend, principal.**—The principal may suspend a pupil who engages in an activity for which suspension is discretionary.

(5) **Authority of teachers.**—If a teacher observes a pupil engaging in an activity for which suspension is discretionary, the teacher may suspend the pupil or refer the matter to the principal.

(6) **Restriction on suspension by teacher.**—A teacher cannot suspend a pupil under this section for a period longer than the minimum duration described in subsection (3).

(7) **Other matters.**—Subsections 306(7) to (10) and 306(12) apply, with necessary modifications, with respect to a discretionary suspension under this section.

(8) **Definition.**—In this section,

"discretionary suspension" means a suspension authorized by subsection (1).

(9) **Commencement.**—This section comes into force on a day to be named by proclamation of the Lieutenant Governor.

2000, c. 12, s. 3

308. (1) **Review of suspension.**—The following persons may request a review of a decision to suspend a pupil, other than a decision to suspend a pupil for one day or less:

1. If the pupil is a minor, his or her parent or guardian.
2. If the pupil is not a minor, the pupil.
3. Such other persons as may be specified in a policy of the board.

(2) **The review process.**—The review shall be conducted in accordance with the requirements established by board policy.

(3) **Same.**—The review shall be conducted by the person specified in the board policy and, for the purposes of the review, the person has the powers and duties set out in the policy.

(4) **Appeal of suspension.**—Following a review, the following persons may appeal a decision to suspend a pupil, other than a decision to suspend a pupil for one day or less:

1. If the pupil is a minor, his or her parent or guardian.
2. If the pupil is not a minor, the pupil.
3. Such other persons as may be specified by board policy.

(5) **The appeal process.**—An appeal under this section must be conducted in accordance with the requirements established by board policy.

(6) **Same.**—The board shall hear and determine an appeal and, for that purpose, the board has the powers and duties set out in its policy. The decisions of the board are final.

(7) **Delegation by board.**—The board may delegate its powers and duties under subsection (6) to a committee of the board, and may impose conditions and restrictions on the committee.

(8) **Commencement.**—This section comes into force on a day to be named by proclamation of the Lieutenant Governor.

2000, c. 12, s. 3

309. (1) **Mandatory expulsion of a student.**—It is mandatory that a pupil be expelled if the pupil commits any of the following infractions while he or she is at school or is engaged in a school-related activity:

1. Possessing a weapon, including possessing a firearm.
2. Using a weapon to cause or to threaten bodily harm to another person.
3. Committing physical assault on another person that causes bodily harm requiring treatment by a medical practitioner.
4. Committing sexual assault.
5. Trafficking in weapons or in illegal drugs.
6. Committing robbery.
7. Giving alcohol to a minor.
8. Engaging in another activity that, under a policy of the board, is one for which expulsion is mandatory.

(2) **Duty to suspend pending expulsion, principal.**—The principal shall suspend a pupil who the principal believes may have committed an infraction for which expulsion is mandatory.

(3) **Mitigating factors.**—Despite subsection (1), expulsion of a pupil is not mandatory in such circumstances as may be prescribed by regulation.

(4) **Action following suspension.**—If the principal suspends a pupil under subsection (2), the principal shall promptly refer the matter to the board or conduct an inquiry to determine whether the pupil has committed an infraction for which expulsion is mandatory.

(5) **Notice of suspension.**—The principal shall ensure that written notice of the suspension under subsection (2) is given promptly to the pupil and, if the pupil is a minor, to the pupil's parent or guardian.

(6) **Conduct of inquiry.**—The principal's inquiry shall be conducted in accordance with the requirements established by a policy of the board and the powers and duties of the principal are as specified by board policy.

(7) **Action following inquiry.**—If, after the inquiry, the principal is satisfied that the pupil committed an infraction for which expulsion is mandatory, the principal shall,

(a) impose a limited expulsion as described in subsection (14) on the pupil; or
(b) refer the matter to the board for its determination.

(8) **Restriction on expulsion by principal.**—The principal cannot expel a pupil if more than 20 school days have expired since the principal suspended the student under subsection (2), unless the parties to the inquiry agree upon a later deadline.

(9) **Hearing by board.**—When a matter is referred to the board under subsection (4) or clause (7)(b), the board shall hold an expulsion hearing and, for that purpose, the board has the powers and duties specified by board policy.

(10) **Conduct of hearing.**—The expulsion hearing shall be conducted in accordance with the requirements established by board policy.

(11) **Duty to expel, board.**—If, after the expulsion hearing, the board is satisfied that the pupil committed an infraction for which expulsion is mandatory, the board shall impose

a limited expulsion as described in subsection (14) or a full expulsion as described in subsection (16) on the pupil.

(12) **Restriction on expulsion by board**.—The board cannot expel a pupil if more than 20 school days have expired since the principal suspended the pupil under subsection (2), unless the parties to the expulsion hearing agree upon a later deadline.

(13) **Delegation**.—The board may delegate its duty to hold an expulsion hearing and its powers and duties under subsection (11) to a committee of the board, and may impose conditions and restrictions on the committee.

(14) **Limited expulsion**.—A pupil who is subject to a limited expulsion is not entitled to attend the school the pupil was attending when he or she committed the infraction and is not entitled to engage in school-related activities of that school until the later of,

(a) the date specified by the principal or the board when expelling the pupil, which date cannot be more than one year after the date on which the principal suspended the pupil under subsection (2); and

(b) the date on which the pupil meets such requirements as may be established by the board for returning to school after being expelled.

(15) **Same**.—A regulation may vary the limit described in clause (14)(a) and may specify a different limit for different circumstances or different classes of persons.

(16) **Full expulsion**.—A pupil who is subject to a full expulsion is not entitled to attend any school in the province or to engage in school-related activities of any school in the province until he or she meets such requirements as may be established by regulation for returning to school after being expelled.

(17) **Effect on other rights**.—A pupil's rights under sections 33, 36, 42 and 43 are inoperative during a full expulsion.

(18) **Minimum duration of mandatory expulsion**.—The minimum duration of a mandatory expulsion is 21 school days and, for the purposes of this subsection, the period of a pupil's suspension under subsection (2) shall be deemed to be a period of expulsion. The minimum duration may be varied by regulation, and a different standard may be established for different circumstances or different classes of persons.

(19) **Factors affecting type and duration of expulsion**.—When considering the type and duration of expulsion that may be appropriate in particular circumstances, the principal or board shall consider the pupil's history and such other factors as may be prescribed by regulation and may consider such other matters as he, she or it considers appropriate.

(20) **Notice**.—The principal or board that expels a pupil under this section shall ensure that written notice of the mandatory expulsion is given promptly to the pupil and, if the pupil is a minor, to the pupil's parent or guardian.

(21) **Policies and guidelines**.—The Minister may issue policies and guidelines to boards to assist boards and principals in interpreting and administering this section.

(22) **School-related activities**.—A pupil who is expelled is not considered to be engaged in school-related activities by virtue of using services to assist such pupils or taking a course or participating in a program that prepares the pupil to return to school.

(23) **Commencement.**—This section comes into force on a day to be named by proclamation of the Lieutenant Governor.

2000, c. 12, s. 3

310. (1) **Discretionary expulsion of a pupil.**—A pupil may be expelled if the pupil engages in an activity that, under a policy of the board, is one for which expulsion is discretionary.

(2) **Suspension pending expulsion, principal.**—If the principal believes a pupil may have engaged in an activity for which expulsion is discretionary, the principal may suspend the pupil.

(3) **Other matters.**—If the principal suspends a pupil under subsection (2), subsections 309(4) to (20) and 309(22) apply, with necessary modifications, with respect to an expulsion authorized by this section.

(4) **Commencement.**—This section comes into force on a day to be named by proclamation of the Lieutenant Governor.

2000, c. 12, s. 3

311. (1) **Appeal of expulsion.**—The following persons may appeal a decision to expel a pupil, including a decision under section 310 respecting the type and duration of the expulsion:

1. If the pupil is a minor, his or her parent or guardian.
2. If the pupil is not a minor, the pupil.
3. Such other persons as may be specified by a policy of the board.

(2) **The appeal process.**—An appeal under this section must be conducted in accordance with the requirements established by board policy.

(3) **Same, expulsion by principal.**—The board shall hear and determine an appeal from a decision of a principal to expel a pupil and, for that purpose, the board has the powers and duties set out in its policy. The decisions of the board are final.

(4) **Delegation by board.**—The board may delegate its powers and duties under subsection (3) to a committee of the board, and may impose conditions and restrictions on the committee.

(5) **The appeal process, expulsion by board.**—A person or entity designated by regulation shall hear and determine an appeal from a decision of a board to expel a pupil, and, for that purpose, the person or entity has the powers and duties set out in the regulations. The decisions of the person or entity are final.

(6) **Same.**—For the purposes of subsection (5), the Minister may by regulation establish an entity to exercise the powers and perform the duties referred to in that subsection, and the Minister may determine the composition and the other powers and duties of the entity.

(7) **Commencement.**—This section comes into force on a day to be named by proclamation of the Lieutenant Governor and different subsections may be proclaimed into force as of different dates.

2000, c. 12, s. 3

312. (1) **Programs, etc., for suspended pupils.**—The Minister may require boards to establish and maintain specified programs, courses and services for pupils who are suspended, and may impose different requirements for different circumstances, different locations or different classes of pupils.

(2) **Same, expelled pupils.**—The Minister may require boards to establish and maintain specified programs, courses and services for pupils who are expelled and may authorize boards,

(a) to enter into agreements with other boards for the provision of the programs, courses and services;

(b) to retain others to provide the programs, courses and services; or

(c) to establish one or more corporations to provide the programs, courses and services.

(3) **Authorization.**—The Minister may impose conditions and restrictions when authorizing a board to engage in an activity described in subsection (2).

(4) **Programs for expelled pupils.**—The Minister may establish one or more programs for expelled pupils to prepare the pupils to return to school and may require boards to give specified information about the programs to expelled pupils.

(5) **Same.**—The Minister may establish policies and guidelines respecting pupils' eligibility to participate in a program established under subsection (2) or (4) and respecting the criteria to be met for successful completion of the program.

2000, c. 12, s. 3

313. (1) **Transition, suspension of a pupil.**—This section applies with respect to a pupil who engages in an activity before section 306 comes into force that may result in his or her suspension under section 23 as it reads on the day the pupil engages in the activity.

(2) **Same.**—Section 23, as it reads on the day the pupil engages in the activity, continues to apply after section 306 comes into force for the purpose of determining whether, and for how long, the pupil is to be suspended and for the purpose of determining any appeal relating to the suspension of the pupil.

2000, c. 12, s. 3

314. (1) **Transition, expulsion of a pupil.**—This section applies with respect to a pupil who engages in an activity before section 309 comes into force that may result in his or her expulsion under section 23 as it reads on the day the pupil engages in the activity.

(2) **Same.**—Section 23, as it reads on the day the pupil engages in the activity, continues to apply after section 309 comes into force for the purpose of determining whether, from where and for how long the pupil is to be expelled and determining the criteria for the pupil's return to school.

2000, c. 12, s. 3

315. (1) **Collection of personal information.**—The Minister may collect and may by regulation require boards to collect such personal information as is specified by regulation from, or about, the classes of persons specified by regulation for the following purposes, and the Minister may specify or restrict the manner in which the information is to be collected:

1. To ensure the safety of pupils.
2. To administer programs, courses and services to pupils who are suspended or expelled and to determine whether an expelled pupil has successfully completed a program, course or service and as a result is eligible to return to school.

(2) **Disclosure**.—A board or other person is authorized to disclose the personal information collected under subsection (1) to the Minister for the purposes described in that subsection, and the Minister may disclose it to such persons or entities as may be prescribed by regulation for those purposes.

(3) **Definition**.—In this section,

"personal information" has the same meaning as in section 38 of the *Freedom of Information and Protection of Privacy Act* and section 28 of the *Municipal Freedom of Information and Protection of Privacy Act*.

2000, c. 12, s. 3

316. (1) **Regulations**.—The Minister may make regulations,

(a) prescribing such matters as are required, or permitted, under this Part to be prescribed or to be done by regulation;
(b) specifying when, during a school day, a suspension of a pupil is permitted to begin and to end.

(2) **Classes**.—A regulation under subsection (1) may impose different requirements on different classes of person, place or thing or in different circumstances.

(3) **Exceptions**.—A regulation under subsection (1) may provide that one or more provisions of this Part or of the regulation does not apply to specified persons or in specified circumstances.

2000, c. 12, s. 3

STATUTORY POWERS PROCEDURE ACT

R.S.O. 1990, c. S.22, as am. S.O. 1993, c. 27, Sched.; 1994, c. 27, s. 56; 1997, c. 23, s. 13; 1999, c. 12, Sched. B, s. 16; 2002, c. 17, Sched. F, s. 1

1. (1) **Definitions.**—In this Act,

"Committee" [Repealed: S.O. 1994, c. 27, s. 56(1)]

"electronic hearing" means a hearing held by conference telephone or some other form of electronic technology allowing persons to hear one another;

"hearing" means a hearing in any proceeding;

"licence" includes any permit, certificate, approval, registration or similar form of permission required by law;

"municipality" has the same meaning as in the *Municipal Affairs Act*;

"oral hearing" means a hearing at which the parties or their counsel or agents attend before the tribunal in person;

"proceeding" means a proceeding to which this Act applies;

"statutory power of decision" means a power or right, conferred by or under a statute, to make a decision deciding or prescribing,

(a) the legal rights, powers, privileges, immunities, duties or liabilities of any person or party, or
(b) the eligibility of any person or party to receive, or to the continuation of, a benefit or licence, whether the person is legally entitled thereto or not;

"tribunal" means one or more persons, whether or not incorporated and however described, upon which a statutory power of decision is conferred by or under a statute.

"written hearing" means a hearing held by means of the exchange of documents, whether in written form or by electronic means.

(2) **Meaning of "person" extended.**—A municipality, an unincorporated association of employers, a trade union or council of trade unions who may be a party to a proceeding in the exercise of a statutory power of decision under the statute conferring the power shall be deemed to be a person for the purpose of any provision of this Act or of any rule made under this Act that applies to parties. S.O. 1994, c. 27, s. 56(1), (2), (3); 2002, c. 17, Sched. F, s. 1.

2. Interpretation.—This Act, and any rule made by a tribunal under section 25.1, shall be liberally construed to secure the just, most expeditious and cost-effective determination of every proceeding on its merits. 1999, c. 12, Sched. B, s. 16(1)

3. (1) **Application of Part 1.**—Subject to subsection (2), this Act applies to a proceeding by a tribunal in the exercise of a statutory power of decision conferred by or under an Act of the Legislature, where the tribunal is required by or under such Act or otherwise by law to hold or to afford to the parties to the proceeding an opportunity for a hearing before making a decision.

(2) Where Part 1 does not apply.—This Act does not apply to a proceeding,

(a) before the Assembly or any committee of the Assembly;
(b) in or before,
  (i) the Court of Appeal,
  (ii) the Ontario Court (General Division),
  (iii) the Ontario Court (Provincial Division),
  (iv) the Unified Family Court,
  (v) Small Claims Court, or
  (vi) a justice of the peace;
(c) to which the Rules of Civil Procedure apply;
(d) before an arbitrator to which the *Arbitrations Act* or the *Labour Relations Act* applies;
(e) at a coroner's inquest;
(f) of a commission appointed under the *Public Inquiries Act*;
(g) of one or more persons required to make an investigation and to make a report, with or without recommendations, where the report is for the information or advice of the person to whom it is made and does not in any way legally bind or limit that person in any decision he or she may have power to make; or
(h) of a tribunal empowered to make regulations, rules or by-laws in so far as its power to make regulations, rules or by-laws is concerned. S.O. 1994, c. 27, s. 56(5), (6).

4. (1) Waiver of procedural requirement.—Any procedural requirement of this Act, or of another Act or a regulation that applies to a proceeding, may be waived with the consent of the parties and the tribunal.

(2) Same, rules.—Any provision of a tribunal's rules made under section 25.1 may be waived in accordance with the rules. S.O. 1994, c. 27, s. 56(7); 1997, c. 23, s. 13(1).

4.1 Disposition without hearing.—If the parties consent, a proceeding may be disposed of by a decision of the tribunal given without a hearing, unless another Act or a regulation that applies to the proceeding provides otherwise. S.O. 1994, c. 27, s. 56(7); 1997, c. 23, s. 13(2).

4.2 (1) Panels, certain matters.—A procedural or interlocutory matter in a proceeding may be heard and determined by a panel consisting of one or more members of the tribunal, as assigned by the chair of the tribunal.

(2) Assignments.—In assigning members of the tribunal to a panel, the chair shall take into consideration any requirement imposed by another Act or a regulation that applies to the proceeding that the tribunal be representative of specific interests.

(3) Decision of panel.—The decision of a majority of the members of a panel, or their unanimous decision in the case of a two-member panel, is the tribunal's decision. S.O. 1994, c. 27, s. 56(8); 1997, c. 23, s. 13(3).

4.2.1 (1) Panel of one.—The chair of a tribunal may decide that a proceeding be heard by a panel of one person and assign the person to hear the proceeding unless there is a statutory requirement in another Act that the proceeding be heard by a panel of more than one person.

(2) Reduction in number of panel members.—Where there is a statutory requirement in another Act that a proceeding be heard by a panel of a specified number of persons, the chair of the tribunal may assign to the panel one person or any lesser number of persons than the number specified in the other Act if all parties to the proceeding consent. 1999, c. 12, Sched. B, s. 16(2)

4.3 Expiry of term.—If the term of office of a member of a tribunal who has participated in a hearing expires before a decision is given, the term shall be deemed to continue, but only for the purpose of participating in the decision and for no other purpose. S.O. 1994, c. 27, s. 56(9); 1997, c. 23, s. 13(4).

4.4 (1) Incapacity of member.—If a member of a tribunal who has participated in a hearing becomes unable, for any reason, to complete the hearing or to participate in the decision, the remaining member or members may complete the hearing and give a decision.

(2) **Other Acts and regulations.**—Subsection (1) does not apply if another Act or a regulation specifically deals with the issue of what takes place in the circumstances described in subsection (1). S.O. 1994, c. 27, s. 56(9); 1997, c. 23, s. 13(5).

4.5 (1) Decision not to process commencement of proceeding.—Subject to subsection (3), upon receiving documents relating to the commencement of a proceeding, a tribunal or its administrative staff may decide not to process the documents relating to the commencement of the proceeding if,

(a) the documents are incomplete;

(b) the documents are received after the time required for commencing the proceeding has elapsed;

(c) the fee required for commencing the proceeding is not paid; or

(d) there is some other technical defect in the commencement of the proceeding.

(2) **Notice.**—A tribunal or its administrative staff shall give the party who commences a proceeding notice of its decision under subsection (1) and shall set out in the notice the reasons for the decision and the requirements for resuming the processing of the documents.

(3) **Rules under s. 25.1.**—A tribunal or its administrative staff shall not make a decision under subsection (1) unless the tribunal has made rules under section 25.1 respecting the making of such decisions and those rules shall set out,

(a) any of the grounds referred to in subsection (1) upon which the tribunal or its administrative staff may decide not to process the documents relating to the commencement of a proceeding; and

(b) the requirements for the processing of the documents to be resumed.

(4) **Continuance of provisions in other statutes.**—Despite section 32, nothing in this section shall prevent a tribunal or its administrative staff from deciding not to process documents relating to the commencement of a proceeding on grounds that differ from those referred to in subsection (1) or without complying with subsection (2) or (3) if the tribunal or its staff does so in accordance with the provisions of an Act that are in force on the day this section comes into force. 1999, c. 12, Sched. B, s. 16(3)

4.6 (1) Dismissal of proceeding without hearing.—Subject to subsections (5) and (6), a tribunal may dismiss a proceeding without a hearing if,

(a) the proceeding is frivolous, vexatious or is commenced in bad faith;

(b) the proceeding relates to matters that are outside the jurisdiction of the tribunal; or

(c) some aspect of the statutory requirements for bringing the proceeding has not been met.

(2) **Notice.**—Before dismissing a proceeding under this section, a tribunal shall give notice of its intention to dismiss the proceeding to,

(a) all parties to the proceeding if the proceeding is being dismissed for reasons referred to in clause (1)(b); or

(b) the party who commences the proceeding if the proceeding is being dismissed for any other reason.

(3) **Same.**—The notice of intention to dismiss a proceeding shall set out the reasons for the dismissal and inform the parties of their right to make written submissions to the tribunal with respect to the dismissal within the time specified in the notice.

(4) **Right to make submissions.**—A party who receives a notice under subsection (2) may make written submissions to the tribunal with respect to the dismissal within the time specified in the notice.

(5) **Dismissal.**—A tribunal shall not dismiss a proceeding under this section until it has given notice under subsection (2) and considered any submissions made under subsection (4).

(6) **Rules.**—A tribunal shall not dismiss a proceeding under this section 25.1 respecting the early dismissal of proceedings and those rules shall include,

(a) any of the grounds referred to in subsection (1) upon which a proceeding may be dismissed;

(b) the right of the parties who are entitled to receive notice under subsection (2) to make submissions with respect to the dismissal; and

(c) the time within which the submissions must be made.

(7) **Continuance of provisions in other statutes.**—Despite section 32, nothing in this section shall prevent a tribunal from dismissing a proceeding on grounds other than those referred to in subsection (1) or without complying with subsections (2) to (6) if the tribunal dismisses the proceeding in accordance with the provisions of an Act that are in force on the day this section comes into force. 1999, c. 12, Sched. B, s. 16(3)

4.7 Classifying proceedings.—A tribunal may make rules under section 25.1 classifying the types of proceedings that come before it and setting guidelines as to the procedural steps or processes (such as preliminary motions, pre-hearing conferences, alternative dispute resolution mechanisms, expedited hearings) that apply to each type of proceeding and the circumstances in which other procedures may apply. 1999, c. 12, Sched. B, s. 16(3)

4.8 (1) Alternative dispute resolution.—A tribunal may direct the parties to a proceeding to participate in an alternative dispute resolution mechanism for the purposes of resolving the proceeding or an issue arising in the proceeding if,

(a) it has made rules under section 25.1 respecting the use of alternative dispute resolution mechanisms; and

(b) all parties consent to participating in the alternative dispute resolution mechanism.

(2) **Definition**.—In this section,

"alternative dispute resolution mechanism" includes mediation, conciliation, negotiation or any other means of facilitating the resolution of issues in dispute.

(3) **Rules**.—A rule under section 25.1 respecting the use of alternative dispute resolution mechanisms shall include procedural guidelines to deal with the following:

1. The circumstances in which a settlement achieved by means of an alternative dispute resolution mechanism must be reviewed and approved by the tribunal.

2. Any requirement, statutory or otherwise, that there be an order by the tribunal.

(4) **Mandatory alternative dispute resolution**.—A rule under subsection (3) may provide that participation in an alternative dispute resolution mechanism is mandatory or that it is mandatory in certain specified circumstances.

(5) **Person appointed to mediate, etc**.—A rule under subsection (3) may provide that a person appointed to mediate, conciliate, negotiate or help resolve a matter by means of an alternative dispute resolution mechanism be a member of the tribunal or a person independent of the tribunal. However, a member of the tribunal who is so appointed with respect to a matter in a proceeding shall not subsequently hear the matter if it comes before the tribunal unless the parties consent.

(6) **Continuance of provisions in other statutes**.—Despite section 32, nothing in this section shall prevent a tribunal from directing parties to a proceeding to participate in an alternative dispute resolution mechanism even though the requirements of subsections (1) to (5) have not been met if the tribunal does so in accordance with the provisions of an Act that are in force on the day this section comes into force. 1999, c. 12, Sched. B, s. 16(3)

4.9 (1) **Mediators, etc., not compellable**.—No person employed as a mediator, conciliator or negotiator or otherwise appointed to facilitate the resolution of a matter before a tribunal by means of an alternative dispute resolution mechanism shall be compelled to give testimony or produce documents in a proceeding before the tribunal or in a civil proceeding with respect to matters that come to his or her knowledge in the course of exercising his or her duties under this or any other Act.

(2) **Evidence in civil proceedings**.—No notes or records kept by a mediator, conciliator or negotiator or by any other person appointed to facilitate the resolution of a matter before a tribunal by means of an alternative dispute resolution mechanism under this or any other Act are admissible in a civil proceeding. 1999, c. 12, Sched. B, s. 16(3)

5. Parties.—The parties to a proceeding shall be the persons specified as parties by or under the statute under which the proceeding arises or, if not so specified, persons entitled by law to be parties to the proceeding.

(1) **Written hearings**.—A tribunal whose rules made under section 25.1 deal with written hearings may hold a written hearing in a proceeding.

(2) **Exception.**—The tribunal shall not hold a written hearing if a party objects.

(3) **Documents.**—In a written hearing, all the parties are entitled to receive every document that the tribunal receives in the proceeding. S.O. 1994, c. 27, s. 56(10); 1997, c. 23, s. 13(6).

5.1 (1) **Written hearings.**—A tribunal whose rules made under section 25.1 deal with written hearing may hold a written hearing in a proceeding.

(2) **Exception.**—The tribunal shall not hold a written hearing if a party satisfies the tribunal that there is good reason for not doing so.

(2.1) **Same.**—Subsection (2) does not apply if the only purpose of the hearing is to deal with procedural matters.

(3) **Documents.**—In a written hearing, all the parties are entitled to receive every document that the tribunal receives in the proceeding. 1994, c. 27, s. 56; 1997, c. 23, s. 13; 1999, c. 12, Sched. B, s. 16(4)

5.2 (1) **Electronic hearings.**—A tribunal whose rules made under section 25.1 deal with electronic hearings may hold an electronic hearing in a proceeding.

(2) **Exception.**—The tribunal shall not hold an electronic hearing if a party satisfies the tribunal that holding an electronic rather than oral hearing is likely to cause the party significant prejudice.

(3) **Same.**—Subsection (2) does not apply if the only purpose of the hearing is to deal with procedural matters.

(4) **Participants to be able to hear one another.**—In an electronic hearing, all the parties and the members of the tribunal participating in the hearing must be able to hear one another and any witnesses throughout the hearing. S.O. 1994, c. 27, s. 56(10); 1997, c. 23, s. 13(7).

5.2.1 Different kinds of hearings in one proceeding.—A tribunal may, in a proceeding, hold any combination of written, electronic and oral hearings. S.O. 1997, c. 23, s. 13(8).

5.3 (1) **Pre-hearing conferences.**—If the tribunal's rules made under section 25.1 deal with pre-hearing conferences, the tribunal may direct the parties to participate in a pre-hearing conference to consider,

    (a)   the settlement of any or all of the issues;
    (b)   the simplification of the issues;
    (c)   facts or evidence that may be agreed upon;
    (d)   the dates by which any steps in the proceeding are to be taken or begun;
    (e)   the estimated duration of the hearing; and
    (f)   any other matter that may assist in the just and most expeditious disposition of the proceeding.

(1.1) **Other Acts and regulations.**—The tribunal's power to direct the parties to participate in a pre-hearing conference is subject to any other Act or regulation that applies to the proceeding.

(2) **Who presides.**—The chair of the tribunal may designate a member of the tribunal or any other person to preside at the pre-hearing conference.

(3) **Orders.**—A member who presides at a pre-hearing conference may make such orders as he or she considers necessary or advisable with respect to the conduct of the proceeding, including adding parties.

(4) **Disqualification.**—A member who presides at a pre-hearing conference at which the parties attempt to settle issues shall not preside at the hearing of the proceeding unless the parties consent.

(5) **Application of S. 52.**—Section 5.2 applies to a pre-hearing conference, with necessary modifications. S.O. 1994, c. 27, s. 56(1); 1997, c. 23, s. 13(9), (10).

5.4 (1) **Disclosure.**—If the tribunal's rules made under section 25.1 deal with disclosure, the tribunal may, at any stage of the proceeding before all hearings are complete, make orders for,

    (a) the exchange of documents;
    (b) the oral or written examination of a party;
    (c) the exchange of witness statements and reports of expert witnesses;
    (d) the provision of particulars;
    (e) any other form of disclosure.

(1.1) **Other Acts and regulations.**—The tribunal's power to make orders for disclosure is subject to any other Act or regulation that applies to the proceeding.

(2) **Exception, privileged information.**—Subsection (1) does not authorize the making of an order requiring disclosure of privileged information. S.O. 1994, c. 27, s. 56(12); 1997, c. 23, s. 13(11), (12).

6. (1) **Notice of hearing.**—The parties to a proceeding shall be given reasonable notice of the hearing by the tribunal.

(2) **Statutory authority.**—A notice of a hearing shall include a reference to the statutory authority under which the hearing will be held.

(3) **Oral hearing.**—A notice of an oral hearing shall include,

    (a) a statement of the time, place and purpose of the hearing; and
    (b) a statement that if the party notified does not attend at the hearing, the tribunal may proceed in the party's absence and the party will not be entitled to any further notice in the proceeding.

(4) **Written hearing.**—A notice of a written hearing shall include,

    (a) a statement of the date and purpose of the hearing, and details about the manner in which the hearing will be held;
    (b) a statement that the hearing shall not be held as a written hearing if the party satisfies the tribunal that there is good reason for not holding a written hearing (in which case the tribunal is required to hold it as an electronic or oral hearing) and an indication of the procedure to be followed for that purpose.
    (c) a statement that if the party notified neither acts under clause (b) nor participates in the hearing in accordance with the notice, the tribunal may proceed without the

party's participation and the party will not be entitled to any further notice in the proceeding.

(5) **Electronic hearing.**—A notice of an electronic hearing shall include,

(a) a statement of the time and purpose of the hearing, and details about the manner in which the hearing will be held;
(b) a statement that the only purpose of the hearing is to deal with procedural matters, if that is the case;
(c) if clause (b) does not apply, a statement that the party notified may, by satisfying the tribunal that holding the hearing as an electronic hearing is likely to cause the party significant prejudice, require the tribunal to hold the hearing as an oral hearing, and an indication of the procedure to be followed for that purpose; and
(d) a statement that if the party notified neither acts under clause (c), if applicable, nor participates in the hearing in accordance with the notice, the tribunal may proceed without the party's participation and the party will not be entitled to any further notice in the proceeding. S.O. 1994, c. 27, s. 56(13); 1997, c. 23, s. 13(13); 1999, c. 12, Sched. B, s. 16(5).

7. (1) **Effect of non-attendance at hearing after due notice.**—Where notice of an oral hearing has been given to a party to a proceeding in accordance with this Act and the party does not attend at the hearing, the tribunal may proceed in the absence of the party and the party is not entitled to any further notice in the proceeding.

(2) **Same, written hearings.**—Where notice of a written hearing has been given to a party to a proceeding in accordance with this Act and the party neither acts under clause 6(4)(b) nor participates in the hearing in accordance with the notice, the tribunal may proceed without the party's participation and the party is not entitled to any further notice in the proceeding.

(3) **Same, electronic hearings.**—Where notice of an electronic hearing has been given to a party to a proceeding in accordance with this Act and the party neither acts under clause 6(5)(c), if applicable, nor participates in the hearing in accordance with the notice, the tribunal may proceed without the party's participation and the party is not entitled to any further notice in the proceeding. S.O. 1994, c. 27, s. 56(14), (15).

8. Where character, etc., of a party is in issue.—Where the good character, propriety of conduct or competence of a party is an issue in a proceeding, the party is entitled to be furnished prior to the hearing with reasonable information of any allegations with respect thereto.

9. (1) **Hearings to be public, exceptions.**—An oral hearing shall be open to the public except where the tribunal is of the opinion that,

(a) matters involving public security may be disclosed; or
(b) intimate financial or personal matters or other matters may be disclosed at the hearing of such a nature, having regard to the circumstances, that the desirability of avoiding disclosure thereof in the interests of any person affected or in the public interest outweighs the desirability of adhering to the principle that hearings be open to the public,

in which case the tribunal may hold the hearing in the absence of the public.

(1.1) **Written hearings.**—In a written hearing, member of the public are entitled to reasonable access to the documents submitted, unless the tribunal is of the opinion that clause (1)(a) or (b) applies.

(1.2) **Electronic hearings.**—An electronic hearing shall be open to the public unless the tribunal is of the opinion that,

(a) it is not practical to hold the hearing in a manner that is open to the public; or
(b) clause (1)(a) or (b) applies.

(2) **Maintenance of order at hearings.**—A tribunal may make such orders or give such directions at an oral hearing as it considers necessary for the maintenance of order at the hearing, and, if any person disobeys or fails to comply with any such order or direction, the tribunal or a member thereof may call for the assistance of any peace officer to enforce the order or direction, and every peace officer so called upon shall take such action as is necessary to enforce the order or direction and may use such force as is reasonably required for that purpose. S.O. 1994, c. 27, s. 56(16), (17), (18); 1997, c. 23, s. 13(14).

9.1 (1) **Proceedings involving similar questions.**—If two or more proceedings before a tribunal involve the same or similar questions of fact, law or policy, the tribunal may,

(a) combine the proceedings or any part of them, with the consent of the parties;
(b) hear the proceedings at the same time, with the consent of the parties;
(c) hear the proceedings one immediately after the other; or
(d) stay one or more of the proceedings until after the determination of another one of them.

(2) **Exception.**—Subsection (1) does not apply to proceedings to which the *Consolidated Hearings Act* applies.

(3) **Same.**—Clauses (1)(a) and (b) do not apply to a proceeding if,

(a) any other Act or regulation that applies to the proceeding requires that it be heard in private; or
(b) the tribunal is of the opinion that clause 9(1)(a) or (b) applies to the proceeding.

(4) **Conflict, consent requirements.**—The consent requirements of clauses (1)(a) and (b) do not apply if another Act or a regulation that applies to the proceedings allows the tribunal to combine them or hear them at the same time without the consent of the parties.

(5) **Use of same evidence.**—If the parties to the second-named proceeding consent, the tribunal may treat evidence that is admitted in a proceeding as if it were also admitted in another proceeding that is heard at the same time under clause (1)(b). S.O. 1994, c. 27, s. 56(19); 1997, c. 23, s. 13(15), (16).

10. Right to counsel.—A party to a proceeding may be represented by counsel or an agent. S.O. 1994, c. 27, s. 56(20).

10.1 Examination of witnesses.—A party to a proceeding may, at an oral or electronic hearing,

(a) call and examine witnesses and present evidence and submissions; and
(b) conduct cross-examinations of witnesses at the hearing reasonably required for a

full and fair disclosure of all matters relevant to the issues in the proceeding. S.O. 1994, c. 27, s. 56(20).

11. (1) **Rights of witnesses to counsel.**—A witness at an oral or electronic hearing is entitled to be advised by counsel or an agent as to his or her rights but such counsel or agent may take no other part in the hearing without leave of the tribunal.

(2) **Idem.**—Where an oral hearing is closed to the public, the counsel or agent for a witness is not entitled to be present except when that witness is giving evidence. S.O. 1994, c. 27, s. 56(21), (22).

12. (1) **Summonses.**—A tribunal may require any person, including a party, by summons,

    (a) to give evidence on oath or affirmation at an oral or electronic hearing; and

    (b) to produce in evidence at an oral or electronic hearing documents and things specified by the tribunal,

relevant to the subject-matter of the proceeding and admissible at a hearing.

(2) **Form and service of summonses.**—A summons issued under subsection (1) shall be in the prescribed form (in English or French) and,

    (a) where the tribunal consists of one person, shall be signed by him or her; or

    (b) where the tribunal consists of more than one person, shall be signed by the chair of the tribunal or in such other manner as documents on behalf of the tribunal may be signed under the statute constituting the tribunal.

(3) **Same.**—The summons shall be served personally on the person summoned.

(3.1) **Fees and allowance.**—The person summoned is entitled to receive the same fees or allowances for attending at or otherwise participating in the hearing as are paid to a person summoned to attend before the Ontario Court (General Division).

(4) **Bench warrants.**—A judge of the Ontario Court (General Division) may issue a warrant against a person if the judge is satisfied that,

    (a) a summons was served on the person under this section;

    (b) the person has failed to attend or to remain in attendance at the hearing (in the case of an oral hearing) or has failed otherwise to participate in the hearing (in the case of an electronic hearing) in accordance with the summons; and

    (c) the person's attendance or participation is material to the ends of justice.

(4.1) **Same.**—The warrant shall be in the prescribed form (in English or French), directed to any police officer, and shall require the person to be apprehended anywhere within Ontario, brought before the tribunal forthwith and,

    (a) detained in custody as the judge may order until the person's presence as a witness is no longer required; or

    (b) in the judge's discretion, released on a recognizance, with or without sureties, conditioned for attendance or participation to give evidence.

(5) **Proof of service.**—Service of a summons may be proved by affidavit in an application to have a warrant issued under subsection (4).

(6) **Certificate of facts.**—Where an application to have a warrant issued is made on behalf of a tribunal, the person constituting the tribunal or, if the tribunal consists of more than one person, the chair of the tribunal may certify to the judge the facts relied on to establish that the attendance or other participation of the person summoned is material to the ends of justice, and the judge may accept the certificate as proof of the facts.

(7) **Same.**—Where the application is made by a party to the proceeding, the facts relied on to establish that the attendance or other participation of the person is material to the ends of justice may be proved by the party's affidavit. S.O. 1994, c. 27, s. 56(23)-(26).

13. (1) **Contempt proceedings.**—Where any person without lawful excuse,

(a) on being duly summoned under section 12 as a witness at a hearing makes default in attending at the hearing; or

(b) being in attendance as a witness at an oral hearing or otherwise participating as a witness at an electronic hearing, refuses to take an oath or to make an affirmation legally required by the tribunal to be taken or made, or to produce any document or thing in his or her power or control legally required by the tribunal to be produced by him or her or to answer any question to which the tribunal may legally require an answer; or

(c) does any other thing that would, if the tribunal had been a court of law having power to commit for contempt, have been contempt of that court,

the tribunal may, of its own motion or on the motion of a party to the proceeding, state a case to the Divisional Court setting out the facts and that court may inquire into the matter and, after hearing any witnesses who may be produced against or on behalf of that person and after hearing any statement that may be offered in defence, punish or take steps for the punishment of that person in like manner as if he or she had been guilty of contempt of the court.

(2) **Same.**—Subsection (1) also applies to a person who,

(a) having objected under clause 6(4)(b) to a hearing being held as a written hearing, fails without lawful excuse to participate in the oral or electronic hearing of the matter; or

(b) being a party, fails without lawful excuse to attend a pre-hearing conference when so directed by the tribunal. S.O. 1994, c, 27, s. 56(27); 1997, c. 23, s. 13(17).

14. (1) **Protection for witnesses.**—A witness at an oral or electronic hearing shall be deemed to have objected to answer any question asked him or her upon the ground that the answer may tend to criminate him or her or may tend to establish his or her liability to civil proceeding at the instance of the Crown, or of any person, and no answer given by a witness at a hearing shall be used or be receivable in evidence against him or her in any trial or other proceeding against him or her thereafter taking place, other than a prosecution for perjury in giving such evidence. S.O. 1994, c. 27, s. 56(28), (29).

(2) [Repealed S.O. 1994, c. 27, s. 56(29)]

15. (1) **What is admissible in evidence at a hearing.**—Subject to subsections (2) and (3), a tribunal may admit as evidence at a hearing, whether or not given or proven under oath or affirmation or admissible as evidence in a court,

(a) any oral testimony; and

(b) any document or other thing,

relevant to the subject-matter of the proceeding and may act on such evidence, but the tribunal may exclude anything unduly repetitious.

(2) **What is inadmissible in evidence at a hearing.**—Nothing is admissible in evidence at a hearing,

(a) that would be inadmissible in a court by reason of any privilege under the law of evidence; or
(b) that is inadmissible by the statute under which the proceeding arises or any other statute.

(3) **Conflicts.**—Nothing in subsection (1) overrides the provisions of any Act expressly limiting the extent to or purposes for which any oral testimony, documents or things may be admitted or used in evidence in any proceeding.

(4) **Copies.**—Where a tribunal is satisfied as to its authenticity, a copy of a document or other thing may be admitted as evidence at a hearing.

(5) **Photocopies.**—Where a document has been filed in evidence at hearing, the tribunal may, or the person producing it or entitled to it may with the leave of the tribunal, cause the document to be photocopied and the tribunal may authorize the photocopy to be filed in evidence in the place of the document filed and release the document filed, or may furnish to the person producing it or the person entitled to it a photocopy of the document filed certified by a member of the tribunal.

(6) **Certified copy admissible in evidence.**—A document purporting to be a copy of a document filed in evidence at a hearing, certified to be a copy thereof by a member of the tribunal, is admissible in evidence in proceedings in which the document is admissible as evidence of the document.

15.1 (1) **Use of previously admitted evidence.**—The tribunal may treat previously admitted evidence as if it has been admitted in a proceeding before the tribunal, if the parties to the proceeding consent.

(2) **Definition.**—In subsection (1),

"previously admitted evidence" means evidence that was admitted, before the hearing of the proceeding referred to in that subsection, in any other proceeding before a court or tribunal, whether in or outside Ontario.

(3) **Additional power.**—This power conferred by this section is in addition to the tribunal's power to admit evidence under section 15. S.O. 1994, c. 27, s. 56(30); 1997, c. 27, s. 13(18).

15.2 A tribunal may receive evidence from panels of witnesses composed of two or more persons, if the parties have first had an opportunity to make submissions in that regard. S.O. 1994, c. 27, s. 56(31).

16. Notice of facts and opinions.—A tribunal may, in making its decision in any proceeding,

(a) take notice of facts that may be judicially noticed; and

(b) take notice of any generally recognized scientific or technical facts, information or opinions within its scientific or specialized knowledge.

16.1 (1) **Interim decisions and orders.**—A tribunal may make interim decisions and orders.

(2) **Conditions.**—A tribunal may impose conditions on an interim decision or order.

(3) **Reasons.**—An interim decision or order need not be accompanied by reasons. S.O. 1990, c. 27, s. 56(32).

16.2 Time frames.—A tribunal shall establish guidelines setting out the usual time frame for completing proceedings that come before the tribunal and for completing the procedural steps within those proceedings. 1999, c. 12, Sched. B, s. 16(6)

17. (1) **Decision.**—A tribunal shall give its final decision and order, if any, in any proceeding in writing and shall give reasons in writing therefor if requested by a party.

(2) **Interest.**—A tribunal that makes an order for the payment of money shall set out in the order the principal sum, and if interest is payable, the rate of interest and the date from which it is to be calculated. S.O. 1993, c. 27, Sched.; 1994, c. 27, s. 56(33).

17.1 (1) **Costs.**—Subject to subsection (2), a tribunal may, in the circumstances set out in a rule made under section 25.1, order a party to pay all or part of another party's costs in a proceeding.

(2) **Exception.**— tribunal shall not make an order to pay costs under this section unless,

(a) the conduct or course of conduct of a party has been unreasonable, frivolous or vexatious or a party has acted in bad faith; and

(b) the tribunal has made rules under section 25.1 with respect to the ordering of costs which include the circumstances in which costs may be ordered and the amount of the costs or the manner in which the amount of the costs is to be determined.

(3) **Amount of costs.**—The amount of the costs ordered under this section shall be determined in accordance with the rules made under section 25.1.

(4) **Continuance of provisions in other statutes.**—Despite section 32, nothing in this section shall prevent a tribunal from ordering a party to pay all or part of another party's costs in a proceeding in circumstances other than those set out in, and without complying with, subsections (1) to (3) if the tribunal makes the order in accordance with the provisions of an Act that are in force on the day this section comes into force. 1999, c. 12, Sched. B, s. 16(7)

18. (1) **Notice of decision.**—The tribunal shall send each party who participated in the proceeding, or the party's counsel or agent, a copy of its final decision or order, including the reasons if any have been given,

(a) by regular lettermail;
(b) by electronic transmission;
(c) by telephone transmission of a facsimile; or
(d) by some other method that allows proof of receipt, if the tribunal's rules made under section 25.1 deal with the matter.

(2) **Use of mail.**—If the copy is sent by regular lettermail, it shall be sent to the most recent addresses known to the tribunal and shall be deemed to be received by the party on the fifth day after the day it is mailed.

(3) **Use of electronic or telephone transmission.**—If the copy is sent by electronic transmission or by telephone transmission of a facsimile, it shall be deemed to be received on the day after it was sent, unless that day is a holiday, in which case the copy shall be deemed to be received on the next day that is not a holiday.

(4) **Use of other method.**—If the copy is sent by a method referred to in clause (1)(d), the tribunal's rules made under section 25.1 govern its deemed day of receipt.

(5) **Failure to receive copy.**—If a party that acts in good faith does not, through absence, accident, illness or other cause beyond the party's control, receive the copy until a later date than the deemed day of receipt, subsection (2), (3) or (4), as the case may be, does not apply. S.O. 1994, c. 27, s. 56(34).

19. (1) **Enforcement of orders.**—A certified copy of a tribunal's decision or order in a proceeding may be filed in the Ontario Court (General Division) by the tribunal or by a party and on filing shall be deemed to be an order of that court and is enforceable as such.

(2) **Notice of filing.**—A party who files an order under subsection (1) shall notify the tribunal within 10 days after the filing.

(3) **Order for payment of money.**—On receiving a certified copy of a tribunal's order for the payment of money, the sheriff shall enforce the order as if it were an execution issued by the Ontario Court (General Division). S.O. 1994, c. 27, s. 56(35).

20. Record of proceeding.—A tribunal shall compile a record of any proceeding in which a hearing has been held which shall include,

- (a) any application, complaint, reference or other document, if any, by which the proceeding was commenced;
- (b) the notice of any hearing;
- (c) any interlocutory orders made by the tribunal;
- (d) all documentary evidence filed with the tribunal, subject to any limitation expressly imposed by any other Act on the extent to or the purposes for which any such documents may be used in evidence in any proceeding;
- (e) the transcript, if any, of the oral evidence given at the hearing; and
- (f) the decision of the tribunal and the reasons therefor, where reasons have been given.

21. Adjournments.—A hearing may be adjourned from time to time by a tribunal of its own motion or where it is shown to the satisfaction of the tribunal that the adjournment is required to permit an adequate hearing to be held.

21.1 Correction of errors.—A tribunal may at any time correct a typographical error, error of calculation or similar error made in its decision or order. S.O. 1994, c. 27, s. 56(36).

21.2 (1) **Power to review.**—A tribunal may, if it considers it advisable and if its rules made under section 25.1 deal with the matter, review all or part of its own decision or order, and may confirm, vary, suspend or cancel the decision or order.

(2) **Time for review.**—The review shall take place within a reasonable time after the decision or order is made.

(3) **Conflict.**—In the event of a conflict between this section and any other Act, the other Act prevails. S.O. 1994, c. 27, s. 56(36); 1997, c. 23, s. 13(30).

22. Administration of oaths.—A member of a tribunal has power to administer oaths and affirmations for the purpose of any of its proceedings and the tribunal may require evidence before it to be given under oath or affirmation.

23. (1) **Abuse of processes.**—A tribunal may make such orders or give such directions in proceedings before it as it considers proper to prevent abuse of its processes.

(2) **Limitation on examination.**—A tribunal may reasonably limit further examination or cross-examination of a witness where it is satisfied that the examination or cross-examination has been sufficient to disclose fully and fairly all matters relevant to the issues in the proceeding.

(3) **Exclusion of agents.**—A tribunal may exclude from a hearing anyone, other than a barrister and solicitor qualified to practise in Ontario, appearing as an agent on behalf of a party or as an adviser to a witness if it finds that such person is not competent properly to represent or to advise the party or witness or does not understand and comply at the hearing with the duties and responsibilities of an advocate or adviser. S.O. 1994, c. 27, s. 56(37).

24. (1) **Notice, etc.**—Where a tribunal is of opinion that because the parties to any proceeding before it are so numerous or for any other reason, it is impracticable,

    (a)   to give notice of the hearing; or
    (b)   to send its decision and the material mentioned in section 18,

to all or any of the parties individually, the tribunal may, instead of doing so, cause reasonable notice of the hearing or of its decision to be given to such parties by public advertisement or otherwise as the tribunal may direct.

(2) **Contents of notice.**—A notice of a decision given by a tribunal under clause (1)(b) shall inform the parties of the place where copies of the decision and the reasons therefor, if reasons were given, may be obtained.

25.0.1 Control of process.—A tribunal has the power to determine its own procedures and practices and may for that purpose,

    (a)   make orders with respect to the procedures and practices that apply in any particular proceeding; and
    (b)   establish rules under section 25.1. 1999, c. 12, Sched. B, s. 16(8)

25. (1) **Appeal operates as stay, exception.**—An appeal from a decision of a tribunal to a court or other appellate body operates as a stay in the matter unless,

    (a)   another Act or a regulation that applies to the proceeding expressly provides to the contrary; or
    (b)   the tribunal or the court or other appellate body orders otherwise.

(2) **Idem.**—An application for judicial review under the *Judicial Review Procedure*

Act, or the bringing of proceedings specified in subsection 2 (1) of that Act is not an appeal within the meaning of subsection (1). S.O. 1997, c. 23, s. 13(21).

25.1 (1) **Rules.**—A tribunal may make rules governing the practice and procedure before it.

(2) **Application.**—The rules may be of general or particular application.

(3) **Consistency with Acts.**—The rules shall be consistent with this Act and with the other Acts to which they relate.

(4) **Public access.**—The tribunal shall make the rules available to the public in English and in French.

(5) *Regulations Act.*—Rules adopted under this section are not regulations as defined in the *Regulations Act.*

(6) **Additional power.**—The power conferred by this section is in addition to any power to adopt rules that the tribunal may have under another Act. S.O. 1994, c. 27, s. 56(38).

26. Regulations.—The Lieutenant Governor in Council may make regulations prescribing forms for the purpose of section 12. S.O. 1994, c. 27, s. 56(39), (41).

27. Rules, etc., available to public.—A tribunal shall make any rules or guidelines established under this or any other Act available for examination by the public. 1999, c. 12, Sched. B, s. 16(9)

28. Substantial compliance.—Substantial compliance with requirements respecting the content of forms, notices or documents under this Act or any rule made under this or any other Act is sufficient. 1999, c. 12, Sched. B, s. 16(9)

29.-31. [Repealed S.O. 1994, c. 27, s. 56(40)]

32. Conflict.—Unless it is expressly provided in any other Act that its provisions and regulations, rules or by-laws made under it apply despite anything in this Act, the provisions of this Act prevail over the provisions of such other Act and over regulations, rules or by-laws made under such other Act which conflict therewith. S.O. 1994, c. 27, s. 56(42).

33. and 34. [Repealed S.O. 1994, c. 27, s. 56(43)]

Forms 1 and 2 [Repealed S.O. 1994, c. 27, s. 56(44)]

TEACHING PROFESSION ACT

R.S.O. 1990, c. T.2, as am. S.O. 1991, Vol. 2, c. 52; 1996, c. 12, s. 67;
1997, c. 31, s. 180; 2000, c. 12, ss. 4-8; 2002, c. 7, s. 7

1. Definitions.—In this Act,

"Board of Governors" means the Board of Governors of the Federation;

"board of trustees" [Repealed 1997, c. 31, s. 180(1).];

"executive" means the executive of the Federation;

"Federation" means The Ontario Teachers' Federation;

"member" means a member of the Federation;

"Minister" means the Minister of Education;

"Ministry" means the Ministry of Education;

"regulations" means the regulations made under this Act;

"teacher" means a person who is a member of the Ontario College of Teachers and is employed by a board as a teacher but does not include a supervisory officer, a principal, a vice-principal or an instructor in a teacher-training institution. S.O. 1996, c. 12, s. 67; 1997, c. 31, s. 180(1), (2).

2. Body corporate.—The federation of teachers known as The Ontario Teachers' Federation is continued as a body corporate, under the name The Ontario Teachers' Federation in English and Fédération des enseignantes et ensignants de l'Ontario in French.

3. Objects.—The objects of the Federation are,

(*a*) to promote and advance the cause of education;

(*b*) to raise the status of the teaching profession;

(*c*) to promote and advance the interests of teachers and to secure conditions that will make possible the best professional service;

(*d*) to arouse and increase public interest in educational affairs;

(*e*) to co-operate with other teachers' organizations throughout the world having the same or like objects; and

(*f*) to represent all members of the pension plan established under the *Teachers' Pension Act* in the administration of the plan and the management of the pension fund.

4. (1) Membership in Federation.—Every teacher is a member of the Federation.

(2) **Associate members.**—The following students are associate members of the Federation:

1. Every student in a college for the professional education of teachers established under clause 14(1)(a) of the Education Act.

2. Every student in a school or faculty of education that provides for the professional education of teachers pursuant to an agreement under clause 14(1)(b) of the *Education Act.*

(3) **Persons receiving pension.**—Every person who was a member of the Federation upon retirement and who is receiving a pension or an allowance under the *Teachers' Pension Act* or a predecessor to that Act may, on request, be an associate member of the Federation.

(4) **Restrictions.**—A person described in paragraph 1 or 2 of subsection (2) or in subsection (3) is not eligible to vote in respect of any Federation matter and cannot be required to pay a fee to the Federation. 2000, c. 12, s. 4

5. (1) **Board of Governors.**—There shall be a Board of Governors of The Ontario Teachers' Federation, to be composed of 40 members as follows:

1. The immediate past president, the president, the first vice-president, the second vice-president and the secretary-treasurer of each of The Ontario Secondary School Teachers' Federation, the Elementary Teachers' Federation of Ontario, the Association des enseignantes et des enseignants franco-ontariens and The Ontario English Catholic Teachers' Association.

2. Five representatives of each of The Ontario Secondary School Teachers' Federation, the Elementary Teachers' Federation of Ontario, the Association des enseignantes et des enseignants franco-ontariens and The Ontario English Catholic Teachers' Association, to be elected annually at the annual meeting of the federation or association from among its members.

(2) **Term of office.**—The members of the Board of Governors shall take office at the conclusion of the annual meeting of the Federation and shall hold office until their successors take office.

(3) **Vacancies.**—If a vacancy occurs on the Board of Governors, it shall be filled by the executive of the affiliated body that the person who vacated the office represented and the person so named to fill the vacancy shall hold office for the remainder of the term of the person who vacated the office. 2002, c. 12, s. 5

6. (1) **Executive.**—There shall be an executive of The Ontario Teachers' Federation, to be composed of 13 members as follows,

1. The immediate past president, the president, the first vice-president, the second vice-president and the secretary-treasurer of The Ontario Teachers' Federation.

2. The president and the secretary-treasurer of each of The Ontario Secondary School Teachers' Federation, the Elementary Teachers' Federation of Ontario, the Association des enseignantes et des enseignants franco-ontariens and The Ontario English Catholic Teachers' Association.

(2) **Term of office.**—The members of the executive shall take office at the conclusion of the annual meeting of the Federation and shall hold office until their successors take office.

(3) **Vacancies.**—If a vacancy occurs on the executive, it may be filled by the Board of Governors from among its members who represent the affiliated body that the person who vacated the office represented, and the person so named shall hold office for the remainder of the term of the person who vacated the office. 2002, c. 12, s. 6

7. President and vice-presidents.—There shall be a president, a first vice-president and a second vice-president of the Federation to be elected annually at the annual meeting of the Board of Governors from among its members in such a manner that the offices of immediate past president, president, first vice-president and second vice-president represent each of the affiliated bodies. 2000, c. 12, s. 7

8. Secretary-treasurer.—There shall be a secretary-treasurer of the Federation appointed by the Board of Governors who may be a member of the Board of Governors and who shall receive such remuneration as may be fixed by the Board of Governors.

9. Functions of executive.—The executive is responsible for carrying on the business of the Federation and may,

(a) subject to the approval of the Minister, acquire and hold in the name of the Federation such real and personal property as may be necessary for the purposes of the Federation and may alienate, mortgage, lease or otherwise dispose of such property as occasion may require;

(b) invest the funds of the Federation in any securities in which a trustee is authorized to invest money in his hands under the *Trustee Act*;

(c) make such grants as it considers advisable to organizations having the same or like objects as the Federation;

(d) act as the representative of the members of the pension plan established under the *Teachers' Pension Act* including carrying out the following functions:

1. Appointing persons to be members of the Ontario Teachers' Pension Plan Board created under that Act.

2. Entering into agreements as described in that Act.

3. Negotiating, agreeing to or directing amendments to the plan as permitted under that Act or an agreement entered into under that Act.

4. Entering into an agreement on behalf of the Federation to indemnify a member of the Ontario Teachers' Pension Plan Board or a member of a committee of the Board against any costs sustained with respect to legal proceedings arising out of an act or omission done in the execution of his or her duties as a member of the Board or committee. S.O. 1991, Vol. 2, c. 52, s. 9.

10. Conferences.—In the interests of the advancement of education and the improvement of teaching conditions in Ontario, the Board of Governors shall meet annually and confer with the Minister and the senior officials of the Ministry on matters touching and concerning the objects of the Federation, and the Board of Governors shall at such meeting and may at any other time make such representations and recommendations either of a general nature or which relate to any particular school, teacher or matter as it considers advisable and as are in keeping with the objects of the Federation.

11. [Repealed 1997, c. 31, s. 180(3).]

12. (1) **Regulations.**—Subject to the approval of the Lieutenant Governor in Council, the Board of Governors may make regulations,

(a) prescribing a code of ethics for teachers;

(b) [Repealed 1997, c. 31, s. 180(4).];

(c) providing for voluntary membership in the Federation of persons who are not members thereof and prescribing the duties, responsibilities and privileges of voluntary members;

(d) prescribing the duties, responsibilities and privileges of associate members;

(e) providing for the suspension and expulsion of members from the Federation and other disciplinary measures;

(f) [Repealed 2000, c. 12, s. 8.]

(g) providing for the holding of meetings of the Board of Governors and of the executive and prescribing the manner of calling and the notice to be given in respect of such meetings;

(*h*) prescribing the procedure to be followed at meetings of the Board of Governors and of the executive;

(*i*) providing for the payment of necessary expenses to the members of the Board of Governors and the executive;

(*j*) conferring powers upon or extending or restricting the powers of and prescribing the duties of the Board of Governors and of the executive;

(*k*) providing for the appointment of standing and special committees;

(*l*) providing for the establishment of branches of the Federation or of the recognition by the Federation of local bodies, groups or associations of teachers which shall be affiliated with the Federation.

(2) **Reporting sexual abuse**.— Despite any regulation made under subsection (1), a member who makes an adverse report about another member respecting suspected sexual abuse of a student by that other member need not provide him or her with a copy of the report or with any information about the report.

(3) **Definition**.— In subsection (2),

"**sexual abuse**" of a student by a member means,

(a) sexual intercourse or other forms of physical sexual relations between the member and the student,

(b) touching, of a sexual nature, of the student by the member, or

(c) behaviour or remarks of a sexual nature by the member towards the student. 2000, c. 12, s. 8; 2002, c. 7, s. 7

13. (1) **Restriction re by-laws.**—A by-law governing the membership of teachers in an affiliated body of the Federation shall not authorize a teacher to be a member of an affiliated body that is not his or her designated bargaining agent, if any, under Part X.1 of the *Education Act*.

(2) **Changes to regulations, by-laws.**—The Minister may request the Board of Governors to make, amend or revoke a regulation or by-law if the Minister considers it appropriate to do so.

(3) **Same.**—If the Board of Governors fails to comply with the Minister's request within 60 days after receiving it, the Lieutenant Governor in Council may, by regulation, make, amend or revoke the regulation or by-law. S.O. 1997, c. 31, s. 180(5).

Transitional Provision — 2000, c. 12, s. 9

9. *Despite the amendments made to the Teaching Profession Act by sections 4 to 8 of this Act and subject to subsections 5 (3) and 6 (3) of that Act,*

(a) *the persons who were members of the Board of Governors of The Ontario Teachers' Federation immediately before this Act received Royal Assent continue to be the members of the Board of Governors until the conclusion of the first annual meeting of the Federation that takes place after this Act receives Royal Assent;*

(b)   the persons who were members of the executive of The Ontario Teachers' Federation immediately before this Act received Royal Assent continue to be the members of the executive until the conclusion of the first annual meeting of the Federation that takes place after this Act receives Royal Assent; and

(c)   the persons who were the immediate past president, president, first vice-president, second vice-president and third vice-president of The Ontario Teachers' Federation immediately before this Act received Royal Assent continue to be the immediate past president, president, first vice-president, second vice-president and third vice-president of the Federation until the conclusion of the first annual meeting of the Federation that takes place after this Act receives Royal Assent.

REGULATION MADE UNDER THE TEACHING PROFESSION ACT*

[Updated to June 1, 1997]

Affiliated Bodies

1. The Ontario Secondary School Teachers' Federation, the Federation of Women Teachers' Association of Ontario, the Ontario Public School Teachers' Federation, l'Association des enseignantes et des enseignants franco-ontariens and the Ontario English Catholic Teachers' Association shall be affiliated with the Federation and known as "affiliated bodies."

Voluntary Membership

2. (1) The Board of Governors shall grant voluntary membership in the Federation to a person who,

    (a) is not a member thereof;

    (b) holds a teacher's certificate;

    (c) is engaged in an educational capacity;

    (d) is a member of an affiliated body; and

    (e) makes application to the Board of Governors for voluntary membership in the Federation.

(2) The Board of Governors shall grant voluntary membership in the Federation to a person who is not a member thereof and who is from outside Ontario and is on an assignment of two years or less as a teacher in Ontario under a teacher exchange program.

(3) The duties of a voluntary member shall be the same as those of a member under Sections 13 to 18.

(4) A voluntary member shall have such privileges as are common to all members of the Federation.

Application for Membership by a Former Member

3. (1) A teacher who has withdrawn from membership under subsection (1) or (2) of Section 4 of the *Teaching Profession Act, 1944*, may make application to the Board of Governors for reinstatement as a member.

---

* Editor's Note: Section 1 of the Regulations Act, R.S.O. 1990, c. R.21 expressly excludes regulations made pursuant to the Teaching Profession Act from the application of the Regulations Act, R.S.O. 1990, c. R.21, and as such, they are required to be published in the Ontario Gazette. Accordingly, the Regulation Made Under the Teaching Profession Act does not have a conventional "R.S.O. 1990, Reg. ***" or an "O. Reg. ***/9*" citation.

The text noted below was updated by verifying its accuracy with the Ontario Teachers' Federation. Section 12 of the Teaching Profession Act gives the Board of Governors of that organization the authority to pass regulations pursuant to that Act.

(2) The Board of Governors shall refer the application to the proper affiliated body for its opinion of the application.

(3) Where the Board of Governors, after considering the opinion of the affiliated body, accepts the application, the secretary-treasurer of the Federation shall notify the Minister and the applicant forthwith.

Fees

4. (1) Subject to subsections 2 and 4, a member shall pay the Federation an annual membership fee as follows:

 1. A secondary school teacher, 1.18 per cent of total annual salary.
 2. A statutory member of the Ontario Public School Teachers' Federation $100.00 plus 1.2 per cent of the total annual salary of the member.
 3. A female public school teacher,
   (i) working more than half-time, $650.00,
   (ii) working half-time or less, $325.00.
 4. A separate school teacher,
   (i) working more than half-time, $675.00,
   (ii) working half-time or less, an amount which bears the same relation to $660.00 as does the teacher's total annual salary the teacher would earn if full-time.
 5. A teacher in a French-language school or class who is a member of L'Association des enseignantes et des enseignants franco-ontariens, 1.5% of the teacher's total annual salary;

where "total annual salary" means salary in accordance with the terms and conditions under which the member is employed, and includes a cost of living or other similar bonus.

(2) A member who is employed by a board exclusively in respect of the continuing education classes provided by the board shall pay the Federation an annual membership fee as follows:

 1. A secondary school teacher, 1.18 per cent of the salary attributable to such teaching.
 2. A statutory member of the Ontario Public School Teachers' Federation, 1.15 per cent of the salary attributable to such teaching.
 3. A female public school teacher $.020 in respect of each day on which the teacher performs teaching duties to a maximum amount of $4.00 for each month in which the teacher performs such teaching duties.
 4. A separate school teacher, 1.25 per cent of the salary attributable to such teaching duties.
 5. A teacher of a French-language school or class who is a member of L'Association des enseignantes et des enseignants franco-ontariens, 1.5 per cent of the salary attributable to such teaching duties.

(3) A member to whom subsection (1) applies who is also employed for the purpose of a class referred to in subsection (2) shall pay an annual membership fee that is the sum of the annual membership fee applicable to the member under subsection (1) and the annual membership fee that would be applicable to the member under subsection (2), if the member were a person employed exclusively for the purpose of a class referred to in subsection (2).

(4) Where a fee, or a portion thereof, that is payable under subsection (1) is not based upon salary, such fee or portion thereof shall be reduced, in the case of a teacher who is not employed for the full school year, by multiplying such fee or portion thereof by the ratio of the member of full and part months that the teacher was employed in the school year to ten.

(5) A board of trustees, in respect of a teacher employed by the board, shall,

(a) where a single deduction is made, remit to the secretary-treasurer of the Federation the full annual fee,
   (i) by the 30th day of November, or
   (ii) in the case of a teacher whose employment commences after the first school day in November, by the last day of the first full month that the teacher is employed by the board; and
(b) where deductions are made in instalments, place the instalment fee on deposit with the Federation on or before the 15th day of the month immediately following the month of deduction.

Meetings of the Board of Governors

5. (1) The annual meeting of the Board of Governors shall be held in each year on the days during the three weeks next preceding Labour Day that are, and at a time and place that is, determined by the president.

(2) Subject to subsection (5), there shall be a special meeting of the Board of Governors on the days during or within two weeks following each of the Christmas vacation and the Easter vacation that are, and at a time and place that is, determined by the president.

(3) The Board of Governors shall meet at such other dates and times as the executive may by resolution determine.

(4) A member of the Board of Governors shall be allowed a leave of absence not exceeding four days a year to attend meetings of the Board of Governor referred to in subsection (2) and (3).

(5) Upon the recommendation of the executive and with the approval of at least thirty-two members of the Board of Governors, the Board of Governors may, by resolution, waive the holding of one of the meetings under subsection (2).

(6) The secretary-treasurer of the Federation shall send to members of the Board of Governors a written notice of the date, time and place of a meeting of the Board of Governors,

(a) at lest fourteen days before the date of a meeting under subsection (1) or (2); and
(b) at least three days before the date of a meeting under subsection (3).

(7) A quorum at a meeting of the Board of Governors shall be thirty-two members thereof.

Meetings of Executive

6. (1) The executive shall meet immediately before and immediately after a meeting of the Board of Governors.

(2) The secretary-treasurer of the Federation shall send to members of the executive at least seven days in advance of a meeting of the executive written notice of date, time and place of the meeting under subsection (1).

(3) The president of the Federation may at any time call a special meeting of the executive.

(4) A quorum at any meeting of the executive shall be six members thereof.

Nominating Committee

7. (1) At the meeting of the executive immediately before the annual meeting of the Board of Governors, the executive shall appoint a nominating committee and include thereon a representative of each of the affiliated bodies.

(2) The nominating committee shall meet on the first day of the annual meeting of the Board of Governors to prepare nominations for the executive for the year next following.

(3) The nominating committee shall present the report of its nominations to the Board of Governors and, upon these and other nominations which may be submitted from the floor by any member of the Board of Governors, a secret ballot shall be taken.

Relations and Discipline Committee

8. There shall be a Relations and Discipline Committee appointed by the Board of Governors.

Standing Committees

9. (1) There shall be standing committees as follows:

1. Educational finance
2. Educational Studies
3. Legislation
4. Pension
5. Teacher Education

(2) A committee under subsection (1) shall,

(a) be composed of the chairman or a member of the corresponding committee of each affiliated body, together with the president and secretary-treasurer of the Federation; and
(b) be convened by a member designated by the executive, following the annual meeting of the Board of Governors.

(3) The Board of Governors may, by by-law, establish such standing committees, in addition to those set out in subsection (1), as it considers expedient, and terminate any standing committee so established.

(4) A by-law passed under subsection (3) establishing a standing committee shall make provision for the composition of the committee.

(5) Clause (b) of subsection (2) applies to a standing committee established under subsection (3).

Special Committees

10. The Board of Governors or the executive may, by resolution, appoint such special committees as it considers necessary from time to time.

Procedure at Annual Meeting of Board of Governors

11. (1) The order of procedure at the annual meeting of the Board of Governors shall be as follows:

1. Call to order.
2. Appointment of committees.
3. Reading and confirming the minutes of the next preceding meeting.
4. Business arising from the minutes.
5. Reading of correspondence and action thereon.
6. Reports of officers.
7. Reception of delegations.
8. Reports from affiliated bodies.
9. Reports of standing and special committees.
10. General business.
11. Elections.
12. Installation of officers.
13. Adjournment.

(2) The Board of Governors may omit one or more items of the order of procedure from the agenda of the annual meeting.

Expenses

12. The Federation shall pay such necessary expenses as members of the Board of Governors and of the executive incur in carrying out their duties under the Act and this Regulation.

General Duties of Members

13. A member shall strive at all times to achieve and maintain the highest degree of professional competence and to uphold the honour, dignity, and ethical standards of the teaching profession.

Duties of a Member to his Pupils

14. A member shall,

(a) regard as his first duty the effective education of his pupils and the maintenance of a high degree of professional competence in his teaching;
(b) endeavour to develop in his pupils an appreciation of standards of excellence;
(c) endeavour to inculcate in his pupils an appreciation of the principles of democracy;
(d) show consistent justice and consideration in all his relations with pupils;

(e) refuse to divulge beyond his proper duty confidential information about a pupil; and
(f) concern himself with the welfare of his pupils while they are under his care.

Duties of a Member to Educational Authorities

15. (1) A member shall,

(a) comply with the Acts and regulations administered by the Minister;
(b) co-operate with his educational authorities to improve public education;
(c) respect the legal authority of the board of trustees in the management of the school and in the employment of teachers;
(d) make in the proper manner such reports concerning teachers under his authority as may be required by the board of trustees; and
(e) present in the proper manner to the proper authorities the consequences to be expected from policies or practices which in his professional opinion are seriously detrimental to the interests of pupils.

(2) A member shall not,

(a) break a contract of employment with a board of trustees;
(b) violate a written or oral agreement to enter into a contract of employment with a board of trustees; or
(c) while holding a contract of employment with a board of trustees, make application for another position the acceptance of which would necessitate his seeking the termination of his contract by mutual consent of the teacher and the board of trustees, unless and until he has arranged with his board of trustees for such termination of contract if he obtains the other position.

Duties of a Member to the Public

16. A member shall,

(a) endeavour at all times to extend the public knowledge of his profession and discourage untrue, unfair or exaggerated statements with respect to teaching; and
(b) recognize a responsibility to promote respect for human rights.

Duties of a Member to the Federation

17. A member shall co-operate with the Federation to promote the welfare of the profession.

Duties of a Member to Fellow Members

18. (1) A member shall,

(a) avoid interfering in an unwarranted manner between other teachers and pupils;
(b) on making an adverse report on another member, furnish him with a written statement of the report at the earliest possible time and not later than three days after making the report;

    (c) refuse to accept employment with a board of trustees whose relations with the Federation are unsatisfactory; and

    (d) where he is in an administrative or supervisory position, make an honest and determined effort to help and counsel a teacher before subscribing to the dismissal of that teacher.

(2) Under clause (c) of subsection (1), the onus shall be on the member to ascertain personally from the Federation whether an unsatisfactory relationship exists.

(3) A member shall not attempt to gain an advantage over other members by knowingly underbidding another member, or knowingly applying for a position not properly declared vacant, or by negotiating for salary independently of his local group of fellow-members.

Relations and Discipline Procedure

19. (1) In this section and Sections 20 to 28

    (a) "Committee" means the Relations and Discipline Committee of the Ontario Teachers' Federation;

    (b) "teaching certificate" means an Ontario Teacher's Certificate or other qualification to teach prescribed under Regulation 269 as amended and revised from time to time.

(2) The Committee shall be composed of ten members who are teachers, appointed by the Board of Governors, two of whom shall be from each affiliated body.

(3) A person is not eligible for appointment to the Committee who,

    (a) holds office on a disciplinary body of an affiliated body;

    (b) holds office on the executive of an affiliated body; or

    (c) is employed by either an affiliated body or the Federation.

(4) The Committee shall appoint one of the members of the Committee to be chairman.

(5) The chairman of the Committee may assign a panel of five members of the Committee to hold a hearing.

(6) Three members of the panel assigned under subsection (5) constitute a quorum for a hearing and all disciplinary decisions require the vote of a majority of members of the Committee present at the hearing.

(7) The secretary-treasurer of the Federation shall act as secretary to the Committee but shall not participate in any decision of the Committee.

20. (1) The Committee shall,

    (a) consider complaints regarding professional misconduct or unethical conduct of a member;

    (b) consider applications for reinstatement of the teaching certificate of a former member or the lifting of a suspension thereof.

(2) A hearing of the Committee shall be held in camera unless the member requests otherwise by notice delivered to the Committee not later than the day before the day fixed for the hearing, in which case the Committee shall conduct the hearing in public except when,

    (i) matters involving public security may be disclosed; or

    (ii) the possible disclosure of intimate financial or personal matters outweighs the desirability of holding the hearing in public.

(3) No hearing in respect of alleged professional misconduct or unethical conduct shall be conducted by the Committee unless;

    (a) a written signed complaint has been filed in the office of the secretary-treasurer of the Federation;

    (b) a copy thereof has been served on the member whose conduct is being investigated; and

    (c) the member whose conduct is being investigated has been served with notice of the time, place and purpose of the hearing.

(4) The secretary-treasurer of the Federation shall,

    (a) prepare and complete or cause to be completed a written complaint and file it in the office of the secretary-treasurer of the Federation;

    (b) serve upon the member whose conduct is being investigated,

        (i) a copy of the complaint; and

        (ii) a notice of the hearing which shall include,

            A. a statement of the time, place and purpose of the hearing;

            B. a reference to the statutory authority under which the hearing will be held;

            C. a statement that if the party notified does not attend at the hearing the Committee may proceed in his absence and he will not be entitled to any further notice of the proceedings; and

            D. a statement that the member may,

               1. be represented by counsel or an agent;

               2. call and examine witnesses;

               3. present arguments and submissions; and

               4. conduct cross-examination of witnesses as reasonably required for full and fair disclosure of the facts in relation to which they have given evidence; and

    (c) make all necessary arrangements for the conduct of the hearing including,

        (i) the appointment of counsel for the Federation;

        (ii) the arrangement for oral evidence to be recorded; and

        (iii) the notification to all members of the Committee of the time and place of the hearing.

21. In proceedings before the Committee, the Federation and the member whose professional misconduct or unethical conduct, or reinstatement is being investigated shall be parties to the proceedings.

22. (1) A member whose professional misconduct or unethical conduct or reinstatement is being investigated shall be afforded an opportunity to examine, before the hearing, any written or documentary evidence that will be produced or any report, the contents of which will be given in evidence at the hearing.

(2) Members of the Committee conducting the hearing shall not,

    (a) have taken part before the hearing in the investigation of the subject matter of the complaint;

(b) have taken part in any previous hearing involving the member whose professional misconduct, unethical conduct or reinstatement is being investigated; or

(c) communicate directly or indirectly in relation to the subject matter of the hearing with any person or with any party or representative of a party, except upon notice to and opportunity for all parties to participate.

23. (1) The evidence before the Committee shall be recorded by a person appointed by the chairman of the Committee.

(2) Nothing is admissible in evidence before the Committee that would be inadmissible in a civil case and the findings of the Committee shall be based exclusively on evidence before it.

(3) No member of the Committee shall participate in the decision of the Committee unless he has been present throughout the hearing.

24. At a hearing before the Committee, a party to the proceedings may,

(a) be represented by counsel or an agent;

(b) call and examine witnesses;

(c) present arguments and submissions; and

(d) conduct cross-examination of witnesses as reasonably required for full and fair disclosure of the facts in relation to which they have given evidence.

25. (1) A member may be found guilty by the Committee of a professional misconduct or unethical conduct if in the opinion of the Committee he has contravened any of the provisions of Sections 13 to 18.

(2) In the case of hearings into complaints of professional misconduct and unethical conduct, the Committee shall,

(a) consider the allegations, hear the evidence and ascertain the facts of the case;

(b) determine whether upon the evidence and the facts so ascertained the allegations have been proved;

(c) determine whether in respect of the allegations so proved, the member is guilty of professional misconduct or unethical conduct; and

(d) determine the penalty to be imposed, as hereinafter provided, in cases in which it finds a member guilty of professional misconduct or unethical conduct.

(3) Where the Committee finds a member guilty of professional misconduct or unethical conduct, it shall,

(a) recommend to the Minister the cancellation of the teaching certificate of the member;

(b) recommend to the Minister the suspension for a stated fixed period of the teaching certificate of the member; or

(c) reprimand the member,

or proceed with any combination of the foregoing.

26. (1) Where the Federation receives a request for a recommendation in respect of the reinstatement of a teaching certificate of a former member or the lifting of the suspension thereof, the secretary-treasurer shall refer the matter to the Committee for a hearing.

(2) Following a hearing under subsection (1), the Committee shall recommend to the Minister that the teaching certificate be reinstated or the suspension lifted, or that the teaching certificate remain cancelled or the suspension not to be lifted, as the case may be.

27. (1) The Committee shall give its decision and recommendation, if any, under subsections 25.(3) or 26.(2) in writing and shall give reasons in writing, therefor, if requested by a party.

(2) The decision of the Committee shall be served upon the parties.

28. Any notice or other document required to be served by this regulation may be served by prepaid first class mail addressed to the person to whom notice is to be given at his last known address and where notice is served by mail, the service shall be deemed to have been made on the fifth day after the day of mailing unless the person to whom the notice is given establishes that he, acting in good faith, due to absence, accident, illness or other cause beyond his control, did not receive the notice or did not receive the notice until a later date.

Evidencing Regulations and Resolutions

29. Regulations made by and resolutions passed by the Board of Governors may be evidenced by the signatures of the president and the secretary-treasurer of the Federation.

Effective Date and Transitional Provisions

30. (1)This Regulation comes into force on the 1st day of January 1986, and applies in respect of any complaint of professional misconduct or unethical conduct filed in the office of the secretary-treasurer of the Federation on or after that date, and in respect referred to in Section 26 received by the Federation on or after that date.

(2) The provisions of the Regulation made under the Teaching Profession Act that are revoked by this Regulation shall continue to apply to any matter or proceeding brought thereunder and no disposed of prior to the 1st day of January 1986 notwithstanding the coming into force of this Regulations.

TRESPASS TO PROPERTY ACT

R.S.O. 1990, c. T.21 as am. S.O. 2000, c. 30, s. 11

1. (1) **Definitions.**—In this Act,

"occupier" includes,

(*a*) a person who is in physical possession of premises, or

(*b*) a person who has responsibility for and control over the condition of premises or the activities there carried on, or control over persons allowed to enter the premises,

even if there is more than one occupier of the same premises;

"premises" means lands and structures, or either of them, and includes,

(*a*) water,

(*b*) ships and vessels,

(*c*) trailers and portable structures designed or used for residence, business or shelter,

(*d*) trains, railway cars, vehicles and aircraft, except while in operation.

(2) **School boards.**—A school board has all the rights and duties of an occupier in respect of its school sites as defined in the *Education Act*.

2. (1) **Trespass an offence.**—Every person who is not acting under a right or authority conferred by law and who,

(*a*) without the express permission of the occupier, the proof of which rests on the defendant,

    (i) enters on premises when entry is prohibited under this Act, or

    (ii) engages in an activity on premises when the activity is prohibited under this Act; or

(*b*) does not leave the premises immediately after he or she is directed to do so by the occupier of the premises or a person authorized by the occupier,

is guilty of an offence and on conviction is liable to a fine of not more than $2,000.

(2) **Colour of right as a defence.**—It is a defence to a charge under subsection (1) in respect of premises that is land that the person charged reasonably believed that he or she had title to or an interest in the land that entitled him or her to do the act complained of.

3. (1) **Prohibition of entry.**—Entry on premises may be prohibited by notice to that effect and entry is prohibited without any notice on premises,

(*a*) that is a garden, field or other land that is under cultivation, including a lawn, orchard, vineyard and premises on which trees have been planted and have not attained an average height of more than two metres and woodlots on land used primarily for agricultural purposes; or

(*b*) that is enclosed in a manner that indicates the occupier's intention to keep persons off the premises or to keep animals on the premises.

(2) **Implied permission to use approach to door.**—There is a presumption that access

for lawful purposes to the door of a building on premises by a means apparently provided and used for the purpose of access is not prohibited.

4. (1) **Limited permission.**—Where notice is given that one or more particular activities are permitted, all other activities and entry for the purpose are prohibited and any additional notice that entry is prohibited or a particular activity is prohibited on the same premises shall be construed to be for greater certainty only.

(2) **Limited prohibition.**—Where entry on premises is not prohibited under section 3 or by notice that one or more particular activities are permitted under subsection (1), and notice is given that a particular activity is prohibited, that activity and entry for the purpose is prohibited and all other activities and entry for the purpose are not prohibited.

5. (1) **Method of giving notice.**—A notice under this Act may be given,

(*a*) orally or in writing;

(*b*) by means of signs posted so that a sign is clearly visible in daylight under normal conditions from the approach to each ordinary point of access to the premises to which it applies; or

(*c*) by means of the marking system set out in section 7.

(2) **Substantial compliance.**—Substantial compliance with clause (1)(*b*) or (*c*) is sufficient notice.

6. (1) **Form of sign.**—A sign naming an activity or showing a graphic representation of an activity is sufficient for the purpose of giving notice that the activity is permitted.

(2) **Idem.**—A sign naming an activity with an oblique line drawn through the name or showing a graphic representation of an activity with an oblique line drawn through the representation is sufficient for the purpose of giving notice that the activity is prohibited.

7. (1) **Red markings.**—Red markings made and posted in accordance with subsections (3) and (4) are sufficient for the purpose of giving notice that entry on the premises is prohibited.

(2) **Yellow markings.**—Yellow markings made and posted in accordance with subsections (3) and (4) are sufficient for the purpose of giving notice that entry is prohibited except for the purpose of certain activities and shall be deemed to be notice of the activities permitted.

(3) **Size.**—A marking under this section shall be of such a size that a circle ten centimetres in diameter can be contained wholly within it.

(4) **Posting.**—Markings under this section shall be so placed that a marking is clearly visible in daylight under normal conditions from the approach to each ordinary point of access to the premises to which it applies.

8. Notice applicable to part of premises.—A notice or permission under this Act may be given in respect of any part of the premises of an occupier.

9. (1) **Arrest without warrant on premises.**—A police officer, or the occupier of premises, or a person authorized by the occupier may arrest without warrant any person he believes on reasonable and probable grounds to be on the premises in contravention of section 2.

(2) **Delivery to police officer.**—Where the person who makes an arrest under subsection (1) is not a police officer, he or she shall promptly call for the assistance of a police officer and give the person arrested into the custody of the police officer.

(3) **Deemed arrest.**—A police officer to whom the custody of a person is given under subsection (2) shall be deemed to have arrested the person for the purposes of the provisions of the *Provincial Offences Act* applying to his or her release or continued detention and bail.

10. Arrest without warrant off premises.—Where a police officer believes on reasonable and probable grounds that a person has been in contravention of section 2 and has made fresh departure from the premises, and the person refuses to give his or her name and address, or there are reasonable and probable grounds to believe that the name or address given is false, the police officer may arrest the person without warrant.

11. Motor vehicles and motorized snow vehicles.—Where an offence under this Act is committed by means of a motor vehicle, as defined in the Highway Traffic Act, or by means of a motorized snow vehicle, as defined in the Motorized Snow Vehicles Act, the driver of the motor vehicle or motorized snow vehicle is liable to the fine provided under this Act and, where the driver is not the owner, the owner of the motor vehicle or motorized snow vehicle is liable to the fine provided under this Act unless the driver is convicted of the offence or, at the time the offence was committed, the motor vehicle or motorized snow vehicle was in the possession of a person other than the owner without the owner's consent. 2000, c. 30, s. 11.

12. (1) Damage award.—Where a person is convicted of an offence under section 2, and a person has suffered damage caused by the person convicted during the commission of the offence, the court shall, on the request of the prosecutor and with the consent of the person who suffered the damage, determine the damages and shall make a judgment for damages against the person convicted in favour of the person who suffered the damage, but no judgment shall be for an amount in excess of $1,000.

(2) **Costs of prosecution.**—Where a prosecution under section 2 is conducted by a private prosecutor, and the defendant is convicted, unless the court is of the opinion that the prosecution was not necessary for the protection of the occupier or the occupier's interests, the court shall determine the actual costs reasonably incurred in conducting the prosecution and, despite section 60 of the *Provincial Offences Act*, shall order those costs to be paid by the defendant to the prosecutor.

(3) **Damages and costs in addition to fine.**—A judgment for damages under subsection (1), or an award of costs under subsection (2), shall be in addition to any fine that is imposed under this Act.

(4) **Civil action.**—A judgment for damages under subsection (1) extinguishes the right of the person in whose favour the judgment is made to bring a civil action for damages against the person convicted arising out of the same facts.

(5) **Idem.**—The failure to request or refusal to grant a judgment for damages under subsection (1) does not affect a right to bring a civil action for damages arising out of the same facts.

(6) **Enforcement.**—The judgment for damages under subsection (1), and the award for costs under subsection (2), may be filed in the Small Claims Court and shall be deemed to be a judgment or order of that court for the purposes of enforcement.

YOUTH CRIMINAL JUSTICE ACT

An Act in respect of criminal justice for young persons and to amend and repeal other Acts

S.C. 2002, c. 1 as am. S.C. 2002, c. 7, s. 274; 2002, c. 13, s. 91
[s. 91(1) to come into force June 1, 2004.]

(Excerpts)

. . .

125. (1) **Disclosure by peace officer during investigation.**—A peace officer may disclose to any person any information in a record kept under section 114 (court records) or 115 (police records) that it is necessary to disclose in the conduct of the investigation of an offence.

(2) **Disclosure by Attorney General.**—The Attorney General may, in the course of a proceeding under this Act or any other Act of Parliament, disclose the following information in a record kept under section 114 (court reports) or 115 (police records):

(a) to a person who is a co-accused with the young person in respect of the offence for which the record is kept, any information contained in the record; and

(b) to an accused in a proceeding, if the record is in respect of a witness in the proceeding, information that identifies the witness as a young person who has been dealt with under this Act.

(3) **Information that may be disclosed to a foreign state.**—The Attorney General or a peace officer may disclose to the Minister of Justice of Canada information in a record that is kept under section 114 (court records) or 115 (police records) to the extent that it is necessary to deal with a request to or by a foreign state under the Mutual Legal Assistance in Criminal Matters Act, or for the purposes of any extradition matter under the Extradition Act. The Minister of Justice of Canada may disclose the information to the foreign state in respect of which the request was made, or to which the extradition matter relates, as the case may be.

(4) **Disclosure to insurance company.**—A peace officer may disclose to an insurance company information in a record that is kept under section 114 (court records) or 115 (police records) for the purpose of investigating a claim arising out of an offence committed or alleged to have been committed by the young person to whom the record relates.

(5) **Preparation of reports.**—The provincial director or a youth worker may disclose information contained in a record if the disclosure is necessary for procuring information that relates to the preparation of a report required by this Act.

(6) **Schools and others.**—The provincial director, a youth worker, the Attorney General, a peace officer or any other person engaged in the provision of services to young persons may disclose to any professional or other person engaged in the supervision or care of a young person — including a representative of any school board or school or any other educational or training institution — any information contained in a record kept under sections 114 to 116 if the disclosure is necessary

(a) to ensure compliance by the young person with an authorization under section 91 or an order of the youth justice court;

(b) to ensure the safety of staff, students or other persons; or

(c) to facilitate the rehabilitation of the young person.

(7) **Information to be kept separate.**—A person to whom information is disclosed under subsection (6) shall

(a) keep the information separate from any other record of the young person to whom the information relates;

(b) ensure that no other person has access to the information except if authorized under this Act, or if necessary for the purposes of subsection (6); and

(c) destroy their copy of the record when the information is no longer required for the purpose for which it was disclosed.

(8) **Time limit.**—No information may be disclosed under this section after the end of the applicable period set out in subsection 119(2) (period of access to records).

. . .

129. No subsequent disclosure.—No person who is given access to a record or to whom information is disclosed under this Act shall disclose that information to any other person unless the disclosure is authorized under this Act.

. . .

146. (1) General law on admissibility of statements to apply.—Subject to this section, the law relating to the admissibility of statements made by persons accused of committing offences applies in respect of young persons.

(2) **When statements are admissible.**—No oral or written statement made by a young person who is less than eighteen years old, to a peace officer or to any other person who is, in law, a person in authority, on the arrest or detention of the young person or in circumstances where the peace officer or other person has reasonable grounds for believing that the young person has committed an offence is admissible against the young person unless

(a) the statement was voluntary;

(b) the person to whom the statement was made has, before the statement was made, clearly explained to the young person, in language appropriate to his or her age and understanding, that

(i) the young person is under no obligation to make a statement,

(ii) any statement made by the young person may be used as evidence in proceedings against him or her,

(iii) the young person has the right to consult counsel and a parent or other person in accordance with paragraph (c), and

      (iv) any statement made by the young person is required to be made in the presence of counsel and any other person consulted in accordance with paragraph (c), if any, unless the young person desires otherwise;

  (c) the young person has, before the statement was made, been given a reasonable opportunity to consult

      (i) with counsel, and

      (ii) with a parent or, in the absence of a parent, an adult relative or, in the absence of a parent and an adult relative, any other appropriate adult chosen by the young person, as long as that person is not a co-accused, or under investigation, in respect of the same offence; and

  (d) if the young person consults a person in accordance with paragraph (c), the young person has been given a reasonable opportunity to make the statement in the presence of that person.

(3) **Exception in certain cases for oral statements.**—The requirements set out in paragraphs (2)(b) to (d) do not apply in respect of oral statements if they are made spontaneously by the young person to a peace officer or other person in authority before that person has had a reasonable opportunity to comply with those requirements.

(4) **Waiver of right to consult.**—A young person may waive the rights under paragraph (2)(c) or (d) but any such waiver

  (a) must be recorded on video tape or audio tape; or

  (b) must be in writing and contain a statement signed by the young person that he or she has been informed of the right being waived.

(5) **Waiver of right to consult.**—When a waiver of rights under paragraph (2)(c) or (d) is not made in accordance with subsection (4) owing to a technical irregularity, the youth justice court may determine that the waiver is valid if it is satisfied that the young person was informed of his or her rights, and voluntarily waived them.

(6) **Admissibility of statements.**—When there has been a technical irregularity in complying with paragraphs (2)(b) to (d), the youth justice court may admit into evidence a statement referred to in subsection (2), if satisfied that the admission of the statement would not bring into disrepute the principle that young persons are entitled to enhanced procedural protection to ensure that they are treated fairly and their rights are protected.

(7) **Statements made under duress are inadmissible.**—A youth justice court judge may rule inadmissible in any proceedings under this Act a statement made by the young person in respect of whom the proceedings are taken if the young person satisfies the judge that the statement was made under duress imposed by any person who is not, in law, a person in authority.

(8) **Misrepresentation of age.**—A youth justice court judge may in any proceedings under this Act rule admissible any statement or waiver by a young person if, at the time of the making of the statement or waiver,

  (a) the young person held himself or herself to be eighteen years old or older;

(b)   the person to whom the statement or waiver was made conducted reasonable inquiries as to the age of the young person and had reasonable grounds for believing that the young person was eighteen years old or older; and

(c)   in all other circumstances the statement or waiver would otherwise be admissible.

(9) **Parent, etc., not a person in authority.**—For the purpose of this section, a person consulted under paragraph (2)(c) is, in the absence of evidence to the contrary, deemed not to be a person in authority.

. . .

147. (1) **Statements not admissible against young person.**—Subject to subsection (2), if a young person is assessed in accordance with an order made under subsection 34(1) (medical or psychological assessment), no statement or reference to a statement made by the young person during the course and for the purposes of the assessment to the person who conducts the assessment or to anyone acting under that person's direction is admissible in evidence, without the consent of the young person, in any proceeding before a court, tribunal, body or person with jurisdiction to compel the production of evidence.

(2) **Exceptions.**—A statement referred to in subsection (1) is admissible in evidence for the purposes of

(a)   making a decision on an application heard under section 71 (hearing - adult sentences);

(b)   determining whether the young person is unfit to stand trial;

(c)   determining whether the balance of the mind of the young person was disturbed at the time of commission of the alleged offence, if the young person is a female person charged with an offence arising out of the death of her newly-born child;

(d)   making or reviewing a sentence in respect of the young person;

(e)   determining whether the young person was, at the time of the commission of an alleged offence, suffering from automatism or a mental disorder so as to be exempt from criminal responsibility by virtue of subsection 16(1) of the Criminal Code, if the accused puts his or her mental capacity for criminal intent into issue, or if the prosecutor raises the issue after verdict;

(f)   challenging the credibility of a young person in any proceeding if the testimony of the young person is inconsistent in a material particular with a statement referred to in subsection (1) that the young person made previously;

(g)   establishing the perjury of a young person who is charged with perjury in respect of a statement made in any proceeding;

(h)   deciding an application for an order under subsection 104(1) (continuation of custody);

(i)   setting the conditions under subsection 105(1) (conditional supervision);

(j)   conducting a review under subsection 109(1) (review of decision); or

(k)   deciding an application for a disclosure order under subsection 127(1) (information about a young person).

. . .

Index